Methods for Assessing
Children's Syntax

Language, Speech, and Communication

**Methods for Assessing
Children's Syntax**

edited by
Dana McDaniel,
Cecile McKee, and
Helen Smith Cairns

The MIT Press
Cambridge, Massachusetts
London, England

First MIT Press paperback edition, 1998

© 1996 Massachusetts Institute of Technology

All rights reserved. No part of this book may be reproduced in any form by any electronic or mechanical means (including photocopying, recording, or information storage and retrieval) without permission in writing from the publisher.

This book was set in Times Roman by Asco Trade Typesetting Ltd., Hong Kong.

Printed and bound in the United States of America.

Library of Congress Cataloging-in-Publication Data

Methods for assessing children's syntax / edited by Dana McDaniel,
   Cecile McKee and Helen Smith Cairns.
     p.   cm. — (Language, speech, and communication)
   Includes bibliographical references and index.
   ISBN 0-262-13325-3 (hc: alk. paper), 0-262-63190-3 (pb)
   1. Language acquisition—Research—Methodology. 2. Grammar,
Comparative and general—Syntax—Research—Methodology.
I. McDaniel, Dana. II. McKee, Cecile. III. Cairns, Helen Smith.
IV. Series.
P118.15.M48   1996
401'.93—dc20   96-33915
                                                          CIP

For Kelley, Merrill, and Chuck

Contents

Contributors

Helen Smith Cairns
Department of Communication
Arts and Sciences
Queens College—G100
Flushing, NY 11367
cairns@qcvaxa.acc.qc.edu

Katherine Demuth
Department of Cognitive and
Linguistic Sciences
Brown University
Box 1978
Providence, RI 02912
katherine_
demuth@postoffice.brown.edu

Jill de Villiers
Psychology Department
Smith College
Northampton, MA 01063
jdevil@smith.smith.edu

Suzanne Flynn
Department of Foreign Languages
and Literature
Massachusetts Institute of
Technology
77 Massachusetts Avenue
Cambridge, MA 02139
sflynn@mit.edu

Claire Foley
Department of Modern Languages
and Linguistics
Cornell University
Morrill Hall
Ithaca, NY 14853
cf14@cornell.edu

LouAnn Gerken
Department of Speech and
Hearing Sciences
Building #71
University of Arizona
Tucson, AZ 85721
gerken@ccit.arizona.edu

Roberta Michnick Golinkoff
Department of Educational Studies
University of Delaware
46 East Delaware Avenue
Newark, DE 19716
roberta@strauss.udel.edu

Helen Goodluck
Department of Linguistics
University of Ottawa
PO Box 450 Stn A
Ottawa, Ontario
Canada K1N 6N5
hgoodlu@aix1.uottawa.ca

Peter Gordon
Department of Psychology
University of Pittsburgh
Pittsburgh, PA 15260
peter@vms.cis.pitt.edu

Kathy Hirsh-Pasek
Department of Psychology
Temple University, 022-29
Philadelphia, PA 19122
v5080e@vm.temple.edu

Jennifer Ryan Hsu
Department of Communication
Disorders
The William Paterson College
300 Pompton Road
Wayne, NJ 07470

Louis Michael Hsu
Department of Psychology
Fairleigh Dickinson University
1000 River Road
Teaneck, NJ 07666

Celia Jakubowicz
Université René Descartes
UFR Institut de Psychologie
Laboratoire de Psychologie
Expérimentale
CNRS URA 316
28, rue Serpente
75006 Paris, France
jakubowi@idf.ext.jussieu.fr

Laurence B. Leonard
Department of Audiology and
Speech Sciences
Purdue University
Heavilon Hall
West Lafayette, IN 47907
xdxl@vm.cc.purdue.edu

Barbara Lust
Department of Modern Languages
and Linguistics
Cornell University
Morrill Hall
Ithaca, NY 14853
bcl4@cornell.edu

Dana McDaniel
Linguistics
University of Southern Maine
96 Falmouth Street
P.O. Box 9300
Portland, ME 04104-9300
rxa364@usm.maine.edu

Cecile McKee
Department of Linguistics
Douglass 200E
University of Arizona
Tucson, AZ 85721
mckee@u.arizona.edu

Thomas Roeper
Department of Linguistics
226 South College
University of Massachusetts,
Amherst
Amherst, MA 01003
roeper@cs.umass.edu

Michele E. Shady
Department of Psychology
SUNY Buffalo
Park Hall
Buffalo, NY 14260

Karin Stromswold
Department of Psychology and
Center for Cognitive Science
Rutgers University
New Brunswick, NJ 08903
karin@ruccs.rutgers.edu

Rosalind Thornton
Department of Linguistics
1401F Marie Mount Hall
University of Maryland
College Park, MD 20742
rt58@umail.umd.edu

Preface

People have studied child language at least since Darwin (1877) reported on his son's early speech. However, in recent years both the scope of the field and the methods used for studying child language have greatly expanded. This is largely due to Noam Chomsky's influence on the study of syntax, where emphasis on hidden competence has taken researchers far beyond the behaviorists' focus on observable phenomena. Changes in the field have entailed changes in methodology:

> It seems clear that the description which is of the greatest psychological relevance is the account of competence, not that of performance, both in the case of arithmetic and the case of language.... Obviously one can find out about competence only by studying performance, but this study must be carried out in devious and clever ways, if any serious result is to be obtained. (Chomsky 1964, 36)

Since Chomsky made this statement, advances in methods for studying competence have led to a more sophisticated conception of the competence/performance distinction itself. When the distinction was first made, competence was seen as a fascinating, hidden, static system, whereas performance was considered an uninteresting overlay of squalor that one had to slog through to discover the underlying competence. It is now recognized that competence is in many ways dynamic and that many performance phenomena, such as referential preferences, are not only interesting but also—although not part of the grammar—clearly linguistic. The sophisticated methods that led to a better understanding of the notions of competence and performance are also able to address new questions that arise as a result of reconceptualization of these notions.

Methodology has therefore played an important role in the development of the field. Although methodology is not an end in itself, methods affect results, which in turn drive conclusions. Methodological differences can often account for seemingly divergent results across studies. In such cases, one must interpret the results in light of the methodological differences. Conversely, to the extent that results converge across a variety of methods, they support conclusions in which one can have a high degree of confidence.

This brings us to the purpose of this book. Though methodology plays an important role in hypothesis testing and though methods have become quite sophisticated and complex, methodological issues are underaddressed in journals. The reason for this is, of course, that journal articles must devote most of their space to the findings and conclusions of specific studies. The relatively small amount of space devoted to methods is not sufficient to convey much to readers about a specific task used in a study or to address general methodological issues. This book takes a step toward filling that void.

In editing the book, we had two general purposes in mind. The first is to help students or researchers who are designing a study to choose a method or to use a method with which they have no experience. For such people, this book can function as a how-to handbook. A method (or combination of methods) can be chosen based on what is measured and who the subjects are. For example, a comprehension task is generally more appropriate than a production task if the goal is to learn about interpretations of sentences; an off-line task is not appropriate for studying midsentence garden paths; and for very young subjects, preferential looking is more effective than most other comprehension tasks. The book should also be helpful in determining the procedures involved in designing and conducting a study, once a task has been selected.

The second general purpose of the book is to aid in the evaluation of research. For example, as noted above, divergent findings are often attributed to methodology. In order to form hypotheses about how differences in methods are responsible for different findings, one must examine the relevant methods in detail. One might ask, for example, what the methods have been used to assess in the past, what the pitfalls of the methods are, and how their results are generally analyzed. This book should provide the information needed to carry out such a comparison.

The work in child syntax represented in this book combines the best features of two approaches to the study of human cognition: the computational-representational approach developed by linguists and the experimental approach developed by experimental psychologists.

A central tenet of experimental psychology is that a phenomenon must occur more often than would be anticipated by chance before it can be considered psychologically "real." Sophisticated quantitative tools are designed to distinguish such genuine phenomena from ambient variability ("noise"). Individual differences are typically considered part of the "noise," and psychological theories, in the main, account for phenomena characteristic of groups of children. Experiments are designed to ensure that the psychological effects they identify are stable and replicable. Data collection must therefore be completely objective, and experimental manipulations must be free of confounding effects.

The philosophy guiding the field of linguistics is quite different. In that field, a phenomenon is considered genuine if it is theoretically interesting and coherent, and often a phenomenon is evaluated by how well it can be accounted for within a particular theory. Under this approach, individual differences signal important differences in grammar, which the theory is responsible for. Linguistics is thus empirical, but not experimental in the sense of experimental psychology. Although data are adduced to test hypotheses, no real attention is given to the methods of data collection.

The field of child language acquisition has combined these two approaches to create methods that in our view are more effective than they would be if they were based exclusively on the philosophy of a single field. Linguistics has contributed rich theoretical questions and attention to the individual. The latter is important because children cannot be assumed to be linguistically homogeneous; individual differences in children's responses must therefore be identified and addressed. Experimental psychology has provided standards for design and analysis that allow one to trust and defend one's data and compare findings across children, age groups, laboratories, languages, and so on, availing oneself of all the power of statistical analysis. Unfortunately, in order to get the best results with children, it is often necessary to modify procedures to create an experimental ambience that maximizes the quality of each subject's data. From a theoretical perspective, the alliance between experimental psychology and linguistics grounds the study of language within the study of human cognition. An overarching cognitive science perspective provides a context for and thus enriches theories of the human language faculty.

The three of us have different academic backgrounds, and we have all experienced firsthand the consequences of this synergy between the fields of experimental psychology and theoretical linguistics. As we have collaborated on this book, we have discovered that in our work with children each of us has a sense of compromising precepts drawn from our basic academic training. On the one hand, we have experienced the tensions of tempering rigorous experimental strictures with the reality of working with individuals. On the other, we have recognized the necessity for more elaborate methods of data collection than those typically employed by theoretical linguists. We recognize that modifying the standard methods of the two fields allows us to do work in the hybrid field of child language that otherwise would not be possible. The methods discussed in this book reflect the influence of both linguistics and experimental psychology. Some are closer to language acquisition's roots in one field or the other, but they all include some aspects of both.

The scope of this book is limited to methods for assessing syntax. However, many of the methods discussed could be, and have been, used to study morphology and the lexicon as well. Furthermore, though many of the contributors work within the Principles and Parameters framework and therefore cite examples of studies conducted within this framework, the methods described would be equally useful for researchers with other theoretical orientations.

The book is organized as follows. Parts I–III contain chapters on specific methods, divided according to the type of data that are collected: production, comprehension, and judgment data, respectively. The chapters in part IV discuss general methodological considerations that arise regardless of which method is used.

Each chapter in parts I–III pertains to one method, characterized by the subject's task. Within each part, the methods are roughly ordered according to the perceived degree of complexity of the task for the subject, starting with the least complex. Each chapter includes some discussion of the history of the method, the types of issues it can address, its advantages and disadvantages, and how-to instructions on its use.

The contributors to this book have extensive experience with the methods they describe, and they base their discussions largely on their own experience. The reader should not assume, however, that the procedures are limited to the uses to which they have been put in the past. All of the methods described can be modified, and probably are being modified, in many ways. As the authors point out, some degree of modification is almost always necessary to meet the requirements of each specific study, depending on the issues that the research project is designed to address. Many studies also use more than one method or combine several methods into one. Furthermore, clear lines cannot always be drawn between the methods described in this book. Take, for example, the truth-value judgment task (chapter 10, this volume), in which subjects are presented with a scenario and a sentence about the scenario and are asked to judge whether the sentence is true within that context. The sentence can be declarative, in which case the subject makes a true/false judgment, or it can be a yes/no question that the subject answers. The declarative variant is quite similar to a grammaticality judgment task concerning judgments of reference, in which subjects have to judge whether a certain sentence can be used to describe a particular scenario (chapter 11, this volume). The question variant is almost identical to the questions-after-stories task (chapter 8, this volume). The only difference is that the former task uses yes/no questions and the latter uses *wh*-questions; in both cases the researcher concludes something about the subjects' structural analyses of the questions based on their answers.

The chapters in part I discuss methods that employ subjects' language production as data. Though this type of method is the oldest used in studying child language, recent developments have enhanced it in numerous ways. Demuth discusses the care with which spontaneous speech data are now collected and the issues that arise in cross-cultural production work. In her chapter on analyzing spontaneous utterances, Stromswold demonstrates how this type of data, which was classically associated with individual subjects, can be analyzed like group data from an experiment. In their chapter on elicited imitation, Lust, Flynn, and Foley demonstrate how a well-established technique can be used to address complex syntactic issues, and in her chapter on other elicited production techniques, Thornton shows how, in spite of subjects' syntactic creativity, it is possible to put them in a situation that induces them to use a specific syntactic construct.

Comprehension tasks, discussed in part II, allow researchers to study children's language apart from their language production, and they exchange greater freedom on the part of the subject for more control on the part of the experimenter. The materials in a comprehension task can be designed in such a way as to test subjects' interpretations of minimal permutations on a construction. The intermodal preferential looking paradigm, described by Hirsh-Pasek and Golinkoff, can be used with young subjects who are not yet saying anything at all. Another nonverbal task, appropriate for slightly older subjects, is the picture selection task, described by Gerken and Shady. They also demonstrate that the picture selection task is not limited to determining interpretations, but, when accuracy scores are evaluated, can also indicate sensitivity to grammaticality. Goodluck argues that the act-out task can determine which interpretations are possible, in addition to which are preferable. De Villiers and Roeper demonstrate that the questions-after-stories task can be used to assess subjects' knowledge of complex constraints on wh-constructions. McKee discusses on-line tasks, which have only recently been modified for child subjects and which arguably offer the only way to explore children's sentence processing as it occurs in real time.

Judgment tasks, discussed in part III, most closely resemble the methods used by syntacticians studying adult language and in fact were not modified for use with children until relatively recently. Gordon emphasizes two variations on the truth-value judgment task, both of which can be used with very young subjects. McDaniel and Cairns discuss the grammaticality judgment task, which allows the researcher to ask subjects directly about ungrammatical sentences and which can be used to study the full range of possible referents for pronominal elements.

The chapters in part IV include general considerations that span the various methods. Until recently most work in child syntax focused on English. Recent crosslinguistic investigations, as discussed by Jakubowicz, are particularly informed by the theory of Universal Grammar. Jakubowicz discusses the methodological considerations that enter into designing a crosslinguistic study. In his chapter on research in clinical settings, Leonard argues that investigations of disordered language can and should be expanded to include researcher-designed instruments like those discussed in this book. Finally, Hsu and Hsu focus on issues of experimental design and quantitative analysis that are especially relevant to the study of child language.

This book is a joint effort involving a number of people. We are grateful to Amy Pierce at MIT Press for the guidance she gave us at every stage. We thank two anonymous reviewers for helpful comments on our initial proposal. We consider ourselves extremely fortunate to have had Anne Mark as our copyeditor and Kelley McDaniel as our indexer. We are also grateful to Sandra Minkkinen, the production editor, for her help in the final stages. We are, of course, indebted to our contributors who have been a joy to work with. Finally, we thank all the many nonacademic people whose cooperation is essential for work in child language to go forward: children who serve as subjects, and teachers and administrators who invite linguists into their schools.

PART I

Production Data

Chapter 1

Collecting Spontaneous Production Data

Katherine Demuth

1.1 Introduction

Much of the earliest work on child language acquisition took the form of longitudinal diary studies, where parents documented developments in their child's grammar and/or lexicon (e.g., Stern and Stern 1907; Grégoire 1937, 1947). Later, with the emergence of tape-recording technology, both parents and nonparent researchers were able to collect spontaneous speech samples from a variety of children. This paved the way for a significant increase in both the amount of material that could be collected and the types of research issues that could be addressed. Many of these issues, such as the path to development of grammatical competence, the contributions of general cognitive abilities, and the role of input, continue to be hotly debated today, not only by linguists and researchers working on language acquisition, but also by learning theorists and cognitive scientists more generally.

Along with a growing interest in the nature of linguistic structure (Chomsky 1957, 1965) came an increasing concern with how these structures are actually acquired. Some of the earliest research on the acquisition of English used spontaneous production data to begin to address this question (e.g., Braine 1963; Brown and Fraser 1963; Miller and Ervin 1964; Bloom 1970). It was also recognized that crosslinguistic data are essential for understanding the nature of language acquisition. This led Slobin and colleagues to the development of *A Field Manual for Cross-Cultural Study of the Acquisition of Communicative Competence* (Slobin 1967). Several studies of children learning other languages followed (Finnish, Bowerman 1973; Samoan, Kernan 1969; and Japanese, McNeill 1966a, McNeill and McNeill 1966). Since that time, the collection of spontaneous production data has become a frequently used method for addressing acquisition questions, and the number of crosslinguistic studies using this technique has continued to grow (e.g., Slobin 1985b, 1992). Many spontaneous production corpora from a variety of languages have been computerized, and an increasing number are available as part of the CHILDES data archive at Carnegie Mellon University (MacWhinney and Snow 1985; MacWhinney 1991). The collection of spontaneous data has already made a significant contribution to language acquisition research. It is not, however, to be undertaken lightly: spontaneous production data are useful only when collected systematically and with careful attention to details that affect the quality of the resulting corpus.

One set of spontaneous production data that has had a significant and continuing impact on the field has been Roger Brown's longitudinal study of the English-speaking children given the pseudonyms Adam, Eve, and Sarah (Brown 1973). This data set continues to be useful because it was carefully collected and documented, because it provides longitudinal evidence for similar stages of development across three children with different developmental rates, and because data collection took place during the morphosyntactically interesting period when the mean length of utterance (MLU) was between 1.75 and 4 morphemes. Although the specific goal of Brown's study was to examine English-speaking children's development of grammatical morphology, these corpora continue to provide researchers with a rich set of production data that can be used to investigate many syntactic issues. For example, they have been used by Stromswold (1990b) in investigating children's acquisition of auxiliary verbs, by Marcus et al. (1992) in examining morphological overgeneralization, and by Bloom (1990) in a treatment of children's subjectless sentences. When collected appropriately, spontaneous production data can provide a wealth of information to be tapped repeatedly over the years. In the following section I discuss the kinds of syntactic phenomena that can most profitably be examined using this type of data.

1.2 Syntactic Phenomena Investigated

A primary goal of language acquisition research has been to assess the Chomskyan notion of grammatical competence. It is often more difficult to assess young children's knowledge of language than adults'. Researchers have therefore devised various methods appropriate for assessing young children's early grammatical abilities, and many of these are discussed in later chapters (see chapter 11, this volume). Spontaneous production data can also be used to determine certain types of grammatical competence, especially in the area of morphosyntactic development.

1.2.1 Pro-Drop and Parameter Setting

Since the early and mid 1980s grammatical morphology has played an increasingly important role in the construction of syntactic theory. This state of affairs has been reflected in the questions researchers have asked about the course of language acquisition. For example, in the development of the Principles and Parameters approach to linguistic structure (Chomsky 1981), it was noted that in some languages (e.g., English) an overt subject is obligatory, whereas in others (e.g., Italian) it is not. Hyams (1986) suggested that the lack of pronominal subjects in early English was evidence of a null-subject stage of development, where young English speakers' initial setting of the pro-drop parameter was hypothesized to be similar to that of null-subject Italian. Spontaneous speech data from English-speaking children have subsequently been used to argue against this view (e.g., Valian 1991) by providing statistics on how frequently young English speakers use lexical and pronominal subjects.

1.2.2 Functional Categories and Syntactic Structure

Grammatical morphology and its role in children's developing grammars have taken on renewed relevance as the distinction between functional and lexical categories (closed- vs. open-class items) has moved into the mainstream of syntactic theory (Abney 1987; Chomsky 1991). A flurry of research activity has ensued examining spontaneous production data from languages as diverse as Italian, English, Swedish, German, Swiss-German, French, Korean, and Sesotho (see Meisel 1992; Lust, Suñer, and Whitman 1994; Hoekstra and Schwartz 1994; and references therein). Researchers have studied how and when children acquire various aspects of grammatical morphology, including the marking of tense, person, number, gender, and case, as well as the placement and use of auxiliaries, negation, determiners, and complementizers. Some of these studies have drawn on original findings from Brown's corpora: Bellugi (1967) studied the emergence of children's use of negation and subject-auxiliary inversion, and Brown (1968) investigated stages in the acquisition of yes/no questions and *wh*-questions. More recently, spontaneous production data have been used by Pierce (1992) and Déprez and Pierce (1993) to investigate negation in French and by Radford (1994) to examine the syntax of early English *wh*-questions. I have also used spontaneous production data from Sesotho (a Bantu language) to explore the development of complementizers and the formation of relative clauses, questions, infinitival complements, and embedded clauses (Demuth 1995).

1.2.3 Passives, Causatives, and Grammatical Relations

Spontaneous production data have also been used to explore how and when passives, causatives, and other grammatical-function-changing operations are acquired. Although passives rarely occur in the spontaneous speech of English-speaking children, they appear much more commonly in the spontaneous speech of children learning Bantu languages (Sesotho, Demuth 1989, 1990; Zulu, Suzman 1985). Children also use ergative marking and antipassive constructions quite early in learning languages such as K'iche' (Pye 1992) and Inuktitut (Allen and Crago 1993). Such findings have called into question previous theoretical notions of grammatical complexity and children's early grammatical abilities. Other studies, including work on the acquisition of causative constructions (cf. Bowerman 1982), shed light on the child's developing lexicon and on lexical interactions with syntactic development. Much of this latter research draws on longitudinal diary studies of children's spontaneous productions and focuses on overgeneralization errors.

1.2.4 Morphological Paradigms and Learning

Spontaneous production data such as Brown's (1973) corpora have also been used in addressing learnability issues such as how seemingly complex inflectional paradigms are learned (e.g., Rumelhart and McClelland 1986; Pinker and Prince 1988). Issues of input become extremely important in such studies, and researchers are beginning to reexamine spontaneous production corpora, looking more closely at the distributional properties of the input and its relationship to the acquisition of morphological paradigms (e.g., Clahsen et al. 1992; Ziesler and Demuth 1995).

In sum, the use of spontaneous production data has been and continues to be extremely important for addressing various issues relating to morphological and syntactic development. As technological and theoretical advances in the area of "corpus-based" linguistics increase, so will the advantages of using spontaneous production data to address acquisition and learnability issues.

1.3   Spontaneous Production Data Collection Procedures

Like any other type of data collection, spontaneous production data collection is useful only if collection methods are carefully planned. Planning must include consideration of both the research questions to be asked and the methods to be used in the process of data collection itself. Given the labor-intensive nature of collecting and coding spontaneous production data, it is advantageous to have both short-term and long-term research goals in mind. This should hold not only for the specific research topic(s) to be addressed, but also for issues relating to the number of children, the ages of the children, the length of the study, the frequency and length of the recordings, and the conditions of the recording situation, including the site, interlocutors, and acoustic quality of the recording itself. Each of these issues is discussed in more detail below.

1.3.1   Number of Children to Include in a Study
Acquisition studies have shown that the course of language development varies to a certain extent from child to child. Although much of this variation is related to when certain constructions are acquired rather than to the course of acquisition, it is generally accepted that a study of several children is more informative than a study of one child. It is therefore preferable to collect spontaneous production data from more than one child. Given a target of three children, it may be advisable to start a study with four. This is especially important in research settings where children and their families may move away before the completion of a longitudinal study, or succumb to sickness or death, as may happen in communities with high early childhood mortality. Furthermore, one or more children or families may drop out of the study for reasons of work, frustration, or other priorities. Brown's (1973) study of three children provides a nice sample of variation, where Eve is much more precocious than either Adam or Sarah. Such diversity is vital to constructing a coherent theory of acquisition.

1.3.2   Age Range of the Children and Longitudinal Scope of a Study
The age range of the children to be recorded and the length of the study should be determined on the basis of the general research questions and the specific grammatical phenomena being investigated. Given individual variation in development, a certain amount of variation in the age of the

children studied should be allowed: individual children's MLU may be a more accurate measure of linguistic ability than age (Brown 1973). This is true even though there may be difficulty calculating MLU crosslinguistically, especially for highly inflected languages such as Hebrew (Dromi and Berman 1982) and West Greenlandic Fortescue 1985; Fortescue and Lennert Olsen 1992).

If little previous acquisition work has been done on the language under study, it might be advisable for the researcher to consult persons in the community who are knowledgeable about child language, or to listen to children of different ages to determine if certain constructions are in use. In general, however, children between the ages of 2 and 3 show rapid phonological, lexical, morphological, and syntactic development. If the study concerns development of grammatical morphology, it is advisable to begin recordings with children younger than 2 years in order to catch the transition stage. If grammatical constructions such as passives, relative clauses, or complementation are to be examined, the study should include older children, perhaps between 2;6 and 4 years. If the study looks at certain types of lexical categorization involving complementation and argument structure relations, children between the ages of 3 and 5 should probably be included.

In situations where it is impossible to follow one set of children for longer than 12 months, it may be useful to collect data from children in one or two age groups, or from children of overlapping ages (e.g., 3;6–4;6, 4–5, 4;6–5;6 years). This may be especially useful when initiating the study of a language where little or no previous acquisition work exists and it is unclear when children acquire certain constructions.

1.3.3 Selecting Children for a Study

Several factors should be considered in selecting children to participate in a longitudinal study of spontaneous speech production. First, if the community is bilingual or multilingual, the language situation in the home and/or day care center should be carefully assessed to ensure that the monolingual/bilingual setting is appropriate to the requirements of the study. This may be a determining factor in selecting the initial research site. For my work in Lesotho, in southern Africa, I decided to base my study in a rural village rather than an urban center to avoid possible English influence on the children's acquisition of Sesotho (Demuth 1984, 1992). Second, it is good to have a gender balance among the children in the study, so that sex-based rates of maturation and gender-based use of language (in some cultures) can be represented. Third, children with a history of ear infection and/or other health problems and children with obvious cognitive deficits should not be included unless the research is specifically designed to study language development in these populations; both cognitive deficits and health problems that affect hearing may have a significant negative impact on children's language development.

Once the age range of the children to be studied has been determined, the researcher should visit several children in the community to determine which children and families are most appropriate for inclusion in the study. These visits are useful in two respects. First, they offer the researcher an opportunity to become familiar with some children and their families. Second, they provide a basis for deciding which children will become part of the study. If MLU is a factor in selecting children for the study, this period of familiarization can facilitate assessment of children's stage of linguistic development. Finally, the families as well as the children will be involved in the study: the researcher will have to arrange times convenient for recording, and if parent-child interactions are required, the parents will have to agree to participating in the research themselves. In some research situations, such as with the Inuit in Canada (Crago 1988), parents work during the day, and recordings have to be carried out with the cooperation of other caregivers. Prerecording visits to families therefore provide the researcher with critical information regarding which families and children will be most appropriate for the study. It is important that the researcher feel at ease with both the families and the children; the quality of the data will be adversely affected if recording sessions are stilted or artificially constructed in any way (see Clark 1982).

1.3.4 Frequency and Duration of Recording Sessions

A decision must be made about the frequency and duration of recording sessions. In Brown's (1973) study, Eve was recorded for at least half an hour every week, and Adam and Sarah were recorded for about an hour every two weeks. In addition, more data were collected more frequently when morphosyntactic changes were occurring at a rapid pace. By contrast, for my work on Sesotho acquisition I collected data less frequently (once a month), but in a variety of discourse situations, resulting in much larger samples per session (3–4 hours). It is useful to have a plan for how often and how long to record, but it is also necessary to be flexible and ready to adapt when recording opportunities arise. It may be advisable to collect more data than actually needed to ensure that at least a certain number of relevant utterances (i.e., utterances containing constructions of a certain grammatical type) are included in every recording session.

The collection of spontaneous production data is at best a sampling technique. An important consideration in determining how much material to collect is to ensure that the data constitute a "representative sample" of the child's productive language capabilities at the time. What counts as "representative" will depend greatly on the grammatical phenomena being studied and how frequently these constructions occur in everyday discourse. For example, more data are needed to examine complex grammatical constructions such as passives, relative clauses, and complementation; fewer data are needed to examine the use of subject agreement or other frequently occurring morphosyntactic phenomena. As will be discussed in the following sections, the recording site and recording procedures often have as much to do with collecting representative samples as do the frequency and duration of the recordings themselves.

1.3.5 The Recording Situation

Several factors, including the site of the recording sessions, the participants, the interactive situations being recorded, and the type of recording equipment used, all play an important role in the quality of the spontaneous production data collected. Many of these issues are similar to those of collecting experimental production data, though others are necessarily different. Each of these issues is discussed more fully below.

Most longitudinal spontaneous production studies take place in and around children's homes rather than in an acoustically treated laboratory. There are several reasons for this. First, the phenomena investigated using spontaneous production data have generally been of a morphological, syntactic, or semantic nature rather than phonological or acoustic. Second, it is generally recognized that young children are more likely to talk freely, and to use more grammatically complex linguistic constructions, when they are in a familiar environment. It is for this reason that studies using spontaneous production data, which have frequently involved upper-middle-class children, have focused on mother-child interaction as being the prototypically "familiar" setting in which the upper end of children's linguistic abilities would be readily observable. However, studies of children learning other languages in other cultural settings have found that children typically interact with a large range of both adults and children on an everyday basis and that recording should not necessarily be confined either to mother-child interactions or to one setting. For instance, in rural Lesotho I found that grandmothers, peers, and older siblings were some of the most frequent interlocutors with young children and that mother-child interactions decreased significantly around the age of 2;6 years, with or without the birth of a younger sibling. In addition, some of the children's most advanced linguistic forms, such as restrictive relative clauses, occurred during peer and sibling interactions where children had to be extremely linguistically sophisticated to get what they wanted (Demuth 1984). Thus, although the home environment may be the site in which children feel most comfortable, that environment may include many more discourse participants than simply the mother. This may be especially true when extended families or peers live nearby, or when the child has older siblings. Such interactions can provide an extremely rich set of production data, from both the child and other caregivers, including fathers, aunts and uncles, grandparents, older siblings, and cousins. One of the challenges for the researcher is to determine, given a particular culture and specific family situations within that culture, which interactive situations are the most productive for collecting children's speech.

Interactions that involve either one or a number of participants may not necessarily be confined to one site. Some of the richest interactive and linguistic situations may be embedded in a range of daily activities including bathing, cooking, eating, and playing outdoors. Noise factors, such as water running into a bathtub, the TV, washing machine, or dishwasher in the background, rain pelting on a tin roof, cooking noises, loud music from next door, or ten preschoolers at a birthday party, can obliterate the speech of the target child; in such situations it is best to stop recording and continue later or the next day. The researcher should be flexible enough to take advantage of different recording opportunities as they arise. Allen (1994) reports that one of her richest recording sessions with Inuit children took place five hours away from home at the family's summer camp.

The picture that begins to emerge here shows the researcher gradually becoming "part of the extended family." Both researcher and family have to make decisions about how this relationship will be negotiated, and it is highly relevant to the quality of data collected. By living and working in a small village of 550 people in Lesotho, I was able to establish a relationship of daily interaction with three families, becoming a member of the extended community and someone the children saw and talked with frequently. My transitions into and out of families' homes, with or without the tape recorder, became normal events in the life of each child, allowing me to record whenever and wherever the collection of spontaneous linguistic productions looked promising. Sometimes this meant joining families for a meal; other times it meant racing after children as they chased chickens or played tag. The resulting data set is grammatically extremely rich, providing an excellent assessment of children's syntactic abilities in a broad range of discourse situations.

The researcher will have to decide whether to be a participant in verbal interactions, or simply an observer. If the researcher is not a native speaker of the language under investigation, interactions should probably be limited. When recording in Lesotho, I rarely initiated conversation with the children, only answering when spoken to, or warning children against activities that might lead to bodily harm, such as falling into the fire pit or playing with a sharp knife. Bowerman (1973), in her study of Finnish children, also took this approach. Even when the researcher is a native speaker of the language being studied, the goals of the research may influence decisions about researcher participation. For example, if one of the goals is to examine the type of input adults provide to children, the researcher will want to keep interaction to a minimum. On the other hand, if the researcher wants to do some informal elicitation to probe for children's knowledge of certain syntactic constructions, specific types of interaction could play a useful role.

In addition to audio recording, the researcher should arrange to take contextual notes or video recordings. This is important because the details of the setting and activities of the participants are often essential to interpreting children's utterances. For example, the use of a relative clause in English may or may not be restrictive, and it may only be notes such as "child looks at three dolls, then picks up the tall one," or the equivalent observed on videotape, that can provide the information needed to evaluate children's use of such constructions. Written or videotaped contextual notes should be keyed to the counter on the tape recorder for easy and accurate retrieval.

1.3.6 Recording Equipment

Spontaneous production data may be collected in a variety of indoor and outdoor settings. The type of recording equipment used should be selected accordingly. Consultation with someone knowledgeable about professional recording equipment, as well as the conditions under which the researcher will be recording, is highly recommended. In general, however, recording equipment should be of high quality, but also portable. Fortunately, researchers today can choose from a number of light, portable audio and video recorders of professional quality. As recording technology becomes increasingly sophisticated, decisions will have to be made about when to move to the latest technology. Again, the goals of the research become important in making this decision. If the project is a preliminary, exploratory study where the long-term preservation of tapes is not critical, traditional analog recordings are probably adequate. If, however, the study is large and potentially of significant long-term interest to the field, like Brown's (1973) study, the use of digital recordings, with long-term archival shelf life, should be seriously considered. In either case, high-quality tape should be used.

New equipment should *always* be tested before the researcher disappears to the field. This is especially true if it incorporates new technologies, since the researcher may need to become familiar with the equipment, and since new products may lack effective quality control. As an additional precaution, backup recording equipment should always be taken to the research site; recording equipment, especially under intensive use, has been known to break and/or suffer the consequences of wear and tear, especially when used outdoors.

More important than the choice of tape recorder is the choice of microphone. Again, knowledge about the recording site will play a significant role in determining which type of microphone is best. If the recordings are to take place primarily in one room, it may make sense to hang an omnidirectional microphone in the middle of the room so that all speakers' voices can be heard. However, if recordings will take place on the go, it is advisable to use either a handheld directional microphone, or a wireless broadcast microphone built into a vest that the child wears, or both if discourse interactions with other speakers are also desired. The quality of the microphones should be good. If recording is done outdoors, microphones should be used with a wind screen.

Given the nature of collecting spontaneous production data from young children, it may be best to power the recorder with batteries rather than relying on an electrical outlet. It is therefore wise to carry extra batteries— nothing is worse than being ready to record only to find that the batteries are dead! Likewise, carrying an extra tape is a good idea: if the child is having a particularly verbose day, it may be worth collecting more than the usual amount of data. Finally, at the end of each recording session it is advisable to verify that recording actually took place and that the tape is intelligible. All tapes should be marked with the recording date and with the age and name of the child.

1.4 Transcribing and Tagging Spontaneous Production Data

Several recent publications have described widely used conventions for transcribing and tagging spontaneous speech data and have discussed which procedures are most appropriate for different types of production data (e.g., MacWhinney 1991; Edwards and Lampert 1993). The purpose of this section is not to repeat the material found there but to offer a procedural perspective on these issues, with specific reference to the types of decisions that will need to be made.

1.4.1 Getting Ready to Transcribe

Once a recording session has been completed, the researcher should begin transcription as soon as possible. This ensures the maximum transmission of contextual information and transcript accuracy. It is probably best to make a copy of the original tape and to transcribe from the copy, keeping the original for archival use or for backup; transcription involves lots of going back and forth, and tapes sometimes break under the strain. If the original recording was digital, the copy can be analog, since most transcribing machines still use analog tape.

If possible, audio recodings should be transcribed directly into a computerized database so that the corpus can be easily used for analysis. The format used for transcription will again depend partly on the goals of the research. Some researchers may decide to transcribe data into a format compatible with the files in the CHILDES data bank at Carnegie Mellon University. CHILDES offers child-language-oriented search-and-analysis programs (such as CLAN) that can calculate MLU and collect statistics on the frequency of occurrence of certain constructions (see chapter 2, this volume, for further details). Furthermore, these search programs are available for both PC and Macintosh computers, complete with documentation (MacWhinney 1991). There may be cases, however, where researchers wish to customize transcription and coding into a format that is more readily usable for immediate research purposes. In this case it is still advisable to code data into some sort of database. Excel and 4th Dimension are databases that some researchers have found useful. Customized search programs can be written for these databases, and the data can be converted to the CHILDES format at a later date.

Each file, or transcript, should include information about the child and the recording situation, such as the child's name (using a preselected pseudonym), the child's age, the date and site of the recording, and participants in the recording session (e.g., mother, siblings, other relatives, friends). If the researcher is not a native speaker of the language being investigated, it may be advisable to transcribe the tape in conjunction with the mother of the child or some other native-speaker adult who knows the child well and might have been present during some of the recording sessions.

Finally, the researcher will have to decide whether to transcribe only the child's utterances or to include both the child and other interlocutors. In my Sesotho corpus I have transcribed all speech from adults, peers, and others who were interacting with the target child. This interaction is invaluable for understanding the context of the discourse and, in some cases, for determining what the child was trying to say.

1.4.2 The Transcription Process

As Ochs (1979) so aptly notes, the very process of transcription has theoretical consequences. At every stage of the data collection and transcription process, certain details are lost, resulting in a product that preserves only certain types of information. Given that researchers generally use only the final transcript when conducting syntactic analysis (and when they use the CHILDES data bank, this transcript is often the only data source available), the type and quality of the information included in the transcript will undoubtedly bias our understanding of how language is acquired. Decisions about what to transcribe and how to transcribe it therefore play a critical role in the types of syntactic and related research questions the data can be used to address. Some of these issues involve the level of phonetic detail transcribed, the inclusion of relevant contextual information, and decisions about what constitutes an "utterance." These and related issues are examined in more detail below.

Given the nonlaboratory nature of most spontaneous production recordings and a research focus on lexical, morphological, and syntactic issues, a broad phonemic (rather than narrow phonetic) transcription is probably adequate. In many cases broad phonemic transcriptions have used the orthographic conventions of the language (e.g., Brown 1973; Bowerman 1973). However, a decision will have to be made about how to transcribe children's phonetically altered forms, and a description of these conventions should accompany the transcripts. Any phonetic information relevant to the syntax should be marked. For example, in languages that use lexical and/or grammatical tone, such as many Southeast Asian and African languages, tone may need to be marked to capture lexical, morphological, or syntactic information. The presence or absence of grammatical function items, including vowel or consonant quality, can also be extremely relevant for addressing certain syntactic questions. Even when transcribing English it may be advisable to use some convention for encoding intonational contours that can capture contrastive stress. Thus, a broad phonemic transcription may need to be carried out with attention to some phonetic detail. In some cases this may involve the use of diacritics not readily available on a keyboard. The CHILDES manual (MacWhinney 1991) has a series of conventions for entering such cases (PHONASCII), and it may be appropriate to use them unless the researcher finds them inadequate in some respect.

Another decision to be made is how to break up conversation into "utterance"-level units for transcription purposes. Again, the choice of transcription technique will vary depending on the research questions being asked. Much of my early work on Sesotho dealt with passive constructions; I therefore coded data according to clauses. Since the material on Sesotho exists in database format, it is possible to recover the complete utterances so that relative clauses and embedded complements can also be examined. Taking a different approach, Allen (1994) transcribed each utterance on a separate line and then counted the number of verbal clauses per utterance. A related issue is how to deal with "repetitions." In the Sesotho corpus I generally coded identical consecutive repetitions as one utterance, with a note in the "comments" column (a separate "field" in the database) about how many times it occurred. If "repetitions" were segmentally or prosodically different, or if utterances by other interlocutors intervened, I counted them as separate utterances. Transcript entries should all be keyed to the original tapes to facilitate easy access; the researcher may find it useful or even essential to return to the original tapes from time to time, either to check the original transcription or to transcribe additional information (such as phonetic or prosodic detail).

Contextual information often provides evidence of the pragmatic intent of the utterance, and this may influence the grammaticality of what was said. This becomes highly relevant to the syntactic investigation of focus constructions such as topicalization, clefting, relativization, the use of stressed pronouns, word order, and the like. Contextual information that has been captured in notes or on videotape should therefore be entered into a "context" field in the transcript.

Even with contextual information, a videotape, and the aid of a native speaker, it may occasionally be difficult to determine what the child actually said. Sometimes little or nothing is recoverable; in this case the researcher should indicate that the child said something, but that it was unintelligible. This will aid in understanding the nature of the discourse within an ongoing conversation. In other cases the child's utterance may sound like actual words, but it may not be clear if what the researcher hears is what the child actually said. In this case the researcher should note in a "comments" field of the transcript that there is uncertainty about what has been transcribed, and include alternatives if there are any. Some of these utterances may become disambiguated once more of the session has been transcribed. If not, and if a second transcriber is unable to shed light on the issue, the researcher may choose to disregard these entries or gloss them as unintelligible utterances.

Once a transcription has been completed, it should be checked and verified by another researcher. It may be advantageous if this person is a native speaker of the language, but one who was not present during the recordings. Verification should be conducted by listening to representative samples of the tape (perhaps 10% of the total data set) and retranscribing it. The two transcriptions should then be checked for validity. Backup copies of all work should be made.

Transcription is a painstaking process. I found that even when I worked with the mother or grandmother of the child, broad phonemic transcription of 1 hour of audiotape of the Sesotho corpus generally took 7 hours. Allen (1994) and Crago (1988) found that Inuktitut speakers transcribed about 2 to 5 minutes of videotape per hour. In other words, transcribing either audio- or videotape requires a large investment of time. The researcher should plan accordingly.

1.4.3   Tagging (Coding) the Corpus

Spontaneous production corpora are most useful if some type of tagging (grammatical coding) is included in the transcript (database). Again, the extent and type of tagging will depend, in part, on both the immediate and long-term goals of the project. Many corpora, such as the transcripts of Adam, Eve, and Sarah, have not been tagged. I have found that tagging is extremely helpful even in corpora from languages one knows well. For example, if one wanted to study the use of auxiliaries in an untagged English corpus, one would have to list all auxiliaries and then exclude main verb uses of *be* and *have*. On the other hand, if auxiliaries have been tagged, a search for AUX will pull out all auxiliaries. Tagging becomes even more important when working with a lesser-known language—especially if the eventual goal is to make the corpus available to a larger audience, for example, by donating it to the CHILDES data bank.

In working with the Sesotho corpus, I have found it most fruitful to have separate fields for the child's utterance, the grammatical adult target form, a detailed set of morphological tags, and an English running gloss. The example in (1) gives an idea of how this can be done, where the different fields are Speaker = the speaker, Session = the recording session, Key = the counter number on the tape, Utterance = the child's utterance, Targe = the adult equivalent target (i.e., what the child was trying to say), Tag = the morpheme-by-morpheme tag (grammatical coding) of the target utterance, English = a running English gloss that captures the meaning of the utterance, Context = contextual information, Comments = notable aspects of the utterance.

(1) Speaker   H
    Session   IIA
    Key   642
    Utterance   ko rata
    Target   ke-a-o-rat-a
    Tag   1sSM-PRES-2sOM-like-IN
    English   I like you
    Context   child looks at doll
    Comments   × 2

The transcript should then also include a separate glossary of all the tagging terms used throughout the corpus. For example, the glossary for the tags used in example (1) would include the items in (2).

(2) 1sSM   1st person singular subject agreement
    2sOM   2nd person singular object agreement
    PRES   present tense
    IN   indicative mood
    × 2   identical consecutive repetition of an utterance

The specific tags used will depend partly on the language being investigated and partly on the research questions being asked. This type of detailed tagging is extremely useful for conducting automatic searches of certain grammatical phenomena, especially in cases where children's pronunciation of "words" or "morphemes" differs from the adult equivalent forms, or in cases of homophony. It is also useful in cases where the orthography of a language is not completely standardized and different transcribers use slightly different orthographic conventions. Furthermore, the inclusion of a field for "adult equivalent forms" provides other non-native-speaker researchers with ready access to where and how the child's utterance deviates from the adult form. This information is often lacking in transcripts and in publications, making it difficult for both researchers and readers who do not have full command of the particular language to understand what the child has omitted or changed.

1.5   Disadvantages of Collecting and Using Spontaneous Production Data

Some potential problems involved with collecting spontaneous production data were discussed in section 1.4. Once the data have been collected, there are also certain limitations on what they can tell us about the course of acquisition. One of the central concerns in the field of language acquisition is to determine the nature of children's underlying grammatical competence. Using production data to determine grammatical competence introduces certain problems of interpretation: how and when does the researcher know that the child has *productive grammatical competence* with certain grammatical forms? These issues are discussed below.

One limitation of using spontaneous production data lies in the nature of the sampling technique itself: if a particular grammatical construction does not occur in the sessions sampled, it is often difficult to determine the cause of its absence. For example, passive constructions occur relatively infrequently in young children's spontaneous use of English. It was initially assumed that their absence was due to grammatical complexity or lack of linguistic "maturation" (e.g., Brown and Hanlon 1970; Borer and Wexler 1987). However, crosslinguistic evidence of early passives in spontaneous production data from languages like Sesotho indicates that English-speaking children should, in principle, be able to comprehend and produce passives by the age of 3 (Demuth 1989, 1990). Thus, spontaneous production data can provide positive evidence for the presence of a grammatical construction, but they are of limited use (without crosslinguistic evidence) in determining whether the absence of a particular grammatical construction is due to lack of linguistic ability, lack of exposure to the construction, or lack of appropriate discourse contexts in the sample.

It has long been realized that children's *comprehension* of some grammatical constructions, especially those pertaining to grammatical morphology, may precede children's *production* of these forms (e.g., Shipley, Smith, and Gleitman 1969). This is especially relevant to the current debate concerning the presence or absence of functional categories and the projection of syntactic structure (see Meisel 1992; Lust, Suñer, and Whitman 1994; Hoekstra and Schwartz 1994). Researchers using spontaneous production data may actually underestimate children's grammatical competence, especially at early stages of development. Spontaneous production data can often provide evidence of children's competence with certain constructions, but finding this evidence may require careful investigation on the part of the researcher. For example, early evidence of person marking in Sesotho comes from tonal evidence rather than from the presence of agreement morphemes, which tend to be phonologically reduced (Demuth 1993).

On the other hand, if a specific construction or grammatical item is present in spontaneous production data, it may be difficult to determine if its occurrence is "productive." For example, some researchers have argued that children initially have limited control of relative clauses (e.g., de Villiers et al. 1979; Tavakolian 1981a) and long-distance *wh*-movement (de Villiers, Roeper, and Vainikka 1990). Furthermore, some grammatical morphemes may initially be produced as lexicalized rather than productive forms. The researcher must therefore look for signs of "productivity," including morphological "errors" such as the overgeneralization of past tense *-ed* (e.g., *goed, catched*) in English. Experimental techniques (like those discussed in this volume) can often provide a more detailed assessment of children's linguistic competence with grammatical morphology and syntactic/semantic phenomena such as anaphoric relations, quantifier scope, island constraints, and the use of embedded and control structures.

1.6   Advantages of Collecting and Using Spontaneous Production Data

The greatest advantage of using spontaneous production data is that they can supply a wealth of information about many aspects of children's grammatical development. Longitudinal spontaneous production studies are particularly useful in identifying general developmental trends, providing an excellent picture of the overall course of development for a given language. This is especially helpful when initiating the study of a language on which little or no previous acquisition research has been done. For example, passive constructions, which were initially thought to be difficult to acquire, turn out to be productively used in the spontaneous speech of 3-year-old speakers of Bantu languages like Sesotho (Demuth 1989, 1990) and Zulu (Suzman 1985). Furthermore, spontaneous production data from Inuktitut (Allen 1994) and K'iche' (Pye and Quixtan Poz 1988) show early acquisition of antipassive constructions in these ergative languages. Spontaneous production data can be used to assess children's grammatical competence in a number of ways: evidence of "productivity" comes from spontaneous overgeneralizations (e.g., regular past tense and plural marking on irregular English verbs and nouns), children's use of other novel forms that they could not have heard, the use of alternating forms (e.g., verbs with various endings), and children's own self-corrections (see Demuth 1989 and Allen 1994 for discussion).

Spontaneous production data that include utterances from interlocutors are especially useful in providing information about how frequently specific grammatical constructions typically occur in a language. They can therefore provide important evidence for determining whether a particular grammatical phenomenon, such as the passive, is linguistically difficult for young children to acquire or whether it simply fails to appear because of language-particular discourse factors such as low frequency, as in the case of English (see Pinker, Lebeaux, and Frost 1987). Ultimately, this type of information is critical for developing a comprehensive theory of acquisition.

Spontaneous production studies can also provide information about individual variation in the course of language development. For example, Brown (1973) found that Eve was very precocious in learning the grammatical morphology of English, whereas Adam and Sarah were much slower. This provides researchers with an idea of the range of what can be considered "normal" in language development, and the time course over which it occurs. Although there is thought to be no direct implicational relationship between input and the course of individual children's linguistic development (e.g., Brown 1973), other studies indicate that certain connections may exist. For example, Peters and Menn (1993) argue that the emergence of certain English prepositions in the early speech of two children is closely related to the different input they receive from their respective parents.

Thus, spontaneous production data can provide information regarding the overall course of language development, language-specific and family-specific aspects of the input, individual variation in the developmental path, and the discourse situations in which language learning takes place. One of the great advantages of collecting and using such data is that they can continue to provide an invaluable source of information regarding various morphological, syntactic, and semantic phenomena as new theoretical questions arise. This is readily attested by the frequent use of Brown's (1973) corpus and others in the CHILDES data bank. In addition, these corpora can provide much-needed information for designing experimental tasks to further tap aspects of linguistic competence. For example, children tend to use restrictive relative clauses in spontaneous speech, yet until Hamburger and Crain 1982, relative clause studies rarely used this type of context in testing children's ability to comprehend and produce relative clauses. As both statistical methods for examining linguistic corpora and connectionist models of learning become more sophisticated, the use of spontaneous production corpora will assume an even greater importance in addressing issues of how syntactic structures are acquired.

1.7 Conclusion

In conclusion, the use of spontaneous production data has had an enormous impact on the field of language acquisition. When carefully collected and coded, these data provide an extremely rich resource for investigating the nature of children's grammatical competence and are invaluable for evaluating hypotheses regarding the acquisition of syntax. The collection of new corpora continues today as emerging theoretical issues call for more data from a larger number of children and a wider range of languages. Recent advances in computer technology, plus the organizational efforts of researchers involved with the CHILDES data archive, provide affordable and widespread access for the use of existing corpora, as well as support for collecting, transcribing, and coding new data sets. These developments lay the groundwork for the continuing importance of spontaneous production corpora for the field of language acquisition.

Note

I thank Shanley Allen, Cecile McKee, and Clifton Pye for comments and discussion.

Chapter 2

Analyzing Children's Spontaneous Speech

Karin Stromswold

2.1 General Issues in Spontaneous Speech Studies

2.1.1 Introduction

Since at least the early part of the 20th century (e.g., Stern and Stern 1907; O'Shea 1907), researchers have investigated language acquisition by analyzing children's spontaneous speech. During the first half of this century, a number of psychologists kept diaries in which they recorded details about children's language development, particularly children's acquisition of vocabulary items. Starting in the early 1960s, researchers took advantage of the availability of inexpensive audio tape recorders and began to record and analyze children's spontaneous speech. Most of these studies were longitudinal, in-depth studies of a few children (e.g., Brown 1973; Bloom 1970, 1973; Clark 1978; Bowerman 1973, 1974; Kuczaj 1976). Working without the aid of computers, these researchers made remarkably rich, accurate, and robust discoveries about how children acquire syntax. In the 1980s the widespread availability of inexpensive computers and optical scanners made it possible to put into computer-readable format the transcripts of children's spontaneous speech collected by these and other researchers (see MacWhinney and Snow 1985 for a description of the Child Language Data Exchange System or CHILDES). The availability of computer-readable transcripts has greatly increased the number of researchers who use children's spontaneous speech data to refine or test theories about the acquisition of syntax.

Although computer-readable transcripts make it easier to use children's spontaneous speech data and make it possible to use these data in ways that are otherwise not feasible, they also make it easier for researchers to fail to notice important regularities in the acquisition of syntax and to (inadvertently) misuse spontaneous speech data in ways that aren't possible when transcripts are not computerized. Before computer-readable transcripts existed, researchers who used children's spontaneous speech data had no choice but to read all of the lines that children and adults said. The necessity of reading entire sections of transcripts meant that researchers made discoveries that they were not specifically looking for. It also decreased the chances of making certain types of errors. For example, when Brown (1973) used Adam, Eve, and Sarah's transcripts to investigate the acquisition of *be*, he could not simply use a computer to cull lines containing *be* allomorphs (e.g., *am, is, are, was, were*). Because Brown had to read entire sections of their transcripts, he knew the context of *be* utterances and could distinguish between utterances that were bona fide uses of *be* and those that were routines, imitations, speech errors, or possible mistranscriptions. Brown developed a sense of how frequent correct and incorrect uses of *be* were at different stages, even in those cases where he did not perform quantitative research to specify exactly *how* frequent a particular type of *be* utterance was. He discovered, for example, that some of the children's earliest uses of *be* are contracted forms of *be* (e.g., *it's*) and that these contracted forms may be unanalyzed units.

This chapter provides guidelines on how to use computer-readable transcripts of children's spontaneous speech to formulate and test theories of syntactic development. The goal of this chapter is to show how to take advantage of the power afforded by computer-readable transcripts, while avoiding the perils associated with this power. I will argue that most of the types of problems faced by researchers who investigate the acquisition of syntax by analyzing children's spontaneous speech are similar to the types of problems faced by researchers who conduct "real" experiments and, furthermore, that the types of factors that must be taken into consideration in order to do competent transcript-based research are similar to those required to do competent experimental work. Section 2.1 will deal with general issues surrounding the use of spontaneous speech transcripts, including its advantages and disadvantages. Section 2.2 will cover methodological concerns associated with analyzing errors in children's spontaneous speech, and section 2.3 will cover issues associated with analyzing the order in which children acquire various aspects of syntax.

2.1.2   Inherent Advantages and Limitations of Spontaneous Speech Studies

Most researchers investigating the acquisition of syntax seek to characterize the development of syntactic competence, rather than the development of performance factors that may influence or limit production. Unfortunately, no currently available method allows us to study competence directly in either the child or the adult. Perhaps the greatest advantage of using spontaneous speech to assess syntactic development is that, of all the methods currently available to language acquisition research, studies of spontaneous speech are the least likely to be affected by extraneous experimental task demands. This is particularly an advantage when investigating the earliest stages of acquisition.[1] Procedures such as those described by Thornton (chapter 4, this volume) that are used to elicit constructions may influence the utterances that children produce.[2] Tasks that involve assessing syntactic competence by assessing comprehension (e.g., act-out tasks, picture selection tasks) must address the possibility that children may understand an utterance without having mastered the aspect of syntax that is being assessed or that, conversely, children may fail to understand an utterance that is generated by their grammar because of additional task demands or limitations of their parser (e.g., see Stromswold 1995b for a discussion of the comprehension of *wh*-questions and Gropen et al. 1989 for a discussion of the comprehension of dative sentences).[3] Another advantage of spontaneous speech studies is that they are well suited for longitudinal studies of language acquisition. Cross-sectional investigations of syntax acquisition must deal with the practical and theoretical problems raised by the possibility that individual children may develop language at different rates and, perhaps, in different ways. Although, in theory, methods other than spontaneous speech studies can be used to study syntax acquisition longitudinally, in practice most researchers are concerned that repeated administration of the same test may influence children's performance on the test. Such problems do not arise for longitudinal spontaneous speech studies: because in spontaneous speech studies children are allowed to say and do whatever they want, one can record a child as many times as one wants.

One problem with using children's spontaneous speech to test theories about syntactic development is that it is possible that a child might simply choose not to produce a particular syntactic construction, even though she has acquired it (i.e., even though the construction can be generated by her grammar). With spontaneous speech studies, one may need to record many hours of speech in order to collect enough spontaneous examples of a syntactic construction to be able to analyze its acquisition. This is particularly likely for constructions that are rare in the input. The problem of what to do about syntactic constructions that children rarely use is alleviated somewhat if the transcripts of children's spontaneous speech are computerized. If the transcripts are computer-readable, researchers can use a computer to cull those lines that are likely to contain utterances that exhibit the aspect of syntax under investigation (see sections 2.1.4 and 2.2.2). Another way of getting around this problem is to use an elicitation procedure such as that outlined by Thornton (chapter 4, this volume) to prod children into producing syntactic constructions that they rarely produce spontaneously (but see note 2). Asking a child to judge the grammaticality of utterances is yet another way of teasing apart whether a child does not use a construction because it is not part of her grammar or because she chooses not to. Unfortunately, the task demands associated with eliciting grammaticality judgments are particularly high and, thus, grammaticality judgments generally cannot be used to investigate early syntactic development. (For methods of eliciting grammaticality judgments from children, see de Villiers and de Villiers 1974; chapter 11, this volume; and Stromswold 1990b.)

Sometimes the fact that children are able to say whatever they want makes it difficult for the researcher to figure out exactly what they actually say. Because transcripts of spontaneous speech provide only limited information about the phonetic form or nonlinguistic context of utterances, the problem of interpreting children's utterances is magnified if the person analyzing the transcripts does not have access to videotapes or audiotapes of the transcribed sessions (e.g., when researchers analyze CHILDES transcripts that they did not collect). The problem of interpreting a child's utterance is reduced if the range of possible topics is reduced, as is the case in elicited production and imitation studies. Another potential problem with spontaneous speech studies stems from the fact that most spontaneous speech studies are longitudinal investigations of the linguistic development of a small number of children. The implicit assumption underlying such studies is that the syntactic development of all children is essentially the same and, therefore, that it is perfectly acceptable to study just one or two children. The conclusions drawn from in-depth studies of a few children's spontaneous speech will be flawed if the assumption is incorrect and the syntactic development of the particular children being studied is unusual. If a large number of children are studied, one is less likely to encounter this problem. The availability of longitudinal, computer-readable transcripts of children's spontaneous speech makes it feasible for researchers to do in-depth longitudinal studies of many children.

2.1.3 Stating the Acquisitional Predictions Entailed by a Theory

The first step in using children's spontaneous speech data to test a theory is to determine what acquisitional predictions the theory entails. A theory may predict than children will make certain types of syntactic errors and not others, that children will acquire certain aspects of syntax before others (ordering predictions), or that children will acquire a number of aspects of syntax at the same time (clustering predictions). If one wants to use transcripts to *test* an acquisitional theory, the predictions entailed by the theory must be stated before one begins to examine children's transcripts: it is no more legitimate to examine a child's transcripts and then concoct a theory that is consistent with what is observed, than it is to look at the results of an experiment and then come up with a theory that is consistent with the results of the experiment. It is, of course, very useful and legitimate to examine the transcripts of a child's utterances to get some sense of the child's syntactic development and, in this sense, to use the transcripts to help formulate one's theory. However, any data that are used to help formulate a theory should not be taken as proof that the theory is correct. Minimally, either one should examine the transcripts of other children and determine whether their data are also consistent with one's theory, or one must enumerate other predictions that are entailed by the theory and determine whether the spontaneous speech data for the first child are consistent with these other predictions. The problem of post hoc analyses (i.e., devising or changing a theory *after* looking at the data; see chapter 14, this volume) seems to be much more pervasive in spontaneous speech studies than in experimental studies of syntactic development. The reason for this is probably that a researcher can examine children's spontaneous speech without having made any commitment about the acquisitional theory being tested (or even what aspect of syntax is under investigation), whereas in order to examine children's performance on an experimental task, the researcher must first design the task. The necessity of designing an experimental task forces the researcher to decide what aspects of syntactic development are under investigation, what theory is being tested, and what predictions are entailed by the theory.

2.1.4 Setting Criteria to Be Used in a Study

One must explicitly set certain aspects of the method to be used prior to beginning either a spontaneous speech study or an experimental study. For example, in traditional experimental studies, one must decide before beginning to test children what stimuli will be used, how many items will be included, what age children will be tested, and so on. The same types of methodological details should be specified before beginning a spontaneous speech study. Assuming that one has access to spontaneous speech data from more than one child, prior to beginning one must decide which children will be included in the study. One must also decide which of the children's utterances will be examined. If only a subset of a child's utterances will be analyzed, care must be taken to ensure that the utterances chosen are an unbiased sample (see section 2.2.4 for a description of one case in which the speech sample chosen inadvertently affected the results obtained). If a theory makes predictions that are testable in most multiword utterances (e.g., predictions about the order of subjects, verbs, and objects in children's utterances), one might choose to analyze every Nth multiword utterance, where the value of N will depend on the total number of utterances available in the transcripts. If the theory makes predictions that are manifested only in certain syntactic constructions (e.g., questions, passives, utterances containing pronouns), it may make sense to examine only those utterances that are likely to contain the syntactic construction under investigation. This can be done by using a simple computer program such as the UNIX utility "grep" (Grab Regular Expression Program) or the CLAN program "kwal" (Key Word and Line; see MacWhinney 1991) to cull all of the utterances that contain letter strings that are likely to be present in utterances that contain the syntactic construction. For example, if one is investigating the acquisition of questions, one could instruct a computer to pull any utterance said by a child that contains a question mark or a *wh*-word. As a general rule, if a computer is used to cull (potentially) relevant utterances, it is far safer to have the computer pull too many utterances (which must then be examined by hand) than too few. For example, if potential *who* questions are culled by searching for lines containing the string "[space]who[space]" rather than the string "who" then lines that contain such words as *whole* and *whoops* will correctly be excluded, but so will many relevant lines (e.g., lines containing strings such as *who's, whom, whose, who're, who'd, who've, who, ... who?*). Because electronic search programs simply pull those lines that contain *exactly* the string being searched for, they are very susceptible to inconsistencies or typographical errors in transcription (see Edwards 1992). One way to get around this potential problem is to use a computer program such as the CLAN frequency program "freq" to generate a list of all of the strings that appear in a transcript and then search this list for any possible variants of the form under investigation (e.g., see Edwards 1993, for a list of the variants of contracted *not* that appear in some versions of the CHILDES transcripts). Electronic searches should then be performed for all possible variants of the target string.

In almost every spontaneous speech study, one must establish criteria for determining whether an utterance is an imitation, a repetition, or a mumbled, unclear, or stuttered utterance. If one uses a computer program to cull utterances that are likely to contain the syntactic construction under investigation (instead of going through the entire transcript by hand looking for examples), it is a good idea to also examine the utterances before and after (potential) target utterances. This is easy to do if one uses a computer program such as the CLAN program "kwal" that can be instructed to pull a specified number of lines immediately preceding and following a target utterance. My experience has been that reading the two or three lines immediately preceding and following a target utterance is usually enough to clarify the meaning of unclear utterances and to identify imitations, repetitions, mistranscriptions, typographical errors, and the like. In analyses of children's spontaneous speech, one must decide whether to ignore or include children's utterances that may be imitations, routines, and so on. Great care must be taken to ensure that the criteria for including and excluding utterances do not (inadvertently) bias a study in a way that favors the hypothesis being tested. If it is impossible to establish criteria that are unbiased, the criteria should be established in a way that works *against* the hypothesis under investigation. Consider, for example, how the treatment of echo questions (e.g., Speaker 1: "I don't like fish"; Speaker 2: "You don't like fish?") might influence the results of an acquisitional study of subject-auxiliary inversion in yes/no questions. If echo questions are not eliminated, the rate at which children fail to invert in yes/no questions will be considerably higher than if echo questions are eliminated. Because echo questions are part of the adult grammar, it makes sense to eliminate any question where the context makes it clear that it is an echo question. What one should do in those cases where it is not clear from context depends on the predictions made by the theory under investigation. If the theory predicts children *will* fail to invert in yes/no questions, all unclear cases should be eliminated. If the theory predicts children will *not* fail to invert in yes/no questions, unclear cases should be retained.

2.1.5 Testing the Statistical Significance of Acquisitional Findings
Whenever possible, statistical tests should be performed on the results of spontaneous speech studies. Spontaneous speech studies must include a large enough number of children and a large enough sample of utterances per child for statistical tests to have sufficient power. How many children must be included in a study depends on the complexity or richness of the predictions being tested, the types of statistical tests being performed, and the size and uniformity of the effect being measured. Consider, for example, a theory that makes the simple prediction that children will acquire construction A before construction B. Because there are two possible orderings of A and B (A > B, B > A), the probability that any single child will have the acquisitional ordering A > B *by chance alone* is 50%. If, however, 5 children are examined and all 5 children acquire A before B, the probability that this is the result of chance alone is less that 5% ($p = .5^5 = .031$). Fewer children will be required if more complicated predictions are being tested. Consider, for example, a theory that predicts children will acquire construction A before construction B and construction B before construction C (order of acquisition: A > B > C). Because there are six different possible orderings of A, B, and C,[4] the probability that any single child will have the acquisitional ordering A > B > C (by chance alone) is 1/6. The probability (by chance alone) that 2 children will have exactly this acquisitional ordering is $(1/6)^2 = .028$.

In the examples just given, the possibility that constructions might be acquired simultaneously was not considered. In some cases it may be appropriate to consider this possibility. For example, if the acquisitional theory being tested entails the prediction that several constructions will be acquired at the same time, it may be appropriate to consider simultaneous acquisition when enumerating the possible orders of acquisition. For example, when simultaneous acquisition is considered, there are exactly three possible patterns of acquisition for two constructions (A > B; B > A; A = B) and, therefore, the probability (by chance alone) that a single child will acquire A before B is 1/3 or .33. If 3 children are studied and all 3 acquire A before B, this result would be statistically significant ($p = .33^3 = .037$). Because when simultaneous acquisition is considered, there are 13 possible acquisitional ordering for three constructions,[5] the probability (by chance alone) that even a single child will exhibit a particular order is quite small ($p = 1/13 = .077$). If one studies 2 children and both children acquire the three constructions in the same order, this would be unlikely to occur by chance alone ($p = .077^2 = .006$). When simultaneous acquisition is considered, there are 75 possible orderings for four constructions and, hence, it is quite unlikely (by chance alone) that even a single child would exhibit the particular order predicted by one's theory ($p = 1/75 = .013$).[6]

In the example given above, nonparametric statistical tests were performed. The main advantage of nonparametric statistical tests is that it is less important to know the shape of the population distribution from which the data are drawn (see Snedecor and Cochran 1980). If one can determine the age of acquisition of constructions A and B (rather than just the relative order of acquisition of the two constructions) and these ages appear to be (at least approximately) normally distributed, more flexible and powerful parametric tests (e.g., a t test) can be used to determine whether children acquired construction A significantly before construction B. The number of subjects required for results to reach statistical significance with parametric tests depends on how different the means of the groups are (i.e., fewer subjects will be needed if the mean ages of acquisition of constructions A and B are very different) and how much variability exists within the groups (i.e., fewer subjects will be needed if all of the children acquire the constructions at approximately the same age). If an acquisitional theory makes predictions about the order of acquisition of more than two constructions, then a series of paired t tests or an analysis of variance can be used. (For a more detailed discussion of the uses and limitations of several commonly used statistical tests, see chapter 14, this volume.)

2.1.6   Ruling Out Plausible Alternative Accounts

Even if statistical tests reveal that one's acquisitional findings are statistically significant, one must consider alternative explanations for why these results might have been obtained. The specific alternative explanations that should be considered will depend on the specific theories under investigation (see sections 2.2.5 and 2.3.3). To get a sense of how input characteristics, sampling biases, pragmatic factors, cognitive factors, processing/performance factors, and other linguistic factors might result in a certain set of findings, consider the following example.[7] Borer and Wexler (1987, 1992) have argued that the ability to form (nontrivial) A-chains must mature and, therefore, that before a certain age, children cannot produce constructions that require NP-movement. Because passive sentences are generally believed to require (nontrivial) NP-movement and active sentences do not, one prediction entailed by Borer and

Wexler's theory is that children should acquire passive sentences later than they acquire active sentences. Consistent with Borer and Wexler's theory, Bever (1970), de Villiers and de Villiers (1973), and others have reported that children acquire *by* passives (e.g., *The cat was chased by the dog*) significantly later than active sentences (e.g., *The dog chased the cat*). Before it can be concluded that Borer and Wexler are correct, a number of alternative explanations must be considered (and ruled out). Children might acquire actives before *by* passives because they hear considerably fewer examples of *by* passives than actives (an *input account*). Children might (appear to) acquire actives before *by* passives because they use active sentences much more frequently than *by* passives and, therefore, samples of their speech are more likely to include examples of actives than *by* passives (a *sampling account*). Children might acquire passives later than actives because the pragmatic/discourse factors governing when passives are appropriate are more complex or restrictive than those involved for actives (a *pragmatic account*). If more resources are required to produce longer sentences and these resources are restricted in the child, children would acquire actives before *by* passives because actives have two fewer words (a *performance account*). Some other linguistic aspect of passives might explain why children acquire *by* passives after they acquire actives. For example, children may have to learn the special case and/or thematic properties of *by* (an *alternative linguistic account*). (For a more complete description and analysis of children's passives, see Stromswold 1989c; Stromswold and Snyder 1995; Snyder and Stromswold, to appear.)

2.2 Error Analyses

Much of what is known about the acquisition of syntax has come from analyses of the errors children make in their spontaneous speech as they are acquiring language. For example, the observation that children regularize the irregular morphological forms of their language (e.g., saying *eated* for *ate*, or *mouses* for *mice*) was one of the first pieces of evidence put forth to support the notion that children use rules for generating inflected forms and do not simply memorize the forms that they hear (e.g., Berko 1958; Brown 1973). More recently the frequency and types of regularized inflected forms that occur in children's spontaneous speech have been taken as evidence for symbolic, rule-based architectures (e.g., Pinker and Prince 1988) and nonsymbolic connectionist architectures (e.g., Rumelhart and McClelland 1987). Similarly, over the years the frequency with which and the linguistic situations in which children fail to invert subject and auxiliaries (e.g., saying "*Why I can't eat more cookies?" rather than "Why can't I eat more cookies?") have been taken as evidence for a derivational theory of language (e.g., Bellugi 1971; Klima and Bellugi 1966), evidence for the VP-internal subject hypothesis (e.g., Déprez and Pierce 1993; but see Stromswold 1995a), evidence for an innate distinction between lexical and auxiliary verbs (e.g., Stromswold 1990b, 1994), and (partial) evidence for a distinction between theta-government and antecedent government of traces (Stromswold 1988b, 1990b).

2.2.1 Errors of Omission and Errors of Commission

Utterances that are ungrammatical because an obligatory element is omitted (*errors of omission*) should be distinguished from utterances that are ungrammatical because an element that is present in the utterance is used incorrectly (*errors of commission*). Examples of errors of omission include utterances such as "*She eating candy," "*Want candy," "*Dog is climbing tree." At least intuitively, each of these utterances is ungrammatical because one or more obligatory elements have been omitted. If the missing obligatory elements were replaced, the resulting utterance would be acceptable. Errors of omission are particularly problematic for researchers because it is possible that the child knows that they are not acceptable, but because of performance limitations, he is unable to produce all of the constituents he knows are required. In errors of commission, an utterance contains one or more elements that are used incorrectly. Examples of errors of commission include utterances that have misplaced elements (e.g., "*Why she is happy?"), utterances that contain elements that are not needed (e.g., "*Did she be happy?"), utterances that contain an incorrect form of an element (e.g., "*She doed that," "*Me want candy," "*Did she went to the store?"). Adding an element (or even several elements) to such utterances will not make the resulting sentences grammatical. Children's errors of commission can also be problematic because it is possible that they do not occur because children have a different type of grammar than adults, but instead are caused by the same mechanisms that cause adults to occasionally make speech errors.

2.2.2 Predicted and Observed Errors

To test an acquisitional theory by examining the errors children make in spontaneous speech, the researcher must begin by specifying the types of errors that the theory predicts should and should not occur in children's

Table 2.1
Using children's patterns of errors to test hypotheses

	Error predicted to occur	Error predicted not to occur
Error present in transcripts	A (Predicted error observed)	B (Inexplicable error)
Error absent from transcripts	C (Predicted error missing)	D (Predicted nonoccurring error)

spontaneous speech. Only once these predictions have been specified should the researcher examine children's transcripts to determine what types of errors children do and do not make. Table 2.1 shows the relationship between observed and predicted errors. To the extent that children make the errors that a theory predicts should occur (cell A in table 2.1) *and* children do not make the errors that the theory predicts should not occur (cell D), results of children's error analyses are consistent with the acquisitional theory. By contrast, if children do not make the kinds of errors the theory predicts they should make (cell C in table 2.1) *or* if children do make errors that the theory predicts they should not make (cell B), the acquisitional theory may not be correct.

Notice that in terms of testing the validity of an acquisitional theory, the errors that children do not make (henceforth, *nonoccurring errors*) can be just as informative as the errors that children do make (henceforth, *occurring errors*). Although occurring and nonoccurring errors may be equally informative, they are not equally obvious to the researcher. If a researcher is proficient in the language a child is acquiring, he or she can readily detect a child's errors merely by noticing when the child's utterances are different from what an adult speaker of the language would say. Nonoccurring errors are more difficult to detect because the researcher must look for the *absence* of a particular type of error. Furthermore, the types of errors that will count as nonoccurring errors (if they are absent) will depend on the theory being tested. Consider the types of errors predicted by two theories of the acquisition of English lexical verbs (e.g., *run, eat, drink*) and auxiliary verbs (e.g., the modals *can, could, will,* and *would,* the *do* in *I do not wash windows,* the *is* in *She is smiling,* the *have* in *They have eaten the cookies*). In English the properties of auxiliary verbs are similar to those of lexical verbs in some ways, but not in others (see Stromswold 1990b). Children could notice the similarities between lexical verbs and auxiliary verbs, and form a single Verb category that encompasses both types of verbs (*single Verb theory*). If they do, they should treat auxiliaries and lexical verbs alike. If children generalize the behavior of auxiliary verbs to lexical verbs, we would expect to find them failing to inflect lexical verbs (e.g., "*She run"), permitting multiple lexical verbs to appear in a single sentence (e.g., "*She wants goes"), permitting the negative marker *not* to appear after lexical verbs (e.g., "*She eats not cookies"), and inverting lexical verbs ("*What eats she for supper?").[8] If children notice the differences between auxiliary and lexical verbs, then instead of forming a single Verb category, they might form distinct auxiliary and lexical Verb categories (*distinct Verb theory*). If they do, they should not invert or negate lexical verbs or allow multiple lexical verbs to appear in a single sentential clause. Notice that the single Verb theory predicts that children *will* invert and negate lexical verbs, whereas the distinct Verb theory predicts that children will not make these sorts of errors. If children do invert and negate lexical verbs, this finding is evidence for the single Verb theory (cell A) and against the distinct Verb theory (cell B). If, on the other hand, children do not invert or negate lexical verbs, this finding is evidence for the distinct Verb theory (cell D) and against the single Verb theory (cell C). (For a longer discussion of the generalizations children might make about the behavior of auxiliaries and the generalizations they actually make, see Stromswold 1989b, 1990b.)

2.2.3 When Is an Error Worth Explaining? The Denominator Problem

In section 2.2.2 an implicit assumption was that any ungrammatical utterance said by a child is the result of the child's grammar being different from the adult grammar. Although having a grammar different from the adult grammar is one possible source of children's errors, errors may be the result of children's stuttering, repeating, hesitating, restarting, or (partially) imitating an utterance, or adults' mishearing, mistranscribing, or misinterpreting children's grammatical utterances. By carefully examining the context in which errors are produced, the researcher may be able to eliminate many such cases. However, even when great care is taken, it may not be possible to determine why a child produced an ungrammatical utterance. When in doubt, the researcher should err on the side of caution and systematically discard or retain such cases, choosing the option that works against the theory being tested: if the theory predicts that a particular questionable error will occur, the error should be discarded; if the theory predicts that the questionable error should not occur, the error should be retained.

What should we make of an error than occurs only once or twice in a child's transcripts? Does such a mistake provide a rare glimpse into the structure of a child's "internalized" language (I-language) or is it just the result of the child's being, for example, distracted or tired? The more frequent a particular error, the more likely it is to result from the child's having a grammar different from the adult grammar. It is not sufficient merely count the number of times a child makes a particular type of error in a transcript or even to calculate what percentage of the child's utterances contain the particular type of error. Rather, one must determine how likely the child is to make a particular error *relative to* the number of opportunities the child had to make the error. In other words, error rates should be calculated by dividing the number of times a child makes a type of error (the numerator) by the number of opportunities the child had to make that type of error (the denominator). In calculating error rates, one must decide what denominator is the most appropriate to use. The following example demonstrates the importance of choosing the appropriate denominator. In his 33rd transcript (at age 3;6), Adam (Brown 1973) failed to invert the subject and auxiliary in four *wh*-questions ("Why you won't let me fly?", Why de tail is gon to break # huh?", "Why your hand is out like that?", "Why he can exercise it [?]?"). In this transcript Adam said a total of 832 utterances, and 178 of these utterances contained a *wh*-word. Thus, *wh*-questions without subject-auxiliary inversion constitute approximately 0.6% (4/832) of all of Adam's utterances and approximately 2.3% (4/178) of Adam's utterances that contain a *wh*-word. However, one could argue that the denominator should not include *wh*-questions that lack an auxiliary (e.g., "What you eat for dinner?"), *wh*-questions that lack a subject (e.g., "What do eat for dinner?"), embedded *wh*-questions (e.g., "Do you know what you can eat for dinner?"), or subject *wh*-questions (e.g., "Who can stay for dinner?") because such questions do not represent opportunities in which Adam could have failed to invert in *wh*-questions.[9] A more appropriate denominator is the number of nonsubject matrix *wh*-questions that Adam asked that contained an auxiliary in either inverted or noninverted position (i.e., questions such as "What she can eat?" and "What can she eat?"). Adam asked only 27 such questions and, thus, he failed to invert in almost 15% (4/27) of his matrix *wh*-questions. He correctly inverted subject and auxiliary in only one matrix *why* question ("Why is dat breaking?"), giving him an inversion error rate of 80% (4/5) for *why* questions.

Another example of the importance of choosing the correct denominator involves analyses of children's double-tensed questions (e.g., "*Did you came home?"). No one denies that children make double-tensing errors. Furthermore, no one denies that children seem to make these errors more frequently in some contexts (e.g., questions with irregular past tense verbs) than in others. The debate concerns the significance of these errors, and the significance of these errors depends critically on their frequency. Some researchers (e.g., Hurford 1975; Fay 1978; Mayer, Erreich, and Valian 1978) have argued that double-tensed questions are evidence that the transformation that moves the auxiliary to sentence-initial position is actually composed of two basic operations, a "copy" operation (which copies the element into its S-structure position) followed by a "delete" operation (which deletes the element from its D-structure position); double-tensing errors result when children correctly perform the copy operation but fail to perform the delete operation. Other researchers (e.g., Kuczaj 1976; Maratsos and Kuczaj 1978; Maratsos 1984; Prideaux 1976; Goodluck and Solan 1979; Stromswold 1989a, 1990a,b) have argued that double-tensing errors are less frequent than a copy-without-deletion theory would predict.[10] For example, in my analyses of the CHILDES transcripts of 12 children, I found that only between 0.04% and 0.4% of the questions that contained a verb were double-tensed (Stromswold 1989a, 1990a,b). (For a possible account of why children make double-tensing errors, and why they tend to occur in certain contexts, see section 2.2.5.)

2.2.4   Statistical Analyses of Error Data

The type of statistical tests that should be performed on children's error data will depend on the particular spontaneous speech study that has been conducted. If a study is designed to test a prediction that different types of errors will occur with different frequencies, a chi-square test could be used to analyze the results for individual children. If the study includes enough children, it may be possible to perform sign tests or t tests on the children's data. If a theory predicts that children will make a certain type of error more during one developmental stage than another, chi-square tests, sign tests, or t tests can be used to determine whether the developmental pattern of errors conforms to the prediction. If one wants to determine whether children make a certain type of error significantly more often during one developmental stage than another, one must have a criterion for determining when the two developmental stages begin and end that is *independent* of the frequency with which the children make the particular error. It is not legitimate to examine the data, find the point at which the error becomes more (or less) frequent, and say that this is the demarcation point between developmental stages.[11] What criterion should be used to decide when one stage ends and another begins will depend on the particular study that is being conducted. For example, developmental stages might be defined in terms of mean length of utterance, age, the appearance of a particular type of error, construction, or aspect of syntax (e.g., embedded clauses, long-distance questions, overregularization), or mastery of a particular aspect of syntax (e.g., using a particular grammatical morpheme in 90% of obligatory contexts; see Brown 1973).

To get a sense of how error data might be analyzed, consider the prediction made by Bellugi (1971) about relative rates of subject-auxiliary inversion in yes/no questions and *wh*-questions. Bellugi noticed that one child (Brown's Adam) seemed to invert in yes/no questions but not in *wh*-questions. Bellugi argued that this reflected the fact that, within the transformational theory of the time (Chomsky 1957), the formation of yes/no questions involves only one transformation (the transformation that moves the auxiliary to presubject position), whereas the formation of *wh*-questions requires two transformations (one to move the auxiliary to presubject position and one to move the *wh*-word to sentence-initial position). Bellugi argued that performing transformations was taxing for children and predicted that all children should go through a developmental stage during which they correctly invert in yes/no questions, but fail to invert in *wh*-questions. In order to test Bellugi's hypothesis, I analyzed the CHILDES transcripts of 13 children and determined the number of times each child asked matrix yes/no and *wh*-questions with inverted and uninverted auxiliaries (Stromswold 1989b, 1990b, 1994). Contrary to Bellugi's prediction that all children should invert auxiliaries in yes/no questions more frequently than in *wh*-questions, individual chi-square tests (or where appropriate Fisher Exact tests) performed on each child's data revealed that 3 children inverted significantly more often in yes/no questions than in *wh*-questions, 4 children inverted significantly more often in *wh*-questions than in yes/no questions, and 6 children were equally likely to invert in yes/no and *wh*-questions. Of the 7 children who had different rates of inversion for yes/no and *wh*-questions, 3 inverted more frequently in yes/no questions ($p > .10$ by sign test). Similarly, across children, parametric statistics revealed no significant difference in the rate of inversion for yes/no and *wh*-questions ($t(12) = .40$, $p > .10$). I also looked for developmental trends in the children's rate of inversion for yes/no questions and *wh*-questions and found that none of the children went through a stage during which they inverted auxiliaries in yes/no questions but not in *wh*-questions. Although I did not find any differences for yes/no and *wh*-questions, I did find differences in rates of inversion in argument and adjunct *wh*-questions (auxiliaries were inverted significantly less often in adjunct questions) and for different types of auxiliaries (e.g., negated auxiliaries, modal auxiliaries, and copula *be* were inverted substantially less often than other auxiliaries). By going back and determining which transcripts Bellugi examined and by reexamining Adam's data for those transcripts, I discovered that the reason Bellugi thought Adam always inverted in yes/no questions but rarely inverted in *wh*-questions is that in the sample of Adam's transcripts that she analyzed, most of Adam's *wh*-questions were *why* questions and other adjunct questions and many of these adjunct questions contained negated auxiliaries (e.g., "Why I can't go to the store?").

2.2.5 Ruling Out Plausible Alternative Accounts

Even if statistical analyses reveal that the patterns of errors made by children are statistically significant, before one can conclude that children have a different grammar than adults, other alternative explanations for the pattern of errors must be considered. The specific alternative explanations that must be ruled out will depend on the particular theory under investigation. The researcher should consider the possibility that the results obtained merely reflect the types of input children receive (*input accounts*). If, for example, children hear more examples of construction A than construction B, it would not be surprising if they make more mistakes on construction B. The commonly reported phenomenon of children referring to themselves by their own name or by the pronoun *you* might be considered special cases of the effect of input. The researcher should also attempt to rule out the possibility that the results obtained are actually just a reflection of the number of opportunities children have for making a particular error or of a particular error's detectability (*sampling accounts*). The first type of sampling account can be ruled out by using the rate of errors *relative to* the number of possible opportunities for errors (see section 2.2.3), rather than using the absolute number of errors (or the rate of errors relative to all utterances). More difficult to rule out is the possibility that certain types of children's errors appear to be more frequent because they are more detectable to the person transcribing the tape (because they are more acoustically salient, they change the meaning of an utterance, etc.).

According to *performance accounts*, children produce errors because their ability to produce utterances is more limited than adults', not because they have a different grammar than adults (i.e., children's errors reflect differences in performance rather than differences in competence or I-language). Although performance accounts could explain some apparent errors of commission (e.g., a child who intends to say "I wonder what she is eating?" and instead says "*What she is eating?"), performance constraints are most likely to cause errors of omission. Researchers who believe that children have adultlike functional projections even in the earliest stages of language acquisition sometimes explain young children's frequent omissions of grammatical morphemes in terms of limitations on performance. Consider, for example, three possible explanations for why children produce matrix questions that lack auxiliaries (e.g., "What Cookie Monster eats?"), an error than Brown (1968, 1973) found to be quite frequent in Adam, Eve, and Sarah's early transcripts. These errors might result from children's failing to raise the verb (i.e., a special type of failing to invert subject and auxiliary) or from their thinking that auxiliaries are optional in matrix questions. Alternatively, like the adult grammar, children's grammars might generate only questions such as "What does Cookie Monster eat?", but occasionally constraints on performance might cause children to fail to say the auxiliary (e.g., "What Cookie Monster eat?"). The fact that when children omit auxiliary *do* in questions, they usually overtly tense the lexical verb (e.g., "What Cookie Monster eats?") suggests that auxiliary-less questions result from their failing to verb-raise, rather than from their having a performance constraint or a grammar in which auxiliaries are optional in matrix questions (see Stromswold 1990a,b).

Some of children's apparent errors might be the result of their imitating adult utterances.[12] For example, if the child imitates the embedded clause of the adult question "Do you know what Cookie Monster eats?", the result will be a question that looks like it lacks *do*-support but contains an inflected lexical verb ("What Cookie Monster eats?"). Similarly, if the child imitates the embedded clause of the adult question "Do you know what Cookie Monster can eat?", the child's resulting utterance will look like an example of failure to invert subject and auxiliary. Unless researchers examine the contexts of children's errors, they will not recognize that these errors are the result of children's partially imitating adult utterances. Certain (apparent) errors could arise because the transcriber or researcher has misunderstood or misinterpreted what a child intended an utterance to mean. For example, if the child says "No I want salad" to indicate that he would prefer to have a salad rather than spinach, but the researcher interprets this utterance to mean 'I don't want salad', the researcher will incorrectly count the child's grammatical utterance as an example of ungrammatical, sentence-initial negation (see Bloom 1970; de Villiers and de Villiers 1979; Stromswold 1995a).[13] Examples of apparent errors of commission can also occur when a child hesitates, corrects, or recasts a sentence in the middle of the utterance. For example, if the transcriber does not reliably indicate retraced utterances, a researcher could erroneously take an utterance such as "I want that - these cookies" as evidence that a child has not mastered basic restrictions on determiners. Similarly, the self-corrected utterance "I did - will clean my room" could erroneously be taken as evidence that a child has not learned what combinations of auxiliaries are allowed in English.

Children might occasionally speak ungrammatically for the same reasons that adults occasionally speak ungrammatically. Clearly, children should not be expected to be any less error-prone than adults and, to the extent that their processing/performance abilities are more limited than those of adults, children might make more speech errors than adults. If speech errors occur because processing/performance capacities are exceeded, the frequency of children's speech errors might be greater for more complex constructions than for less complex constructions. Furthermore, to the extent that there are regularities in the types of speech errors that appear, one cannot assume that children's ungrammatical utterances that result from speech errors are randomly distributed and merely add noise to error data. (For a discussion of regularities in adult speech errors and what they reveal about adult language processing, see Garrett 1980.) Some errors might reflect children's knowledge or beliefs or their cognitive capacity (*cognitive accounts*). For example, if a child thinks the sun is alive and sentient (or if she pretends that it is), she might use the pronoun *he, she,* or *who* to refer to the sun, rather than the pronoun *it* or *what.* Patterns of errors might also reflect pragmatic or discourse effects (*pragmatic accounts*). For example, Hyams (1986) has argued that the reason very young English-speaking children frequently omit grammatical subjects is that they think that English, like Italian, does not require phonetically realized subjects (a *linguistic account*). Other researchers (e.g., Bloom

1993) have argued that children produce sentences without overt subjects because their capacity for producing morphemes is limited (i.e., a performance constraint): children omit subjects more frequently than objects or verbs because it is easier to use the context of an utterance to infer the subject of a sentence than the object or verb of a sentence (a *pragmatic account*).

Finally, linguistic factors other than those under investigation could cause children to make a particular type of error (*alternative linguistic accounts*). Children's syntax may be identical to that of adults, but because they have not mastered specific aspects of lexical items, they make certain types of errors that appear to be syntactic. For example, children could use count noun syntax with mass nouns (e.g., *two milks*) because they have yet to acquire the syntax required of count and mass nouns, or because they think *milk* is a count noun (i.e., *milk* means 'a container of milk"). Similarly, children who have mastered the syntax of datives and the semantic and phonological restrictions under which verbs can appear in double object dative constructions could still make dative alternation errors if the lexical entries for particular verbs are incorrect. For example, if children mispronounce or have incorrect meanings for the verbs *donate* or *whisper*, they might produce utterances such as "*She donated him the painting" or "*She whispered him the secret" (Gropen et al. 1989). Gropen et al. (1991) have also proposed that one reason children make errors such as "*I poured the glass with water" is that they erroneously think that the word *pour* means 'fill'. Children's errors (particularly their errors of commission) might also be the result of incorrectly or incompletely parsing adult utterances. Noticing that double-tensing errors often involve irregular verbs (e.g., "*Did you came home?"), a number of researchers (e.g., Maratsos 1984; Maratsos and Kuczaj 1978; Stromswold 1990a,b) have argued that these errors result from children's incorrectly analyzing verbs like *came* as being infinitival forms, not past tense forms. In a similar vein, noting that many of the purported examples of copying without deletion (virtually all of the examples in declarative sentences) involve *didn't* (e.g., "*Didn't I kicked the ball?" or "*I didn't kicked the ball"), researchers have suggested that these errors result from children's incorrectly analyzing *didn't* as simply being a negation marker, rather than correctly analyzing it as an irregular past tense auxiliary verb. The finding that the frequency of double-tensed sentences with irregular verbs or *didn't* is greater than would be expected based on the frequency of these verbs in the children's transcripts suggests that children utter double-tensed sentences not because they have a different grammar than adults or copy without deleting but because they have misanalyzed particular lexical items (Stromswold 1990a,b).[14]

2.3 Patterns of Acquisition

Studies of children's syntactic errors such as those reported in section 2.2 can simultaneously be too sensitive and too crude as indicators of the nature of children's syntax. As was just discussed, error analyses may be too sensitive in that having a different grammar is only one possible cause of children's errors. Looking at errors can also be too crude an indicator of children's grammars because children's errors only show us cases in which children's grammars differ from the adult grammar in ways that result in errors. By examining the acquisitional time course for the various aspects of syntax, one may be able to learn how children's grammars develop. For example, consider how studying *acquisitional clusters* in auxiliary and lexical verbs could shed light on the types of categories children form. One could determine whether all members of an auxiliary subtype exhibit certain linguistic behaviors at the same time. One could also determine whether auxiliaries that are acquired late immediately exhibit all of the traits associated with that subtype, or whether these traits have to be learned anew for each auxiliary. If, for example, a child is willing to generalize what he knows about the auxiliary *does* to the auxiliaries *do* and *did*, then he should acquire auxiliary *do*, *does*, and *did* at about the same age and he should begin to use all three forms of auxiliary *do* in the same contexts (e.g., inverted or negated contexts) at approximately the same age. In effect, clusterings in the acquisition of auxiliaries provide clues about children's grammar. Which particular clusterings we predict we will find depends on which of the divisions of auxiliaries (and lexical verbs) we predict children will consider (see section 2.2.2). If, for example, children make no distinction between auxiliaries and lexical verbs, we would predict that they would acquire all the auxiliaries and lexical verbs at the same time. A more refined prediction would be that children would acquire auxiliary and lexical verb homophones (e.g., lexical and auxiliary *do*) at the same time. If, instead, children distinguish between lexical verbs and auxiliaries, but make no further divisions within the auxiliary verbs, we would not predict acquisitional clustering for auxiliary and lexical verb homophones, but we would expect clustering of all of the auxiliary verbs. Studying *acquisitional orders* of auxiliary and lexical verbs could also shed light on children's grammars. For example, if a theory entails that children cannot learn the specific behavior of auxiliaries in their language until they have learned how lexical verbs are marked for tense and aspect in the language, the theory would predict that children will acquire lexical verbs before auxiliary verbs.

2.3.1   Measures of Acquisition

Researchers who investigate acquisitional orders and clusters must choose the criterion they will use for determining when a child has acquired a component of syntax. What criterion is most appropriate will depend on the particular study and aspect of syntax under investigation. The most important aspects of establishing which criterion will be used are (1) to make the decision *prior* to looking at the data and (2) to choose a criterion that is not biased to give results consistent with one's hypothesis. One criterion for acquisition that is frequently used is *mastery*, defined as the percentage of the time a child correctly uses an aspect of syntax when it is obligatory. The particular percentage required varies, but the general idea is to establish a certain percentage as a cutoff above which a child is said to have acquired whatever is under investigation. The particular percentage required is arbitrary. There is nothing magical about 90% correct use in obligatory context (the percentage used in Brown 1973), 75% (the percentage used in a large number of studies), or 50%. Language is not a fixed-choice experiment where there are a finite number of possible choices that can be made.[15] However, this implicit assumption seems to underlie many researchers' choice of 90% or 75% correct use in obligatory contexts. What these researchers fail to realize is that there are an infinite number of choices a child could make about use of a construction, inflection, and so on. All the child has to demonstrate is that she uses the aspect of syntax only where it is required. Imagine, for example, a child who only uses the -*ed* form in 10% of obligatory contexts. One could argue that if she uses -*ed* only to mark the past tense on verbs and never applies it to an adjective, noun, adverb, and so on, she has acquired the past tense inflection, even though in 90% of the cases where it is required, she does not use it.[16] One problem with using measures of mastery as the criterion for acquisition is deciding what cutoff to use. In addition, if one is interested in the acquisition of a particular type of syntactic construction (e.g., passives, long-distance questions, datives), mastery measures cannot be used because it is never obligatory to use a particular construction.

When mastery measures cannot be used, one can examine when children use particular constructions to determine when they acquire these constructions. It is an empirical question how many times (or how frequently) a child must use a construction before the child should be given credit for having acquired the construction. I examined when 12 children in the CHILDES database first used, repeatedly used, and regularly used *for* infinitivals, exceptional case-marking constructions, double object datives, questions with preposition stranding, and passives with preposition stranding (Stromswold 1989c). For the purposes of the three measures, only utterances that were clear (i.e., not stuttered) were included, and both imitations and routines were excluded. Age of first use was defined as the age at which a child first used a clear, novel example of a construction. Age of repeated use was the age by which a construction either had appeared five times or had appeared twice in one month, whichever occurred earlier. Age of regular use was the age at which a child began to use a construction regularly. This was determined by graphing the number of occurrences of a construction and visually inspecting the graph for points of inflection. For all five of these constructions, all three measures of acquisition were very highly correlated (all r's > .85, all p's < .01).

None of these measures is perfect. The age of first use is the most sensitive measure of acquisition because it measures the earliest age at which a child could be said to have acquired a construction. As such, it should be less affected by performance constraints than measures of acquisition that require repeated or regular use of a construction. It is possible, however, that the first use of a particular construction is actually a speech error, an unanalyzed routine, or an imitation. These possibilities can be minimized—but not eliminated—by checking the context of children's utterances. An advantage of measures of acquisition that require repeated or regular use is that they are less susceptible to the problem of children's being given undue credit for speech errors, unanalyzed routines, and the like. The limitation of such measures is that for relatively rare constructions (e.g., embedded questions), requiring regular or repeated use may inflate the age of acquisition or, in the case of extremely rare constructions (e.g., long-distance *wh*-questions), the child may not qualify as having acquired a construction for years after having clearly used it. (For further discussion, see Stromswold 1989c, 1990b.)

2.3.2   Testing Acquisitional Ordering and Clustering Predictions

Correlations, sign tests, and t tests can be used to test the acquisitional predictions about whether children acquire various aspects of syntax in a certain order (*ordering predictions*) or at the same time (*clustering predictions*). If a theory makes clustering predictions, it may be useful to characterize the amount of time that elapses between the acquisition of two constructions and not to distinguish between acquiring construction A x months before construction B and acquiring B x months before A. The term *temporal gap* can be used to refer to the absolute difference between the ages of acquisition of two constructions. If the acquisition of two constructions is significantly *correlated*, roughly speaking, there is a relationship between the ages of acquisition for the two constructions such that knowledge about the age of acquisition of one construction can be used to predict at better than chance level the age of acquisition of the second construction. If two constructions are acquired at approximately the same age, the two constructions can be said to be acquired *concurrently*. In general, if two constructions are acquired concurrently (i.e., if they form an acquisitional cluster), there should be no significant difference in the ages of acquisition for the constructions, the ages of acquisition will be correlated with one another, and the temporal gap between the ages will be small.[17]

If two constructions depend on exactly the same language-specific properties, there should be a significant correlation between the ages of acquisition for the two constructions. In addition, the two constructions should be acquired concurrently. Thus, one would not expect to find that one of the two constructions is consistently acquired before the other (as measured by a sign test), nor would one expect to find a significant difference in the ages of acquisition for the two constructions (as measured by a t test). One would also expect that if any time elapses between the acquisition of the first construction and the acquisition of the second, this temporal gap will be small. On the other hand, if two constructions share one property (X), but differ in that only one of the constructions depends on the acquisition of a second property (Y), then one still might expect to find a significant correlation between the ages of acquisition for the two constructions, but one would make an additional prediction: the construction that requires only property X should be acquired either before, or at the same time as, the construction that requires both property X and property Y. Assuming that the acquisition of properties X and Y is freely ordered, and hence that property X will be acquired before property Y approximately half of the time, one would expect the acquisition of the two constructions to exhibit an ordering effect in which both the sign test and the t test reveal significant differences in the ages of acquisition for the two constructions. Finally, if two constructions have no properties in common, then one would not expect to find a significant correlation in the ages of acquisition for the two constructions. One also would not (necessarily) expect to find that the two constructions are acquired concurrently. One would not be surprised if there was a large temporal gap in the acquisition of the two constructions, or if there were significant differences (measured by sign and t tests) in the ages of acquisition for the two constructions.

2.3.3   Ruling Out Plausible Alternative Accounts

Before an observed ordering effect between two constructions can be interpreted, one needs to evaluate the possibility that the order is an effect of frequency rather than acquisition of syntactic knowledge (*input account*). If frequency in the input affects age of acquisition, then children who hear many examples of construction A should acquire construction A at a relatively early age and children who hear few examples of construction A should acquire it at a later age. In other words, the input account predicts that the age of acquisition of two constructions will be significantly correlated with the relative frequency of these constructions in the input. Apparent ordering effects may merely be the result of sampling two constructions that occur with different frequencies (*sampling account*). The logic goes as follows: if a child uses three times more examples of construction A than construction B, then even if the child acquires both constructions at the same age, when one searches the transcripts, one has a 75% chance of coming across an example of construction A before coming across an example of construction B (i.e., $p_i = p(A|A \cup B) = .75$). Although this is certainly true for a single child, if one studies many children and all of the children acquire construction A before construction B, then the likelihood that differences in frequency in the output account for the ordering becomes much smaller. If, for example, one studies 11 children and all 11 children use three times as many examples of construction A as construction B, the probability that this ordering is the result of chance alone is less than 5% ($.75^{11} = .04$). If, for each child, one determines the proportion of the child's A and B utterances that are A utterances (i.e., p_i), the probability that by chance alone all 11 children acquired A before B can be calculated by multiplying together the p_i's for all of the children ($p_{overall} = (p_1)(p_2)(p_3)(p_4)(p_5)(p_6)(p_7)(p_8)(p_9)(p_{10})(p_{11})$).

Furthermore, if the sampling account is incorrect and children actually acquire A before B, then children should use a considerable number of examples of construction A before they use their first example of construction B. Consider the following example. If, for a given child, one determines that the frequency with which that child uses construction A relative to the frequency with which the child uses construction B is $2:1$ (i.e., $p(A|A \cup B) = .67$) and one finds that the child uses 10 examples of construction A before he uses his first example of construction B, the probability (by chance alone) of getting this result for this single child is less than $.05$ ($p^n = .67^{10} = .018$). If, for each child i, one determines the number of times the child uses examples of construction A prior to her first example of construction B (n^i) and the proportion of the child's A and B utterances that are A utterances (p^i), then the overall probability of finding the observed number of examples of construction A before the first example of construction B can be calculated by multiplying together the values of p^n for all of the children ($p_{overall} = (p_1{}^{n1})(p_2{}^{n2})(p_3{}^{n3}) \times (p_4{}^{n4})(p_5{}^{n5})(p_6{}^{n6})(p_7{}^{n7})(p_8{}^{n8})(p_9{}^{n9})(p_{10}{}^{n10})(p_{11}{}^{n11})$).

Ordering effects might also be due to one construction's being more difficult for children to produce than another (*performance account*). For example, very young children might be restricted in the number of phonologically realized morphemes they can utter or they might have more difficulty producing some phonemes than others. If this is true and construction B requires more overtly realized morphemes (or more difficult-to-pronounce morphemes) than construction A, children could acquire construction A before construction B. For example, in our study of the acquisition of English datives, William Snyder and I found that in spontaneous speech, children begin using double object datives before they begin using *to* datives (Stromswold 1989c; Stromswold and Snyder 1995; Snyder and Stromswold, to appear). Before we could conclude that this ordering reflected a grammatical difference between the two types of datives, we had to rule out the possibility that the children acquired double object datives first because double object datives require one morpheme fewer than *to* datives (cf., e.g., *I gave him the book* and *I gave the book to him*). We did this by showing that children did not produce *to* datives that lacked the preposition *to* prior to acquiring adultlike *to* datives (i.e., young children did not utter sentences such as "I gave the book him") and by showing that the acquisition of the preposition *to* was not a good predictor of the acquisition of *to* datives.

The order of acquisition of constructions could also be due to the relative cognitive complexity of the constructions (*cognitive accounts*). For example, in my analyses of children's spontaneous *wh*-questions, I found that children acquire argument *wh*-questions before adjunct *wh*-questions (Stromswold 1988a,b, in preparation). Before I could conclude that this acquisitional order reflects grammatical differences between argument and adjunct questions (namely, differences in the way argument and adjunct traces are governed), I had to rule out the possibility that it merely reflected the fact that, intuitively, argument questions (e.g., most *who*, *what*, and *which* questions) are conceptually simpler than adjunct questions (e.g., *why*, *when*, *how*, and *how come* questions). I was able to rule out a cognitive account by showing that, even though argument *where* questions (e.g., *Where did he put it?*) and adjunct *where* questions (e.g., *Where did he find it?*) have equal cognitive complexity, children acquire argument *where* questions significantly before they acquire adjunct *where* questions. Ordering effects can also be the result of pragmatic or discourse effects (*pragmatic/discourse accounts*). For example, children might begin asking argument questions before adjunct questions because it is more important for them to learn the answers to *who* or *what* questions than to learn the answers to *why* or *when* questions. Notice, however, that the results of the argument and adjunct *where* analyses rule out this pragmatic account. The order of acquisition of constructions might be due to some linguistic factor other than the one under investigation (*alternative linguistic accounts*). For example, perhaps the reason children acquire argument questions before adjunct questions has nothing to do with how argument and adjunct *wh*-traces are governed, but rather merely reflects when children acquire argument and adjunct constituents. This alternative linguistic account can be ruled out to the extent that children begin to use argument and adjunct constituents at the same age in declarative sentences. By showing that children began using locative adjuncts in declarative sentences (e.g., "He found it *on the table*") at the same age that they began using locative arguments in declaratives (e.g., "He put it *on the table*"), I was able to rule out this alternative linguistic account.

2.4 Summary

In summary, the guidelines for doing competent transcript-based acquisitional research are very similar to those required for doing competent experimental research. One must begin by formulating an acquisitional theory that makes clear, testable predictions. The predictions entailed by the acquisitional theory should be stated prior to examining children's transcripts. Data from transcript studies should be analyzed statistically. This requires that certain criteria and methodological details be set at the start of a transcript study (e.g., which utterances from which subjects' transcripts will be examined, what criterion will be used for acquisition, how error rates will be calculated) and that they be established in a manner that is not biased in favor of the theory under investigation. Studies must include enough subjects (and enough data per subject) that the results can be analyzed statistically. The number of subjects required will depend on the richness or complexity of the predictions to be tested, with more complex predictions requiring fewer subjects. Even if transcript analyses yield statistically significant results that are consistent with one's theory, one should determine whether the findings are the result of input characteristics, sampling biases, pragmatic factors, cognitive factors, processing or performance factors, or linguistic factors other than those under investigation.

Notes

Preparation of this chapter was supported by a grant from the John Merck Foundation. I am grateful for helpful comments and suggestions made by Helen Cairns, Jacob Felman, Dana McDaniel, Cecile McKee, Steven Pinker, William Snyder, Polly Tremoulet, and members of the audience at the 14th Annual Boston University Conference on Language Development (where an earlier version of some of this work was presented).

1. Spontaneous speech studies yield relatively uncontaminated data only if children are recorded in settings where they feel comfortable to talk in a normal fashion. Preferential looking tasks (see chapter 5, this volume) also have few task demands associated with them and can be used with very young children. However, preferential looking tasks can be used only when the syntactic phenomenon under investigation has a clear semantic effect (e.g., they cannot be used to evaluate Wexler's (1994) proposal that there is an optional infinitive stage in early acquisition).

2. For example, it is striking that in spontaneous speech children very rarely produce the types of long-distance *wh*-questions with medial *wh*-words that Thornton and her colleagues frequently elicit (see chapter 4, this volume). Although it is possible that at a certain stage of syntactic development English-speaking children's grammars generate medial *wh*-questions but in spontaneous speech children simply don't happen to produce them, it is also possible that these constructions are *not* part of their grammar, but are the result of the elicitation

procedure. Even if one takes the rather pessimistic view that at least some of the utterances elicited are not part of the grammar, it is important to note that the types of utterances that can be elicited appear to be quite restricted. Specifically, at first blush, children do not seem to produce utterances that violate Universal Grammar.

3. Getting statistically reliable responses in comprehension studies does not ensure that one is getting a picture of a child's competence any more than getting statistically reliable spontaneous speech data means that one is getting a picture of a child's competence (see sections 2.1.6, 2.2.5, 2.3.3 on ruling out competing hypotheses). For example, as Gropen et al. (1989) point out, given that most comprehension studies of datives use datives with full lexical NPs, it is not surprising that these studies show that (similar to adults) children have more difficulty interpreting double object datives (e.g., *The tiger gave the giraffe the elephant*) than *to* datives (e.g., *The tiger gave the elephant to the giraffe*).

4. The number of unique orderings of N constructions is $N!$.

5. The 13 possible acquisitional orders are $A > B > C$, $A > C > B$, $B > C > A$, $C > B > A$, $B > A > C$, $C > A > B$, $A = B > C$, $C > A = B$, $B = C > A$, $A > B = C$, $B > A = C$, $A = C > B$, $A = B = C$.

6. If one allows for the possibility of simultaneous acquisition of constructions, a lower bound for the number of different orders of acquisition can be calculated using the following formula, where N is the number of constructions:

$$N! + \sum_{k=2}^{N} \binom{N}{k}(N - k + 1)!$$

Although one can enumerate the number of possibilities for any N, there is no closed-form expression for the *exact* number of possible orders of acquisition. For a discussion of the problems associated with finding a closed-form expression for the number of partitions of a set, see Rota 1964.

7. Just as one may get the results predicted by one's theory for reasons having nothing to do with the theory (a type I error), so one may fail to get those results even if the theory is correct (a type II error). Consider again a theory that predicts children will acquire construction A before construction B. If construction B is much more frequent (in the input or the output) than construction A, or if pragmatic, cognitive, production/processing, or additional linguistic factors are involved in construction A that are not involved in construction B, the theory might be correct, but children might still acquire construction B at the same time as or even before construction A.

8. Alternatively, children might generalize the behavior of lexical verbs to auxiliary verbs and make the inverse set of errors, such as applying incorrect inflections to auxiliaries (e.g., "*She musts eat"), allowing auxiliaries to appear by themselves (e.g., "*She must it"), overregularizing the inflections of auxiliary and lexical verbs (e.g., "*She haves eaten" and "*She haves dinner"), and failing to invert any auxiliaries (e.g., "*What she can eat?").

9. If Brown (1973) is correct and many of children's early contracted auxiliaries are unanalyzed units (see section 2.1.1), then *wh*-questions with contracted auxiliaries (e.g., "Where's Mommy?", "What it's doing?") should also be excluded. I have done this in the analyses presented here and elsewhere (Stromswold 1989b, 1990b, 1994).

10. Furthermore, some errors that are predicted to occur under the copy-without-deletion theory are never found. For example, *wh*-word in situ errors such as "*I can eat what?" and matrix *wh*-questions with two *wh*-words such as "*What can I eat what?" are inexplicably missing or cell C cases. See Maratsos 1984, Stromswold and Pinker 1986.

11. The classic analogy used to explain what is wrong with doing this compares the researcher with the Texas sharpshooter who shoots the side of a barn and *then* draws a bull's-eye around the bullet holes.

12. Given that the vast majority of adult utterances are grammatical, children will not make errors if they exactly imitate adults' utterances. However, the fact that an utterance is ungrammatical does *not* mean that the utterance is novel, because children's inexact or incomplete imitations could result in ungrammatical utterances.

13. One cannot rely on the presence or absence of a comma between the words *no* and *I* to distinguish anaphoric negation from sentential negation because the person who transcribes the child's speech is not immune to misinterpreting the child's meaning.

14. The labels given to accounts are merely descriptive. Multiple factors may be necessary to explain the appearance of certain types or patterns of errors. For example, Bloom's (1993) explanation for why English-speaking children produce null-subject sentences requires the interaction of performance and pragmatic factors. In other cases, different types of factors might be interrelated. For example, children may be more likely to misparse utterances that overtax their processing/performance abilities (e.g., see Pinker 1984 for a discussion of how processing limitations might result in double-tensing errors).

15. At first blush, this may seem to be exactly the claim entailed by parametric theories of language (e.g., Chomsky 1981), according to which languages differ only in the particular parametric settings that are chosen. Notice, however, that although the number of parametric settings may be fixed and finite, the way that these parametric settings can be expressed is essentially infinite. For example, across languages, the particular inflectional or free-standing morpheme used to indicate past tense can vary just as much as the choice of word used to express the concept "cat."

16. Because, in many ways, studies that use mastery measures of acquisition are more similar to error analyses than patterns-of-acquisition analyses, the guidelines given in section 2.2 may be more relevant for such analyses than the guidelines given in section 2.3.

17. Whether the ages of acquisition of two constructions are correlated with one another and whether the ages of acquisition are significantly different from one another are logically independent. The acquisition of two constructions can be significantly correlated without there being a significant difference in the ages of acquisition for the two constructions; the acquisition of two constructions can be correlated and there can be a significant difference in the ages of acquisition; and the ages of acquisition of two constructions can be significantly different, without there being a significant correlation between the two.

Chapter 3

What Children Know about What They Say: Elicited Imitation as a Research Method for Assessing Children's Syntax	Barbara Lust, Suzanne Flynn, and Claire Foley

3.1 Introduction

3.1.1 Linguistics as a Science

Methodology in modern linguistics must meet the fundamental purpose of current linguistic theory: to validly characterize the grammatical knowledge represented in the mind. More specifically, in keeping with current linguistic theory, it must validly characterize Universal Grammar (UG) as that content of language knowledge which is biologically programmed, and truly universal to the human species. Study of first language acquisition pursues this purpose directly, given that UG is hypothesized to provide a theory of the "initial state" and the basis for an explanation of first language acquisition (Chomsky 1986b; cf. Lust, to appear, in preparation).

In this chapter we discuss one experimental task that has been developed to access children's syntactic competence in a manner that allows scientific test of precise hypotheses generated by linguistic theory, namely, *elicited imitation*.

Throughout, we assume that analyses of linguistic data must be subjected to the rigors of behavioral science, whether the data are collected from child or adult. We hold this assumption even though the study of linguistic theory and cognitive competence can and must go beyond the study of behavior. (We return to this issue below. See also Lust, Flynn, et al., to appear.)

3.1.2 Imitation

Some capacity for imitation appears to be innate, having been observed even in the newborn (Piaget 1968; Meltzoff and Moore 1985). At the same time, it is not the case that anything can be imitated at any time in the child's development. (This is consistent with a rationalist approach to knowledge.) Imitation of new, complex behavior appears to wait until the child mind has developed the "cognitive structure" required for generation of the behavior. For example, although newborns may initially imitate simple tongue protrusion of the type in their own behavioral repertoire, they would not be found to imitate a new sequence or combination of new tongue movements they did not already have the competence for (Piaget 1968). Imitation is therefore not a passive copy, but a reconstruction of the stimulus.

In the area of language development, similar findings exist. Much research has replicated the paradoxical finding that in order for the child to "imitate" a structure, the structure must apparently be part of the child's grammatical competence, for example, as evidenced in the child's natural speech (see, e.g., Bloom, Hood, and Lightbown 1974). Again, imitation is not a passive copy; it reflects cognitive competence.

3.1.3   Rationale for Elicited Imitation as a Research Method for the Assessment of Syntactic Knowledge

3.1.3.1   General Rationale   Given this essential nature of imitation, the researcher should be able to test for the nature of grammatical competence by eliciting imitation of language. For example, given a specific syntactic theory, the researcher should be able to precisely design the sentences for which imitation is elicited, in order to precisely test specific hypotheses regarding the child's knowledge of components of grammar. Given innate competence for imitation in the infant, it should be possible to use this method to test young children close to the "initial state," when they are first able to combine words.

Now, years of development of elicited imitation as an experimental research method in the study of language acquisition have confirmed an early intuition: "[T]he child's ability to repeat sentences and nonsentences . . . etc. might provide some evidence as to the underlying system that he is using" (Chomsky 1964, 39).

3.1.3.2   The Nature of Elicited Imitation Data: Grammatical Factors Elicited imitation allows researchers to assess children's knowledge of precise *grammatical factors*. In linguistic theory, overt evidence for the reality of a purely theoretical constraint or principle is both desirable and scarce. Elicited imitation offers this kind of evidence. In this task, children "imitate" (repeat) sentences that are designed to differ only with respect to a particular grammatical factor.

(1) a. Bert bought [the car [which Max chose]].
    b. Bert bought [the thing [which Max chose]].
    c. Bert bought [what Max chose].

(1a) and (1b) differ in only one respect: the lexical head of the relative clause (*car*) has specific semantic content in (1a) that is lacking in (1b), where the head is the more semantically indeterminate *thing*. The two sentences share the same syntactic relativization structure. In an elicited imitation task (Flynn and Lust 1981), children were asked to repeat structures similar to (1a) and (1b) (under identical conditions, as described further below).[1] Any significant difference in success at imitating (1a) and (1b) can only have been due to a semantic *factor*—namely, the semantic content of the head noun—not to the syntactic factor that the two sentences share.[2]

On the other hand, (1b) and (1c) differ with respect to syntactic structure: one relative clause has a lexical head, and the other does not ((1c) is referred to as a "free" or "headless" relative). Any significant difference in success at imitating (1b) and (1c) must be due to this syntactic factor. (1a) and (1c) also differ with regard to semantic indeterminacy, but because (1b) is also tested, effects due to this semantic factor can be dissociated from those due to the syntactic one.

This example illustrates the ability of elicited interpretation, when used in conjunction with experimental design, to test the reality of a grammatical factor. If a particular factor is the only possible explanation for the (significant) variation in imitation success across two types of structures, then strong evidence is provided for the reality of that factor. The status of these factors in a grammatical theory is a separate issue: the experiment must be grounded in a theory, and in particular syntactic analyses, so that the difference between structures being tested has relevance for the theory.

3.1.4 History of the Method

3.1.4.1 Anecdotal Origins Early anecdotal applications of the elicited imitation method had revealed fundamental properties of elicited imitation in the child (see Lust, Chien, and Flynn 1987 for review of earlier studies). Slobin and Welsh's (1973) classic child "Echo" (2 years old), for example, provided data revealing the *reconstructive* and *analytic* aspects of elicited imitation in the child.

Evidence for *reconstruction* of the model sentence is provided by Echo's "elaboration" of gaps in the model. In this case the child clearly cannot be simply passively copying the model, which is itself "empty" (as suggested by ∅ in our transcription of the model). The examples in (2) and (3) are taken from Slobin and Welsh 1973.

(2) *Adult* The red beads (∅) and brown beads are here.
    Child Brown beads here an' a red beads here. (2;3;3)

(3) *Adult* The owl eats candy and (∅) runs fast.
    Child Owl eat candy ... owl eat the candy and ... he run fast.
             (2;4;3)

Such reconstructive results were later replicated experimentally over large groups (Lust 1977) in more controlled and focused studies on the acquisition of coordinate structures.

More specifically, even anecdotal evidence shows that children's elicited imitation responses are *analytic*: children isolate *syntactic* factors and *semantic* factors of the stimulus sentence independently. The child's response may maintain meaning and lexicon at the expense of syntactic form, or, as illustrated in the anecdotal exchange in (4) (from Slobin and Welsh 1973), it may isolate syntactic factors at the expense of semantic ones.

(4) *Adult* Mozart got burned and the big shoe is here.
    Child Mozart got burned an-duh ... big shoe got burned.

Even in this primitive response, the child gives evidence of having analyzed the syntactic coordinate structure of the model, as in (5), at the same time having partially lost the lexicon and the semantics of the original. (We assume that all full clauses are CPs, or complementizer phrases, although this is not critical to our point.)

(5) [[ ]$_{CP}$ and [ ]$_{CP}$]$_{CP}$

3.1.4.2 Experimental Development of Elicited Imitation Subsequently elicited imitation has been developed in the Cornell Language Acquisition Lab (CLAL) as an experimental method, and subjected to standardized procedures of design, administration, and analysis. Elicited imitation has been developed in conjunction with precise hypotheses regarding syntactic competence, generated by linguistic theory. In general, as we will sketch below, this use of elicited imitation has been found to allow assessment of children's analysis and reconstruction of the language they hear spoken, and therefore of their grammar. More specifically, when used in conjunction with experimental design and method, elicited imitation has been found to allow precise testing of children's knowledge of *specific hypothesized grammatical factors* involved in UG.

The elicited imitation method has now been used widely in experimental research on first language acquisition. It has also been applied in the study of language pathology (e.g., Bloom and Lahey 1978), special populations such as the hearing deprived (e.g., Pinhas and Lust 1987), and adult second language acquisition (e.g., Flynn 1987). See also more recent work by Gerken, Landau, and Remez (1990).

3.1.4.3 Overview of the Experimental Method As it is currently used, the elicited imitation task elicits imitation of particular sentences by young children: children are asked to repeat a "story" (sentence) exactly as the adult said it. The set of sentences for a particular experiment is carefully designed: *the model sentences vary only in critical grammatical factors, with all others controlled or held constant.*

Results are analyzed both quantitatively and qualitatively. Major quantitative results include comparisons in number of "correct" imitations across sentences that vary in a critical grammatical factor (examples given below). The assumption is that if the child can correctly reproduce the full sentence structure, then it can be inferred that the child has the full grammatical competence for this structure. Without the grammatical competence by which to analyze and reconstruct the stimulus sentence, the child could not (productively) repeat it successfully. Qualitative analysis includes study of spontaneous conversions that children make on the model. These spontaneous conversions (see note 2) provide more precise evidence of the child's analysis and reconstruction of the adult sentence, and thus provide the basis for discovering more precisely the nature of the child's own theory, which may be different from the adult's. It is these spontaneous changes that are the most critical elements of the elicited imitation data. With informed linguistic analyses, they may provide evidence for principles, parameters, or constraints in the child's grammar.

For example, consider (6a) and (6b).

(6) a. [When he sat down], Johnny read the book.
   b. Johnny read the book [when he sat down].

(6a) is a left-branching structure; the adverbial subordinate *when* clause is preposed, to the left of the main clause. (6b) reflects the right-branching structure that adheres to the right-branching parameter setting of English phrase structure. When asked to imitate a left-branching structure like (6a), a child acquiring English not only may imitate it less successfully than (6b) but also may spontaneously repeat it as (6b). Children acquiring a left-branching language, however, may and frequently do convert (6b) to (6a) and imitate (6a) more successfully. Complete experimental designs can and do allow the researcher to consider other factors (e.g., pronoun direction) independently in interpreting these results (e.g., Lust 1981a, in preparation; Lust and Mazuka 1989).

3.2   Aspects of Syntax That Have Been Investigated with Elicited Imitation

Several aspects of syntax have now been studied using elicited imitation (often in conjunction with other methods to provide converging evidence, and often in a series of different experiments, in order to dissociate various factors involved in the child's competence in particular grammatical domains). We will briefly discuss a few of these; see the references for a more precise report of the results of each study.

3.2.1   Constituent Structure and Phrase Structure

Studies using elicited imitation have analyzed the child's acquisition of coordinate structures, the role of coordinate structure in the child's development of phrase structure, and the principles, parameters, and constraints that underlie this role. Early studies involving the acquisition of English coordination (e.g., Lust 1977, 1981a,b; Beilin and Lust 1975) have been complemented by parallel crosslinguistic studies involving coordination in Japanese (Lust and Wakayama 1979, 1981), Chinese (Lust and Chien 1984), and Sinhalese, Hindi, and Arabic (Lust, Bhatia, et al., to appear; Lust et al. 1980; Lust 1994).

Various subordinate or embedded forms of phrase structure have also been analyzed using elicited imitation, including relative clauses in English and French (e.g., Flynn and Lust 1981; Foley, in preparation) and adverbial subordinate clauses in English, Japanese, Sinhalese, Hindi, Arabic, and Korean (e.g., Lust 1981a; Lust, Solan, et al. 1986; Gair et al., to appear; Lust and Mazuka 1989; Lust, Mangione, and Chien 1984; Lust and Lee 1988; Lust 1983; Lust and Mangione 1983; Lust, Bhatia, et al., to appear). Snyder (1987) provides a test of young Japanese children's knowledge of embedding in phrase structure, including relativization.

Other embedding types have been tested by undertaking elicited imitation study of control structures like those in (7), which involve VP complements, and systematically comparing them to still other types like the sentential complements in (8) (Cohen Sherman 1983; Cohen Sherman and Lust 1993).

(7) a. John told Max [to eat].
    b. John promised Max [to eat].

(8) a. John told Max [that he would eat].
    b. John promised Max [that he would eat].

(Cohen Sherman compared subordinate and coordinate structures experimentally. See also Nuñez del Prado et al. 1994 for a related study in Spanish.)

3.2.2 Linear Order

The elicited imitation task has proven to be particularly sensitive to word or constituent order or directionality. Results generally suggest that children know and prefer the "unmarked" or underlying order of a constituent structure. For example, in a study of Japanese acquisition (Lust and Wakayama 1989), children were tested on elicited imitation of sentences with the unmarked SOV order of Japanese, as in (9), and with right-dislocated order, as in (10).

(9) [S + S] V
     Raion-to tora-ga hashiru.
     'Lion(s) (and) tiger(s) run.'

(10) V [S + S]
     Hashiru-yo, usagi-to kame-ga.
     'Run, rabbit (and) tortoise.'

In this study, a large proportion (51%) of errors on elicited imitation of dislocated sentences like (10) consisted of a spontaneous attempt to move the dislocated constituent(s) back to their unmarked position (corresponding to (9)). Similar results, showing a preferred order on the part of the child, have been found in experiments that vary order of adverbial subordinate clauses in Japanese (e.g., Lust, Wakayama, et al. 1986). See also Barbier 1995 on Dutch word order.

3.2.3 Anaphora

Numerous studies have used elicited imitation to provide evidence with
regard to anaphora and its underlying grammatical principles (or the
relation between antecedents and proforms, e.g., pronouns or empty categories of various types). (In fact, most of the studies cited above also
involve anaphora.)

These studies test directionality of anaphora (e.g., Lust 1981a; Lust,
Solan, et al. 1986) and interactions among directionality, phrase structure
location (e.g., depth of embedding), and distance in anaphora (e.g., Lust
and Clifford 1986).

They also test constraints on anaphora, such as Principle C of the
binding theory. The structural relation between the pronoun and the noun
is the source of this constraint. Surprisingly, reduced elicited imitation
success has been found with sentences like (11a), which violate Principle
C, in contrast to (11b) (see Lust, Loveland, and Kornet 1980; Lust, Eisele,
and Mazuka 1992, for review).

(11) a. He$_{*i,j}$ turned around when Snuffles$_i$ found the penny.
      b. When he$_{i,j}$ closed the box, Cookie Monster$_i$ lay down.

Presumably, this reduced elicited imitation success with (11a) reflects the
fact that the impossibility of an anaphoric relation between the pronoun
and the name in this sentence makes the sentence more difficult to interpret, mentally represent, and reconstruct in production.

3.2.4 Interaction of Phrase Structure and Anaphora

In another study, children acquiring Mandarin Chinese were tested for
their knowledge of grammatical constraints on empty categories in "equi"
constructions. The elicited imitation stimulus sentences involved redun-
dant noun phrases that children could reduce to empty categories in their
responses. Children were highly selective in these spontaneous reductions:
in their sentences, the reductions appeared in configurational contexts
where the resulting empty category was grammatical, but not where it was
ungrammatical (see Chien 1983; Chien and Lust 1985). For further examples, see Lust, Mangione, and Chien 1984 and Nuñez del Prado et al. 1994.

3.3 Strengths of Elicited Imitation

The strongest advantage of the elicited imitation method is that it can
provide overt, direct evidence of the child's grammar construction for

particular targeted aspects of grammar, and can do so in highly (linguistically) focused ways. Since producing an elicited imitation requires the child actually to construct constituent/phrase structure and establish linear order, elicited imitation must tap grammatical competence.

3.3.1 Converging Evidence

The best test of the strength of a particular method lies in whether or not the evidence it provides converges with evidence from other methods. This converging evidence provides the strongest possible argument that grammatical competence is being tapped (i.e., formal competence that exists above and beyond the performance or processing involved in any particular task or use of language).

The evidence from elicited imitation converges with other production data (e.g., natural speech). Lust and Mervis's (1980) study of natural speech corroborates results regarding the acquisition of coordination that were obtained through experimental elicited imitation. Hamburger's (1980) study of natural speech and relativization corroborates experimental elicited imitation results observed by Flynn and Lust (1981).

Elicited imitation evidence also converges with comprehension data (e.g., act-out tasks or truth-value judgment tests of comprehension). For examples of studies reporting matched elicited imitation and act-out task results, see Lust, Solan, et al. 1986, Lust and Clifford 1986, Cohen Sherman 1983, Cohen Sherman and Lust 1993, and Lust, Loveland, and Kornet 1980. For studies reporting matched results from elicited imitation and a truth-value judgment test of comprehension, see Lust, Eisele, and Mazuka 1992 and Eisele and Lust, to appear.

3.3.2 Disambiguating Comprehension Data

Elicited imitation data can also disambiguate results from tasks that would provide misleading results if used alone. For example, researchers using elicited imitation have discovered that children's representations of particular structures may differ significantly from what the adult had assumed. These discoveries have been particularly important in cases where comprehension data alone might have led to incorrect conclusions about children's grammatical knowledge.

Elicited imitation has been used in studies of children's hypotheses regarding the Japanese reflexive *zibun* 'self' (Mazuka and Lust 1994). Japanese children productively converted the model *zibun* sentences into structures with *zibun de*, as illustrated in (12).

(12) a. *Adult*

　　　Papa-ga　　　sakana-o yaku toki, zibun-ga　mado-o
　　　Papa-NOM fish-ACC grill　when self-NOM window-ACC
　　　aketa.
　　　opened
　　　'Papa grilled the fish when he opened the window.'

　　b. *Child*

　　　Papa-ga　　　sakana-o yaku toki　∅ zibun-de mado-o
　　　Papa-NOM fish-ACC grill　when　　self-(de)　window-ACC
　　　aketa.
　　　opened
　　　'Papa grilled the fish when he opened the window by himself.'

In (12b) *zibun* appears to represent an emphatic, where *zibun* is in non-argument position (in the *zibun de* 'by self' postpositional phrase). This result clearly showed that the child's representation of the adult model differed from the adult model itself, where *zibun* was in subject argument position. The Japanese child was not representing *zibun* as a binding theory anaphor, which would have had to occur in an argument position.

If the Japanese children had been tested with a comprehension task and not with elicited imitation, they probably would have interpreted *zibun* as coreferential with the subject in these sentences. This is the interpretation they would give the sentence whether they had represented *zibun* as an emphatic or as an anaphor. Without the elicited imitation results, the experimenter could have, and probably would have, drawn an incorrect conclusion: for example, that Principle A of the binding theory applies to *zibun* in Japanese-speaking children's grammars in a straightforward manner. In a comprehension task, the experimenter would simply have assumed the child was "acting out" the adult's intended representation of the stimulus sentence (16a).[3]

For other examples of studies where elicited imitation corroborates and disambiguates comprehension data, see Lust, Solan, et al. 1986, Cohen Sherman 1983, and Cohen Sherman and Lust 1993.

3.3.3　Linguistic Precision and Control

Another strength of elicited imitation is that it allows the researcher to focus on a specific syntactic factor and to obtain data directly related to that factor. It makes clear and overt the *model* or "*target*" that the child is attempting to represent and reconstruct. Therefore, the researcher can make direct inferences from the child's utterance regarding particular aspects of syntactic competence, allowing precise comparison between adult and child syntax. Elicited imitation allows *precise design* of the target stimulus sentences in such a way that factors can be isolated. It is especially suitable when the researcher is led by specific, focused theoretical hypotheses.

3.3.4 Statistical Analyses and Scientific Control

Elicited imitation results allow parametric *statistical factorial analysis*, which separates behavioral variance due to linguistic factors from that due to chance, or from that due to nonlinguistic factors. These analyses can be general, comparing "correct" and "incorrect" responses, but they can also be specific, examining precise changes the child makes in the stimulus sentences.

Elicited imitation allows scientific control in that reliability and replicability can be ensured by audiotaping (and/or videotaping) every child's response to every stimulus. Independent transcribers and scorers can check each other's work. Standardized conditions are imposed for design, administration, and scoring.

3.3.5 Power and Validity

Since elicited imitation is especially sensitive to linear order and constituent structure, it is sensitive to the most fundamental aspects of syntax. Elicited imitation can reveal the *child's representation of an adult sentence*, including possible differences from the adult representation. Thus, it can more precisely reveal the true nature of a child's syntactic competence.

3.3.6 Applicability

Elicited imitation is readily accessible and natural to children even as young as 1 to 2 years of age. Thus, it is often possible to test younger children with elicited imitation than with other experimental methods, and it is usually not necessary to invest a large amount of time and effort in "teaching the rules of the game," as with other experimental methods. Elicited imitation can be used with large samples of children in a standardized manner, allowing tests for generalization of results.

Elicited imitation can be applied *cross-culturally and crosslinguistically*, with only minimal variation in methods of administration and analysis. This crosslinguistic validity is critical to the attempt to distinguish UG from specific language grammar.

Elicited imitation can also be used for developmental analyses, where hypotheses must be tested against different age groups, including very young ones, with a common method.

3.3.7   Calibration with Other Methods

As noted above, elicited imitation tests can easily be calibrated with other methods in order to test for converging evidence—for example, with comprehension tests, where stimulus sentences can be experimentally designed to match those tested using elicited imitation, or with other methods of testing language production, such as natural speech analyses. The latter, for example, could allow calibration with certain structural measures of language development (e.g., mean length of utterance), as well as age.

3.4   Advantages of Elicited Imitation

In summary, elicited imitation allows the researcher to focus selectively on specific aspects of grammatical knowledge, which can be precisely manipulated in the stimulus sentences. Compared with other methods, elicited imitation allows more scientific control over administration and analysis, and thus more direct and valid inference regarding precise grammatical factors. Elicited imitation reveals the child's own representation, rather than assuming the adult's.

With elicited imitation, the measurement of grammatical competence is not confounded with other nonlinguistic cognitive competence, as it is when other tasks are used. This is not to say that no nonlinguistic cognition is necessary for elicited imitation; rather, elicited imitation succeeds better at controlling for these nonlinguistic factors and thus allows more direct access to syntactic competence.

3.4.1   Natural Speech Analyses

Although natural speech is a rich source of data, the problems of analysis for this method are well known. Studies of natural speech often require the researcher to painstakingly analyze thousands of utterances in a child's natural speech sample in order to have sufficient evidence to even begin to ground an inference regarding the child's grammatical competence. This often forces the researcher to depend on single case studies rather than large numbers of subjects. Testing for possible disconfirmation of a particular hypothesis may never be possible with natural speech data, although it is with elicited imitation.

3.4.2 Elicited Production

Elicited production methods provide data similar to elicited imitation data. They stand as an intermediary between elicited imitation and a natural speech method; thus, they may be expected to provide evidence that converges with evidence from elicited imitation. However, whereas elicited imitation allows precise identification of the model that the child is attempting to produce, elicited production can never ensure what the child will attempt to say in the context given, or exactly what the child's utterance attempts to produce. The researcher may assume that the child is attempting to say what the adult would say in the same context. However, this in a sense begs the issue.

Elicited production methods face problems of replicability: the exact interaction between experimenter and child would usually be difficult to replicate exactly. In contrast, the strict controls on the administration of elicited imitation tasks allow close to exact replication of experiments.

3.5   Disadvantages of Elicited Imitation

3.5.1   Complexity of Design Refinement

Designing the stimulus sentences in an experimental use of elicited imitation requires precise manipulation of the syntactic factors being tested and precise control over all syntactic factors other than the ones being manipulated and tested. Also, all processing or general cognitive factors in the stimulus sentences must be controlled in order to isolate effects due to the selected grammatical factors. Thus, design of sentence batteries is complicated. Length and complexity of sentences must be taken into account; this includes word and syllable length, internal syntactic structure of every phrase, and morphological complexity of every word. The semantics of the lexical items chosen for every stimulus sentence must also be controlled. (See section 3.8 for details.)

3.5.2   Analysis of Converging Evidence across Tasks

Although converging evidence for grammatical factors from various methods is the strongest paradigm for assessing syntactic competence, the method of analyzing converging evidence can itself be complex. For example, since each task (measuring production or comprehension) is mediated by different sets of processing and general cognitive factors, and since each more directly taps some distinct set of factors in language knowledge, results of the same experimental design using different methods will not always replicate straightforwardly. Analysis of converging evidence can be highly abstract (see, e.g., Lust, Loveland, and Kornet 1980).

3.5.3 Relation Between Elicited Imitation Behavior and Competence

Elicited imitation behavior may quite directly allow the researcher to make inferences regarding the child's grammatical competence and/or syntactic knowledge. This was the case, for example, in the study of Japanese *zibun* discussed earlier. Another example comes from German. Boser (1989) found that children learning German who were asked to imitate (13a) often produced (13b).

(13) a. *Adult*

Suzanne warf den Ball als   Manfred den Schneeball warf.

Suzanne threw the ball as/when Manfred the snowball   threw

   b. *Child*

Suzanne tat den Schneeball werfen.

Suzanne did the snowball   throw

(13b) provides direct evidence that children know the VP auxiliary structure, which is often null in natural speech (and which is certainly null in the model, (13a)), since here the children spontaneously produce an auxiliary verb that does not occur in the model sentence. (See also Boser et al. 1992.)

In other cases, however, elicited imitation may only indirectly relate to grammatical competence. For example, Gerken, Landau, and Remez (1990) asked children to imitate sentences with functional categories (e.g., determiners). Although children frequently omitted these functional categories in their elicited imitation, they more often correctly imitated model sentences that contained the functional items than those that did not. (Here, "correct imitation" meant "maintaining the basic content and lexical structure.") This elicited imitation result shows that the child must know about the role of functional categories, although these functional categories themselves may be absent in elicited imitation or natural speech utterances.

In an elicited imitation study, the child may convert model sentences from subordinate structures to coordinate structures (e.g., Lust 1981a). It has been argued, however, that this result in itself does not require the conclusion that the child does not have the grammatical competence for phrase structure subordination as well as coordination (e.g., Lust 1994). For example, children may differ in how many coordinate responses they produce depending on the subordinate structure of the model. This shows indirectly that the child must know about subordination (Nuñez del Prado et al. 1994).

Adults may make the same conversion to coordination in elicited imitation, under processing constraints (see Flynn and Epstein, in preparation). Again, this means that a specific elicited imitation behavior may not always in itself directly allow a conclusion about the child's grammar. Each elicited imitation behavior must be evaluated in conjunction with others in an experimental design that provides a factorial analysis, and in conjunction with a grammatical theory.

3.6 Criticisms of Elicited Imitation

A first criticism is that elicited imitation behavior reflects simply rote behavior (i.e., passive copy without reconstruction). Thus, it is suggested, the child's elicited imitation behavior reflects only performance, not grammatical competence. The results reviewed above clearly show that this criticism is untenable. They demonstrate that the child's elicited imitation behavior is reconstructive, interpretive, and analytic; it is not random, and it does not reflect only "list" memory behaviors (e.g., serial position effects). In general, results such as those described earlier have confirmed that there are significant, consistent differences in children's elicited imitation behaviors across structures that differ according to a precise grammatical factor. Therefore, the child's elicited imitation responses must consult these abstract grammatical factors; and if they do so, they cannot be rote repetitions. The fact that comprehension tasks provide results that converge with those of elicited imitation also belies this criticism.

A more interesting criticism of elicited imitation data has been provided by Lasnik and Crain (1985). They question how children in an elicited imitation task can make seemingly intelligent conversions on the adult model sentence if they do not have grammatical competence for the adult model. Thus, they suggest that children's elicited imitation behaviors should not be interpreted as reflecting any limitations on their grammatical competence; rather, the children must be converting from one "language" to another, as in a translation of French to English, presumably with full grammatical competence for both languages (see, e.g., Lasnik and Crain, p. 149). For example, Lasnik and Crain suggest that directionality effects found in elicited imitation tests must be specific to the method, and again could not reflect any aspect of grammatical competence. As reviewed above, however, directionality effects can be replicated with other methods, such as truth-value judgment tasks of comprehension (see chapter 10, this volume). This result suggests that the effects of directionality in elicited imitation tasks do not simply reflect a specific performance measure.

Although the question that Lasnik and Crain raise is interesting, we think it provokes a more general one, which is not linked to any one method more than another. If UG exists prior to any language experience, then how does the child intelligently analyze her first language data (sometimes referred to as primary language data or PLD)? This initial analysis cannot be assimilated to the paradigm of "translation" from one language to another since the child does not yet know any language.

A third criticism is suggested by Smith and van Kleeck (1986, 403): "... an imitation task mainly taps short term memory." Smith and van Kleeck have conducted an important investigation of the interaction between general cognitive factors and syntactic factors in various tasks used to study language acquisition. These factors affect elicited imitation tasks as they do all tasks that attempt to test linguistic knowledge. As the evidence reviewed above shows, elicited imitation results reflect grammatical factors involved in design of stimulus sentences, and not only memory factors (even though memory—short-term as well as more long-term—may also be involved). The converging results from elicited imitation tests and tests of comprehension also provide critical evidence against the claim that an elicited imitation task is vitiated by effects of memory limitations. Smith and van Kleeck suggest that "the results of elicited imitation cannot be taken as more than partial evidence of children's language knowledge" (p. 404). As the evidence we have reviewed suggests, this conclusion is true, but it may be no more true of elicited imitation than of any other method used to test grammatical competence.[4]

3.7 Description of the Elicited Imitation Procedure

3.7.1 Description of the Task

In general, successful application of the elicited imitation method involves designing stimulus sentences that induce reconstructive behavior by the child. The stimulus sentences must tax the child's processing ability (e.g., by their length) just enough so that children can and do attempt reconstruction, thus overtly involving their grammar.[5]

In most current research, elicited imitation is used with a repeated measures design. At least two sentence batteries are designed, identical except for lexical content for each condition being tested. (That is, the syntactic structures of the sentences in each battery are identical, but the words are different in replication items across batteries.) This allows the researcher to evaluate whether it is in fact the grammatical factors underlying structure, not lexical items or specific meanings, that critically affect children's behavior. All sentences must be of similar, if not identical, length (generally differing in length by no more than two words or two syllables), in order to dissociate the effects of this aspect of processing in a child's response. (Note, however, that sentence length and sentence complexity interact.) Sentences must also be balanced for semantic content. Although different words are used across replication items, these words must not differ in any important semantic sense, and all must be accessible to the children being tested.

The two sentence batteries of identical design (for convenience, batteries A and B) will allow tests for consistency across a particular syntactic structure and will allow statistical analyses of results. (A minimum score variance of 0–2 is required for parametric statistics.)[6] The order of the structures tested within each battery must differ and must be basically random.[7]

Pilot testing should be conducted in order to reveal unexpected problems in design—for example, in order to eliminate lexical items that may cause unexpected difficulty for the child.

No props are required in this task. The experimenter asks the child to play a game: "I will tell you a little story. Can you tell me the story back exactly the way I say it?" The experimenter then reads a sentence and waits for the child to repeat it. The response is recorded on audiotape (sometimes on videotape as well).[8] Transcription is carried out by two independent transcribers as soon as possible after administration.

3.7.2 Analysis

Quantitative statistical analyses may be performed on various dependent variables defined over the elicited imitation data. First, the number of correct responses may be analyzed in terms of the factorial experimental design of the stimulus sentences (e.g., by analyses of variance). (See note

2 for discussion of the term *correct*.) Subsequently, different types of changes made by the children may be analyzed with regard to the factors varied in the experimental design. Qualitative linguistic analyses may then be performed on the types of changes the children make. Statistical analyses of the significance of grammatical factors on elicited imitation data within a group of subjects may be complemented by within-subjects analyses. (See chapter 14, this volume, for further discussion of statistical analysis.)

3.8 Instructions for Applying Elicited Imitation as an Experimental Method

3.8.1 Training Subjects
The elicited imitation task (a set of experimental sentences) should be preceded by a set of pretraining sentences. This set must be carefully designed to allow the child to get used to the "game" and to ensure that the child expects to be asked to repeat sentences of the same syllable length and general complexity as the experimental test sentences. (These pretraining sentences may not involve the experimental factors being tested.) As much as possible, pretraining should be used to break any response strategy that may occasionally appear (e.g., giving just a last word).

The experimenter may coach children during administration of the pretraining sentences, encouraging them and supplying words if children forget them. The pretraining sentences may be repeated many times.[9]

Children who complete the pretraining sentences (at least with general success) are given the experimental test batteries. During administration of the test batteries, the experimenter may not coach children or lead them toward their responses in any way. After the model sentence is read, the experimenter may only wait for the child's response. Regardless of what the response is, when the child is finished, the experimenter praises the child (e.g., "Very good!"). After this, the experimenter may talk informally with the child, but extensive talk between test sentences should be avoided. It is very important that the child feels he has done a good job, regardless of his response.

If the child does not respond, or provides only one word, the experimenter may ask, "Do you want me to read it again?" Only one repetition is allowed, and only under these circumstances. (Uncontrolled numbers of administrations of stimulus sentences across children may make the responses across different children incomparable.) If the child becomes distracted, testing should be broken up into shorter segments. If the child repeats only part of a sentence, this must be accepted as the response, although the experimenter may then periodically ask, "Is that all?"

The purpose of these controls is to ensure replicability and to allow statistical analysis. With this method, the context and environment can be controlled to the extent possible in a psycholinguistic experiment. Each child hears exactly the same introduction to the task, and during the administration of the task each child undergoes almost exactly the same experience. No coaching or coaxing is given to one child that is not given to every child. This allows the assumption that random variation in responses comes from within the children and that sources of variation are not introduced by the experiment or the experimenter.[10]

3.8.2   Pitfalls to Avoid in Design

If the sentences do not tax a child's processing constraints at all (e.g., if they are extremely short), elicited imitation results may be completely uninteresting. All sentences will simply be correctly imitated, with no variance between grammatical structures or factors. If stimulus sentences are too long for a child's processing capacity, the child may respond as though the experimenter had read the Declaration of Independence, and again no significant data will result. In a successful elicited imitation design, stimulus sentences must tax the child just enough to cause a reconstruction effort, but not enough to discourage a constructive response. Sentences should be grammatical.[11]

Care should be taken in designing the sentence batteries to omit structural complexity that is unrelated to the grammatical factors being tested. Care should also be taken in details of designing stimulus sentences for elicited imitation (e.g., to ensure that the beginnings and ends of words are phonologically distinct). (For example, a design that tests English-speaking children's use of auxiliaries should avoid verbs that begin with /s/, since this could be easily confused with the auxiliary *is*.) Every noun phrase referent makes the stimulus sentence cognitively more complex and therefore the reference of noun phrases must be controlled.

3.8.3   Pitfalls to Avoid in Administration

Experimenters should be taught never to intervene between initial administration of the stimulus sentence and the child's elicited imitation. The child may take a long, silent time before responding. Intervention confounds interpretation of results and changes the cognitive complexity of the child's task. Sentences must be administered as a whole, not in parts. Experimenters should also be careful to regulate intonation, giving even, natural emphasis to all parts of the sentence.

3.8.4 Pitfalls to Avoid in Transcription

Often, untrained researchers transcribe the child's utterance in terms of what they think the child "is trying to say." Transcribers need to be taught that the most interesting aspect of the elicited imitation data is what the child actually says, which may be different from the adult model. Reliability measures (e.g., having different transcribers compare their results) and training are essential to accurate transcription.

3.8.5 Pitfalls to Avoid in Scoring

Scoring criteria must be defined for each experimental study using elicited imitation. These scoring criteria should be available in written form for tests of replicability of elicited imitation results. For example, if a researcher is interested in relative clause structure, and in a particular imitation the child changes only inflectional morphology (e.g., saying *choosed* instead of *chose*), then it would not make sense to score this response as "incorrect." Such scoring would make it difficult to evaluate variance that may be due to structural factors related to relative clauses.

3.9 Conclusions and Discussion

Here, we articulate several fundamental assumptions regarding the link between linguistic theory and first language acquisition that are implied in the research paradigm that has been developed in conjunction with the scientific standardization of the elicited imitation method. (For further development of these points, see Lust, Flynn, et al., to appear.)

1. It is assumed that convergence across studies and different methods will identify abstract constraints on the course of acquisition, and not grammars of particular children. Experimental designs using elicited imitation attempt to test significance (or nonsignificance) of abstract linguistic factors and do not attempt to characterize a child or a set of children per se.

2. Similarly, experimental designs using elicited imitation do not attempt to characterize a child's knowledge of particular structures directly.

Rather, elicited imitation results are interpretable in accord with the assumption that structures (e.g., relative clauses, coordinate structures) are epiphenomenal in themselves (Chomsky 1993) and are reflexes of underlying grammatical principles and parameters and their interaction.

3. Only if scientific methods apply to them can acquisition data be attributed independent status and therefore test theoretical hypotheses about UG.

4. Designs using elicited imitation assume that real development may take place in the child's knowledge of language. They assume that elicited imitation results may reveal a child's representation of specific language grammar, which a priori may exhibit differences from the adult grammar. In addition to seeking to define the nature of a priori knowledge, they seek to test if and when language development truly occurs and to identify the locus of this development.

5. In summary, the elicited imitation method is used with the assumption that arguments for the content of UG (i.e., for biological programming of principles and parameters of the language faculty) cannot be validated on the basis of any single piece of language performance (e.g., production, comprehension, or grammaticality judgment), from any particular child on any particular structure. Rather, inferences regarding such biological programming can be justified only on the basis of results that generalize over large populations of children, over more than one method and more than one type of language performance. Ideally, arguments for the content of UG must be validated over more than one language, in order to distinguish UG from specific language grammar.

Notes

1. Note that in an experimental battery, as described below, the lexical content of the subjects and verbs varies across replication items.

2. Throughout the chapter we refer to "correct" or "successful" imitations as those involving no significant change in the stimulus sentence. Which changes are insignificant (if any are insignificant) must be determined for each particular study. We refer to changes as "errors." Among possible errors in an elicited imitation study are conversions, where a child changes a stimulus sentence into a sentence that is structurally different.

3. This result may reflect the adult grammar also; that is, emphatic *zibun* may in general be unmarked.

4. A final criticism of elicited imitation is implied by Crain and Thornton (1991, 321), who suggest that elicited production "yields a new perspective on children's acquisition, one that is more in keeping with the precepts of current linguistic

theory." This implies that elicited imitation is not in keeping with "precepts of current linguistic theory." However, as we have suggested, the experimental design of elicited imitation studies in principle allows scientific testing of any hypothesized linguistic principle, parameter, or constraint.

5. Only pilot testing can determine the appropriate sentence length for the age of the children being studied.

6. More than one replication item for each condition may be included, but this will increase the length of sentence batteries. We have found that 16–20 sentences broken into two batteries is a limit for many young children.

7. Randomness should be constrained—for example, to prevent long sequences of a particular structural type that may arise randomly. As with all experimental designs, subjects must be randomly assigned to two groups; one receives battery A first, and the other, battery B first.

8. As with any experimental task, not all children will be amenable to elicited imitation, especially in the youngest age groups. As with all experimental procedures, no child who is fundamentally uncomfortable in the experimental situation should be included in an elicited imitation study, since the child's well-being must always be the paramount concern.

9. Since some children require more practice with pretraining sentences than others, it is wise to include several alternative sentences for each structure in the pretraining battery. This prevents excessive repetition of the same sentence, which may be dull for children.

10. Reluctant children may need coaxing during the pretraining battery, as described above. As with all experimental methods, children who are fundamentally uncomfortable with the setting must be eliminated from study, and only interviewers who are trained in basic child care and safety should be allowed to work with the children being tested.

11. Although Chomsky's (1964) intuition quoted earlier ("[T]he child's ability to repeat sentences and nonsentences ... etc. might provide some evidence as to the underlying system that he is using") suggested that ungrammatical sentences may also be used in elicited imitation, we do not recommend it. This is because the child must assume that this "game" concerns well-formed sentences, in order that the responses can be interpreted as reflecting the child's theory of how grammar works.

Chapter 4

Elicited Production   Rosalind Thornton

This chapter introduces the methodology of elicited production. The goal of the chapter is to illustrate how this experimental technique can be used to investigate children's grammatical knowledge. The focus will, therefore, be on elicitation of syntactic structures. The chapter will not discuss how the technique might be modified to study properties of discourse, or word-level properties, for example.

Elicited production is an experimental technique designed to reveal children's grammars by having them produce particular sentence structures. The syntactic structures of interest are elicited in the broader context of a game, frequently one in which the child interacts with a puppet. The game is orchestrated to incorporate situations or contexts that are associated with a specific meaning and are designed to be uniquely felicitous for production of the structure being investigated. The utterance that the child associates with the particular meaning is elicited following a "lead-in" statement from the experimenter. For example, suppose that the goal of the experiment is to elicit (truncated or full) passive sentences. To elicit a passive structure, a game is designed in which the child asks a puppet a question about a scenario acted out with toys. Suppose there are two zebras in the workspace, one of which is being tickled by a crane (who is using one of his own feathers). The experimenter might proceed as follows:

(1) *Experimenter*   In this story, the crane is tickling *one* of the zebras.
    Ask the puppet which one.
    Child   Which zebra is getting tickled by the crane?

Notice that the idea of the experimenter's lead-in is to provide the context and "ingredients" for production of the structure *without modeling it*. This is an important difference between elicited production and elicited imitation (regarding which, see chapter 3, this volume).

The chapter is organized as follows. Section 4.1 introduces the elicited production technique. Section 4.2 discusses previous research, briefly sketches some variations in how the task can be applied to address particular issues, and outlines the factors that should be taken into consideration when planning an elicited production experiment. Section 4.3 presents an experiment that tests a constraint on form by investigating the "*wanna* contraction" paradigm. Finally, section 4.4 discusses children's long-distance questions. Throughout the chapter possible solutions to problems that might be encountered in conducting an elicited production experiment are discussed.

4.1 Properties of Elicited Production

In this section some of the methodological strengths of the elicited production technique are outlined, with the intent of clarifying when it is appropriate to use this technique.

One general advantage of production data is that they reveal the child's grammar without the need to make inferences from "yes" and "no" responses, as is necessary in a judgment task. In general, comprehension tasks that rely on "yes" versus "no" responses by children must take additional steps to ensure that these responses truly reflect children's grammatical knowledge. In the sense that the grammar does not need to be inferred from "yes" or "no" responses, elicited production data can be considered to more "directly" reflect the child's grammar. It is highly unlikely that a child could put words together in a particular way accidentally. The consistent appearance of a particular sentence type in a child's speech is strong evidence that the sentence is generated by the child's grammar. This is especially true in cases where the child's utterance is not evident in the adult input. For example, the elicitation technique has uncovered the fact that many young children produce negative questions with two auxiliary verbs, such as "What did he didn't eat?" (Thornton 1993; Guasti, Thornton, and Wexler 1995). Since such questions do not appear in the adult grammar, it could not be argued that children are mimicking the input or parroting fixed phrases. Rather, such productions can be taken to expose a difference between the child's grammar and that of an adult.

A distinguishing feature of the elicited production technique is that it enables the experimenter to control the meaning that is to be associated with the targeted utterance. The meaning is controlled by presenting a particular scenario, acted out with toys and props, on each trial of the experiment. Such experimental control of the context offers several obvious benefits. Most importantly, it eliminates many of the difficulties that arise in attempting to interpret a child's intended meaning, a problem that is frequently confronted in investigations based on transcripts of children's spontaneous production data.

Another virtue of the task is that it enables the experimenter to evoke sentences corresponding to complex syntactic structures, ones that occur only rarely, if at all, in children's spontaneous speech (and possibly in adults' speech as well). The context that is uniquely felicitous for certain complex sentences might be quite exotic in day-to-day conversation. Moreover, contexts encountered every day might not be *uniquely* felicitous for a given construction, so that children may avoid using the construction and choose an alternative, simpler means of expression. This may lead to serious underestimates of children's linguistic competence. By presenting situations that are felicitous only for the construction that is targeted, the elicited production technique can help uncover the full extent of children's grammatical knowledge.

Also useful is the fact that the elicited production technique allows a robust data sample of the targeted structure to be gathered within a single experimental session. Sufficient data can be collected to draw solid conclusions about the child's grammar at a particular point in time. By contrast, in database searches of transcripts from children's spontaneous speech, this is often not possible. In order to collect a sufficient data sample, researchers frequently have to search files that cover months or years, leaving open the possibility that important grammatical stages are obscured.

The elicited production methodology is appropriate for evaluating scientific hypotheses. In addition to target sentences, a range of control sentences can be included in the planned battery of structures for elicitation. The production data from children reveal what children *do* say, and when correct controls are included in the experiment as well, they also reveal what children *cannot* say. In many cases it is possible to identify sentences that are excluded from children's grammars by principles of Universal Grammar (UG).

4.2 The Elicited Production Task

The elicited production task has been in service in one form or another for more than 30 years. An early and much celebrated use of the task was an experiment by Berko that investigated children's morphological knowledge (Berko 1958). The aim of Berko's study was to assess children's ability to create new linguistic forms, ones that follow from the application of rules. To this end, Berko introduced children to novel words that they could not possibly have heard before. Children between the ages of 4 and 7 were shown pictures of an object, such as a cartoon bird, and were told what it was: "This is a 'wug.'" Then the children were shown a second picture with another token of the same object, and were told, "Now there are two of them." To elicit the target responses, children were invited to finish the experimenter's sentence: "There are two ____." From most children, this carrier phrase elicited the correct form, "wugs," which was interpreted as evidence that children had internalized the process (e.g., a rule) for supplying the plural ending to nouns. In any event, we see how the experimental results could be used to argue that children's productions of real plural nouns are not the result of memorizing forms they have heard in the input.

Another early use of the elicited production methodology was an experiment by Bellugi (1967, 1971), who studied the syntactic development of the well-known children Adam, Eve, and Sarah (Brown 1973). The technique was used to supplement data from spontaneous speech, in order to probe Adam's knowledge of subject-auxiliary inversion in positive and negative questions. One experimenter played the role of an "old lady" puppet and spoke in a high quavering voice. The game is reported as follows (Bellugi 1971):

(2) *Adult*   Adam, ask the Old Lady why she can't sit down.
    Adam   Old Lady, why you can't sit down?
    Old Lady   You haven't given me a chair.

Having fallen out of fashion for some years, the elicited production task has recently been resurrected to study many other aspects of children's grammars, in the areas of both syntax and semantics. A partial list of the grammatical properties and syntactic structures that have been studied includes structure dependence (Crain and Nakayama 1987); the *wanna* contraction and *that*-trace paradigms (Thornton 1990; Crain 1991); clitics in Italian (McKee and Emiliani 1992); passives (Crain, Thornton, and Murasugi 1987; Pinker 1989); subject-auxiliary inversion (Erreich 1984; Sarma 1991); negation in English questions (Guasti, Thornton, and Wexler 1995) and in Italian questions (Guasti, in press); properties of referential versus bare *wh*-phrases in questions (Thornton 1995); relative clauses in English (Hamburger and Crain 1982); relative clauses in Italian (Crain, McKee, and Emiliani 1990); relative clauses in French (Labelle 1990; Guasti and Shlonsky, in press) and in Spanish (Pérez-Leroux 1995); control properties of infinitival sentences (Eisenberg and Cairns 1994); negative polarity (O'Leary and Crain 1994); and universal quantification (Crain et al., in press).

It is important to appreciate that although the studies listed above have many features in common, there are in fact many elicited production techniques. That is, the elicited production task can, and sometimes must, be modified to accomplish the goals of a particular experiment. Nevertheless, many variations of the task have incorporated the strategy of involving children in a game in which they interact with a puppet. For example, a child might be invited to direct a puppet to do something (such as "Point to ..."), or the child might be directed to question the puppet about scenarios acted out with toys, or even to correct a statement that the puppet makes about the scenarios. In other variants of the task, children are involved in some activity with an experimenter, rather than a puppet. For example, in the task used by Labelle (1990) to elicit relative clauses from French-speaking children, child subjects were involved in a game placing stickers on pictures. The relative clauses were elicited in response to the experimenter's question asking children where they wanted to place the sticker. Another variation, used recently by Eisenberg and Cairns (1994), required children to complete a sentence started by the experimenter.

The technique of elicited production works well for children aged about 3 years and older. With effort, it can be used with many children as young as $2\frac{1}{2}$. For children younger than this, however, it is difficult to maintain the needed degree of experimental control to reliably evoke consistent data; some compromise between elicited and spontaneous speech production data may be necessary for most children younger than around $2\frac{1}{2}$.

4.2.1 Experimental Preliminaries

As with any kind of experiment involving young children, one of the key ingredients to successful data collection is the comfort of the child; higher priority should be given to the child's enjoyment than to the goals of the experiment. This is especially true of production studies, because children are being asked to be active participants and talk, not just observe. If children are comfortable in the experimental situation, they will want to participate over and over in these "games," in sessions that can last up to

30 minutes. It goes without saying, moreover, that attention to the child's well-being gains the confidence of parents and teachers, fostering the kind of productive working relationship that is most conducive to research.

In order to achieve the optimal level of comfort for children in an elicited production experiment, it is crucial for the experimenters to know the child subjects well. Generally, the experimenter should have interacted extensively with each child in the classroom setting (or at the child's home). These interactions take place in the weeks before children are invited to "play the game." If the experiment requires taking children to an unfamiliar research room, it is often worthwhile to invite them to preview the room and to give them a short introduction to the "game." This practice session should be fun, so that the child will want to return to play in the "real" testing session. For a child who is hesitant to leave the familiar classroom setting, it is sometimes helpful to invite the teacher along with the child to the practice session.

Elicitation experiments can sometimes be carried out by a single experimenter, but it is usually worthwhile to recruit a colleague to play the role of a puppet. The main reason for including a puppet is that children are often more willing to interact with a puppet than with an adult (even though they know that an adult is posing as the puppet character). This means they are more likely to be verbal in an elicitation task, and this is, after all, critical.

There is another reason for using a puppet: it makes the session more enjoyable for the child. It often takes time to set up a story, and this momentarily takes the experimenter's attention away from the child. Alone, the experimenter would have to ask the child to just sit quietly; but the puppet engages the child between trials, assuming the role of an interesting character who tells jokes, or gets easily mixed up, or is shy, and so on. The puppet also entertains the child between scenarios, while the experimenter puts away props from one trial and prepares the props that are needed for the next. The result is that the child relaxes and enjoys the interludes between trials. During an experimental trial, however, the puppet's role changes. The puppet helps the experimenter to keep the child's attention focused on the story. During this part of the "game," then, the puppet doesn't entertain the child subject, but attends to the story along with the child. With the hand that isn't occupied, the experimenter playing the role of the puppet may also monitor the audio equipment, change the audiocassettes, and do a limited amount of scorekeeping, note taking, and so on.

A research strategy that has proven quite successful in eliciting questions from children is to explain that the puppet is shy of grown-ups. Selecting the right puppet also helps. One puppet that has worked well is a snail puppet, which withdraws into its shell every time the "grown-up" experimenter gets too close or attempts to ask it a question. Another successful puppet is a newborn dinosaur that has just broken out of its shell. Because the puppet is too shy to talk to grown-ups and will only talk to kids, the experimenter can explain the dilemma that this creates and can enlist the child's help in finding out various things about the puppet. An advantage of this set-up is that "You ask him" is not a possible response, since it has already been established that the puppet won't talk to grown-ups. Without the child's help, the game cannot continue.

In the course of an elicited production experiment, children sometimes have difficulty in accessing the targeted structure. This situation often demands quick thinking on the part of the experimenter and may call for certain deviations from the planned presentation of experimental items. When a child is struggling or fails to come up with the target structure, repetition of part of the acted-out story is sometimes warranted, to allow the child another attempt at producing the target structure. If the experimenter decides to repeat the story, however, a reason should be given for doing this, so that the child does not think she failed to do what the experimenter wanted. Here the puppet can come to the rescue and claim, for example, that it had found that particular story hard and would like to hear it again.

If a child does not produce the targeted structure on the second attempt, it is best to move directly on to another "story." It is often wise to insert a filler item before moving to the next target item. Several such fillers should be prepared ahead of time, and kept to one side in case they are needed. A filler should elicit an unrelated sentence type, preferably a structure that the child finds easy. A success experience with the filler story will usually renew a child's confidence, and the child will be prepared to have another try at producing whatever structure is needed on a target trial. Such deviations from the experimenter's ideal plan are essential if data collection is to be successful. The drawback to repeating certain trials and inserting fillers as they are needed is that some children's sessions end up differing slightly from those of other children. Some researchers may find it disquieting to abandon the usual rigid procedures, but there is no reason to believe that this compromises the investigation, since repeating a story or adding a filler item does not "cue" the child about the target structure.

On the subject of "cueing" the child, it should be noted that to the extent possible, the experimenter avoids using the targeted structure. If the goal of the experiment is to elicit passive sentences, the experimenter avoids using passives. In other cases it is more difficult to safeguard against using the target structure. Suppose the experiment is studying children's use of subject-auxiliary inversion in *wh*-questions, for example. To avoid using subject-auxiliary inversion would be to avoid asking the child any questions, or to use only intonation to mark questions. This may not be possible.

It is essential to audiotape the entire session, using high-quality and reliable equipment. It is critical to check that everything is ready and working properly before the child subject is brought into the research room. If the production data do not end up being recorded on the tape, the session is wasted. When the child is brought into the room, the experimenter should mention the child's name to the puppet ("Amy has come to see you"), to remind the puppet, who may have forgotten the child's name, and to guarantee that the audiotape can be correctly catalogued for later transcription. Children are not usually bothered by the presence of the tape recorder and microphone on the table. If they are curious about it, they are usually satisfied with the explanation that the experimenter is making a tape to listen to later on.

The following practical tips may be useful for first-time experimenters:

- When making up stories or scenarios for an experiment, it is often helpful to lay out all of the toys you have available and use these for inspiration. Making up stories in the abstract while sitting at the computer often leads to frustration. When it comes time to get the toys ready for the experiment, inevitably some of them are missing. The toys for each story can be placed in a resealable plastic bag, so that everything is kept together for a particular story and there are no delays in finding toys.
- Buy toys with big feet so that they won't keep falling down as you try to tell your story.
- Mix up unusual combinations of characters in stories, so that children do not have preconceived ideas about how certain characters should act. Children are rarely bothered if Superman, Pocahontas, and Goldilocks all feature in the same story.
- Encourage children to watch the stories and not pick up the toys during the narration. After the story has ended, they can handle the toys and participate by helping to put them away.

- Having the child choose the next story is a convenient way of ensuring a random presentation order if this is the design of the experiment.
- To the extent possible, the story should be told exactly the same way to each child subject. Rehearse the stories out loud first, and practice on a friend to ensure smooth presentation when it comes to testing children. Test the adults and older children before moving to younger subjects.
- If the plot of the stories is complex, it helps to have a reminder of the order of events in each story, at least at the start of testing when the stories aren't ingrained in memory. For a recent experiment investigating children's comprehension of questions like "What didn't every rabbit buy?", I had written a story about three rabbits going to a spare parts store, where spare noses, tails, eyes, ears, and so on, were on sale. Three actions took place, and to remind myself of the order, I had the following notes:

"What didn't every rabbit buy?"
(i)   every rabbit buys a gold heart
(ii) no rabbit buys spare elephant ears
(iii) 2 of the 3 rabbits buy a spare tail

4.2.2   Felicity Conditions

In designing an elicited production experiment, it is essential to understand the pragmatic conditions that are both necessary and sufficient to produce the structure under investigation. Identifying the properties of the uniquely appropriate situation for a target construction usually requires a considerable investment of time; the time is spent piloting the experiment with adults and older children. It is important to take the step of establishing that adults produce the target structure in the experimental context before testing the target population of young children. The point cannot be overemphasized: pilot work is essential if the experiment is to achieve its goal. In fact, pilot work often takes more time than conducting the actual experiment.

As adults, our intuitions about the conditions necessary for producing a particular structure are frequently dull. This is because, as adults, we have the ability to "accommodate" pragmatic infelicities. That is, adults can often fill in the missing inferential steps in response to speakers who fail to establish the presuppositions that underlie their statements. The downside of having the ability to readily accommodate presuppositional failures is that adults, linguists among them, find it difficult to diagnose those aspects of a pragmatic context that are needed to elicit a particular type of sentence.

Young children 3, 4, and 5 years old apparently do not have the same capacity as adults to understand sentences produced in infelicitous circumstances. Children cannot accommodate presuppositional failures as well as adults (see, e.g., Hamburger and Crain 1982, for discussion). In one sense, this makes it look as though children are more sensitive to pragmatics than adults. If an experimental context does not fulfill the presuppositions for an utterance, children may have difficulty producing it. In fact, they will probably not understand what is being asked of them.

Children have frequently been found to make errors in comprehension experiments that tested structures in infelicitous circumstances. A good example is provided by studies of restrictive relative clauses. In early experiments, children's knowledge of relative clauses like the one in *The lion kissed the zebra that jumped over the fence* was examined in situations where only one zebra was available, instead of a set of zebras. In acting out the sentence, children often made the lion kiss the zebra and then jump over the fence (instead of making the zebra jump the fence). Hamburger and Crain (1982) pointed out that a restrictive relative clause like *the zebra that jumped over the fence* entails that at least two zebras be present, one that jumped over the fence and one that didn't. Hamburger and Crain found that with the simple addition of an extra zebra, children performed more accurately than had been reported for previous experiments (e.g., Tavakolian 1981a). They also found that children were able to produce restrictive relative clauses without difficulty once this presupposition was satisfied. Hamburger and Crain did not attempt to elicit relative clauses in the pragmatically infelicitous situation with only one zebra, but it is likely that children and adults alike would not have come up with a restrictive relative clause in this circumstance.

In elicitation experiments focusing on question structures, experimenters frequently find that some children have what is commonly labeled the "ask/tell problem" (see C Chomsky 1969). That is, in situations where they are supposed to query the puppet, children respond by telling the puppet the answer to the question they should have posed. This problem occurs more acutely with younger children, in the 3-year-old range. It usually arises only in contexts that, on examination, fail to satisfy certain felicity conditions for asking questions. Specifically, it is most felicitous to ask a question if the person who is asking doesn't know the answer, and if that person has reason to believe that the one being asked *does* know the answer. Therefore, in the ideal situation, each question should request information that is unknown to the child subject.

The ask/tell problem can be sidestepped for some children if the felicity conditions are satisfied at the beginning of the experimental session. This can be thought of as satisfying the felicity conditions at the "global" level. One way to set the stage for question asking is to introduce children to a puppet they know nothing about and have never seen before. This ploy was used successfully in Crain and Nakayama's (1987) experiment eliciting yes/no questions. Instead of a puppet, the Star Wars character Jabba the Hutt was used. Jabba the Hutt was from another planet and had never been to Earth before. The experimenter began the session by wondering what Jabba the Hutt knew about our world and by raising a lot of unknowns. The experimenter's patter might go something like this:

(3) *Setting the stage for the game*
    Experimenter   I wonder if Jabba the Hutt can walk or talk ... I
    don't know. Look at his body, it's got funny bumps on it. Maybe
    he's part animal. Could be! I don't know. He looks quite friendly.
    Maybe he likes people. I wonder if he gets hungry. I have a
    hamburger here. I wonder if he likes hamburgers. I don't know if
    they have hamburgers on the planet he comes from. Maybe you
    could help me find out ...

Having set the stage as shown, the experimenter can provide a lead-in for each individual question. For example, the experimenter might say, "Ask him if they have hamburgers on his planet."[1] This lead-in would evoke the question "Do you have hamburgers on your planet?" Notice that when the child asks whether or not there are hamburgers on Jabba the Hutt's planet, he is genuinely requesting information for which he does not know the answer.

It is not always simple to set up target questions to request new information, however. Suppose that among the question forms targeted are *wh*-questions with third person singular subjects. In this case it is not possible to have the child ask Jabba the Hutt a question about himself, or his planet, because such a question would take the form "Do you ..." or "What do you ..." To elicit a question with a third person subject of the form "What does she ..." or "What does he ...," the child needs to ask Jabba the Hutt about someone else. This extra character might be part of a scenario staged with toy props, say, one in which Fido eats a cookie but not a bone. Following this scenario, the experimenter might say, "Ask

Jabba the Hutt what Fido ate." The difficulty is that the question no longer requests new information. The child already knows that Fido ate a cookie and not a bone, and there is a danger that the ask/tell problem might reemerge.

There are at least two ways to rescue such an experiment. One way is to do a little more work at the global level. Having asked Jabba the Hutt some questions about himself, the experimenter can suggest they find out if Jabba understands about "Earth things." The object of the game could be to find out if he can pay attention to and understand stories (such as the story about what Fido ate). In this way, it at least makes sense to ask Jabba a question about an event or character that doesn't directly relate to him. This doesn't solve the problem that the child knows the answer to the question, however. Another angle on this problem is to modify the story. Perhaps Fido is given a bone and a cookie, and he takes them behind a wall to hide them. The child can't see behind the wall, but Jabba the Hutt can. Fido eats the cookie and buries the bone for later. In this situation it would make perfect sense for the child to ask, "What did Fido eat?"

For a child with an extreme ask/tell problem, it might be necessary to set up every target question so that the answer remains a mystery to the child. For most children, this last step isn't necessary. As long as the experiment starts off with the felicity conditions being satisfied at the global level, the child gets involved in the question game and will continue to ask questions, even if the answers are already known. Often it is then possible to switch to stories like the first Fido scene, without running into an ask/tell problem.

4.3   A Constraint

This section presents an experiment investigating children's knowledge of the constraint on contraction across *wh*-trace in the *wanna* contraction paradigm. The experiment is introduced primarily to show how the elicited production technique can be used to assess children's syntax. The section ends by considering when elicited production cannot be used to test a constraint.

4.3.1   *Wanna* Contraction

For experimenters working within the Principles and Parameters model of UG (Chomsky 1981, 1986a, 1991), the elicited production technique can be used to examine children's knowledge of grammatical constraints on production. In the theory of UG, principles (constraints) and parameters are part of the knowledge that is innately specified. Parameters account for crosslinguistic variation. Constraints are of two types. One kind of constraint restricts the *meanings* that may be assigned to an utterance; another kind of constraint restricts the *form* that an utterance can take. The elicited production task is suitable for assessing children's knowledge of constraints on the form of sentences (see Crain 1991 for further discussion of constraints of both kinds).

An example of a constraint on form is the principle that limits contraction across a trace of *wh*-movement (Wasow 1972; Bresnan 1978; Chomsky 1976; Lightfoot 1976; and many others). In English this constraint places restrictions on the environments in which sequences like *want to* can be contracted to *wanna, supposed to* can be contracted to *sposta, have to* can be contracted to *hafta*, and so on. Below, *wanna* contraction is used as the paradigm case to illustrate how to test children's knowledge of the constraint. Further details of this experiment can be found in Thornton 1990.

Let us examine the phenomenon in more detail. To see the effect of the constraint, we need to compare *wh*-questions in which the *wh*-phrase is extracted from object position of the infinitival complement to the verb *want*, with those in which the *wh*-phrase is extracted from subject position of the infinitival complement. In object extraction questions like (4a), *wanna* contraction is permitted, but in subject extraction questions like (5a), it is not. In corresponding declaratives like (6a), the constraint is irrelevant, because such sentences contain no traces of *wh*-movement. As a result, declaratives are grammatical both with and without contraction.

(4) a. Who do you want to kiss *t*?   object extraction
    b. Who do you wanna kiss *t*?

(5) a. Who do you want *t* to kiss Bill?   subject extraction
    b. *Who do you wanna kiss Bill?

(6) a. I want to kiss Bill.   declaratives
    b. I wanna kiss Bill.

In (4) the *wh*-phrase *who* is moved from object position, and a trace (shown by *t*) is left behind in this position. When the trace is in object position, it does not interfere with contraction of *want to* to *wanna*. This is not the case in (5), however. Here the *wh*-phrase is moved from subject position of the lower clause (cf. *You want who to kiss Bill*), leaving a *wh*-trace between *want* and *to*. Thus, contraction is prohibited.

Suppose the constraint on contraction across a *wh*-trace is specified as a constraint in UG. We can assume that the constraint could not be learned (except with a good deal of trial and error) because negative evidence would be needed to master it, and it is assumed that negative evidence is unavailable (Brown and Hanlon 1970; Travis and Morgan 1989; Marcus 1993). Positive evidence, in the form of adult *wh*-questions like (4a), (4b), and (5a), would not be sufficient to inform the child of the prohibition on contraction in the environment when the *wh*-phrase is moved from subject position (i.e., (5b)). If the constraint is part of UG, however, children should be steadfast in their adherence to it. That is, as soon as they can be tested, all children should be observed to avoid contraction of *want* and *to* in their subject extraction questions, irrespective of the level of contraction in declaratives and in object extraction questions.

Assuming that we are working in the UG framework, our *experimental hypothesis* (i.e., the hypothesis to be tested in the experiment) is that children are equipped with innate knowledge of the constraint. The opposing *null hypothesis* is that the constraint is not innate. According to the null hypothesis, children have to *learn* the facts of the paradigm. Therefore, we would expect many errors, that is, illicit instances of contraction in subject extraction questions like (5b).

How can we test the experimental hypothesis—that children know the constraint on contraction across a *wh*-trace? Would it be sufficient, for example, to show that children produce only questions like (5a), but never questions like (5b), with the ungrammatical contraction? This demonstration would be suggestive, but it leaves a crucial question unanswered. The possibility would remain that children's failure to produce questions like (5b) results from a preference to avoid contraction, even though contraction is tolerated in the child's grammar. However unlikely this scenario might appear to be, it would clearly be preferable to make a stronger case for the innateness hypothesis—that children know the constraint in the absence of decisive evidence from experience. To make a convincing case, we need to disprove the hypothetical proposal that children prefer to avoid contraction when they can. For this purpose, the experiment should include object extraction questions like (4a) and (4b) as experimental controls. Since both contracted and noncontracted forms of (4) are permissible, each individual child's preference for contraction can be assessed. If it can be shown that children prefer to contract in object extraction questions like (4b), but avoid contraction in subject extraction questions, this would be compelling evidence that they adhere to the constraint.

Before the experimental hypothesis can be evaluated, the object extraction control questions from each individual subject must be examined carefully. Suppose the control sentences evoked from children revealed that there were some children who never contracted, producing questions like (4a) but not ones like (4b). These children would have to be excluded from the experiment, because their data would not be relevant for assessing the experimental hypothesis. If these children do not contract in object extraction questions, the fact that their subject extraction questions also lack contraction is of little consequence.

As it turns out, however, it is very unlikely that the experiment would expose a child who avoids contraction. This is because, as speakers, we have a tendency to use reduced forms of expression whenever possible (and the assumption is that children and adults have the same universal parser). This tendency to reduce forms favors contraction in object extraction questions like (4), where both forms are possible. As noted before, the demonstration that contraction is favored in object extraction questions like (4), but avoided in subject extraction questions like (5), would provide the critical evidence that children abide by the constraint on contraction across a *wh*-trace.

4.3.2 The Experimental Design
With the logic behind the experiment in mind, let us turn to its implementation. In conducting an experiment, it is important to be conservative as research scientists. Conservativity means that we should take the necessary steps to ensure that the experimental hypothesis is not favored by the experimental design; that is, we should avoid type I errors (see chapter 14, this volume, for more details). In the present case we would want to avoid designing the experiment so that children were encouraged to refrain from contracting in subject extraction questions for reasons that have nothing to do with adherence to the grammatical constraint. The best way to avoid favoring the experimental hypothesis is often to bias the experiment in ways that favor the null hypothesis instead. In the present case we might encourage children's use of contracted forms in order to favor the null hypothesis. To do this, the experimenter might begin with the object extraction trials, which are known to evoke contraction by adults. Once a sufficient number of object extraction questions have been elicited, the experimenter can switch to eliciting subject extraction questions. The issue

then becomes whether or not children manage to override their preference
for contraction, as established in the earlier object extraction trials, in
order to obey the grammatical constraint.

The experiment should be piloted with adults (or older children who are
adult with respect to the aspect of grammar being tested). It is also a good
idea to test a group of adults in addition to children in the actual experiment, so that their responses can be used for comparison. There is no
hard-and-fast rule; whether or not the use of adult controls is crucial
depends on the experimental hypothesis. But one can never go wrong by
including adults. In the case of the *wanna* contraction experiment, it is
advisable to include adult controls, so that the degree to which adults
favor contraction can be established.

The next step is for the experimenter to decide how many target structures (i.e., subject extraction questions) and how many control structures
(i.e., object extraction questions) to elicit. A reasonable goal would be a
minimum of four of each type. Because children may not produce what
the experimenter is hoping for on every trial, it is a good idea to have
about six experimental items prepared, in order to ensure that a total of
four tokens of the target structure are elicited from each child. In addition, a number of "warm-up" items and fillers should be prepared.

The targets, controls, and fillers can all be elicited in the context of a
game. When the experiment discussed above was actually conducted, the
ploy mentioned earlier of using a shy puppet who won't speak to grown-
ups was successful. I explained that the puppet—in this case a rat puppet
named Ratty—had come to live at my house, and I didn't know anything
about him. I solicited the child's help in finding out about him, and later,
when the puppet was feeling less shy, the child invited him to play various
games. The session began with simple warm-up questions to find out if the
rat was a boy or a girl, how old he was, where he lived, and so on. No
props were required for the warm-up questions. The control object extraction questions were elicited by the experimenter as shown in the following
protocol. In the situation set up to elicit "What do you wanna eat?",
various items of plastic food were laid out in the workspace.

(7) *Protocol for object extraction questions*
   Experimenter   The rat looks kind of hungry. I bet he wants to eat
   something. Ask him what.
   Child   What do you wanna eat?
   Ratty   Is that pepperoni pizza over there? I'll have some of that.

Similar questions could investigate what the rat wants to drink, what game he wants to play, and so on. With some thought, the experimenter can find a way to join the target items into one continuous discourse sequence. For example, after the rat has requested pizza to eat (as shown in the protocol), the experimenter might note that pizza often makes people thirsty, and then the scenario above can be repeated, substituting *drink* for *eat*.

Since the whole idea of elicited production is to investigate the child's grammar, the experimenter avoids using the *want to* sequence that is being tested. Notice in the protocol shown in (7) that the experimenter uses *wants to* (i.e., third person), but this is not a sequence that can be contracted to *wanna*, so it provides the child with no clues concerning when contraction is, and is not, permitted.

In response to the experimenter's lead-in, however, it is possible that the child might just ask "What do you want?" instead of "What do you wanna eat?" This question would not be useful for evaluating whether or not children contract the sequence *want* plus *to*. If this happens, the experimenter playing the role of the rat can ask for a repetition by saying "What?" or "Excuse me?" (see Valian and Wales 1976). In most cases this request for clarification elicits a full question.

For the subject extraction questions critical to testing the constraint, two protocols were prepared: a "simple" protocol, and a more complex protocol whose purpose was to encourage children to ask a full question. The questions using the simple protocol were elicited as part of the ongoing engagement with the rat. For example, after the rat had had a lot to drink and eat, the experimenter might say he should probably brush his teeth because he didn't want to get cavities. The experimenter put a toothbrush in the workspace, and the protocol might go as follows:

(8) *Simple protocol for subject extraction questions*
   Experimenter   I bet the rat wants someone to brush his teeth for him. Ask him who.
   Child   Who do you want to brush your teeth?
   Ratty   You!

The more complex protocol involved the child and the rat puppet in a "choosing" game. In this game, three toys were placed in the workspace, and the rat's task was to match each one up with one of three alternative actions described by the experimenter. The idea was that if more than one potential event could take place, the child would realize that a full question was needed to distinguish between them.

(9) *Complex protocol for subject extraction questions*
     Experimenter   In this game, there's a baby, a dog, and Cookie
     Monster, OK? And some different things are going to happen, and
     the rat gets to choose who gets to do those different things. Now,
     one of these guys gets to take a walk, one of these guys gets to take a
     nap, and one of these guys gets to eat a cookie. So, one of these guys
     gets to eat a cookie, right? Ask the rat who he wants.
     Child   Who do you want to eat a cookie?
     Ratty   Cookie Monster!

4.3.3   Data Analysis

Care must be taken in presenting data from elicited production experiments because each child's session will be a little different. Among the subjects will be children who produced all of the questions the experimenter was hoping for, children who were successful some proportion of the time, and possibly children who had difficulty with the targeted structures. Depending on the goal of the experiment, children who produce little relevant data can be excluded, as long as this is noted in the results. For example, a child in the present experiment who always used the expression "What would you like to ..." instead of "What do you want to/wanna ..." could be excluded on the grounds that her data were irrelevant to the null and experimental hypotheses. There are cases where exclusion would not be legitimate, however. If, for example, the point of the experiment was to see whether 3-year-old children's grammars can generate questions with an embedded infinitival clause, then all their attempts at questions from the *wanna* contraction paradigm would need to be included in the data analysis.

Before the subject and object extraction questions produced by each child are counted, certain decisions need to be made about how children's questions are coded. Will only full sentences (questions) be counted? If the child repeats a question, will it be counted as one instance of a question or two? If a child stutters and changes the structure midway through the question, does this count as a performance mistake? A criterion also needs to be established for deciding whether a particular child's data set should be included in the analysis of adherence to the constraint. One possible criterion for inclusion would be production of sufficient relevant data, say, at least four object extraction questions with contraction. Usually, the experimenter will have the criterion for inclusion in mind at the start of the experiment. On occasion, it is necessary to adjust the criterion once the data are all gathered. This step is legitimate, once again, as long as all the data are reported: those that are included in the analysis of children's adherence to the constraint, and those that are not. Whatever decisions the experimenter makes should be adhered to consistently for each child and described clearly in the report of the experimental findings.

In most cases an experimenter analyzes his or her own data. For an elicited production experiment, the tapes must be transcribed, and for the *wanna* contraction experiment, the child's questions carefully coded as *want to* or *wanna*. Because of the subjective nature of this decision, it is wise to call on outside judges, to ensure that there is a high degree of agreement in the judgments of the experimenter and other impartial parties. This was in fact done in the experiment reported in Thornton 1990.

The list of productions gathered for each child differs slightly in elicited production experiments, and for this reason group data can be misleading unless complemented with individual subject data. For the sake of illustration, let us say that the children's productions of object extraction questions were tallied, and of the 100 questions produced by the children, 62 exhibited contraction (i.e., 62%). From this percentage, it is not possible to infer that all of the children who participated in the experiment favor contraction. The group percentage could include some children who never contracted and other children who contacted most of the time. As noted earlier, for the *wanna* contraction experiment, it is crucial to show that every child whose data are used for evaluating the experimental hypothesis had a *preference* for contraction in the control object extraction questions. It would therefore be essential to include a table showing how many questions each child produced and how many of these showed contraction, so that readers could verify the preference for themselves.

For the record, the results of the *wanna* contraction experiment reported in Thornton 1990 showed that children do obey the constraint on contraction across *wh*-trace. That is, the experimental hypothesis was supported, even though the experiment was biased in favor of the null hypothesis. The experiment tested a total of 26 children, 14 of whom met the criterion for inclusion in the data analysis. These children all showed a strong preference for contraction in their object extraction questions, as a group contracting 88% of the time. In their subject extraction questions, children contracted 8% of the time.[2] This figure is sufficiently small to attribute to experimental error.[3] In short, the experimental hypothesis was confirmed.

4.3.4 Limitations of Elicited Production as a Tool for Investigating Constraints

As the discussion above has shown, elicited production can be used very successfully to test children's knowledge of constraints on form. In the particular experiment just reviewed, the technique was successful because the experimenter was able to establish a preference for contraction that was overridden in the critical subject extraction case. This response pattern clearly constituted convincing support for the innateness of the constraint. As noted, if children had not demonstrated a preference for contraction in the object extraction controls, it would have been difficult to make a strong case for innate knowledge of the constraint. It might have been possible to show that the data were *compatible* with knowledge of the constraint, but the data might equally well have been explained by other factors, such as a preference for noncontraction.

It might be helpful to illustrate the point with an example where elicited production cannot be used to provide convincing evidence for innate knowledge of a constraint. The Empty Category Principle (ECP) is such a case, at least if it is tested by investigating the well-known *that*-trace paradigm.

The *that*-trace paradigm consists of long-distance questions like those given in (10) and (11). Long-distance questions are questions in which the *wh*-phrase is moved from an embedded clause that is tensed. In the *that*-trace paradigm, the ECP constrains the appearance of the complementizer *that*. In the questions in (10), the *wh*-phrase is extracted from object position of a tensed embedded clause, and the questions are grammatical either with or without the complementizer. In questions in which the *wh*-phrase is moved from subject position, however, the question is grammatical only when the complementizer is omitted, as in (11a). In the ungrammatical question form in (11b), in which the complementizer is present, the complementizer *that* is followed by a *wh*-trace (hence the name "*that*-trace paradigm").

(10) a. What do you think flies eat *t*?   object extraction
     b. What do you think that flies eat *t*?

(11) a. What do you think *t* eats flies?   subject extraction
     b. *What do you think that *t* eats flies?

There are several accounts of why the complementizer in (11b) makes the sentence ungrammatical (for two of these, see Lasnik and Uriagereka 1988 and Rizzi 1990). For present purposes, it is sufficient to note that the ungrammaticality of (11b) is due to a putative constraint of UG.

As noted earlier, an experiment testing a constraint should establish a preference for the phenomenon that is then suppressed in syntactic environments where the constraint is at work. In the case of the ECP, the experimenter would need to establish a preference for complementizers in object extraction questions that disappears when the ECP disallows them in subject extraction questions. The problem is that it is difficult to establish a preference for use of complementizers in the control object extraction environment. In this particular case, the parsing preference to produce reduced forms runs counter to the goals of the experiment. In the *wanna* contraction experiment, the tendency to use reduced forms encouraged contraction, and this was what was needed. In the present experiment, the same tendency to reduce forms encourages *omission* (not *insertion*) of complementizers, making it impossible to show that children have a preference for use of complementizers in the control object extraction environment.[4] For this reason, elicited production cannot provide data that are robust enough to argue strongly for the innateness of the ECP, although it can provide data that are compatible with innate knowledge of the constraint.

Given the difficulties encountered by elicited production, one might want to turn to other techniques to test children's knowledge of the ungrammaticality of questions like (11b). The grammaticality judgment technique of McDaniel and colleagues is one possibility (for this method, see McDaniel, Chiu, and Maxfield 1995; chapter 11, this volume).

4.4 Long-Distance Questions

This section demonstrates that elicited production can be used for in-depth investigations of aspects of children's grammars. The discussion centers on the *form* of children's long-distance questions, which are reported to appear very rarely in children's spontaneous speech. According to de Villiers, Roeper, and Vainikka (1990), only 16 such questions can be found in Adam's transcripts on the CHILDES database over a period of $3\frac{1}{2}$ years. For this reason, it is interesting to see whether children ask questions extracting from an embedded clause when put in situations that are uniquely felicitous for the long-distance question structure. As it happens, children readily produce long-distance questions, but many of them are "nonadult" in form (Thornton 1990; Thornton and Crain 1994). One purpose of this section will be to show how an experimenter might pursue the source of the nonadult responses. Let us begin by examining the protocols that elicit long-distance questions.

4.4.1 Experimental Technique

In the long-distance question experiment, as in the *wanna* contraction experiment, questions are elicited from children by having them find out information from a rat puppet, Ratty, that is too shy to communicate with grown-ups. The child is encouraged to invite Ratty to participate in a "guessing game" in which he is asked his opinion in questions of the form "What do you *think* ...". For completeness, questions should be elicited from varying extraction sites, in case one or another proves to be more problematic for children. Here, we will consider subject and object extraction questions.

In an experiment eliciting long-distance questions, to elicit questions extracting from subject position, the child has Ratty cover his eyes. The experimenter and the child then hide a series of items (say, a toy bear, a marble, and a toy Grover) in various places (in a box, under a blanket, and in a yogurt carton). Ratty is then allowed to uncover his eyes, and the guessing game proceeds. (One experimental context is sufficient to elicit three long-distance questions.)

(12) *Protocol for subject extraction questions*
    Experimenter ⟨in low voice to child, so that Ratty can't hear⟩ We
    know where all the things are hidden, right? We know that there's
    a marble in the box, a bear under the blanket and we know that
    Grover is under the yogurt carton. Let's see if Ratty can guess
    where we hid them. Let's do the box first, OK? We know that
    there's a marble in the box, but ask the rat what *he* thinks.
    Child What do you think is in the box?
    Ratty Can you rattle the box for me? Hmm, I think that there's a
    marble in the box.
    Child You're right!
    Experimenter Hey, he made a good guess. Now let's do the
    blanket ... ⟨game continues in the same way⟩

The experimenter needs to be careful to avoid using the target long-distance *wh*-questions in his or her own speech. The final lead-in to the child in (12) contains an embedded question followed by an elided long-distance *wh*-question (i.e., "Ask the rat what *he* thinks").[5] Since the crucial long-distance *wh*-question is elided and therefore not overt input to the child, this lead-in cannot be said to give the child any clues to the targeted structure.

The protocol for object extraction questions proceeds on similar lines. Again, the rat is asked to hide his eyes while the experimenter and the child settle the items to be guessed about. There are three characters (say, Cookie Monster, a baby, and a Ninja Turtle). The experimenter tells the child that the puppet has to guess what Cookie Monster eats, what babies drink, and what Ninja Turtles like to eat. The protocol proceeds as follows:

(13) *Protocol for object extraction questions*
   Experimenter ⟨to child in a low voice so that Ratty can't hear⟩
   We know about all these guys, right? We know that Cookie
   Monster eats . . .
   Child Cookies.
   Experimenter And babies drink . . .
   Child Milk.
   Experimenter And Ninja Turtles like . . .
   Child Pizza.
   Experimenter Right! Now let's find out if Ratty knows all those
   things. Let's do Cookie Monster first. We know that Cookie
   Monster eats ⟨whispered⟩ cookies, but ask the rat what *he* thinks.
   Child What do you think Cookie Monster eats?
   Ratty Well, Cookie Monster is a monster, so I think he eats
   monsters.
   Child No! Cookies!
   Experimenter He's silly, isn't he? Cookie Monster eats cookies,
   just like you said. Let's do another one . . . ⟨game continues⟩

4.4.2 Potential Ask/Tell Problems

Earlier it was noted that an experiment eliciting questions must satisfy the felicity conditions for a question "game" in order to prevent the ask/tell problem from arising. As noted also, it is often desirable that every target question request new information; children should not know the answers to the questions they are posing to the puppet. In the protocols for eliciting long-distance questions in (12) and (13), the child does not know what *Ratty thinks* babies drink, Cookie Monster eats, and so on. Nevertheless, the child does know what Cookie Monster actually eats, babies actually drink, and so on, because this was established along with the experimenter. In a sense, then, the child knows the "real" answer, and this could possibly prompt a "tell" response. These protocols rarely cause a problem to surface, however, provided that the game starts off satisfying the felicity conditions. If a problem were to arise with a particular child, it would be simple to modify the game so that the child does not know the answer to the questions. To elicit subject extraction questions, for example, the experimenter could hide the objects and have both the child and the puppet cover their eyes. The experimenter could have the child guess what was in each place and then ask Ratty for his guess. The protocol could be adjusted as follows:

(14) *Adjusted protocol for subject extraction questions*
Experimenter ⟨to child and the rat puppet⟩ I'm going to hide some things, and then you and the rat guess. Hide your eyes! ⟨experimenter hides objects⟩ OK, you can come out now. There's something in this box, something under this blanket, and something in the yogurt carton. Let's do the box first. You guess first, and then the rat can have a turn. OK. What's your guess?
Child I think there's a Smurf in there.
Experimenter OK, you had your turn. You think that there's a Smurf in the box, but ask the rat what *he* thinks.
Child What do *you* think is in the box?
Ratty A hamburger?
Experimenter I'll show you what's really in the box. It was Grover!

4.4.3 Findings

Using the technique of elicited production, it can be shown that children as young as 2;6 can produce long-distance questions. Apparently, children do not produce them often in their spontaneous speech because a simpler form of communication is usually available—a matrix question. By orchestrating special situations in which the issue is what someone else thinks, the technique of elicited production is able to show that children can produce long-distance question structures.

The elicitation experiment revealed that many of children's productions of long-distance questions are nonadult in form, however (see Thornton

1990). Some children insert complementizers where they are not permitted according to the ECP, as in (15b), and other children insert an extra *wh*-phrase in "medial" position, as in (16).[6]

(15) a. What do you think that Cookie Monster eats?
     b. *Who do you think that's in the box?

(16) a. *What do you think what Cookie Monster eats?
     b. *Who do you think who's in the box?

These findings may have been observed anecdotally in previous literature (e.g., Stromswold 1990b), but the nonadult forms did not appear frequently enough in children's spontaneous speech to draw any conclusions about whether they were performance errors or part of the child's grammar.

Elicitation experiments targeting long-distance questions show that for some children, the nonadult question forms appear consistently. These consistent insertions of elements that do not appear in adults' long-distance questions are meaningful, because they clearly go against the tendency to reduce forms. This suggests that the uncalled-for complementizers and extra *wh*-phrases are obligatory for these children, and occur for grammatical reasons. How might elicited production be used to test a series of hypotheses that would lead to an explanation of these forms?

First, it would be important to look closely at the individual subject data, to see whether all children produce nonadult questions or only some. If only some children do, it would be premature to claim that such productions represent a "stage" of development. Making this claim would involve following a group of children longitudinally and testing their long-distance question forms periodically. In fact, not all children make this error.

To understand the source of the nonadult questions, the best idea would be to examine the grammars of such children in depth. A range of structures could be elicited to determine which syntactic environments the extra complementizers or extra *wh*-phrases appear in. For example, do the extra complementizers and *wh*-phrases appear only in questions, or also in declaratives? Do they appear in yes/no questions? Do they also appear in long-distance questions in which the *wh*-phrase is moved from an infinitival clause (such as those in the *wanna* contraction paradigm)? This would be an important question for theoretical reasons beyond the scope of this chapter (see Thornton 1990 for more details). Where the data differ from the adult grammar of English, the experimenter could look to other languages, to see whether UG allows the structure.

This kind of investigation is clearly quite different from the *wanna* contraction experiment in which the goal was to test a constraint. The experiment on long-distance questions provides informative data by investigating a range of structures that allow us to home in on the reason for the error. In such an investigation, there is no single control structure, as in the *wanna* contraction experiment. A child's productions of a variety of structures contribute to the total picture of the child's grammar, enabling us to hypothesize what the child can and cannot say.

4.5 Conclusion

The technique of elicited production, described in this chapter, can be used to test children's knowledge of syntax. In particular, it can be used effectively to study children's knowledge of constraints on form, such as the constraint on contraction across *wh*-trace observed in the *wanna* contraction paradigm, and to explore individual children's grammars in depth.

Notes

1. For some of the children, the verb *find out* is less likely to induce the ask/tell problem than *ask*. In this case the child can be prompted to "Find out if they have hamburgers on his planet."

2. Individual subject data are not presented here for lack of space. See Thornton 1990 for a table of individual subject data and for criteria used for including children's data in the analysis for adherence to the constraint.

3. Crain and Wexler (to appear) propose that when testing constraints of UG, researchers should expect a 90% accuracy level, up to 10% of responses being attributable to noise.

4. Complementizers are optional in English, unlike in some other languages. This means they can be omitted, in keeping with the parsing preference to reduce forms, without violating the grammar.

5. The suggestion is that the sentence can be naturally expanded to "Ask the rat what he thinks *is in the box*." In this case a long-distance question is embedded inside an indirect question.

6. For related references on this phenomenon, see McDaniel, Chiu, and Maxfield 1995 and de Villiers, Roeper, and Vainikka 1990. See Thornton and Crain 1994 for experiments that argue that the comprehension phenomenon discussed by de Villiers, Roeper, and Vainikka is not the same phenomenon as the "medial" *wh*-phrase produced by children in their long-distance questions.

PART II
Comprehension Data

Chapter 5

The Intermodal Preferential Looking Paradigm: A Window onto Emerging Language Comprehension	Kathy Hirsh-Pasek and Roberta Michnick Golinkoff

Early language comprehension is mostly an uncharted landscape. Researchers suspect that children know much more than their speech reflects, but it has proven notoriously difficult to substantiate this claim. Methods of studying language comprehension have often been undermined by toddlers who prefer to play with the psycholinguist's toys than to perform requested actions. Hence, measures of comprehension often become measures of compliance rather than of language development. In this chapter we review a relatively new but well-tested procedure for peering into the rich store of language structures that unfold in language comprehension before they are available in language production. In writing the chapter, we have four goals. First, we briefly outline the rationale for using comprehension as an avenue to understanding language development. Second, we present a new method for examining grammatical and lexical comprehension, the intermodal preferential looking paradigm. Third, we briefly review some of the studies that have been completed using this paradigm. Fourth, we evaluate the paradigm's strengths and weaknesses.

5.1 Reasons for Studying Language Comprehension

There can be little doubt that studies on young children's language production in the past 25 years have provided a solid base for language acquisition theories. Language production, the observable half of the child's language performance, is only part of the story, however. Just as astronomers were not satisfied to study only the light side of the moon, so researchers in language acquisition have long recognized that access to data from the "dark" side of their topic—namely, language comprehension—illuminates the language acquisition process far more than the study of production alone. In particular, language comprehension data serve three useful purposes. First, by looking at comprehension, researchers can obtain a more accurate picture of the content of the child's emerging language system. It has sometimes been assumed, for example, that the syntactic variability found in a set of transcripts accurately reflects the breadth of the child's grammatical knowledge. However, since children talk in environments that are rich in contextual and social supports, it is likely that their productions underrepresent their grammatical knowledge. That is, children typically select speech topics from the "here-and-now." Because of this, and because of willing adults who interpret for them, children can often get away with saying less, and saying it in a less sophisticated manner, to achieve their goals. Without comprehension assessments, the researcher is forced to wait for the child to spontaneously produce the structure of interest.

A second reason for focusing on the study of comprehension is that it provides an alternative window onto the *process* of language acquisition. Arguably, by the time children are producing a particular structure, they have already acquired it. Yet the steps leading up to the analysis and mastery of that structure would be less visible without studies of comprehension. By studying language comprehension we can ask, for example, what kinds of organization a child imposes on a word string or what strategy a child is using to interpret a new word (see chapter 9, this volume).

The third reason why comprehension data are useful has to do with *methodological control.* In the real world there may be circumstances in which children appear to comprehend certain structures when in fact they do not. With comprehension experiments, researchers interested in a certain structure and the circumstances under which it is used can create situations of a type that control for extraneous variables. For example, Shatz (1978) argued that children are biased to respond to sentences with action, whether or not an action is being called for. To test this hypothesis, Shatz created conditions in which it was clear to *adults* that an action was *not* being called for to see whether children could resist the temptation to act (e.g., when asked, "Do you know how to jump?", would the child respond by jumping or—as an adult would—by saying "yes"?). The results showed that children indeed overwhelmingly choose to respond to sentences with actions. They seem to interpret questions as indirect requests for action.

In sum, studies of language comprehension have three advantages over studies using spontaneous production: they permit researchers to probe for structures that are not yet produced; they offer a new window onto the process by which the child acquires a particular structure before that structure emerges full-blown; and they permit a degree of methodological control not available from observing production.

Despite the relative advantages of studying comprehension, it has been exceedingly difficult to find methods that can tap into emergent grammar through comprehension. Prior methods have often been plagued by two problems: (1) they require children to act on command when toddlers are notorious for their noncompliance; and (2) they are hampered by the constraints of static stimulus displays that cannot adequately assess the child's growing knowledge of action words (verbs) or propositional relationships (sentences). The intermodal preferential looking paradigm was developed to overcome these hurdles.

5.2 The Intermodal Preferential Looking Paradigm: Rationale and Description

5.2.1 Rationale

The intermodal preferential looking paradigm was adapted from the work of Spelke (1979), who developed it to study intermodal perception. In Spelke's version, 4-month-old infants saw two events (e.g., a person clapping hands and a donkey falling onto a table) and heard a nonlinguistic auditory stimulus that matched only one of the events (say, the sound of hands clapping). The infants tended to look more at the screen on which the event matched the auditory stimulus than at the screen on which it did not.

In our adaptation of the paradigm (Golinkoff and Hirsh-Pasek 1981), an infant is seated on a blindfolded parent's lap exactly between and 2'6" back from the center of two television monitors, which are 30" apart. A concealed audio speaker midway between the two monitors plays a linguistic stimulus that is consonant with or "matches" only one of the displays shown on the screens. Mounted atop the speaker is a light that comes on during each intertrial interval to ensure that the infant makes a new choice about which screen to look at on each trial. The infant's task is to look at one of the two video screens. An observer (either on-line or off-line, watching videotape) records all looking responses. In all such studies the logic is the same as in Spelke's experiments: infants should choose to allocate more attention to the video event that matches what they are hearing (in this case, a linguistic message) than to a video event that does not match. In this linguistic version of the preferential looking paradigm, children can show relatively more visual attention to the match than to the nonmatch only if they *understand* the language that is used.

To see how the paradigm works, consider a pair of stimuli in what is arguably the simplest case: noun comprehension (Golinkoff et al. 1987). In one trial a shoe appeared on one screen and a boat on the other. The linguistic message (produced in child-directed speech) was "Where's the shoe? Find the shoe!" The hypothesis, which was confirmed, was that infants would look more quickly and longer toward the screen displaying the shoe than toward the screen displaying the boat.

Figure 5.1 depicts the paradigm used in a slightly more complicated case: a study on children's perception of constituent structure (Hirsh-Pasek and Golinkoff 1996). On one screen children see a woman kissing keys while holding a ball in the foreground; on the other screen they see a woman kissing a ball while dangling keys in the foreground. The audio that they hear is "Hey! She's kissing the keys." The hypothesis in this study was also confirmed: 14-month-old infants looked longer at the screen that depicted the woman kissing the keys (as opposed to just holding the keys), a response we interpreted to mean that infants understand that language maps to "packages" of events in the world.

The intermodal preferential looking paradigm seems capable of revealing linguistic knowledge in young children for two reasons. First, unlike many other assessments of language comprehension, this paradigm does not require children to point, answer questions, or act out commands. Children need merely employ a response already in their repertoire—visual fixation—in order to fulfill the task requirements. Second, the paradigm usually does not set natural cues for comprehension in conflict with each other, nor does it omit the contribution of these sources. That is, in this paradigm children have access to syntactic, semantic, prosodic, and contextual information. When these are all provided, children may take advantage of what we have called the "coalition" of cues normally used in language comprehension to demonstrate the upper limits of their knowledge (see Hirsh-Pasek and Golinkoff 1996).

It could be argued that the rationale behind the paradigm—namely, that infants will prefer to watch the screen that matches the linguistic stimulus more than the screen that does not—apparently contradicts much of the research indicating that infants prefer to watch novel or

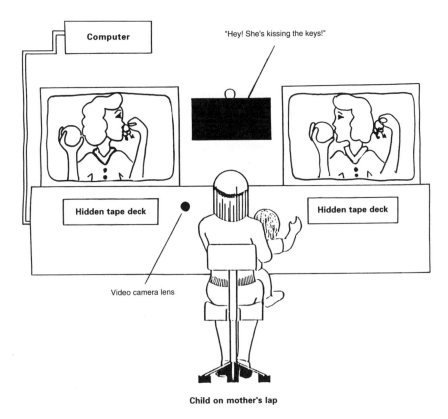

Figure 5.1
The intermodal preferential looking paradigm

discrepant stimuli (see Cohen, DeLoache, and Strauss 1979). However, techniques that have found a preference for novelty differ from the one presented here in two fundamental ways.

First, novelty preference appears to be the rule for *intra*modal experiments in which two visual events are paired and presented with no accompanying auditory stimulus. In addition, intramodal experiments specifically manipulate novelty by presenting the same stimuli repeatedly and then varying the next stimulus in some systematic way to see if the child can discriminate the new from the old. *Inter*modal experiments do not manipulate novelty but ask a different question: Can children find the invariance or link between stimuli presented in two different modalities (e.g., visual and auditory)? Throughout the literature on intermodal perception, studies show that infants prefer to find the matching rather than the nonmatching stimulus. For example, Starkey, Spelke, and Gelman (1983) showed that 10-month-olds, presented with two screens, would watch the one that displayed the same number of objects (randomly arranged) as the number of taps they heard. Similarly, Meltzoff and Borton (1979) found that 29-day-old infants would look longer at a shape they had explored by touch than at one they had not explored. Finally, Kuhl and Meltzoff (1982) found that 4-month-old infants preferred to look at a face whose mouth was moving in concert with a speech sound they heard rather than at a face whose mouth was articulating another sound.

Second, unlike intramodal experiments, intermodal experiments are not designed as discrimination tasks in which a concept or category is built up and then altered systematically. (An example of an intramodal experiment is that of Younger and Cohen (1986), who showed that infants constructed a concept of a novel type of animal that had a certain set of correlated attributes (e.g., tail length and ear height). Infants showed significant dishabituation to animals that did not share the same set of correlated attributes.) In intermodal experiments (like ours) that yoke symbolic stimuli with referents, researchers ask not whether infants can distinguish between two concepts, but whether they can use a symbolic stimulus to find a referent. That is, these studies do not address the issue of novelty and discrimination—indeed, they present two equally novel stimuli. The question is whether children can use their understanding of the language to find the corresponding stimulus presented in the visual modality.

In a sense, the intermodal preferential looking paradigm duplicates the language-learning situation. When a parent says, "See the dog!", for example, the child's task is to *match up* the linguistic stimuli he is hearing (the word "dog") with something in the environment (a dog). Thus, this paradigm may work because its requirements mimic those found in language learning: infants might prefer the matching screen over the nonmatching screen because there is some ecological validity in looking for a "match" in the environment when they are presented with symbolic stimuli like words. For this reason and the reasons stated above, in no studies performed in our laboratories have children ever shown a significant (or even approaching significant) preference for the nonmatch.

5.2.2 Description
In this section we provide a detailed description of the paradigm.

5.2.2.1 Construction of the Video Events Two videotapes are developed for each study. The videotapes are constructed so that they work in synchrony, trial for trial, down to the same number of frames. This level of precision is essential given that the paradigm relies on preferential visual fixation, which can be biased by a number of incidental factors—not the least of which is one tape in a pair coming on before the other. Trials on a pair of tapes start and end at the same time, and the tapes stay in synchrony as they are played. In addition, although achieving perfect control is impossible, every effort is made to balance the amount of action and color on the two screens so as to reduce any potential salience problems. For example, the characters used in each tape in a pair are of approximately equivalent size, and if a repetitive action is being performed on one screen, it is balanced against another repetitive action —taking place the same number of times—on the other screen.

In a perfect world, it would be preferable to test each video scene in the paradigm without accompanying audio to ensure that the stimuli are indeed equally salient—that is, that children watch each video in a pair for an approximately equal amount of time. As a practical matter and without unlimited time or funds, we chose instead to try to balance the salience as best we could before making the video stimuli and then, as will be detailed below, to assess the salience as a control trial within the paradigm. This practice has served us well and allows us to check for salience between the tapes and to control for any imbalances (which are rare) in our final analyses.

Videotapes for the studies are filmed with a color camera against a white background. The best exemplars of each type of desired event are then selected and duplicated exactly for the number of trials needed for a particular study. Editing is done at the University of Delaware's Media Services Center. The videotapes used for the original footage and editing are $\frac{3}{4}''$ performance-quality tapes, although the $\frac{1}{2}''$ medium works as well. Copies of the original edited masters to be used for testing are then made on both $\frac{1}{2}''$ tape (for the Temple University laboratory) and $\frac{3}{4}''$ tape (for the University of Delaware laboratory).

5.2.2.2 Trials and Intertrial Intervals Table 5.1 shows a typical layout of a pair of tapes using a set of stimuli designed to test children's appreciation of constituent structure. There are three kinds of trials, all 6 seconds in length, called "sequential trials," "simultaneous trials," and "test

Table 5.1
The video events and linguistic stimuli for one block of trials

Tape 1	Linguistic stimuli	Tape 2
	Sequential trials	
Woman kissing ball while dangling keys in foreground	"Oh, what's going on?"	Blank screen
Blank screen	{Center light} "Hey, what's going on?"	Blank screen
Blank screen	"Look! What is she doing?"	Woman kissing keys while holding ball in foreground
	Simultaneous trial	
Blank screen	{Center light} "Wow, what's happening!"	Blank screen
Woman kissing ball ...	"What are they doing?"	Woman kissing keys ...
	Test trials	
Blank screen	{Center light} "Hey, she's kissing the keys!"	Blank screen
Woman kissing ball ...	"Wow, she's kissing the keys!"	Woman kissing keys ...
Blank screen	{Center light} "Where is she kissing the keys?"	Blank screen
Woman kissing ball ...	"Oh! She's kissing the keys!"	Woman kissing keys ...

trials," and one type of intertrial interval in which the child sees a blank screen. A trial is defined as the time between two intertrial intervals.

Intertrial Intervals Each trial is preceded and followed by a 3-second intertrial interval. During this period both screens are blank, and a low-wattage light bulb (mounted atop the hidden speaker centered between the two screens) is illuminated. The intertrial interval serves an important function: it draws the child's attention back to the center area between the two screens, allowing the child to make a "clean," independent choice for each trial. If children do not attend to the central fixation light for longer than .30 seconds during the intertrial interval before the test trial, their data for that trial are discarded. (Well over 97% of all trials are retained using this criterion.)

The low-wattage light bulb has been very effective in attracting children's attention to the center. One version of the paradigm (Naigles 1990) employs a coiled circular blinking light for the same purpose. These lights do not function like the reward rabbits reported in Kuhl's (1985) conditioned head-turn paradigms; in those cases the lights served as feedback and reinforcement to the children's responses.

Sequential Trials As table 5.1 shows, in the sequential trials the child first sees an event on only the left screen while the right screen remains blank. This is followed by a 3-second intertrial interval. Then the child sees an event on the right screen while the left screen remains blank. These trials serve to (1) introduce the video events before the child has to find the match for the linguistic stimulus, and (2) create the expectation that something will appear on each screen. The audio presented during sequential trials, as well as the audio presented during the intertrial interval that precedes each sequential trial, is "neutral" in the sense that it "matches" or is equally consistent with both events. For example, as in table 5.1, it might be something like "What's going on?"

Simultaneous Trials A simultaneous trial, during which the video scenes are presented synchronously on both screens, follows the sequential trials. Simultaneous trials show the child that events will appear concurrently on both screens and, as shown in table 5.1, are composed of the same events the child has seen in the sequential trials. They also provide a check on stimulus salience. That is, if the visual stimuli have been well balanced for perceptual factors, and while the linguistic stimulus is still neutral (see above), it is predicted that attention should be distributed approximately equally to each member of the simultaneous pair across children.

Test Trials Two pairs of test trials always follow the simultaneous trial. The test trials differ from the simultaneous trial in a single way: the linguistic stimulus that accompanies these trials now exhorts the child to look at the screen that matches the linguistic stimulus (e.g., "Hey, she's kissing the keys!"). The linguistic stimulus, which describes one of the video events, is first heard during the 3-second intertrial interval that precedes the test trials and again during the test trials themselves.

5.2.2.3 Linguistic Stimuli The linguistic stimuli for the test trials are given first during the intertrial interval that precedes the test trials and then during we the test trials themselves. The rationale for presenting the linguistic stimulus during the intertrial interval is that by the time the intertrial interval that precedes the first test trial comes on the screen, the child has already had ample opportunity to observe the scenes on both screens.

Depending on the particular study, the linguistic stimulus is presented either once or twice during each test trial. From pilot work it became clear that the linguistic stimulus should be present for the duration of the event to maximize the amount of time the infant looks toward the matching screen.

All studies use "motherese" or child-directed speech produced by female voices. Many research findings indicate that infants prefer to listen to child-directed rather than adult-directed speech (Fernald 1985; Kemler Nelson et al. 1989; Cooper and Aslin 1990)—even in nonnative languages (Werker, Pegg, and McLeod 1994). Further, despite the added linguistic complexity, all the linguistic stimuli are full sentences. The rationale for the use of full sentences again comes from the literature on child-directed speech: young children are more likely to be addressed in sentences that are grammatically complete than sentences that are incomplete and grammatically incorrect (Shipley, Smith, and Gleitman 1969).

5.2.2.4 Independent, Dependent, and Counterbalanced Variables The independent, dependent, and counterbalanced variables are more often than not the same across experiments.

Independent Variables Typical between-subjects independent variables in these studies are age and sex. Sometimes children of the same age are also divided on the variable of linguistic level. The within-subjects variables are match versus nonmatch and stimulus. "Stimulus" refers to a pair of test events. Most of the studies have used four pairs of events to test the structure in question. Each pair is seen twice and the data are always averaged across these two trials to increase the reliability of children's responses.

The Dependent Variable Visual fixation time or the total amount of time in seconds (measured to the tenth of a second) the child spends watching the matching versus the nonmatching screen is the dependent variable. It is cumulated from the time that the child looks at the light between the screens for more than .30 seconds during the intertrial interval. Recall that the linguistic stimulus for a test trial is first heard during the intertrial interval that precedes it. By that time children have seen (in most of our studies) two sequential trials and one simultaneous trial, so they presumably know what events to expect on each screen. Thus, we have found that children look to the matching screen even *before* the test trials come on. Furthermore, analyses that began measuring the dependent variable during the intertrial interval or that measured only during the test trials had the same results. In order for a look at either screen to feed into the cumulation of visual fixation time, it must exceed .30 seconds, considered the lower limit on the observer's reliable judgment of visual fixation.

The hypothesis in each study is that significantly more visual fixation time will be allocated to the matching than to the nonmatching event. Note that it is never hypothesized that the child will look *exclusively* at the matching screen. In fact, looking times are expected to be distributed between the two video events since, for control purposes, visual displays in a pair are designed, as much as possible, to contain equivalent activity, bright colors, and complexity.

Coding of the Dependent Variable   Infants' visual fixation responses are recorded either off-line (and coded after the child's visit) or on-line by a hidden observer. When visual fixation is coded *off-line*, the child's viewing of the tape is recorded on another videotape by an observer manipulating a video camera whose lens protrudes slightly from between and below the two monitors. The observer, hidden from the child's view, keeps the camera focused on the child's face. After the child's visit, a coder sets up the computer to receive the data and then plays the child's record back without sound. The coder, blind to the sequence of matches the child has seen, depresses hand-held buttons that correspond to the left and right screens to record the child's visual fixation on the tapes. The coder holds down the appropriate button for the duration of the child's gaze at a screen; both buttons simultaneously if the child looks to the center; and neither button if the child looks at neither screen. A computer program, especially designed for the purpose of calculating the data and depicting them trial by trial, receives the output of the coder's button presses. (This program was written for an Apple IIe and is available from either author on request.)

When visual fixation is coded *on-line*, the observer is behind the apparatus holding the visual fixation coding buttons. The observer can hear the audio but is blind to the sequence of matches the child is seeing. In both the on- and off-line cases, observers report that they cannot keep track of the sequence of the matches; capturing the direction and duration of the child's gaze is all-consuming. Further, since sequential and simultaneous trials intervene between test trials, there is no easy pattern of matches to be memorized. Interrater reliability is quite high in this paradigm (for details, see Hirsh-Pasek and Golinkoff 1996).

Missing Trials Averaging across studies, approximately 3% of children's trials are not included in the data analysis. Trials can be missed for two reasons. First, if a child fails to watch the center light for at least .30 seconds during the intertrial interval that precedes each test trial, that trial is not counted. Second, if a child looks at neither screen for the duration of a trial, that trial is not counted. When a missing trial occurs, the child's mean visual fixation time to the matching and nonmatching screens across all the other test events is entered into the empty data cell.

Counterbalanced Variables Five factors are counterbalanced in all experiments within a pair of videotapes. First, the first sequential trial (see table 5.1) appears half the time on the left screen and half the time on the right screen within the four blocks of trials. Second, the match occurs the same number of times on the left screen as on the right screen. Third, for half of the subjects tape 1 is shown in the left deck; for the other half of the subjects, it is shown in the right deck. This has the effect of producing two orders of the matching events that are mirror images of each other. Fourth, the linguistic message matches one stimulus of a test pair for half of the subjects and the other stimulus of a test pair for the other half. This is achieved by rerecording the audio message. Thus, if positive results emerge in a study, this critical counterbalance allows us to conclude that they are not a function of some peculiar synergism between the linguistic stimulus and the video event. Fifth, when a study requires two actors on a screen, the left-right position of the actors is counterbalanced so that location on the screen cannot serve as an artifactual cue to the matching screen.

Matches always occur in the order left-right-right-left (or its mirror image) to ensure that subjects are basing their performance on finding the match for the linguistic stimulus and not on ordering strategies. Orders avoided are a strict alternating pattern (e.g., left-right-left-right) and starting out with two "winners" on the same side (e.g., left-left-right-right).

5.2.2.5 Additional Experimental Controls Two additional controls are built into the studies. First, the parent (usually the child's mother) wears a visor so as not to be able to see the stimuli and unwittingly influence the looking patterns of the infant. The observers who code infants' eye fixations (either on- or off-line) discard the data from any child whose parent directs more than a passing glance toward the videotapes. Second, the parent sits facing forward with uncrossed legs, having been instructed not to speak to the child so as not to unduly bias the infant's looking preference.

5.2.2.6 Apparatus and Lighting All equipment—except for the two 20″ color monitors—is shielded from the child's view. The videotapes (filmed with a Newvicon 3150 color video camera) are shown on either $\frac{1}{2}″$ or $\frac{3}{4}″$ video decks, at the Temple and Delaware laboratories, respectively. The linguistic stimulus, dubbed onto the first channel of the videotape, is shunted to an audio speaker between the two monitors (see figure 5.1). Thus, infants cannot find the match by looking at the monitor that plays the linguistic message.

Videotapes have two auditory channels. The first channel contains the linguistic message the child hears. The second, inaudible channel contains a 1-kHz tone recorded for the duration of each trial. Thus, when any of the three types of trials is playing, the tone is on; when there is an intertrial interval (blank screen), the tone is off. These tones are "read" by a specially designed tone decoder that has two functions: (1) it turns the light on during the intertrial intervals and off during the trials; and (2) it signals the beginning and end of each trial to the computer that has been programmed to compile a record of each child's looking responses throughout all trials and the intertrial intervals. The output from the observers' button presses enters the computer through the game port control panels.

Ambient lighting in the testing room is kept dim to heighten the salience of the monitors, minimize other distractions, and maximize attention to the screens. Although overall attention to the videotapes can be affected by the ambient lighting, these overall differences in visual fixation do not affect looking preferences to the matching screen.

5.2.2.7 Subject Solicitation Subject families are found through birth announcements in local newspapers or through purchased mailing lists. They are contacted first through a letter explaining the project and then by phone to set up an appointment. Parents are fully informed about the purpose of the study and sign a release form at the laboratory before testing begins. After their visit parents receive a letter thanking them for their participation. Later they receive another letter summarizing the results of the study. Thus far children ranging from 12 months to 4 years of age have been studied using the paradigm.

5.2.2.8 Procedure The children come to our university laboratories, where they first play with an experimenter using a small set of toys. For some of the studies, items relevant to the tapes children are about to see are among the toys used. While the child plays, the parent hears an explanation of the research. The parent signs a human subjects release form and then fills out either the Rescorla Language Inventory (1991), the MacArthur Inventory for Infants, or the MacArthur Inventory for Toddlers (see Fenson et al. 1994). Both require checking off the words that the child understands or produces (depending on the child's age) from a large set of words. (Depending on the child's age, parents are differentially reassured that their children are not expected to know more than a subset of the words.) The parent is also asked to report examples of the longer word combinations that the child has used. Children's utterances during the laboratory visit are recorded by an experimenter so that the children can be crudely classified as one-, two-, or three-word speakers.

The parent is then asked to put on a tennis visor that will be pulled down to block vision during the actual testing. Putting the visor on in the playroom removes some of the novelty of the "hat" so that it does not distract the child's attention during testing. The vast majority of parents comply readily with the request to keep the visor over their eyes during testing.

Parents sit facing forward with uncrossed legs and are asked to keep their children centered on their lap and not to speak to them during the video presentation. If the child seems to want to get off the parent's lap, the parent is told to say something neutral to the child, like "Just another minute." The experimenter darkens the laboratory, starts the two videotapes, and leaves the room. Testing is stopped and the child considered a lost subject if at any point the child becomes fussy or upset. Finally, the parent and child are invited to see the experimental tapes immediately after each test is completed.

5.2.2.9 Subject Loss Subject losses in this procedure parallel those found in other studies of infant development and, in particular, in other studies that use visual fixation as a dependent variable (e.g., Cohen and Oakes 1993). They run between 15% and 50%, with younger subjects responsible for higher losses. Although this procedure has an advantage in that it often uses movement in its visual displays, infants are notoriously difficult subjects.

Criteria used for discarding children's data are as follows. The most obvious reason to discard a child's data is fussiness. Clearly, this decision requires a judgment call. In our view, the goal is for the child and parent to have a positive experience. If the child perseveres in leaving the parent's lap or begins to squirm and/or cry, we stop the testing, reassuring the parent that our tapes are "very boring." Another reason to discard data is equipment failure or experimenter error. For example, an experimenter who observes the testing from behind the parent and child discards the child's data if the tapes are not well synchronized. This can only happen if the tapes are not synchronized well at the outset of the experiment. When inserting the two tapes in their separate videotape players, the experimenter must align both tapes by the synchrony number on the lead prior to each tape. If this is not done properly, the tapes will remain unsynchronized, with one coming on consistently before the other. Data are also discarded from any child who shows a side preference for one screen that exceeds 75% of the total looking time or who watches the tapes less than 35% of the time (these criteria, calculated by the software, enable us to discard subjects who are not responding to the task); from any child whose parent watches the tapes; and from any child who fails to return to the central fixation point on more than 33% of the trials in a given experiment. Failure to return to the central fixation point might imply that the child is watching the same screen (perhaps in a daze?) across several trials.

Of course, the possibility always exists that when children's data are discarded for their failure to engage in the task, it is because they do not understand the linguistic stimuli. On the other hand, the children who complete our studies are not a homogeneous group. Their productive and receptive language varies widely, as do their visual fixation patterns.

The experience level of the laboratory can also affect subject losses. For example, we lost more subjects in earlier studies because of experimenter error and equipment failure than in later studies.

5.3   Studies Using the Intermodal Preferential Looking Paradigm

The intermodal preferential looking paradigm has been successfully used to investigate early language comprehension in numerous studies. The first studies conducted in the paradigm (Golinkoff et al. 1987) were designed to see whether it would work for both syntactic and lexical assessments: we found that 28-month-olds who were using two- and three-word utterances in their own speech showed word order comprehension, and that 17-month-olds showed noun and verb comprehension.

Further work in our laboratories has investigated a number of grammatically relevant constructs. We have already described how 14-month-olds were shown to comprehend basic sentential constituent structure in the "kiss keys" experiment. In another study (Hirsh-Pasek and Golinkoff 1996), 17-month-olds were found to comprehend word order. Children heard the sentence "Where's Cookie Monster tickling Big Bird?" and preferred the scene in which Cookie Monster was the actor and Big Bird the object of the action over one in which Big Bird was the actor and /ookie Monster the object of the action. Early knowledge of the subcategorization frames surrounding verbs showed a developing pattern: 24-month-olds comprehended the implication of transitive verbs (both known and unknown), whereas 27-month-olds appreciated the implications of subcategorization frames for both transitive and intransitive verbs (Hirsh-Pasek, Golinkoff, and Naigles, in press). Interestingly, the 27-month-olds were so sophisticated that they demonstrated their knowledge of these two verb types even when the basic order of the content words remained stable, as in "Cookie Monster is blicking Big Bird" versus "Cookie Monster is blicking WITH Big Bird." In the former case, these children looked longer at the "matching" screen that depicted Cookie Monster performing some causal action ("blicking") on Big Bird. In the latter case, the children overwhelmingly looked at the scene in which Cookie Monster and Big Bird were engaged in a parallel action of "blicking."

The intermodal preferential looking paradigm has also been used to study the ability of 3-year-olds to use Principles A and B of the binding theory (Hirsh-Pasek et al. 1995). As was true for the other syntactic and lexical phenomena studied, the paradigm found evidence for comprehension of these principles earlier than most other assessments.

Finally, Naigles (1990) and Naigles and Kako (1993) have used the paradigm to investigate 2-year-olds' knowledge of verb meaning and sensitivity to the meaning implications of transitive and intransitive sentence frames; and Naigles and Gelman (1995), Fernald, McRoberts, and Herrera (in press), and Golinkoff et al. (1992) have used it to investigate lexical comprehension and production.

In short, the potential for use of the intermodal preferential looking paradigm is great. It has been used to test children of various ages and to investigate a wide range of linguistic phenomena, from lexical development to syntactic development to the role of prosody in language learning.

5.4 Advantages and Disadvantages of the Intermodal Preferential Looking Paradigm

Like all methods of investigation, the intermodal preferential looking paradigm has both strengths and weaknesses. The only way to fully appreciate these is to compare the paradigm with those methods that have dominated the psycholinguistics literature. Because many of these methods are reviewed elsewhere in this volume, this discussion will be brief. The first and most popular method for studying comprehension is referred to as the "enactment task" (see chapter 7; this volume), in which researchers provide children with dolls or miniature objects and ask them to (for example) "Make the boy kiss the girl!" A second, related technique is the "act-out task" in which children are asked to carry out actions themselves: for example, "Kick the ball!" These enactment and act-out tasks are easy to administer and are fun for children. Yet comprehension tasks that require children to either act out events or follow commands may underestimate children's linguistic knowledge because of their competing action biases. As noted earlier, children have a tendency to act, and to act in particular ways, when surrounded by objects (see, e.g., Shipley, Smith, and Gleitman 1969; de Villiers and de Villiers 1973; Shatz 1978). Alternatively, young children may simply refuse to act on command. Therefore, a biased response or a failure to respond cannot be taken as evidence of noncomprehension, but only as evidence of noncompliance. In the intermodal preferential looking paradigm, the bias to act is all but nullified because the child need only provide a looking response.

Other studies have used a third method for generating comprehension data: picture selection tasks (see chapter 6, this volume). Children are presented with a choice of pictures and are asked to point to the picture that a sentence describes (Fraser, Bellugi, and Brown 1963; Lovell and Dixon 1967).

Although easy to administer, picture selection tasks pose some problems. In addition to requiring the action of pointing, pictorial displays may fail to provide young children with sufficient motivational incentive and may fail to make sought-after distinctions salient and unambiguous. Studies by Friedman and Stevenson (1975) and Cocking and McHale (1981), for example, have shown that young children do not understand the function of conventions such as curved lines around joints to indicate that movement is taking place. Thus, the depiction of dynamic relationships involving action is problematic. The intermodal preferential looking paradigm not only reduces the action bias but also allows researchers to present dynamic stimuli so that verbs and sentence relationships can be explored.

A fourth method is to infer children's comprehension by observing their comprehension in situ and recording the resulting observations in diaries (Nelson 1973). These studies may overestimate the young child's grammatical knowledge. For example, a mother may state that her child understands the sentence "Go get a diaper." Yet when she typically utters this sentence, she performs a unique action (e.g., peering into the child's diaper), which signals that a diaper change is about to occur. The child may understand no more about the sentence frame than does a dog who sees his master pick up a leash while uttering the sentence "Do you want to go for your walk?" Credit for comprehension can come only from tests in a controlled setting. The intermodal preferential looking paradigm provides such a setting.

Fifth, a parent report measure of children's language comprehension, the MacArthur Communicative Development Inventory (Fenson et al. 1994), can be administered to parents of infants between the ages of 8 and 16 months. Parental responses on this checklist have been shown to correlate positively and significantly with later language ability (Dale et al. 1989; Fenson et al. 1994). Further, this measure requires nothing from the child and can be used to ask parents about children's knowledge of nouns, verbs, and closed-class items such as prepositions. However, other than the questions on closed-class items, the version for infants ("Words and Gestures") was not designed to explore early syntactic sensitivities—sensitivities that can be explored in the intermodal preferential looking paradigm.

In sum, a number of methods have been used to probe early language comprehension. None of them, however, enables researchers to look at grammatical development in ways that require no overt action on the part of the child *and* that can portray grammatical relationships through dynamic stimuli. The intermodal preferential looking paradigm incorporates both of these advantages and permits the experimenter to look at emerging syntax in a wide range of ages.

Still, the procedure also has some drawbacks. The first is simply that it is more difficult and time-consuming to make exciting, well-controlled videotapes than it is to show children novel toys or pictures. The second and third, noted by Bates (1993, 228), concern the inability of the method either to investigate individual differences in grammatical development or to examine more than a few stimuli at any given time.

Although this method works well for group studies, it has proved impossible (at least so far) to adapt the preferential looking technique for use with individual children. In the experiments they have conducted to date, Golinkoff and Hirsh-Pasek can obtain no more than four to six crucial target trials for any linguistic contrast. Although the results are quite reliable at the group level, the predicted pattern (i.e. preferential looking at the pictures that match the language input) is typically displayed by only two thirds of the children with looking biases that average 66% for individual subjects. It should be clear why this kind of hit rate would be unacceptable for individual case studies.

Although Bates's point is well taken, we would note that one reason that children do not look exclusively at the screen depicting the action that matches the linguistic stimulus is that the tapes in a pair are *designed* to be equally salient and to encourage active looking. Thus, by its very design, the intermodal preferential looking paradigm may not be well suited to the study of individual differences.

5.5 Summary

In this chapter we have suggested that studies of language comprehension may offer researchers a unique view of the emergent language system and of the strategies that children use to discover their native language. In fact, comprehension procedures have a number of advantages over those that rely on production, not the least of which is that they allow the researcher to probe for particular language structures that are not yet produced. Despite these advantages, many comprehension studies have been plagued by having to rely on children's willingness to act in particular ways and by the inability to represent dynamic relations.

The intermodal preferential looking paradigm avoids these pitfalls. It requires minimal action (a looking response), and it can portray dynamic relationships in a video format, thereby making available new ways to study the mapping between language and events. Further, it has been used successfully to examine a number of lexical and grammatical developments in children of many different ages and levels of linguistic competence and thus has proven effective in unveiling young children's hidden linguistic competencies. To be sure, the paradigm does have some drawbacks: only four to six pairs of stimuli can be examined in any study, given current designs and subject fatigue; all stimuli are presented in a forced-choice procedure so that very few alternatives can be examined at a single time; and use of the paradigm requires a relatively complacent child. Nevertheless, the advantages of the paradigm seem to outweigh the disadvantages for those who are interested in studying lexical and syntactic sensitivities in very young children, whose language competencies have so far been hidden from view. It is our hope that this paradigm, in concert with other creative measures, will assist in mapping the uncharted landscape of emerging language comprehension.

Note

The order of authorship on this chapter is completely arbitrary. This experimental paradigm is also described in chapter 3 of Hirsh-Pasek and Golinkoff 1996.

We gratefully acknowledge the following grants, which supported the development of this paradigm: a National Institute of Child Health and Human Development grant (HD15964) awarded to Golinkoff and Hirsh-Pasek; another grant from that agency awarded to Golinkoff, Hirsh-Pasek, Paula Malone, and Charles Bean (HD19568); three Pew Memorial Fund grants awarded to Hirsh-Pasek; a University of Delaware Research Foundation grant and Bio-Medical grants from the University of Delaware awarded to Golinkoff. Golinkoff also received a James McKeen Cattell Sabbatical Award and a John Simon Guggenheim Memorial Fellowship. The writing of this chapter was supported by a National Institute of Child Health and Human Development grant (HD25455-0552) awarded to Marsha Weinraub and Hirsh-Pasek and by a Center for Advanced Study Fellowship awarded to Golinkoff by the University of Delaware. Furthermore, the development of this method would never have come to fruition without the inestimable help of many support services at the University of Delaware and the numerous undergraduate and graduate students who have worked in our laboratories over the years.

Chapter 6

The Picture Selection Task	LouAnn Gerken and Michele E. Shady

6.1 Uses of the Picture Selection Task

One of the methods most commonly used to assess children's linguistic capabilities is a comprehension task in which the listener is presented with some linguistic stimulus (e.g., a word or a sentence) and asked to select from a set of pictures the one that best corresponds to it. The *picture selection task* has been used to assess nearly all types of linguistic comprehension abilities in both normally developing children and various clinical populations. It has been used especially in cases where subjects fail to *produce* particular linguistic forms or maintain particular production contrasts. For example, numerous researchers and clinicians have used picture selection to assess young children's abilities to comprehend phonological distinctions, such as the one between the /r/ in *crown* and the /l/ in *clown*, which many children fail to produce (e.g., Barton 1980; Morgan 1984; Provonost and Dumbleton 1953; Snyder and Pope 1970; Strange and Broen 1981; Templin 1957; Wepman 1960). Other researchers and clinicians have used picture selection, often in the form of standardized measurement instruments, to assess lexical comprehension (e.g., Gardner 1985; Miller and Yoder 1974; Carrow-Woolfolk 1985; Kay and Anglin 1982; Newcomer and Hammill 1977; Rescorla 1980).

The picture selection task has also been used to assess the effects of morphosyntactic manipulations on children's sentence comprehension. This use of the task is the focus of our chapter. In sections 6.1.1 and 6.1.2, respectively, we consider two basic versions of the task: one that assesses the *semantic interpretation* of particular morphosyntactic contrasts in sentence comprehension and another that assesses the effects of morphosyntactic *grammaticality* on sentence comprehension. For each version, we present some examples of how the picture selection task has been used by various researchers, what questions the researchers attempted to address, and what their findings might say about the possible relations between language behaviors (e.g., comprehension and production) and grammar. In section 6.2 we discuss some issues to keep in mind when using either version of the picture selection task, compare the two versions of the task, and compare both versions with other comprehension tasks as well as with judgment and production tasks.

6.1.1 Assessing Children's Semantic Interpretation of Morphosyntactic Contrasts

The most frequent use of the picture selection task, with both normally developing children and clinical populations, has been to assess the semantic interpretation of particular morphosyntactic contrasts (e.g., Carrow-Woolfolk 1985; Lee 1970; Miller and Yoder 1974). Researchers who use the task in this way typically have in mind at least one of four goals. One goal is to determine if children can comprehend particular linguistic contrasts, especially contrasts they do not maintain in their own utterances (e.g., *chase* vs. *chased*). A second and related goal is to determine the developmental sequence in which children come to comprehend particular linguistic forms (e.g., active sentences vs. passives). A third goal is to determine the developmental relation between children's production of a particular form and their comprehension of it. A fourth goal is to infer the nature of children's morphosyntactic representations by examining the types of comprehension errors that they make.

An example of the picture selection task employed to test children's semantic interpretations of contrasts that they fail to produce can be seen in the work of Katz, Baker, and McNamara (1974; also Gelman and Taylor 1984). They sought to determine if 17- to 24-month-olds, who do not produce determiners in their own speech, treat novel words as common or proper nouns based on the presence or absence of a determiner. Although Katz, Baker, and McNamara used real objects, as opposed to pictures, research by Cocking and McHale (1981) suggests that object selection and picture selection tasks yield comparable results. In Katz, Baker, and McNamara's task, children were taught a new word applied to either an animate surrogate (a doll) or an inanimate object (a block). They were then asked to select the object from an array containing similar objects. The new words were either preceded by an article (1a), and thus used as common nouns, or preceded by no article (1b), and thus used as proper names.

(1) a. This is the dax. Find the dax.
   b. This is Dax. Find Dax.

Children who learned the new word applied to a block did not perform differently for the two labels, presumably because blocks do not typically have proper names. However, children who learned the new word applied to a doll used the presence or absence of an article to treat the new word appropriately as a common noun or proper name, respectively. These results suggest that even very young children can use the morphosyntactic forms of utterances to restrict their hypotheses about the meanings of new words (also see Naigles 1990). More importantly for the current discussion, the results suggest that failure to maintain a particular linguistic contrast in production does not necessarily imply lack of sensitivity to that contrast.

Fraser, Bellugi, and Brown (1963) used the picture selection task to determine both the developmental sequence in which children comprehend different morphosyntactic forms and the developmental relation between comprehension and production (also imitation). To test a range of morphosyntactic contrasts that might affect young children's sentence comprehension, Fraser, Bellugi, and Brown created pairs of sentences that differed from each other in a single aspect of morphosyntax. The list of contrasts they tested, along with sample sentence pairs, appears in table 6.1. Fraser, Bellugi, and Brown also created pairs of pictures corresponding to each of the sentences in a pair. During testing, they presented 37- to 43-month-olds with one of the sentences from a pair, along with the two pictures associated with that sentence pair, and asked the children to point to the picture that corresponded to the sentence.

Fraser, Bellugi, and Brown's study yielded two findings that are of interest for the current discussion. The first is that children demonstrated better comprehension (more frequently selected the correct picture) for some contrasts than for others (note that the contrasts in table 6.1 are listed from most to least frequently comprehended). Thus, at the extreme, children selected the correct picture for the negative/affirmative contrast much more frequently than for the indirect/direct object contrast. Fraser, Bellugi, and Brown interpreted such differences in the rate of correct responses to mean that the picture selection task is sensitive to children's representations of and/or access to particular morphosyntactic forms. For example, children might have greater mastery over the syntax involved in negation than that involved in double object constructions. On such an

Table 6.1
Some morphosyntactic contrasts tested with the picture selection task (Fraser, Bellugi, and Brown, 1963). Contrasts listed from most to least frequently comprehended

Sample sentence pair	Contrast tested
The girl is cooking. The girl is not cooking.	Affirmative vs. negative
The train bumps the car. The car bumps the train.	Subject vs. object active
The girl is drinking. The girl will drink.	Present progressive vs. future tense
That's his wagon. That's their wagon.	Singular vs. plural possessive pronouns
The paint is spilling. The paint spilled.	Present progressive vs. past tense
There's some mog. There's a dap.	Mass noun vs. count noun
The deer is running. The deer are running.	Singular vs. plural auxiliary *be*
The boy draws. The boys draw.	Singular vs. plural inflections
The car is bumped by the train. The train is bumped by the car.	Subject vs. object passive
The girl shows the cat the dog. The girl shows the dog the cat.	Indirect vs. direct object

interpretation of the data, children should show increasing sensitivity to all morphosyntactic contrasts as they develop more adultlike linguistic representations. We discuss potential problems with this interpretation in section 6.2.2.

The second finding by Fraser, Bellugi, and Brown that is of interest here concerns the developmental relation of comprehension, production, and imitation. With regard to comprehension versus production, all children selected the correct picture for each contrast more frequently than they produced the contrast in a nonimitative sentence elicitation task. On the other hand, comparison of the comprehension and imitation tasks revealed that nearly all children were able to imitate more contrasts than they were able to comprehend. These results suggest that the ability to comprehend a particular linguistic construction may precede the ability to produce it spontaneously and that imitating a linguistic string may be easier or draw on different processes than either comprehension or spontaneous production. We discuss these issues more fully in section 6.2.5.

Several studies have used the picture selection task to infer the nature of children's morphosyntactic representations by examining the types of comprehension errors that they make. For example, McKee, Cripe, and Campos (1995) tested children's semantic interpretation of several O-type adjectives (i.e., adjectives like the one in (2) that are associated with the object of an infinitive).

(2) The boy is hard to catch.

Previous studies demonstrated that children as old as 7 or 8 years consistently misinterpret such sentences as though the subject (e.g., *the boy*) is the one performing the action (Cambon and Sinclair 1974; Chomsky 1969; Cromer 1970). McKee, Cripe, and Campos sought to determine if children perform differently for different adjectives.

In their experiment, McKee, Cripe, and Campos showed two pictures to 2-, 3-, 4-, and 5-year-olds and adults and asked them to say what was the same about them. For example, one picture might show a boy with the line from his fishing pole wrapped around a tree branch, and the other might show the same boy running away from an old man. The experimenter would say, "What's the same about these two pictures? Right! There's a boy in both of them. In this picture, the boy is trying to catch fish, but he can't because his pole is stuck in this tree. And in this picture, an old man is trying to catch the boy, but he can't because the boy is running super fast. So both pictures are about catching. But in one of them, *the boy is hard to catch*. Which one?" The data showed that although children generally improved with age in correctly interpreting these adjectives, their performance differed significantly from adjective to adjective. McKee, Cripe, and Campos interpret this finding to mean that children do not discover the correct syntactic analysis of O-type adjectives all at once; instead, this representation emerges slowly through the interaction of syntactic and lexical knowledge.

Deutsch, Koster, and Koster (1986) used the picture selection task to determine when children come to comprehend particular linguistic forms and to infer the nature of children's morphosyntactic representations, by examining the types of comprehension errors that they make. In particular, they sought to determine whether children correctly interpret reflexive pronouns (e.g., *himself*) sooner than nonreflexives (e.g., *him*) and also to understand children's linguistic representations of these two forms. In the linguistic theory that motivated Deutsch, Koster, and Koster's research (Chomsky 1981), the coreferring noun bears a particular structural relation to the reflexive within the sentence (i.e., c-command; Reinhart 1976). The noun does not bear this relation to coreferring nonreflexives, and it may in fact occur in a sentence preceding the one containing the pronoun. For example, the correct interpretation of the reflexive sentence (3a) is that the brother washes himself, whereas the correct interpretation of the nonreflexive sentence (3b) is that the brother washes Peter or some third person, not himself.

(3) a. Peter's brother washes himself.
    b. Peter's brother washes him.

To determine when children appropriately interpret reflexive versus nonreflexive pronouns, Deutsch, Koster, and Koster presented 6- to 10-year-old Dutch-speaking children with sentences like (3a) and (3b). Accompanying each sentence was a set of four pictures. On the test trials, two of the four pictures showed a reflexive activity in which a child was performing an action on himself (e.g., washing), and two showed a nonreflexive activity in which a child was performing the same action on another child. Two different actors were shown in each set of pictures, one of which was appropriate for the sentence and one of which was not. There were also filler trials that did not contain pronouns.

As Deutsch, Koster, and Koster predicted, the 8- and 10-year-olds selected the correct picture more frequently for the reflexive sentences than the nonreflexive sentences. Because there was always a systematic relation between the stimulus sentence and the accompanying picture set, it was possible to examine what types of errors children made when selecting the incorrect picture. Interestingly, the most frequent error that children made on the nonreflexive sentences was to choose the picture showing a nonreflexive activity performed by an incorrect actor. The authors' interpretation of the latter finding is complex and beyond the scope of this chapter. However, it is important to note that the construction of the picture sets in this study allowed for possible interpretations of both correct and incorrect responses and therefore potentially sheds light on children's developing linguistic representations.

6.1.2 Assessing the Effects of Morphosyntactic Grammaticality on Children's Sentence Comprehension

Note that in the uses of the picture (or object) selection task discussed in section 6.1.1, particular morphosyntactic manipulations had direct referential/semantic counterparts. Thus, the stimulus contrast between "This is the dax" and "This is Dax" has a referential counterpart in an object that is part of a general category containing other similar objects or an object that is not part of a general category. The contrast between "The deer *is* running" and "The deer *are* running" has a referential/semantic counterpart in one deer or more than one deer. And the contrast between "Peter's brother is washing himself" and "Peter's brother is washing him" has a referential counterpart in Peter's brother being washed or Peter being washed. Thus, in each case an adult would presumably respond to the different linguistic forms by choosing a different picture or object.[1] Distinct from these uses of the picture selection task, another version of the task does not manipulate aspects of morphosyntax that have direct referential/semantic counterparts. Rather, the *grammaticality* of particular morphemes is manipulated in order to determine the effect on overall sentence comprehension. This is the version of the picture selection task that has been used most extensively in our laboratory.

Our use of the picture selection task to assess the effects of morphosyntactic grammaticality is related to early psycholinguistic research in which adult listeners were found to perceive or remember grammatical sentences better than syntactically unstructured word strings (Epstein 1961; Marks and Miller 1964; Miller and Isard 1963; also see Tyler and Marslen-Wilson 1981 for similar research with children). Thus, adult listeners appear to use grammatical organization to encode and recall linguistic stimuli. Our use of the picture selection task is also related to earlier developmental research by Shipley, Smith, and Gleitman (1969; also see Petretic and Tweney 1977), whose goal was similar to that of Katz, Baker, and McNamara (1974), namely, to determine if children who do not produce grammatical morphemes in their own utterances are sensitive to these morphemes in comprehension. But unlike Katz, Baker, and McNamara, who used the presence or absence of a morpheme to cue a semantic contrast, Shipley, Smith, and Gleitman used the presence or absence of morphemes to create grammatical versus ungrammatical sentences. They reasoned that if children are like the adult subjects studied by Miller and others and use morphosyntax when encoding linguistic stimuli, they should perform better on grammatical sentences.

Shipley, Smith, and Gleitman did not use picture selection per se, but rather examined whether or not children selected the named object (e.g., ball). The stimulus sentences that are relevant for the current discussion were grammatical sentences containing all required grammatical morphemes (4a), utterances from which grammatical morphemes were omitted, leaving only a verb and noun (4b), and utterances composed of only the object noun (4c).

(4) a. Give me the ball.
     b. Give ball.
     c. Ball.

Children in the experiment were assigned to one of two groups based on the form of their spontaneous speech. Children who produced multiword utterances that did not contain grammatical morphemes were classified as "telegraphic" talkers, and children who produced almost no multiword utterances were classified as single-word talkers. Thus, the two nongrammatical forms corresponded to forms that young children themselves produce. Shipley, Smith, and Gleitman found that telegraphic talkers selected the correct object more frequently in response to grammatical sentences, whereas single-word talkers performed better on utterances that did not contain grammatical morphemes ((4b) and (4c)). These results suggest that at least some children who do not produce grammatical morphemes in their own speech (telegraphic talkers) are sensitive to the presence or absence of these elements in sentence comprehension. The finding that telegraphic talkers performed better on grammatical sentences, whereas single-word talkers performed better on ungrammatical sentences, might be further taken to suggest that there is a developmental lag between when a child is able to show sensitivity to a particular aspect of morphosyntax in comprehension and when the same child is able to produce it. However, this interpretation of Shipley, Smith, and Gleitman's findings is challenged by research using a somewhat different form of the picture selection task, which we present below.

Shipley, Smith, and Gleitman's goal was to determine the relationship between children's comprehension and production of particular linguistic forms, which led them to use child-produced forms as stimuli. Gerken and McIntosh (1993b) used the picture selection task to ask a somewhat different question, namely, whether children who do not produce grammatical morphemes in their own speech nevertheless show sensitivity to the *typical linguistic patterns* in which these morphemes appear. To do this,

Table 6.2
The effect of morphosyntactic grammaticality on children's sentence comprehension (Gerken and McIntosh 1993b). Data from children with mean lengths of utterance under 1.50 morphemes who heard synthesized female voice

Sample sentence	Correct picture selection
Show the dog to me.	86%
Show dog to me.	75%
Show was dog to me.	56%
Show gub dog to me.	39%

they presented 21- to 28-month-olds with sentences in which a target noun was preceded by either a grammatical article (*the*), no grammatical morpheme (similar to Shipley, Smith, and Gleitman's stimuli), an ungrammatical auxiliary (*was*), or a nonsense syllable (*gub*). Examples of each type appear in table 6.2. The sentences were created with DECTalk Speech Synthesizer in order to control for stress and naturalness differences that might be introduced by a human talker (see section 6.2.1). Other unpublished studies have employed tape-recorded natural speech and obtained the same pattern of results (Stetzer 1992).

Children were introduced to a toy robot and told that the robot would tell them about the pictures in a special book. On each trial the experimenter opened to the blank page preceding the relevant picture page in the stimulus book (a large three-ring binder with laminated picture pages separated by blank sheets; see section 6.2.1) and played the sentence through a speaker placed next to the robot. At the end of the sentence, the experimenter flipped up the blank page to reveal a page with four pictures, one of which represented the target word. Two practice trials preceded the stimulus trials. The nouns referring to the three nontarget pictures were phonetically and semantically unrelated to the noun referring to the target (e.g., in one picture set the target was a dog and the distractors were a cart, a girl, and a mailbox). The experimenter encouraged the child to point to the picture that the robot had named. Gerken and McIntosh found that even children who had mean lengths of utterance (MLUs; Brown 1973) under 1.50 morphemes per utterance and produced no articles in their spontaneous speech performed better on grammatical sentences than when either an ungrammatical morpheme or a nonsense syllable preceded the target word.

Two aspects of these data are of interest for the current discussion. First, note that, as in Shipley, Smith, and Gleitman's experiment, children could have pointed to the named picture more frequently if they had simply listened for a familiar concrete noun in each sentence. If this were the case, they should have demonstrated no difference across the conditions. Therefore, the fact that they performed worse for ungrammatical and nonsense sentences than for grammatical sentences suggests that their overall ability to comprehend sentences is affected by morphosyntactic grammaticality. The second point to note is an apparent difference between Gerken and McIntosh's findings and those of Shipley, Smith, and Gleitman. This difference is almost certainly due to the format of the selection task used in the two studies. In particular, even single-word talkers in Gerken and McIntosh's study distinguished grammatical from ungrammatical sentences when the latter contained an incorrectly used morpheme. In contrast, the single-word talkers in Shipley, Smith, and Gleitman's study did not show better comprehension of grammatical sentences than ungrammatical sentences when the latter were produced without function morphemes. Thus, it appears that children at this stage in language development are very sensitive to the incorrect use of a morpheme and less sensitive to its absence. The finding that even single-word talkers perform worse in the presence of an incorrectly used morpheme calls into question the notion that there is a simple temporal lag between comprehension of a particular stimulus and its production. We discuss this issue further in section 6.2.5.

In addition to testing normally developing children's sensitivity to morphosyntactic grammaticality, the grammaticality version of the picture selection task has been used to examine the joint effects of morphosyntax and prosody on young children's comprehension of sentences like those shown in table 6.2, by placing prosodic breaks in prosodically natural or unnatural locations (Shady 1994; Shady and Gerken 1995). This version of the task has also been used to assess morphosyntactic sensitivity in children who manifest atypical patterns of language development. Gerken and McIntosh (1993a) used the stimuli exemplified in table 6.2 to test 3- to 4-year-old children who demonstrated normal nonverbal intelligence, but who produced many fewer of the required grammatical morphemes than their normally developing peers.[2] These children performed as well as age-matched control subjects on sentences with a grammatical article preceding the target word; however, they performed significantly worse on sentences with an ungrammatical auxiliary verb. The normally developing control group performed equally well on all four sentence types. Thus, whereas normally developing 3- to 4-year-olds appear to be able to avoid or recover from the effects of ungrammaticality, children with atypical language development appear to be severely affected by such input.

In summary, the grammaticality version of the picture selection task has been useful in revealing sensitivity to morphosyntactic usage patterns in children whose spontaneous utterances do not include many or any grammatical morphemes.

6.2   Evaluation of the Picture Selection Task

The two versions of the picture selection task have been used to examine several issues in morphosyntactic development in several populations. In the following sections we discuss some general considerations to be aware of when using the picture selection task. We also contrast the two versions of the task discussed in section 6.1 and compare the picture selection task with other tasks for assessing children's syntax.

6.2.1   General Considerations When Using the Picture Selection Task
There are at least six considerations a researcher or clinician should be aware of when using the picture selection task to assess children's morphosyntactic representations. These concern the linguistic stimuli, the picture stimuli, and the child's responses.

With respect to presentation of the linguistic stimuli, many researchers and clinicians simply read the stimulus to the child on each trial. Although this procedure is the easiest and requires the least equipment, it admits the possibility that the experimenter's prosody or other factors that are difficult to control might influence the child's picture choice. For example, if the experimenter unconsciously stresses the auxiliary verb in a sentence like "The deer are eating," the child might be more likely to select the correct picture than if the experimenter had stressed the main verb. The problem of controlling prosody and overall naturalness becomes a serious concern in the grammaticality version of the picture selection task, in which producing a fluent reading of an ungrammatical sentence can be quite difficult. Another choice is to use tape-recorded natural speech (but not that of the experimenter who is testing the child, which young children appear to find confusing). This procedure has the advantage that each child will hear the same stimuli, but it has the disadvantage that children sometimes refuse to respond to tape-recorded speech. We have been able to overcome this problem to a great extent by using a "talking" toy robot, which we introduce to children at the beginning of the session and place next to a portable speaker during testing (see the description of Gerken and McIntosh 1993b in section 6.1.2). Providing a rationale about who is talking to them appears to make children less inhibited than asking them to respond to speech coming out of a speaker. The robot may be especially useful when using the grammaticality version of the picture selection task, because children may be more willing to have a robot speak ungrammatically than a human. A third choice for stimulus presentation is to use tape-recorded synthesized speech or acoustically altered natural speech. This procedure allows for very tight control over the acoustic properties of the linguistic stimulus, and we have found that young children are remarkably eager to listen to synthetic speech. However, this option requires the most special equipment and expertise and is mainly indicated when the researcher is concerned about controlling specific acoustic properties of the stimulus.

Another consideration when using the picture selection task is the nature of the pictures themselves. When the target and distractors are all common nouns, like those in the research by Gerken and McIntosh (1993b), simple brightly colored pictures of similar sizes can be found in books and magazines (see below for a discussion of picture salience considerations). If the pictures come from several sources, having them duplicated on a color photocopier can make them appear more uniform in style. When more complex pictures are required, such as those involving specific actions, it might be necessary to have them drawn by an artist. However, with increasingly accessible computer graphics capabilities, creating almost any kind of picture from clip art collections and scanned images becomes increasingly feasible. Once the pictures are created, it is often useful to laminate them to keep them from being torn or marked.[3]

A third consideration when using the picture selection task is the relative salience of the target and distractor pictures and therefore whether each of the pictures in a set constitutes the correct response to some linguistic stimulus used in the study. Consider the following example: A pair of picture stimuli comprises one of Big Bird chasing Cookie Monster and another of Cookie Monster chasing Big Bird. One possible procedure is to present sentences that correspond to each of these pictures on separate trials (i.e., (5a) on one trial and (5b) on another).

(5) a. Big Bird is chasing Cookie Monster.
   b. Cookie Monster is chasing Big Bird.

The advantage of this procedure is that the salience or interest value of a particular picture is controlled. That is, if children simply liked the picture with Cookie Monster chasing Big Bird better, they would respond to one sentence correctly and to the other incorrectly, yielding chance-level performance. However, if only the sentence corresponding to the favored picture was presented, they would achieve perfect performance. Clearly, the result obtained from presenting both sentences in this case more accurately reflects children's abilities than the one obtained from presenting only one of the sentences.

Unfortunately, there is also a potential disadvantage of having each picture of a set associated with a linguistic stimulus. It is possible that children's evaluation of pictures presented on an earlier trial will be quite different from their evaluation of the same pictures presented on a later trial (i.e., because of repeated exposure). For example, if a child sees the two Big Bird and Cookie Monster pictures described above in the context of sentence (5a) and then sees the same two pictures again later in the context of (5b), the likelihood of choosing the correct picture for the second sentence might be influenced by the choice made for the first sentence.

One way to avoid this problem while still equating the two pictures for overall salience is to create two different lists of linguistic stimuli, such that one picture in a pair is the correct choice on one list, and the other is the correct choice on the other list (also see chapter 5, this volume). For example, in an experiment with 16 subjects, one group of 8 children would hear sentence (5a), and the other group of 8 would hear (5b), the same two pictures being seen by both groups of children.

A fourth consideration when using the picture selection task is the number of pictures presented and how this number affects the statistical analysis of the data. Researchers who use this task typically use either two or four pictures (usually with only one being the "correct" choice). Using two pictures means that chance performance is 50%, and large numbers of subjects or stimulus tokens may be needed to determine if performance is reliably above chance. Using four pictures means that chance performance is 25%, which increases the tester's ability to detect nonrandom behavior. However, creating three equally plausible distractor pictures is not always possible, and if the distractors are not equally plausible, then deciding what constitutes chance performance is extremely difficult. Consider, for example, Fraser, Bellugi, and Brown's (1963) stimulus sentence "The deer is eating," whose purpose was to contrast singular and plural readings (see section 6.1.1). A researcher might present pictures of one deer eating, two deer eating, one giraffe eating, and one deer playing the piano. However, the last two pictures hardly seem equally plausible compared to the second as distractors, and it is therefore difficult to argue that 25% constitutes chance performance in such a situation. Therefore, using four pictures is desirable, but only if the distractors are equally plausible.

A fifth consideration when using the picture selection task is the temporal relation between linguistic and picture stimuli. Most researchers and clinicians present the picture array and then present the linguistic stimulus while the pictures are still displayed. In contrast, Gerken and McIntosh (1993b) presented the linguistic stimulus first and then presented the picture array. When the latter procedure is used, if a child fails to select a picture on the first presentation of the stimulus, the linguistic stimulus can be presented again while the pictures are still displayed, although this is rarely necessary after the practice trials. We do not know of any systematic comparison of presenting pictures before and after linguistic stimuli. However, pilot testing in our laboratory suggests that we obtain clearer effects of grammaticality when the linguistic stimulus is presented without any contextual support. Perhaps requiring the child to remember the sentence long enough for the picture to be revealed heightens the effects of grammaticality.

A final consideration when using the picture selection task is how to handle "unusual" responses. The most frequent of these is that the child refuses to select a picture; this is especially likely to occur with very young children or children with attention problems. One possible approach is to simply skip that trial and move on to the next. The disadvantage of this approach is that some children will take it as permission to simply stop attending to the task altogether. Another possible approach is to repeat the same trial a set number of times (e.g., 2 or 3) before moving on to the next, by re-presenting the linguistic stimulus and encouraging the child to select a picture. This approach has the advantage of discouraging the child from "dropping out" without applying undue pressure. Regardless of which option the tester chooses, it is important note that children may *systematically* fail to select a picture for some types of linguistic stimuli. Therefore, it is useful to record which trials are skipped or require multiple presentations of the linguistic stimulus in order to discern any pattern.

Another, somewhat less frequent "unusual" response is that a child will occasionally point to several pictures on a single trial. In our laboratory we take the first picture the child points to as the response. Sometimes, however, it is difficult to decide which picture was selected first (e.g., when the child points with both hands), in which case we discount that trial.

6.2.2 Comparisons of the Two Versions of the Picture Selection Task

We have identified two versions of the picture selection task: one that assesses the semantic interpretation of morphosyntactic contrasts in sentence comprehension and another that assesses the effects of morphosyntactic grammaticality on sentence comprehension. Which version of the task a researcher or clinician chooses depends largely on the question being asked. If the question concerns how children *interpret* particular morphemes or syntactic structures, clearly the first version of the task is the one to use. An advantage of this version of the task is that any aspect of syntax that affects sentence interpretation in a picturable way can be tested. Furthermore, if properties of the incorrect picture choices are carefully manipulated, children's patterns of correct and incorrect picture selection can be very informative.

Using the picture selection task to assess semantic interpretations also has three potential disadvantages. One is that some syntactic contrasts are easier to depict than others, especially in static representations. For example, the syntactic contrast that children comprehended most successfully in Fraser, Bellugi, and Brown's (1963) study was affirmative versus negative. Children were least successful in comprehending double object constructions. From consideration of the picture pairs associated with these sentences, it seems possible that the pictures associated with the affirmative/negative contrast would be easier to interpret, even for an adult, than those associated with the double object construction. Thus, one must be aware that if children fail to perform well on a particular contrast with the picture selection task, the locus of the problem could be in relating the sentence to the picture, and not in comprehending the sentence, per se.

The second potential disadvantage with the semantic interpretation version of the picture selection task concerns the number of pictures presented. As noted in section 6.2.1, presenting children with four pictures on each trial offers some statistical advantages. However, most researchers who have used this version of the task have used two pictures, one correct and one incorrect, because it is often difficult to create three equally plausible and picturable distractors for many morphosyntactic contrasts.

The third potential disadvantage of the semantic interpretation version of the task also concerns the feasibility of creating appropriate pictures. In particular, it is often desirable to determine if children distinguish between a correct form and a semantically indistinguishable incorrect form that they themselves produce. For example, many young normally developing children and older language-delayed children produce sentences like "Her is eating" instead of "She is eating." In such cases it is not possible to create two pictures to represent the incorrect and correct forms and therefore not possible to test the child's relative comprehension of the two forms using the semantic interpretation version of the picture selection task.

Let us now consider the advantages and disadvantages of the grammaticality version of the picture selection task. Unlike the semantic interpretation version, the grammaticality version is not useful for determining a child's sensitivity to a morphosyntactic *contrast* (e.g., singular vs. plural). Rather, it is used to address the more basic question of whether or not a child perceives or attends to the *existence and usage pattern* of a particular morpheme during sentence comprehension. Such a question is likely to arise when the child fails to produce the morpheme. The question is also likely to arise if the child is very young and therefore potentially sensitive to the existence of a particular morpheme and the contexts in which it typically appears, without yet being sensitive to the semantic/referential properties of this element. For example, a very young child might have a tacit awareness that *the* is a frequently occurring syllable in her language and that this syllable occurs at the beginning of utterances but not the end (Gerken 1994; Shafer et al. 1993; Shady, Gerken, and Jusczyk 1995). These properties of *the* might allow the child to distinguish it from other syllables and even other grammatical morphemes, but not to appreciate its role in distinguishing proper from common nouns. Such a representation is better assessed with the grammaticality version of the picture selection task than the semantic interpretation version. Conversely, the contrast between *the* as a marker of definite nouns and *a* as a marker of indefinites is better assessed with the semantic interpretation version (e.g., see the discussion of Katz, Baker, and McNamara 1974 in section 6.1.1).

Because the grammaticality version of the task does not test the semantic effects of particular contrasts, it does not have the problem that aspects of the pictures themselves can potentially cue the child to the contrast being tested (see above). It also does not have the problem of being potentially limited to two picture choices. Conversely, it has the disadvantage that, in the way the task has been used so far, the distractor pictures have not been designed to reveal anything about children's sentence processing. Although it is possible that the distractors could be created so that they are phonetically or semantically related to the target, such a modification might entail some of the same disadvantages observed in the semantic interpretation version of the task.

Another potential disadvantage of the grammaticality version of the picture selection task is that, in the way it has been used so far, the upper age limit for testing normally developing children appears to be about 30 to 36 months. To see why this is so, consider the normal control group in the study of language-delayed children presented in section 6.1.2 (Gerken and McIntosh 1993a). These children performed equally well for all of the forms presented in table 6.2, whereas normally developing 2-year-olds and language-delayed 3- to 4-year-olds performed better on the grammatical than the ungrammatical sentences. Should we interpret these findings to mean that normally developing 3- to 4-year-olds are not sensitive to the contexts in which *the* can occur, whereas normally developing 2-year-olds and language-delayed children are? Almost certainly not. Rather, it is reasonable to hypothesize that normally developing 3- to 4-year-olds, like adults, are aware that "Find was dog for me" is not a grammatical sentence of their language, but can nevertheless ignore or overcome the form of the sentence to arrive at its plausible meaning within the task. Perhaps adding a reaction time component to the grammaticality version of the picture selection task would allow for a broader range of cross-age and cross-population studies. This might be achieved by showing the picture array under a transparent pressure-sensitive plate that could detect the listener's touch. Using such a technique might reveal that normally developing 3- to 4-year-olds respond more slowly to an ungrammatical sentence than to a grammatical one, even though their ability to select the correct picture does not differ for the two sentence types.

6.2.3 Comparison of Picture Selection with Other Comprehension Tasks

What are the advantages and disadvantages of the picture selection task as compared with two other comprehension tasks, act-out and preferential looking? Let us first consider the act-out task. Because this task requires the child to make a semantic interpretation of a sentence and then enact it, it is most similar to the semantic interpretation version of the picture selection task. One advantage of the picture selection task over the act-out task is that children who are too immature or too shy to act out a sentence on their own might be able to demonstrate their comprehension abilities in a picture selection task. Also, because performance in the act-out task is potentially open-ended, it is difficult to determine what constitutes chance level performance. The open-ended nature of the task also potentially makes it difficult to code children s responses in such a way that interpretable patterns of performance are revealed. However, if an appropriate coding scheme can be created, the act-out task allows for a richer analysis of children's linguistic processing than the picture selection task. Another potential advantage of the act-out task is that it does not depend on the interpretability of adult-created pictures to assess children's comprehension.

The preferential looking task is typically used with infants and very young children, whereas picture selection is used with children starting at age 20 to 24 months. Thus, the choice of which task to use depends largely on the age of the subjects to be tested. Although the most frequently used version of the task examines listeners' ability to interpret morphosyntactic contrasts (e.g., sentences (5a) and (5b); Golinkoff et al. 1987; chapter 5, this volume), a grammaticality version of the task has also been used (Dan Swingley and Ann Fernald, personal communication).[4] The near complementarity in subject age appropriate for the two tasks and the existence of semantic interpretation and grammaticality versions of both tasks suggest that preferential looking and picture selection might be useful for a longitudinal examination of sentence comprehension. However, it is important to consider whether or not these two tasks actually tap the same processes, simply at different ages. It is possible that looking longer at a picture associated with a particular linguistic stimulus is simply an easier version of picture selection, because the former does not require the child to make a conscious choice, whereas the latter does. However, it is also possible that making a conscious selection among a set of pictures requires a different type of representation of the linguistic stimulus than preferential looking.

6.2.4 Comparison of Picture Selection with Judgment Tasks

At a conceptual level, the picture selection task may be most similar to the grammaticality/reference judgment task described in chapter 11 of this volume. The semantic interpretation and grammaticality versions of picture selection appear to parallel the reference and grammaticality versions of the judgment task, respectively. This parallelism is only superficial in the case of the semantic/referential versions of the two tasks. Whereas the picture selection task (like the act-out task) typically requires children to choose the best interpretation of a sentence, the main advantage of the judgment task is that it allows a researcher to probe for multiple interpretations.

The grammaticality versions of picture selection and judgment tasks are much more similar. Each task manipulates the morphosyntactic forms of sentences in order to determine if children notice. One difference between the grammaticality versions of the tasks is whether "noticing" is measured in terms of relative sentence comprehension or in terms of sentence acceptance. Another difference is the age at which subjects can be tested: under about 30 months in the case of picture selection and over about 33 months in the case of judgments. One interesting project for future research would be to use a reaction time measure with older children in the picture selection task (see section 6.2.3) and compare the pattern of results with grammaticality judgment data from the same group of children. Such a comparison might help to determine if processing difficulty is one of the factors that causes children to reject some types of ungrammatical sentences.

6.2.5 Comparison of Picture Selection with Production Tasks

What are the advantages and disadvantages of the picture selection task as compared with examinations of children's productions? As noted several times in this chapter, one of the most frequent uses of the picture selection task is to test children's sensitivity to aspects of language that they do not produce. For example, the observation that young English speakers fail to produce articles and other grammatical morphemes in their early utterances has led to proposals that their grammars do not include these elements (e.g., Bowerman 1973; Gleitman et al. 1988; Gleitman and Wanner 1982; Grimshaw 1981; Lebeaux 1988; Pinker 1982; Radford 1990; Schlesinger 1971). However, picture/object selection experiments have suggested that children's failure to produce a particular linguistic element does not mean that they do not perceive or represent it (e.g., Fraser, Bellugi, and Brown 1963; Gerken and McIntosh 1993b; Katz, Baker, and McNamara 1974; Shipley, Smith, and Gleitman 1969). Therefore, it appears that when a child *omits* a particular linguistic element, spontaneous production data may provide a misleading picture of the child's linguistic sensitivity.

On the other hand, a detailed examination of spontaneous, elicited, or imitative production data can sometimes provide a richer picture of a child's linguistic representations than the picture selection task can. For example, researchers examining the spontaneous and imitative speech of young children have been able to infer a detailed representation of the prosodic structure of their language and of the interface between prosody and syntax (e.g., Demuth 1996; Gerken 1991, 1993; Wijnen, Krikhaar, and den Os 1994). It is difficult to imagine how such a representation could be uncovered from examinations of the same children's comprehension.

A final consideration when comparing comprehension tasks (such as picture selection) and production tasks concerns the developmental relation of comprehension versus production abilities, and the relation of both of these to the child's developing grammar. Observations in which young children show sensitivity to a linguistic form in comprehension before they produce the same form have often been taken to support a widely assumed model of language development. In this model, a particular linguistic representation can be used in comprehension at time T, but can be used in production only at time T + 1, because of greater constraints on production than on comprehension (also see section 6.1.2). Thus, if a child produces a particular form today, it is often assumed that that form became part of the child's grammar at some point in the past. Therefore, this model interprets differences between children's performance on comprehension tasks and their performance on production tasks to indicate that the former provide a more developmentally accurate view of language acquisition than the latter.

However, another model of language development is possible as well. On this model, comprehension and production abilities develop relatively independently, although both are influenced by the child's linguistic input and regularities that the child discovers there. Therefore, no necessary developmental relation exists between comprehension and production (e.g., Bever 1975; Gerken and McIntosh 1993b). This model is consistent with the finding that 2-year-olds omit grammatical morphemes from their utterances but use them in sentence comprehension, whereas 4-year-olds (and probably adults) produce grammatical morphemes correctly but appear to ignore them in some comprehension tasks. Such an alternative model necessarily entails a rather complex relation among comprehension, production, and grammar. That is, neither comprehension nor production tasks are superior at revealing the child's linguistic representation, or grammar. Rather, this representation must be pieced together from information yielded by tasks of different types.

Notes

We thank Janet Nicol and David Snow for thought-provoking discussions and Dana McDaniel, Helen Cairns, Cecile McKee, and David Snow for helpful comments and suggestions on previous drafts. Manuscript preparation was supported by NSF grant SBR9411185.

1. Although we have categorized the study by McKee, Cripe, and Campos (1995) as one in which a morphosyntactic manipulation has a direct referential counterpart, it may not appear to fit that description as well as the other studies presented in section 6.1.1. Changing a noun phrase from common to proper, a copula from singular to plural, and a pronoun from reflexive to nonreflexive all result in minimal pairs in which, arguably, only morphosyntax is altered. Changing an adjective from an S-type (e.g., *eager*) to an O-type (*easy*) more clearly alters the semantics as well as the syntax. The difficulty entailed in creating minimal adjective pairs stems from the fact that adjectives are content words and introduce their own semantic information into a sentence. Therefore, McKee, Cripe, and Campos were not able to manipulate morphosyntax independently of lexical items (which is related to their point that the syntactic properties of adjectives are learned as part of the meaning of individual words). Despite its difference from other studies presented in section 6.1.1, the study by McKee, Cripe, and Campos does examine the effects of particular linguistic manipulations (i.e., adjective type) on listeners' semantic interpretation of sentences, which distinguishes it from the studies presented in section 6.1.2.

2. Although the standardized test scores of the language-delayed children in this study were not available to the researchers, the children appear to fit the criteria for specific language impairment (see chapter 13, this volume).

3. In our laboratory we place the laminated pictures in a book or binder to make the task similar to talking about a book. We often begin the experimental session by looking at real books that we bring or that the child has in order to prepare for presenting our "special book."

4. Unlike the picture selection task used by Gerken and McIntosh (1993b), in which the linguistic stimulus was presented *before* the pictures, the preferential looking task used by Swingley and Fernald presented the linguistic stimulus a few seconds *after* the two pictures had been presented. As noted in section 6.2.1, differences in the temporal relation of linguistic and picture stimuli might lead to different types of processing in the two tasks.

Chapter 7

The Act-Out Task   Helen Goodluck

7.1 Introduction: The Procedure and Its Uses

The *act-out task* was first used to study children's knowledge of syntax by
Chomsky (1969). Chomsky used act-out to study the acquisition of missing subject (PRO) and object constructions and definite pronoun interpretation. In the 1970s and 1980s act-out was used in numerous studies of
syntactic development in children and, to a lesser extent, adult second
language learners. In addition to being used in many studies on the topics
first tackled by Chomsky, the technique has been applied to the study of
relative clauses, passive sentences, and constraints on question formation,
as well as to semantic phenomena, particularly the meaning of prepositions. Table 7.1 lists (nonexhaustively) studies in each of these areas.

The act-out task is not a complicated procedure. The experimenter
reads (or plays a recording of) a sentence to the subject, who then acts out
his or her interpretation of the sentence, using a set of props provided.
(Section 7.3 gives more details of variants of the act-out task.)

7.2 Advantages and Disadvantages of the Act-Out Task

7.2.1 Six Advantages
First, the act-out procedure has a good track record, having proved sensitive to quite fine-grained syntactic distinctions. The task is particularly
well suited to testing of binding possibilities for empty and pronominal/
anaphoric categories, since it provides a clear indication of the subject's
interpretation of such categories.

Second, the procedure is nonintrusive; that is, it allows subjects to
volunteer their interpretations of sentences, without presetting a range of
interpretations for them to choose from. This is an important advantage

Table 7.1
Selected child language studies using the act-out technique

Constructions tested	Grammatical principles and/or interpretive strategies tested	Studies	Age of subjects (years)
Missing subject (PRO) constructions	Minimal Distance Principle; c-command restrictions on obligatory control	Chomsky 1969	5–10
		Maratsos 1974b	4–5
		Goodluck 1981	4–6
		Hsu, Cairns, and Fiengo 1985	3–8
		Goodluck and Behne 1992	4–6 &10
Missing object constructions (*easy* and purpose clause constructions)	Lexical selection of missing object complements; c-command restrictions on operator binding	Chomsky 1969	5–10
		Cromer 1970	5–7
		Cromer 1987	7–9
		Goodluck and Behne 1992	4–6
Relative clauses	Parallel function hypothesis; conjoined clause analysis	Sheldon 1974	3–5
		Solan and Roeper 1978	4–5
		de Villiers et al. 1979	3–6
		Tavakolian 1981b	3–5
		Goodluck and Tavakolian 1982	4–5
		Hamburger and Crain 1982	3–5
Sentences with pronouns and anaphors	Effects attributable to Principles A, B, and C of the binding theory (Chomsky 1981)	Chomsky 1969	5–10
		Solan 1983, 1986	5–7
		Lust 1986, 1987	various
		Stevenson and Pickering 1987	5–6
		Chien and Wexler 1990	2–6

Wh-questions	*That*-trace effects	Phinney 1981	3–6
Passives	N - V = actor - action strategy; effects of verb semantics on passive comprehension	Bever 1970	2–5
		Maratsos 1974a	3–4
Meaning and syntax of prepositions	Semantic feature hypothesis; order-of-mention strategy; pragmatic clues to word meaning	Armidon and Carey 1972	5–6
		E. Clark 1973	3–5
		Johnson 1975	4–5
		Grieve, Hoogenraad, and Murray 1977	2–3
		Stevenson and Pollitt 1987	2–4

of the task, granted that child grammars may deviate to a greater or lesser extent from adult grammars, conceivably in ways currently beyond the imaginations of linguists.

Third, because the act-out task requires the subject to perform actions that vary from sentence to sentence, it may be less prone to response bias than tasks in which there is a fixed and restricted set of responses (e.g., judgment tasks or picture verification tasks in which the subject classes a sentence as "good" or "bad" as a description of an action or picture).

Fourth, act-out tasks are quite easy to administer. No extensive training is needed, either for the subject or for the experimenter. Usually, at age 3 and older children are able to act out sentences successfully after seeing only two or three demonstrations performed by the experimenter and acting out two or three practice sentences themselves. Most experiments on syntactic topics require only a rather simple scoring procedure (e.g., marking the reference of a pronoun or empty category and whether or not the basic action of the clause(s) has been performed correctly). Since most child subjects do well on basic actions from age 3 onward, most scoring can be done by the experimenter as the experiment goes along. The ease with which act-out experiments can be administered gives the task an edge in situations where high reliance on even simple equipment such as an audio tape recorder is undesirable. Video and/or audio recording is more or less the norm for experiments, though, and can provide a helpful backup to the experimenter's on-the-spot scoring and a means of checking for errors in the presentation of stimuli, where the stimuli are not prerecorded.

Fifth, because of its simplicity, the act-out procedure has the important advantage of being inexpensive, compared with some other procedures. Thus, it is a task that makes doing an acquisition experiment feasible for virtually anybody.

Sixth, act-out tasks are fun. It is true that young children may be turned off by having to act out a long sequence of similar, boring sentences (though it is not clear to me that a certain amount of tedium really impairs the effectiveness of the task). But given an engaging set of props, the task is one that both children and adults alike often enjoy. It is thus well suited (although underused) as a measure of second language learning by adults as well as first language learning by children. (See Flynn 1987 and Finney 1994 for examples of act-out tasks used in second language acquisition research.)

7.2.2 Six Disadvantages

The act-out task has a number of actual and potential disadvantages.

First, there are certain types of construction (e.g., questions) that do not easily lend themselves to the task, and certain types of predicates are difficult to act out, such as predicates expressing mental states or feelings (e.g., *want, hope, be happy, feel sad*). It is up to the researcher to decide how detailed an act-out is needed to answer the research question at hand. Even if a predicate is difficult to act out, an indication of who the actor is can nonetheless often be given (by moving a prop, for example), and the experimenter can also follow up the act-out with questions (e.g., "who was happy?").

Second, the nonintrusive property of the task carries with it a disadvantage, namely, that certain interpretations may be available to the subject, but the subject may choose not to act these out. The task thus has the potential to give only a partial view of the child's grammar.

Third, although act-out tests are quite easy to administer and score, the results may not always be easy to interpret. In particular, the task runs the risk that the subject does not act out what the experimenter said, but instead acts out some mentally readjusted version of the sentence (Grieve, Hoogenraad, and Murray 1977; Gerken 1982). For example, suppose the experimenter asks a child to act out a sentence like (1),

(1) He fell down after Fred left.

in which coreference between *he* and *Fred* is barred in the adult grammar, and the child makes *Fred* the subject of both clauses. Does that mean that the child does not know the relevant restrictions on pronoun interpretation, or does it mean that what he acted out was a readjusted version of the sentence, (2),

(2) Fred fell down after he left.

in which coreference is permitted? Thus, ironically, a child's "error" of interpretation may be prompted by a desire to avoid the ungrammatical interpretation that the experiment intended to test knowledge of. Such readjustments may not always be so devastatingly misleading. The child may struggle to readjust a sentence so as to avoid an ungrammatical reading and fail to come up with a complete act-out; or the child may produce an act-out of what is transparently a readjusted form, for example, adjusting (3) to (4) to achieve a sentence in which the pronoun and the subject of the subordinate clause are allowed to corefer.

(3) He hugged Tom before Fred left.

(4) Tom hugged him before Fred left.

(Readjustment of (3) to (4) with a coreferential reading of the pronoun and the subordinate subject is reported in Goodluck 1987, note 11; Goodluck and Solan (1995) report a similar pattern of error responses.) Since act-out errors may cluster systematically around certain sentence types, it is important to examine the patterns of incorrect act-outs and not to be afraid to interpret children's apparent mistakes as evidence of grammatical knowledge.

Fourth, although act-out tasks are easy to administer and easy for subjects to catch on to, it still can be said that act-out is a cognitively complex task. As Saddy (1992, 408) puts it with respect to the version that he employed (in which subjects created a cartoon; see section 7.3):

[A]ct-out ... requires that the subject hold the interpretation of the sentence he is presented with in working memory.... [I]t is necessary to decode the sentence, decide on a picture that will match his understanding and also plan the actions that will result ... in depicting the meaning of the sentence...

(See also Hamburger and Crain 1987.)

Act-out tasks do indeed put quite a few demands on the subject; in planning any act-out experiment, it is a worth while exercise for the experimenter to try out the task, to get a feel for exactly how hard a thing subjects are being asked to do.[1]

Fifth, related to the one just mentioned, a further disadvantage of act-out tasks is that they are not well suited for studying syntax in children younger than 3. The cognitive complexity of the task and the requirement that the child actively participate make act-out studies difficult for very young children. Moreover, children under 3 have been shown to be biased toward performing actions with the props made available, even when the stimulus sentence does not necessarily call for an action (e.g., in response to a question such as "Do you want to ...?"; Shatz 1978).

Sixth, the act-out task is potentially prone to certain response biases particular to the task. One frequently discussed potential bias is the "bird-in-the-hand" strategy (Legum 1975). When a child incorrectly makes the subject of the first clause (*the dog*) the subject of the relative in sentences such as (5),

(5) The dog kissed the horse that patted the sheep.

is this because she has a nonadult rule for relative clauses or is it because she just hangs onto the toy she has used as actor of the main clause when acting out the relative clause? Although the possibility that some such biases enter into the data cannot be ruled out, I think it is fairly clear by now that a bird-in-the-hand strategy cannot be the whole source of some characteristic errors, such as the misinterpretation of (5) just described. Very few children who give a bird-in-the-hand response to relative clauses like the one in (5) will persevere with such a response when faced with an obligatory control PRO sentence such as (6).

(6) The dog told the pig [PRO to pat the sheep].

The fact that putative agrammatical strategies for act-out depend on the particular sentence types being tested argues that their use is filtered through the child's grammar and is confined to cases where the child's grammar permits them to be used, either because the child does not have any firm rule yet for the particular construction or because the response given fits with a nonadult rule.

However, response bias is a real contributor to the second disadvantage noted above, namely, the danger that children's responses may not give a full picture of their grammars. For example, if a child is presented with a sequence of two sentences like (7a–b) and chooses the same (nonmentioned) toy as referent of the pronoun (*him*) and PRO,

(7) a. For him to kiss the pig would please the dog.
    b. PRO to hug the tiger would upset the horse.

is this because the child does not have the adult preference for construing the PRO subject of a sentential subject as referring to an entity mentioned in the main clause, or is it because there is a carryover effect from the previous act-out? We will come back to this problem and how to deal with it.

7.2.3 Summary
For children 3 years of age and older, the act-out task has been shown to be an effective measure of many aspects of syntactic structure, particularly the interpretation of pronominal and empty categories in noninterrogative constructions. The absence of a preset range of responses may discourage response bias and allows the child to reveal interpretations that the experimenter had not anticipated. Act-out experiments are easy to administer and score, and they are inexpensive and generally fun. However,

act-out is a relatively difficult task and as such is not well suited for very young children, who may be prone to act without fully processing or understanding the stimuli. Nor is the task well suited as a measure of certain aspects of syntactic and semantic structure, for example, questions and certain predicate types. The freedom of response the act-out task gives the subject opens the door for mental readjustment of the stimulus, which may or may not be detectable from the response; it also allows the subject to stick with particular interpretations of the stimuli, that is, to demonstrate only a subset of the range of meanings his or her grammar permits for a particular construction.

7.3   Parameters of Design

Various changes have been rung on the act-out procedure. These have aimed at reducing the burden the task places on the subject, spicing up the interest of the task, and/or making the task more suitable for a particular subject group. For example:

- In a study of pronoun interpretation, Solan (1983, chapter 5) reduced the burden of the task by requiring subjects to act out only the second clause of a conjoined sentence; the experimenter acted out the first clause.
- In a study of pronoun and reflexive interpretation, Chien and Wexler (1990) involved the subject as a character in the act-out. For example, children were asked to act out sentences such as (8a) and (8b).

  (8) a. Kitty says that [child's name] should point to herself.
      b. Kitty says that [child's name] should give herself a car.

  Presumably, involving the child as a character in the act-out enhances the interest of the task for the child.
- In a study of an adult aphasic patient, Saddy (1992) asked the subject to act out a variety of sentence types by affixing body parts of characters mentioned in the test sentences to a template to create a cartoon, a variant of the act-out task that potentially reduced the burden of act-out and perhaps is more "adult" than simple toy manipulation.

Plainly, decisions such as how much of the sentence needs to be acted out must be driven by the linguistic goals of the individual experiment. If the most pertinent information can be obtained by asking the subject to act out only one clause, for example, all well and good. Where the goals of the experiment require that the subject act out both clauses of a complex sentence, the locutionary force of the stimuli is a significant factor. In a test of children's interpretation of temporal prepositions (*before/after*), Johnson (1975) demonstrated that error patterns in act-out depended on whether the test sentence was declarative or imperative. If the test sentence was presented as a declarative, as in (9),

(9) The girl bounced the ball before she ate the cookie.

children were less likely to omit acting out the subordinate clause than they were if the test sentence was presented in the form of a command, as in (10).

(10) Move the green car before you move the pink car.

As Johnson notes, the child may have obeyed the command in the main clause in sentences such as (10) and then waited for another command to perform the action of the subordinate clause, failing to act out the subordinate clause when no such second command was given.[2] Thus, in studies in which the acting out of all parts of a complex sentence is important to the point of the study, imperative stimuli should be avoided.

A form of act-out that engages the subject's interest is likely to elicit more data from the subject than one that does not. One format I have found particularly successful in capturing the interest of subjects is to use a doll family or families; various sets that include mom, dad, kids, babies, and/or dog are available in toy stores. For whatever reasons, adults as well as children often seem to melt at the chance to play with doll families and particularly it seems for adult male subjects, the chance is sometimes an irresistible invitation to fool around. It should go without saying that the dolls and props used in any stimulus sentence should be chosen to avoid pragmatic bias toward a given interpretation of the sentence (where such effects are not under investigation). The toys should also be easy to manipulate; for example, they should be ones that stand up easily.

A child's interest and willingness to stick with an act-out experiment can often be maintained by explaining that the child is helping the experimenter with his or her work. Keeping the props in a fixed array and asking the child to return the props to their place after each act-out also helps maintain discipline. Requiring the child to wait until the whole sentence has been presented before touching any of the dolls can help prevent failure to act out the sentence completely. When a clause is not acted out at first, prompts from the experimenter (e.g., "Can you show the pushing part?") can be effective in getting the child to complete the act-out. When nothing at all is acted out on first presentation of a sentence, the rule I have followed in my own experiments is to allow up to two repetitions of the stimulus; two repetitions are rarely necessary for a subject who is paying attention. Although it is good to engage the child's interest in the task, some versions of act-out may be interesting to the point of distracting the child's attention from the stimuli, as Johnson (1975) found when she asked children to create a picture of the stimulus sentence, using crayons and other materials. Thus, the task should not allow children too much leeway in how they do the act-out, or be such that the act-out takes too long to accomplish.

By age 4, most children can act out 20 to 30 sentences with ease, and I have administered batteries of more than 40 to children that age. Thus, it is possible to test several constructions and administer several tokens of each construction within the same experiment. Use of multiple tokens is desirable in child language experiments for various reasons (in addition to the advantage of increased statistical power): it allows the experimenter to divide children by degree(s) of success or degree of use of particular response(s) and it helps minimize the effects of failures to respond and/or experimenter error in administering the test. Act-out experiments during the 1970s and early 1980s characteristically used within-subjects designs, each subject responding to every construction tested, thus minimizing the risk that differences between constructions would arise as an artifact of differences between subjects. Influenced by H. H. Clark 1973, many experiments during the late 1970s also used stimuli that varied the lexical items in each sentence presented, creating a unique set of sentences for each subject. This procedure, although time consuming, increases the probability that the results obtained are a genuine reflection of syntactic structure, rather than the effect of some individual lexical item(s) used in the tokens of a particular construction.[3] In addition, the use of a variety of lexical items in principle contributes to the interest of the test sentences and hence to the subject's interest in the task; it also helps minimize carryover effects from one sentence to the next.

Although the points just mentioned remain important ones to bear in mind in designing an experiment, within-subjects, multiple-token designs with unique stimuli for each subject may not be the be-all and end-all of constructing an act-out experiment. First, by its nature, the act-out task places limits on the range of vocabulary items that can be effectively used, entailing that even when each subject receives a unique set of sentence tokens, those tokens are not necessarily a representative sample of the population of sentences in which the syntactic construction under investigation can occur. Moreover, the limits on vocabulary and on number and type of prop that can be used mean that even if each subject receives a unique set of sentences, the effectiveness of the variety achieved in blocking carryover effects and maintaining interest may be no greater than what can be achieved with a limited set of sentence tokens, arranged to avoid potentially biasing sequences of presentation.

Second, although it is certainly the case that act-out experiments of the 1970s using within-subjects, multiple-token designs with unique sets of sentence tokens for each subject established children's sensitivity to many aspects of syntactic structure (see, e.g., Tavakolian 1981b), it is also the case that experiments of that period and more recently have produced results that argue that the design features just mentioned do not provide much protection against some types of response bias, which may best be obviated by other types of design.

As noted earlier, one disadvantage of the act-out task is that a child's act-outs may not reveal the full range of interpretations permitted in the child's grammar. Several experiments suggest that a bias for a particular response may set in early in the experiment and may persevere despite attempts to distract the subject from it. For example, in Goodluck 1987 I reported two experiments testing, among other things, children's interpretations of the PRO subject of a preposed temporal clause such as that in (11).

(11) Before PRO jumping up and down, the girl kisses the boy.

Many experiments have shown that the adult rule for interpreting the PRO subject of a temporal clause as referring to the main clause subject is not mastered until into the school years, but the manner in which children deal with this construction has been shown to vary considerably from experiment to experiment. The results of the two experiments reported in Goodluck 1987 were radically different. In one experiment children strongly preferred to interpret the PRO subject in sentences such as (11) as referring to an entity not mentioned in the sentence (contrary to the rule in the adult grammar); in the other experiment children the same age completely eschewed such a response, picking either the main clause subject or (incorrectly) the main clause object as referent of PRO. The only (tentative) explanation I was able to give for this large contrast in behavior for the two experiments was that the overall composition of the test battery in the two experiments differed considerably, and that the experiment in which children preferred external reference of PRO in sentences such as (11) contained a high proportion of sentences such as (7a–b) and similar sentence types, in which external reference of the pronoun/PRO is permitted in the adult grammar and is preferred by most children. Thus, children appeared to select a response for sentences such as (11) under the influence of the overall battery of test constructions. In both experiments a unique set of sentence tokens was created for each subject and in both experiments multiple (three) tokens of each sentence type were presented. These measures then did not prevent the child from displaying only one type of interpretation. Moreover, in one of the experiments the act-out task was interrupted after every fourth sentence and the child did a different experiment with a different task. This too evidently did not break the bias established for that test. Further evidence that a bias for a particular reading may set in early comes from a study reported by Goodluck and Solan (1995). We found that adult subjects will act out the coreferential interpretation of sentences such as (4) (with the pronoun and *Fred* coreferring) *if* they are presented with that sentence type as the first (nontraining) sentence to be acted out; if, however, a sentence such as (3), for which a coreferential reading of the pronoun and *Fred* is blocked, is presented as the first sentence in the test battery, then the coreferential reading for (4) becomes opaque and the noncoreferential reading is acted out.

Bias to a particular interpretation in the acting out of a construction can potentially be avoided by judicious use of filler/distractor sentences. For example, a bias toward external interpretation of a definite pronoun or null subject might be broken by interspersing reflexive sentences (*John shaved himself*), which require internal construal of the anaphor, with definite pronoun sentences. Similarly, a bias toward internal construal of a definite pronoun or null subject might be avoided or broken by presenting training and filler sentences in which use of an unmentioned entity is the only way to act the sentence out, as for example in (12).

(12) He ran away.

(Such training did not, however, prevent a bias toward internal reference by young children in the study by Goodluck and Solan (1995).)

Obviously, a strategy of using distractors to help avoid bias toward a particular interpretation affects the maneuvering space for the experiment, given that there are limits on the total number of sentences that a child can act out. This brings up another, separate question with respect to act-out design, namely, whether multiple testing sessions are desirable. Although it is possible to split an experiment into two or more sessions, the possibility of doing so may be limited by practical considerations (e.g., the willingness of children and schools to cooperate). In addition, the act-out task (as opposed to production tasks) exposes the child to the constructions under investigation; given that learning through exposure is a real possibility (see Cromer 1987), multiple-session experiments run a higher risk than single-session experiments of misrepresenting the time (age) at which certain behaviors are typically observed.

In sum, where the research deals with constructions for which the adult and/or child grammar does not yield a single interpretation, the act-out task may run afoul of bias toward a particular interpretation. There is no simple solution to this problem, and the researcher is well advised to pilot heavily to check for such bias. If the cost of getting rid of bias toward one interpretation (e.g., by manipulating the test battery) is the introduction of bias toward another interpretation, then between-subjects designs with only one or two trials may be useful as a way to see the full range of interpretations permitted in children's grammars at a given stage. Given the variation observed in act-out experiments with some constructions, I believe it is a good idea if possible to include in the test battery one or two constructions for which performance has been shown to be quite stable and adultlike from a relatively early age (e.g., control of the PRO subject of the complement to verbs such as *tell*, with both active and passive main clauses; see Maratsos 1974b; Goodluck 1981; Goodluck and Behne 1992). This allows a check on the general level of development of the subjects and the efficacy of the particular test against which variable or unexpected behavior with other constructions can be evaluated.

It is worth keeping in mind that the existence of certain biases for interpretation may itself be of developmental interest. In the experiment reported in Goodluck 1987 in which children generally preferred to interpret pronouns and PRO subjects as referring outside the sentence, a small number of children did, however, prefer an internal interpretation. These children tended to be younger than those who preferred to make the pronoun/PRO refer outside the sentence, a tendency found in a number of experiments on pronoun/PRO interpretation (see references in Goodluck 1987, 1990). The moral with respect to design appears to be that although it may be possible to fiddle with the experiment to get rid of a bias toward a particular interpretation, nonetheless such bias may itself be worth knowing about, because it is part of a developmental pattern.

Again, such bias may be most efficiently revealed by between-subjects comparisons and/or multiple small experiments.

7.4 Syntax, Semantics, and Discourse

The act-out task has a good track record with respect to tests of many aspects of syntactic knowledge (see references in table 7.1). One area that deserves more attention with respect to the utility of the act-out task is the degree to which the task is sensitive to semantic, pragmatic, and discourse-related factors. The just-mentioned tendency for younger children to prefer a sentence-internal construal of a pronoun or PRO may possibly be a reflex of a general orientation among younger children toward sentence-level syntax, as opposed to discourse/pragmatic representations. Somewhat at odds with this view, Hamburger and Crain (1982) argued that performance on the acting out of relative clauses such as the one in (5) could be improved by adjusting the felicity conditions on the use of restrictive relative clauses; specifically, they proposed that performance on the acting out of such relatives was improved by providing a reference set of more than one toy of the type of the (adult) head of the relative, thus visually meeting the condition that a restrictive relative clause normally serves to identify a particular entity in a set. Although providing such a set may increase the degree of success in acting out such clauses (Hamburger and Crain 1982; Goodluck 1990), it has not yet been established that performance improves because felicity conditions are met, rather than because, for example, attention is drawn to the correct head of the relative by the visual prominence of a reference set for the head. By its very nature, the act-out task emphasizes action and thus may not be best suited to test aspects of linguistic knowledge that depend on mental states and discourse knowledge of the speaker/hearer (an extension of the first disadvantage noted in section 7.2.2).

7.5 Act-Out versus Other Tasks

Act-out has both advantages and disadvantages when compared with other tasks, some of which have already been mentioned:

- Act-out can give a clear indication of who does what to whom, and in this sense can be superior to production tasks as a test of many aspects of syntactic knowledge.

- Because the cognitive complexity and physical requirements of act-out limit its use with very young children, act-out is inferior to tasks such as preferential looking (see chapter 5, this volume) as a measure of syntactic development in the earliest stages.
- The lack of a preset range of responses may give act-out an edge over tasks such as situation-sentence judgment in avoiding bias toward a particular response and in allowing the child to reveal interpretations the experimenter has not thought of.
- Act-out is less expensive and easier to administer than many other tasks, particularly on-line tasks.
- Where it is important to establish syntactic effects independently of lexical content (see the discussion in section 7.3), act-out has the advantage that it is relatively easy to create unique sets of sentences for each subject (compare, for example, the labor involved in creating 20 unique sentences per subject with that involved in creating 20 unique sentences and matching pictures per subject for a picture verification test).

One question about which, in my opinion, the jury should still be out is whether act-out is any more prone than some other tasks to tap only preferred readings of sentences (see the second disadvantage discussed in section 7.2.2). In principle, situation-sentence judgment tasks and picture verification tasks, in which the experimenter presents the subject with an interpretation of a sentence in the form of an act-out, a verbal description of the intended meaning, or a picture, have an advantage over act-out in that the experimenter can check with judgment/verification whether a subject accepts an interpretation that may not be revealed if the subject is only asked to act out the sentence. Although the rationale in favor of judgment/verification tasks in this regard is impeccable, one can doubt how effective such tasks really are in picking up nonpreferred readings. For example, Arhonto Terzi and I have been studying children's knowledge of the fact that in Greek the phonetically null (pro) subject of the complement to a verb such as *want* may refer to an entity outside the sentence, as in (13).

(13) O   Yiannis$_i$ theli $pro_{i/j}$ na   fai.
     DET John   wants pro   PARTICLE eats
     'John wants to eat.'

Both adult and child speakers of Greek tend to reject the sentence-external interpretation of the pro subject in (13) when asked to judge the appropriateness of an act-out performed by the experimenter or of a picture showing the external reading (Goodluck and Terzi 1995). Thus, even judgment tasks are not always capable of verifying dispreferred readings (this issue is also discussed in chapters 10 and 11 of this volume).

Finally, in comparing the advantages of various tasks, it is important to keep in mind that for whatever reasons, one child may show his knowledge of grammar with task X and another child may show it with task Y. For example, in the study of Greek just mentioned, some children acted out external reference for the embedded subject of sentences such as (13) but rejected pictures showing such an interpretation; other children accepted such pictures but failed to show the external reference reading in their act-outs.

7.6 Conclusion

Act-out has a valuable place in the array of available tests of syntactic knowledge. Because act-out has been used extensively, its pitfalls are fairly well understood, as are its advantages. A body of act-out results now exists on a range of syntactic phenomena, providing a useful baseline for crosslinguistic work and for comparison with other techniques.

Notes

1. The reader who consults the paper just quoted will find that in Saddy's study of an adult aphasic patient, act-out produced a considerably lower level of performance (correct responses) than did a picture verification task. Saddy attributes this difference to the fact that the patient studied had a severe short-term memory deficit, which impaired his ability to plan the actions for an act-out more seriously than his ability to verify a picture as fitting a given sentence. Thus, the advantage of act-out over tasks such as picture verification in discouraging response bias and/or unreflective responses may be nullified by special characteristics of the population studied.

2. The subordinate clause was omitted with imperative stimuli approximately as often for *before* and *after* clauses in Johnson's study, even though, as Dana McDaniel (personal communication) points out, one might expect the subordinate clause to be omitted more frequently with *before*.

3. The design of act-out experiments was and is frequently sufficiently complex to limit the number of tokens of each sentence type presented to four or fewer, thus restricting the use of statistical remedies (in particular, treatment of items as a random effect) that Clark discusses as a solution to the problem of generalizing from the set of stimuli.

Chapter 8

| Questions after Stories: On Supplying Context and Eliminating It as a Variable | Jill de Villiers and Thomas Roeper |

8.1 Introduction

In the philosophy of science considerable attention has been paid to the question of how to be sure that a given experimental result can be taken as supporting evidence for a theory. That is, theorists are prone to see the causal path in a rather straightforward manner:

Theory → Experimental result

If the experimental result occurs, they rejoice in the confirmation of the theory. But Duhem (1906), Quine (1953), and many others have written about the necessity of paying attention to the methods, measurement procedures, and even assumptions about the apparatus being made by the scientist in subjecting the theory to the test. That is, the result might have occurred not because the theory was true, but because other aspects of the experimental or methodological set-up made it likely to happen:

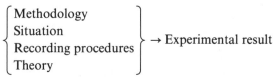

In other words, it must be recognized that every test of the theory is also a test of the "auxiliary assumptions."

Even more problematic is the notion of a confirmation of a theory by a result. Popper (1959) and his followers argued that only disconfirmation is scientific progress: the theory must predict that something will *not* occur, and if it does occur, then that theory can be proven wrong:

Theory → *Not* experimental result

For Popper, true progress in science came with the rejection of theories by such tests. Popper's early work also discussed the importance of theories that made "risky predictions"—namely, ones that seemed counterintuitive or would be highly unlikely on the basis of common sense:

Theory → *Not* experimental result
Common sense/intuition → Experimental result

Much subsequent work raised doubts about achieving certainty by seeking disconfirming evidence, because it can be shown to involve the same problems of induction as positive evidence (Reichenbach 1978): namely, accumulation of compatible instances never guarantees the truth of the theory. Furthermore, negative evidence too is subject to the Duhem-Quine problem. The failure of the prediction might be due to some other assumption: maybe the apparatus was wrong, or the recording technique, or the environment for testing:

$$\left.\begin{array}{l} \text{Methodology} \\ \text{Situation} \\ \text{Recording procedures} \\ \text{Theory} \end{array}\right\} \rightarrow \textit{Not} \text{ experimental result}$$

In general, it is a combination of the evidence and the inherent logic of the theory that makes an experiment persuasive. In the absence of a set of theoretical commitments and beliefs, explanations for experimental results are considered ad hoc. In the most famous case of this problem, the experimenters (Michelson and Morley; see Michelson 1881) tried to test for the drag of ether on the speed of light by testing the speed of light at different angles to the earth's motion through space. Ether was held to be the medium through which electromagnetic "waves" like light must travel. The assumption of the theory was that the apparatus was swimming in a stream of ether, and as with a swimmer attempting to swim in a river, the direction of flow should make a difference to the speed of light. When the expected result did not occur, and instead light seemed to travel at the same speed in both directions, Fitzgerald (1895) and Lorenz (1895) independently invoked an explanation involving the rather miraculous-sounding expansion and contraction of the arms of the apparatus, which was supposed to compensate exactly for the expected difference in speed, thus rescuing the theory about ether. The explanation remained ad hoc until Einstein's theory of relativity provided the new paradigm to accommodate the results, in which the speed of light was constant.

How do we escape from this dilemma in our linguistic research? How can we know that a certain set of results is evidence on behalf of a theory and not due to the auxiliary assumptions required for the test? We have tried to do acquisition studies on aspects of reasonably refined linguistic theories, so that there are other kinds of evidence already articulated in their defense. In our experiments, the auxiliary assumptions are held constant across two conditions that elicit different responses, so the minimal difference between the two conditions must be held responsible for the responses. If the auxiliary assumptions are appealed to as explanation for one phenomenon, they can be shown to make precisely the wrong predictions for a second phenomenon within the same experiment.

We have described this as our ideal strategy; as researchers, we have undoubtedly slipped off this bandwagon of ideal methodology and at times placed greater emphasis on theoretical coherence than methodological rigor. Let us illustrate the strategy in its purest form, and then describe its history.

Suppose there is a sentence, S, that is subject to two interpretations; it is inherently ambiguous. Suppose further that it is preceded by some context that makes either interpretation readily available. One might then expect that subjects hearing this sentence would interpret it either one way or the other, depending on their personal predilections, how they saw the salience of the events in the context, and so on. Ideally, given 10 such sentence/context pairs, they might interpret 5 one way and 5 the other way. Even more ideally, if we looked at the behavior of 10 subjects, it would turn out that each story was interpreted one way five times and the other way five times. Given that result, it would be hard to claim either that individual stories contained biases or that individual subjects had parsing biases. We take this as proof that the stories are pragmatically balanced.

Suppose next that there is a sentence, S′, that is also subject to two interpretations. However, one of the potential interpretations is forbidden by linguistic theory; it would violate some universal constraint. The context preceding S′ is precisely the same as the context preceding S; it contains the same readily available interpretations. However, when the same subjects are presented with S′, they find only one interpretation of the sentence. The scenario has been constructed then in such a way as to rule out the contribution of context to the change in interpretation; since the context stays the same, it is implausible to argue that it is responsible for the shift in choice of interpretation.

Of course, in actuality, the same subject would not be given the same tokens of S and S'. Perhaps for one group of subjects S would be given for one set of five contexts and S' for the other, and for a second group S' would be given for the first set and S for the second. The groups would then be compared to ensure that the sets of tokens made no difference to the outcome.

This design underlies the first in a series of studies we have conducted in the domain of *wh*-question acquisition with young children. In the next section we trace the somewhat mottled history by which we achieved this design.

8.2 Putting It into Practice: History of the Procedure

Consider what is involved in the real-world comprehension of a complex sentence.

(1) How did John ask who to paint?

The situation semantics require at least two characters, some indecision on the part of one of them, and the need for two questions, one indirect.

The result is a situation that cannot be set up in a single sentence; rather, a story is necessary if the referential domain is to be included. Now, however, we have introduced all the problems of memory. Will the child retain the story as we wrote it? In fact, adults are sometimes boggled by a story if there is no visual context to which it can be anchored.

The presentation pragmatics of the experiment now become relevant. We need pictorial support for a child to remember the story that contains the context, but if we present the pictures to children in a sequential manner, perhaps they will pay attention only to the last picture. Should we then create a guarantee that they survey the entire array?

Finally, discourse pragmatics are relevant. Should we ask the children questions to which they know that we know the answers? Is it not pragmatically odd to ask for information that the questioner already possesses? Does the fact that parents constantly ask "test" questions mean that most children will be quite used to this situation?

These are not only possible questions—they are questions that we addressed very seriously in the first phase of our research when we were unsure that we could elicit responses at all to complex questions. In effect, we have introduced a totally uncontrollable set of variables were one to evaluate our work in terms of the variables themselves. Should we independently determine the nature of each of these variables before we begin research? We argue instead that if we design the study in the right way, these methodological issues should assume a lesser importance. How? We use the classic logic of minimal pairs. *All other things being equal, any response difference must be due to the theoretically motivated difference between the two sentences.*

In our first study on *wh*-questions (de Villiers, Roeper, and Vainikka 1990) we presented children with stories followed by ambiguous questions that permitted the children a choice between two interpretations. For example, children might hear the following short story (accompanied by pictures like those in figure 8.1):

This boy loved to climb trees in the forest.

One afternoon he slipped and fell to the ground. He picked himself up and went home.

That night when he had a bath, he found a big bruise on his arm. He said to his dad, "I must have hurt myself when I fell this afternoon!"

Figure 8.1
Typical pictured story from de Villiers, Roeper, and Vainikka 1990

Story

This boy loved to climb trees in the forest. One afternoon he slipped and fell to the ground. He picked himself up and went home. That night when he had a bath, he found a big bruise on his arm. He said to his dad, "I must have hurt myself when I fell this afternoon!"

Question

(2)   When did the boy say he hurt himself?

Given the story, the question has two possible interpretations, depending on where the listener interprets the trace to be for the *wh*-question *when*. Is it connected as an adjunct to *say*, as in (3), or to *hurt*, as in (4)?

(3)   When$_i$ did he say t_i he hurt himself?

(4)   When$_j$ did he say he hurt himself t_j?

That is, a subject might answer "At night" (if (3)) or "That afternoon" (if (4)), depending on the interpretation. The answer corresponding to (3) is referred to as a *short-distance movement*, because the *wh*-word moves within the first clause (from the position marked as the trace t_i). By contrast, the answer to (4) involves *long-distance movement*, because the *wh*-word moves from a position in the embedded clause (t_j).

For that study, we designed stories containing information that made both possible interpretations salient, but we were worried that given the choice, children would choose the short-distance interpretation. Hence, we introduced a source of bias in the context: we made a point of having a second "stooge" experimenter who secretly showed the child a picture containing the information needed to answer the long-distance question from the first experimenter, hoping in that way to increase its salience and plausibility as an answer. For example, for the question in (5)

(5)   How did Big Bird ask to help?

the "stooge" experimenter showed the child (but not the questioning experimenter) a picture in which Big Bird was helping by cutting out the cookie dough—in other words, a picture that provides the "long-distance" answer about how Big Bird helped. The 3- to 6-year-olds (de Villiers, Roeper, and Vainikka 1990) were quite happy to provide either answer, suggesting that their grammars do readily permit long-distance movement. We dropped these extra features in later work when we discovered that they made no difference in the results obtained. And, as is often the case, the evolution of the experiment itself pointed to progressive simplifications.

The main point of the study, however, was to test whether children in this age range obey the subtle constraints on movement that are so central to contemporary syntactic theory. In long-distance questions, the *wh*-word moves in two steps, so if another *wh*-word is present, the first move is blocked; in contemporary terms, there is a *barrier* to movement (Chomsky 1986a). If the medial position in a question is already filled by a *wh*-word serving as the complementizer (the embedding connective), a *wh*-question cannot cycle through that position and leave a trace (t_i), so the resulting sentence is ungrammatical.

(6) *When$_i$ did he say how he hurt himself t_i?

The long-distance interpretation 'in the afternoon' was all right for (4), but it is not permissible as an answer for (6). The question in (6) sounds grammatical, but only under the interpretation of 'when did he say it', not 'when did he hurt himself'; the long-distance reading is excluded. The concept of *local* movement is a feature of Universal Grammar; hence, a child should have that option available. We controlled the stimuli so that for any given story, half of the children heard a story followed by a sentence *without* a medial *wh*-word, and the other half heard the same story followed by a sentence *with* a medial *wh*-word. By designing the study this way, we approached some of the ideals discussed above. First, we had a theory that forbids certain things to happen. If the child did permit long-distance movement in the condition forbidden by the theory, the child's response would be strong evidence against that theory of grammar for young children. However, if a theory survives such a test, it is not proven by it; it merely remains in the set of possible theories. Second, the theory suggests a result that is counterintuitive: adults naive to linguistics are always surprised by the contrast between (4) and (6) and usually resort to ad hoc semantic explanations once they notice it. Third, because the method, context, and measurement are identical, any difference between performance on (4) and performance on (6) must be a consequence of the subtle difference between the two sentences, namely, a medial *wh*-word occupying the specifier of CP position.

The findings of that study revealed that 3-year-old children know the Universal Grammar principles, in that they only rarely give long-distance answers to questions such as (6), which contains the medial *wh*-word. There was a consistent, often tenfold difference between the percentages of long-distance interpretations for questions with and without the barrier. There were further subtle outcomes such as a contrast between adjunct (e.g., *how, why, when*) and argument (e.g., *what, who*) questions that is also strongly counter to lay expectations but precisely predicted by contemporary formulations of barrier theory (e.g., Chomsky 1986a; Rizzi 1990; Cinque 1990).[1] We were not the first to use the story-and-ambiguous-question technique; earlier projects exploited the same procedure. Chomsky (1969) used ambiguous questions; Maratsos (1976) used stories to explore sensitivity to subtle contrasts in determiners. Others put the two techniques together. Otsu (1981) was among the first to use the combined technique, to test directly whether children obey constraints on *wh*-extraction from relative clauses and prepositional phrases in a comprehension task. His preschool subjects heard short pictured stories followed by a *wh*-question. For example:

Story
Jane is drawing a monkey with a crayon. The monkey is drinking milk with a straw.

Question
(7)   What is Jane drawing a monkey that is drinking milk with?

Adult speakers of English can find only one possible meaning for the question, namely, one that links the question to the main clause and construes the preposition as being associated with that clause.

(8) What$_i$ is Jane drawing [a monkey that is drinking milk] with t_i?

However, notice that the question is potentially ambiguous, if the child lacks the constraint on extraction from a relative clause: it could mean 'What is the monkey using to drink the milk?' *if* the trace of *what* is construed as inside the relative clause.

(9) What$_i$ is Jane drawing [a monkey that is drinking milk with t_i]?

If the child's grammar had no constraints on extraction, the answer "A straw" would reveal the availability of the embedded site. In addition to relative clause sentences, Otsu tested the children on simple questions with prepositional phrases. These questions followed simple pictured stories.

Story
James is painting a picture of a boy with a book. James is painting a picture of the boy with a brush.

Question

(10) What is James painting a picture of a boy with?

Actually, Otsu's results showed that 3- and 4-year-olds did rather poorly on this task, often answering the questions in a manner that violated the barrierhood of the relative clause or the prepositional phrase. However, he also included a test of comprehension of the relative clause, which revealed the very interesting finding that those children who showed mastery of the structure in comprehension where more likely to respect the barrierhood of the relative clause. Some of the reasons for the relatively poor performance of children on Otsu's experiment are discussed in de Villiers and Roeper 1995; we found striking obedience when adjunct questions were used instead. Notice that Otsu's procedure, although consisting of the same general idea of a story followed by an ambiguous question, has no built-in control for the influence of the story on the interpretation.

Phinney (1981) also used the ambiguous-question technique to explore children's understanding of *that*-trace restrictions in English. Her task involved short pictured stories with two potential referents for a question such as (11) that would be ambiguous if the child lacked the *That*-Trace Filter.

(11) Who did the lion know that swam in the pond?

If this question is construed as having a trace following *that*—

(12) Who$_i$ did the lion know that t_i swam in the pond?

in other words, who did the lion *witness swimming* in the pond—it violates the *That*-Trace Filter. However, the child had the alternative of choosing a relative clause reading for the sentence.

(13) Who$_i$ did the lion know t_i [that swam in the pond]?

In this case, the lion knew someone, who swam in the pond unbeknownst to the lion. The pictured story defined different referents for the two readings, but the children only rarely chose the reading that would correspond to a violation; that is, they didn't choose the creature witnessed swimming. Phinney's evidence could therefore be considered in keeping with the notion that English-speaking children obey the *That*-Trace Filter. Notice that, like Otsu's, this procedure lacks the control against bias in the story favoring one interpretation. But in Phinney's case subjects did choose the witnessed swimmer in answer to the question lacking *that*.

(14) Who did the lion know swam in the pond?

The work of Otsu and Phinney thus tested precise, theoretically important distinctions by the use of potentially ambiguous questions.

8.3   Assumptions and Controls

In this section we discuss some of the underlying requirements of the task so that experimenters who wish to use this method to test their own theoretical questions can decide whether it is appropriate for that purpose. What are we assuming about the cognitive and linguistic processes in the task?

The child has several problems to solve. First, she must understand the story: the characters, their motives, the order of events, the paths of causation. Information for this is coming from two sources: the story being read, and the sequence of pictures laid down in order as the story is read. The pictures are snapshots capturing critical events; time and motions are lost, and presumably important clues given in real life by facial expression and nonverbal cues from participants are captured only grossly by the artist. Nevertheless, we assume that the average 3-year-old has some practice in this art of narrative construction from being read to both at home and at school.

Second, the child must retain enough of the narrative in memory to search for the answer to the question asked. Again, it is presumptuous to conclude that 3-year-olds have exactly the same skill level in this regard as 5- or 6-year-olds; however, we try to keep the stories short enough to be within their grasp, and of course the pictures are still present as recall clues.

Third, the child must parse the question and arrive at an interpretation for the site of the trace. In our theoretical work, we tend to talk as though that is the only task involved. But how does it interact with the other two tasks above?

Consider a question such as (15).

(15) How did the mother say she cooked the pie?

One possibility is that sentence processing is extremely modular. On that scenario, the child hears the question as an entirely isolated piece of language, and identifies the trace location and arrives at an interpretation in complete independence from the story or pictures that have just been presented. Suppose that this process identifies the first possible gap (after *say*) as the site of the trace. Having arrived at an interpretation, the child must then look at her memory representation to find the answer to, for example, *How did the mother speak?*, and having found such an answer, she gives it.

Consider a second possibility, which is that the processing of the question is completely permeable to the context created by the story. On that description, the child might have already paid greater attention in the story to the manner of speaking, say, than to the manner of cooking. When she hears the question, she immediately construes it to be about the act of speaking rather than about cooking, and again searches her memory representation (presumably it is already primed) and retrieves the answer.

A third position is a compromise between these two: perhaps the sentence interpretation is encapsulated, but in the search process one "manner" is much more salient than the other and the child might backtrack to a different interpretation if the first interpretation offers no immediate answer.

These are important alternatives to be pursued, but we have not yet spent research time in exploring them. Is this a shocking neglect? No, for the following reason. Whatever the process is, it will have to be common both to sentences with a barrier to *wh*-movement and to sentences without. The presence of, say, a medial *wh*-word, or an adverb, in the final question cannot plausibly change the salience of events already coded from the story, or the accessibility of the events from memory. There must be a parsing difference, but that is a reflection of the grammatical constraint, and any theory must accommodate that. Hence, any systematic differences that we detect between these sentences cannot be an artifact of the kind of story processing being undertaken, but must instead reflect the child's grammatical parsing alone.

Why, then, do we attend to the design of the stories so carefully? We do so because it is our goal to minimize the memory and comprehension demands for young children so that failures to arrive at an answer do not confound the results. Remember that no child sees a story twice. The child who hears story A followed by a question with no barrier will hear story B followed by a question with a barrier. Another child will hear story A followed by the question with a barrier and story B followed by the question without one. If we have ensured the comparability of pairs of stories with and without a barrier, then differences that we obtain can be attributed to knowledge of the barrier. In other words, we have achieved the goal we set out with: *we have supplied context and yet removed it as a variable*.

There is one final source of difference that it is natural to attach importance to: the prosody of the question. Much has been written about the important role of sentence prosody as a bootstrap to sentence parsing for young children, though the case is presently built from rather indirect evidence. If it is true that children are highly sensitive to the intonation pattern across a sentence for providing major clues to, say, the location of gaps or the coindexation of anaphora, then it is essential to control that variable in presenting matched pairs of questions.

The usual judgment for many adults is that a speaker can bias a two-clause question to a lower-clause interpretation by using a "long rise" type of intonation with no special stress on the matrix verb.

(16) When did she say she ate?

Alternatively, a speaker can bias the question to a short-distance interpretation by using a slightly falling intonation and a light emphasis on the matrix verb.

(17) When did she say she ate?

In our own work we have tried to control intonation as reliably as possible. Nevertheless, experimenters are human, and the vagaries and stress of presenting 50 or 60 stories and questions over the course of a morning mean inevitable variation in prosody. Fortunately, we videotape our sessions and have all the questions stored on tape. Last year a research assistant blind to the hypothesis at hand went back and coded a random sample of 180 questions for their prosodic characteristics: either long rise or fall or unclear/neutral. The children's responses to those questions were then analyzed to see if the prosody influenced their choice of answer. Results were as follows: the sample included 65 ambiguous *wh*-questions with no medial barrier, of which 36 were presented with rising intonation, 24 with falling intonation, and 5 with neutral intonation. Figure 8.2 shows the distribution of answers to those questions, and it does seem that long-distance answers are more readily provided under the long-rise prosody. The sample also included 168 questions that involved *wh*-barriers, and here the distribution of prosody was different: 33 questions were produced with rising intonation, 87 with falling intonation, and 48 with neu-

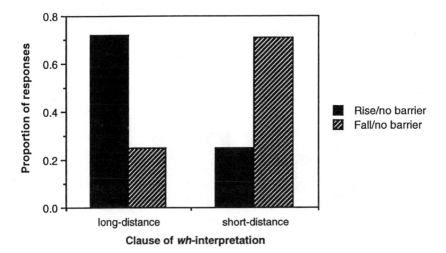

Figure 8.2
The effect of prosody on the interpretation of *wh*-questions with no barriers

tral intonation. Apparently the experimenter found it hard to produce the long-rise prosody reliably with a medial barrier. Figure 8.3 shows the distribution of responses to those questions: the children resist long-distance answers appropriately, and do so even for the long-rise intonation.

Given the less than systematic presentation of the prosody, the intuition about prosody needed further exploration. Another experiment was therefore conducted in which prosody was systematically varied. Children were presented with eight stories followed by questions, half of which had long-rise prosody and half of which did not. The stories were presented in the usual manner. There were two sets: in one set a group of children heard half the questions with a medial *wh*-barrier, in the other they heard those questions without a barrier.

The results were discouraging for the idea that prosody exerts a strong influence. In fact, they were unexpected: the falling intonation actually marginally encouraged long-distance answers in the case of questions with no barriers. In the case of questions with barriers, prosody had no effect. Given that the two studies were conducted by different experimenters, perhaps prosody is a feature that varies idiosyncratically. More work comparing adults and children might reveal interesting changes. Nevertheless, the results from both studies suggest that children can resist long-distance answers that would violate barriers even in the face of misleading

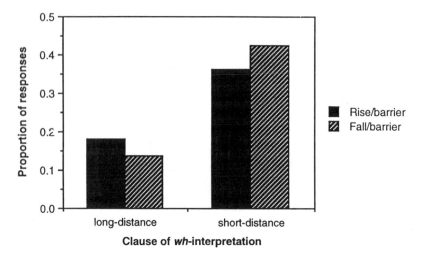

Figure 8.3
The effect of prosody on the interpretation of *wh*-questions with barriers

prosody. Our advice would still be to control prosody as far as possible
unless it is the focus of interest.

8.4 Constructing an Experiment

8.4.1 An Example
How do we actually construct an experiment? Our previous work on
barriers to *wh*-question movement had investigated "strong" barriers to
movement such as medial *wh*-questions (18) or nominals (19) (see Roeper
and de Villiers 1992).

(18) *When$_i$ did the boy say how he hurt himself t_i?

(19) *How$_i$ did the friends see the boy's dancing t_i?

There is a class of barriers to *wh*-movement that is even subtler for adults,
namely, "weak" barriers such as adverbs of quantification like *always*.

(20) Why did he always say he won?

Adults struggle to get the reading 'why he won', but it is easy to get the
reading 'why did he say it'. The barrier is considered "weak" because it
applies to adjunct *wh*-questions such as *why*, *when*, *where*, and *how*, but

not to arguments such as *who* or *what*. For (21), it is easy to get a long-distance reading.

(21) What did he always say he won?

The details of the theories devised to account for this matter do not concern us here. The main point is, How might one investigate whether children know weak barriers?[2]

Philip and de Villiers (1992) set out to investigate just this question with respect to adverbs of quantification such as *always*. They sought to find out whether children would block an interpretation of an adjunct question from a lower clause if an adverb of quantification intervened. To limit other sources of variability, they focused on a single adjunct question, *why*. They did this because the other candidates were less suitable: *when* would interfere with the use of an adverb such as *always* in awkward ways.

(22) When did he always say he won?

However, since there was not much previous work on *why* as a long-distance question, they needed to be sure that children would readily give long-distance and short-distance answers to *why* questions if no barrier was present. This need led to part of the design: roughly identical stories would be constructed that contained answers both to the question "Why did someone say something happened?" and to the question "why did something happen?" For one of them, the question would be simply as shown in (23), and for the other, a quantificational adverb would be added, as in (24).

(23) Why did x say y happened?

(24) Why did x always say y happened?

The predictions would then be as follows: For (23), if the stories were constructed to be free of bias, the children should be equally prone to answer with long- or short-distance interpretations. For (24), even though the children heard the same stories, the question should lead to only short-distance answers if children understood the barrierhood of the adverb. By comparing answers to (23) and (24) for the same children, it would be possible to assess the degree of obedience to the barrierhood of adverbs.

The goal, then, was to devise stories that had the right properties: equal likelihood that a short- or long-distance answer would be given if the question were of type (23). The events in the stories had to be balanced so that the reasons for speaking and the reasons for the event spoken about were equally salient. The rationale for undertaking this kind of balancing has already been discussed. However, here the design was counterbalanced to test the influence of position and type of connective on biasing children's answers to the ambiguous questions (i.e., type (23)).

The design should not allow one type of reason to be lost in the middle of the story and the other to be either highlighted by being at the end or subject to undue emphasis. For example, if the reason for speaking was always embedded in the middle of the story, but the reason for the event was always the last thing mentioned, the child's memory might be biased in such a way that the last reason mentioned was always the first reason to pop into mind. Having no evidence either way on such a matter, Philip and de Villiers chose to counterbalance where the reason occurred within the story and test position as a factor influencing the answers given to type (23) questions.

It was also of concern that some types of causal connection might be more familiar than others to young children. Previous work on naturalistic production (e.g., Bloom et al. 1980) had discovered that different connectives appear at different times in children's speech, so the reasons should not be confounded with types of connective. The connectives chosen were *because* and *so that*, and the stories were balanced in such a way that the type of reason was introduced by either connective. Once again, stories were counterbalanced to test the influence of type of connective on the answers to type (23) questions.

In fact, no one knows whether such biases really exist, and this issue has not been explored to date except in the study just described. In all other cases, we have taken care to balance the stories or to disentangle the variable of interest from other extraneous influences such as order of mention or salience. It may be impossible to foresee every potential confound. Why should certain factors, such as intonation or order of mention, always be considered more likely candidates for explanation, though highly ad hoc, than the variables derived from serious theoretical work? Philip and de Villiers (1992) decided it may be more productive to confront the variables head-on and test for effects than to try to balance all kinds of potential confounds. This approach makes the results more plausible, but since the set of potential pragmatic variables is infinite, ultimately reliance on the intrinsic strength and coherence of the theory is unavoidable.

In the end, Philip and de Villiers controlled intonation, controlled salience, and counterbalanced position in the story and connective. The latter two variables proved to be insignificant variables in the children's choice of answer for sentences of type (23) when tested in an analysis of variance.

Each child heard 4 stories followed by questions of type (23) and 4 followed by questions of type (24) containing an adverb. Four cases were also included with strong medial-*wh* barriers like (18). Each child thus received 12 example stories and questions, usually in two sessions of about 10 minutes each. (In this study the children were asked to complete another task as well.) As in all our work, the stories, were randomized anew for each child (by shuffling the set) so they were not presented in the same order. The remaining parts of this experimental set-up were sufficiently general that we highlight them in a separate section.

8.4.2 More General Procedures

A further aspect of the design concerns the pictures that accompany the stories. We endeavor to have a layout that consists of at most five pictures, because it is hard to scan across a larger set. Usually a simple story can be captured with three pictures that depict the most salient events. Again, the pictures should ideally depict both events discussed, without being biased to favor one reading rather than another. We have used a variety of artists and find that cartoonists, provided their style is not outlandish, produce pictures more suited to the task than other kinds of skilled artists who may pay too much attention to the aesthetics and not enough to what is salient in the story. We have used both black-and-white and colored pictures. In most cases the backgrounds are very minimal and the activities are the focus. An example was provided in figure 8.1.

For most of our studies, we pilot: test our stories and pictures first on college students, who are tested in (almost) the same way as the children. On occasion we have given these as group tests using an overhead projector, but it has been our experience that college students sometimes take these tests as opportunities for having fun if they write the answers and are assured anonymity! We get more sober and reasonable answers with one-on-one interaction in which we can explain the purpose of collecting adults' data for comparison with young children's data.

Finally, there is the manner in which we interact with the child in the sessions. It is imperative to have a quiet place to record the session free of interruption. We first welcome the child informally and introduce ourselves, then draw attention to the fact that we are recording on a video camera by asking the child to "watch for the blinking light to make sure it's working." It is preferable to make this explicit and then ignore the camera rather than adjust the focus (or whatever) without talking to the child about it. The child is seated at a small table on which we can lay out the pictures relevant to the story. It is important to videotape the sessions to record nonverbal responses (e.g., pointing to a picture).

We ask the child if she likes to listen to stories, and say that we will read a story and then ask a question about it. As the story is read, one experimenter lays out the relevant pictures from left to right in front of the child, leaving them all visible at the time of questioning. At the end of the story, the experimenter pauses briefly, then asks the question. A second experimenter records the child's answer verbatim and later checks it against the videotape.

If a child hesitates, acts shy, or looks bewildered, the first experimenter repeats the question. If met with the same response, the experimenter asks if the child would like to hear the story one more time, then repeats it. If a child just points to a picture, the experimenter attempts further clarification by asking, for example, "What? Can you tell me instead?" Once a question is answered, the experimenter proceeds to the next. Children of this age are prone to interrupt with comments or questions of their own, and we do not discourage natural conversation of this sort. If the interruption has been prolonged or off topic, we typically start the story from the beginning after it. With stories this brief, we find most children reserve their conversation for the pause between stories.

Children's pleasure in doing the tasks is relevant; we take it to mean that they are engaged and using their abilities. When the task has been completed, we thank the child profusely and regardless of performance we make some congratulatory comment such as "How come you know so much stuff already? I bet you're really six years old!" The purpose of this is to send the child back to the classroom with a feeling of accomplishment and goodwill. We do not lack for volunteers the next day (of course, we are restricted to choose from the children who have permission to participate).

Date analysis is the next task. We transcribe all responses and enter them in a relational database (4th Dimension) on the computer, with separate files for information on the children (age, gender, school), the stories (type, question), and the data (actual statement by the child, then codes).

Figure 8.4
Typical picture from Philip and de Villiers 1992

In the particular study conducted by Philip and de Villiers (1992), the children's answers to questions like (25), which accompanied the following story and figure 8.4, were coded as shown below.

Story
Last year on his birthday Bobby made his own birthday cake. He wanted it to be green so he made it out of spinach. When his sister Lucy saw it she laughed and laughed. "You can't make a cake out of spinach," she said. *Because Lucy thought it was so funny* she always told people Bobby had made a cake out of spinach *so that it would be green*.

Question
(25) Why did Lucy often/always say Bobby had made a cake out of spinach?

The response was coded as one of the following types:

1. Short-distance (e.g., "Because she thought it was so funny")
2. Long-distance (e.g., "So that it would be green")
3. Global, that is, ambiguous between 1 and 2 ("Because it was a funny green cake")
4. Other (e.g., "I had a chocolate one")
5. "I don't know"
6. *Why/How* confusion ("She laughed and laughed"/"He made it out of spinach")

Using the database allows us to sort along many variables, for instance, to print a report of all the answers to one particular story, or all the "short-distance" answers from 4-year-olds. It is not a necessary step but it is one that has illuminated several phenomena that might have stayed hidden in the original score sheets. In addition, the data set can still be coded along new dimensions of interest. As just one example, we became interested in whether children were prone to answer with an appropriate constituent or not. Consider question (26).

(26) How did the mother say the boy rode the bike?

Let's suppose that in the story the mother said it on the telephone, and the boy rode the bike through the mud. For the upper clause, a child could give the answers in (27a), and for the lower clause, the answers in (27b).

(27) a. "Telephone."
     "By telephone."
     "That." ⟨pointing⟩
     "She spoke in the telephone."
   b. "Through mud."
     "Mud."
     "He rode it through mud."

We coded the constituent form of the answer (e.g., PP, N, NP, S) to test the hypothesis that the occasional mis-answer (e.g., a violation of a barrier) was less likely to be a constituent than a correct answer was, because that might suggest the child was retrieving the answer by some means that circumvented grammar and used inference. We have no strong evidence yet on behalf of that idea, but the database allowed us to recode data along a new dimension to answer a new theoretical question.

After the data are entered, we make a new data sheet suitable for analysis by a statistical package (e.g., analysis of variance). Philip and de Villiers 1992 were interested in the number of lower-clause answers to questions of type (23) without the adverb, versus type (24) with the adverb. Therefore, for each child the number of lower-clause answers to each type of question was counted. Since the contribution of position in the story and connective was found to be insignificant, those differences were collapsed in the final analysis. In other studies such variables as gender and age or school might be of interest, and these would be entered, as between-subjects variables in the analysis of variance.

In the Philip and de Villiers study, the weak barriers created by adverbs were not respected by 4- and 5-year-old children. The children were just as likely to give a lower-clause reading as an upper-clause reading regardless of whether a quantificational adverb was present in the question. The same children were tested on "strong" barriers—medial-*wh*-islands—and respected them completely, suggesting that different mechanisms or modules are at work in the two cases (see Philip and de Villiers 1992).

8.4.3 When Is the Method Most Useful?

The technique as described has been used most successfully in, and is perhaps best suited to, the following kinds of circumstances:

- If one can test children on matched pairs of sentences (e.g., one with a barrier and one without) and control all the other features. However, it may also be useful for a contrasting pair of sentences for which, if a child knows the contrast, one answer would be given for one question and the other for the other question. At present it seems best suited to studying *wh*-interrogatives, but it might be extended with some imagination to other constructions.
- If children can be given enough examples to allow robust statistical analysis: at least four examples of each type, six or more if individual grammars are of interest rather than group data.
- If the materials are suited to age $3\frac{1}{2}$ and upward. Below that age we have encountered difficulties with getting children to give full answers rather than pointing; we have also found that children have trouble concentrating on the story and tend to lack the basic world knowledge and lexical and syntactic proficiency to follow the events and the question.
- If the events are picturable and do not involve subtle issues of intentionality and theory of mind, which confound the picture of syntactic development in this age range (for examples, see de Villiers 1995).

These limitations have not stopped us from pursuing other questions, however. For example, we have attempted a longitudinal study to explore how individual grammars of *wh*-movement change over time. Working in a cooperative campus nursery school, we tested the same children over the course of one year on a variety of *wh*-question forms, to see if we could follow how their grammars changed (see de Villiers and Roeper 1995, for a partial report). We learned from this experience how important it is to present enough exemplars of a type in any one testing session, but were driven by a rival desire to get as much information on as wide a variety of phenomena as possible in any one round of testing. As a result, the goal of diagnosing a particular child's grammar at any one point is compromised by the small number (usually two examples) of a type of sentence presented at any one time. In addition, since we had to make up new examples every three months, the stories and pictures were unevenly matched and some of the fluctuations in performance may be due to the materials rather than to real growth or regression. Obviously, the lessons learned were valuable ones: we realized the importance of selecting, balancing, and pilot-testing the materials in advance for each round. In addition, we recognized that to use this procedure to "diagnose" a child's grammar of questions would require presenting probably six examples of each given type, to allow us to set criteria on mastery at one moment in time. If a child answered two out of only two questions with short-distance answers, could we conclude that the did not permit long-distance answers? If he answered one of the two "barrier" questions with a long-distance answer, could we conclude that he did not know the barrier effect? The more examples, the more secure these decisions can be for an individual child. Yet the limit for testing most children around age 3 seems to be about 15–20 short stories in a session, which can take only 10 minutes or so. Careful planning is necessary if enough data are to be gathered to be useful at the individual level.

Despite the shortcomings, we discovered some phenomena of interest through this longitudinal study and would recommend it again to others who had the opportunity to test changes over time. One interesting methodological note: children of this age remember pictures with astonishing accuracy. In one story we reused part of a set of pictures that a child had seen one year previously, and the child said, "I've already seen this one." We do not know if children would remember their answers, but it is a possibility to be beware of.

8.4.4 Pitfalls

Before we consider the pitfalls of the technique, let us mention some rather specific difficulties that have concerned us in the work on *wh*-questions. Confusions of meaning among the *wh*-words make it difficult to interpret some answers from the youngest group. Consider question (28).

(28) When did the boy say he hurt himself?

If a child answers this question by saying, "On the tree," can we be certain how to analyze the same child's answer to (29)?

(29) When did the boy say how he hurt himself?

If the child again says, "On the tree," is this phrase a long-distance answer to *when*, with a confusion of meaning, or an answer to the medial *how*?

The most prevalent answer that created coding difficulties involved a confusion of meaning for the adjunct question *how*, which may relate to an interesting theoretical perspective on adjuncthood (see de Villiers 1991). Children were very prone to interpret *how* as *why*, either by giving an answer that referred to a reason rather than a manner, or by answering, "Because." Hearing the question in (30),

(30) How did the dog run?

children often answered, "Because he stole the bone" (the reason) or (less often) "Because he was fast" (the manner). We do not know why this particular direction of confusion occurred; perhaps *how* questions are asked of children less often than *why* questions, or perhaps the semantics of *how* are harder to grasp. The control for this is to ask some simple questions at the beginning of the session that might reveal whether the child has mastered the meanings of the *wh*-words. We did this in the longitudinal study mentioned above, at concomitant sacrifice of attention to enough "interesting" examples.

The verb in the question has well-known effects on the youngest children's question answering. Children have been shown to be influenced by the probability that certain verbs will occur in certain *wh*-questions (Tyack and Ingram 1977; Winzemer 1981), and they will answer the "expected" question. For example, *where* is a likely question in conjunction with the verb *go*, so a young child who is asked, "When did they go?" is quite likely to mis-answer, "To the movies."[3] Of course, controlling for this problem introduces new design questions.

A similar difficulty plagued us with what we came to call *quotation* answers. Let us suppose the question is as follows:

(31) How did the mom say she stirred the cake?

If the child pipes up in a squeaky voice, "I stirred it with a spoon!", how should that be scored? The long-distance answer is contained within the quoted reply, but by mimicking the mother's voice, is the child not telling *how* the mother said it? We ended up creating a special category for such answers; fortunately, they were not especially frequent and did not seem to occur only in one particular category (e.g., only in barrier-type sentences). The issue remains for future work but points out again the difficulty with particular adjunct questions such as *how*.

When questions create difficulties of their own, because children's grasp of time at this age is rather fragile, as may be their memory for order of events. However, their marking of major periods of the day (*night, afternoon, next morning,* etc.) may be more dependable, as may their understanding of the names of various times of year (*spring, summer, winter, fall, on his birthday*) or the moment of events (*at the start of the race, when he climbed the tree, after she got home*). However, 3-year-olds do not seem very accustomed to being asked *when* questions, and they sometimes resort to pointing at the pictured events, which is ambiguous in itself. The experimenter can ask for clarification (e.g., "Do you mean then?"), but it is hard to do so without leading the witness. Our solution has been to doubly mark events in the story for time (e.g., by saying, "when she got home that night" or "in the morning before she got up"), thus providing children with a richer context and more opportunities to refer to the time in whatever manner they prefer.

However, these particular difficulties concern not so much the story-and-ambiguous-question technique per se as the domain of *wh*-questions and their interpretation. A more important criticism can be leveled at the method itself: can we be sure that a child is "avoiding" the answer that would violate adult grammar? We have tried to argue that we can have confidence in this conclusion in the ideal situation described: if the child does not avoid such an answer in the absence of a barrier or constraint, and given a precisely equivalent story. The result should probably be backed up with other methods: judgment tasks and elicited production have been used for this purpose by others (McDaniel, Chiu, and Maxfield 1995; Thornton 1990) and have produced similar results.

8.5 Conclusion

We have argued that if one builds an experiment around a contrast that constitutes a minimal pair, then one can risk the use of an intricate context, that is, a story and accompanying pictures. If the results show a clear contrast, as they do, then the potentially "uncontrolled" features of the context have no consequence.

This does not argue that traditional methodological concerns are irrelevant. In fact, as described here, we use these practical insights about experimental design in attempting to balance our stories. Should another researcher decide that the results are due to a methodological feature not accommodated by the linguistic theory, then it is that researcher's obligation to elevate the methodological feature into a countertheory. Such a countertheory must then meet the requirements of a theory: it must predict all the results. On this view, all experiments contrast rival theories; however, rival theories can be compared only if they make predictions of equivalent precision. It is, of course, not possible for us to articulate all rival theories, and new linguistic theories will surely be developed that may cast a different light on these results.

Notes

1. Together with colleagues we have explored children's knowledge of these barriers in other *wh*-movement languages: German and French (Weissenborn, Roeper, and de Villiers 1991), African American English (Seymour et al. 1992), Caribbean Spanish (Pérez-Leroux 1991), and Greek (Leftheri 1991). Kudra, Goodluck, and Progovac (1994) have also reported obedience to barriers in child speakers of Serbo-Croatian. Young children hearing translations of the test sentences into their own languages have provided convincing evidence of long-distance movement, barrier effects, and the argument/adjunct distinction (Roeper and de Villiers 1994; Maxfield and Plunkett 1991; see also Goodluck, Sedivy, and Foley 1989, and for application to the study of parasitic gaps, Maxfield and McDaniel 1991).

2. Theories of the phenomenon vary and include both syntactic and semantic accounts (Rizzi 1990; Szabolsci and Zwarts 1990).

3. This unexpected result has suggested the interesting hypothesis that children fix the *wh*-feature prior to learning the full meaning of the lexical item.

Chapter 9

On-Line Methods   Cecile McKee

9.1 Introduction

The defining feature of on-line studies is their examination of language use as it occurs, an approach that is especially illuminating for syntactic processes. Unfortunately, children are rarely included in such research. And yet, in contrast to methods aimed primarily at finding out whether a learner knows a piece of the adult grammar, on-line methods can also examine the relation between the child's developing grammatical knowledge and the processes that implement that knowledge.

Processing systems for production and comprehension impose their own constraints, and these affect what any given task can reveal of linguistic competence. One significant factor is the time course of normal sentence processing: it is incremental and occurs in approximately real time, with analysis options being considered, and discarded or selected, as the words of a sentence are being input or output. Hence, an important methodological issue for all psycholinguistic research—including tests of children's linguistic knowledge—is the *time* at which performance is measured: the measurement can be taken after a sentence is processed (as in most tasks described in this volume) or at various points during its processing (as in the cross-modal priming task detailed in this chapter). A robust finding in sentence-processing research with normal adults is that postsentence measures of comprehension often present a different picture from on-line measures (see Garrett 1990, and references therein). Since postsentence measures reveal the product of comprehension processes, the steps to a final interpretation are only indirectly reflected in response patterns. This is especially likely when influences on interpretation compete, as when syntactic, semantic, pragmatic, and task-strategic factors do not converge. Thus, some lexical or syntactic processes can occur without being reflected in a measure taken after sentence processing is completed. On-line measures, on the other hand, reveal such processes (Forster 1979, 1989; Frazier 1987; Swinney 1979) and so can sort out various influences on language performance. Despite this promising possibility, studies of children's real-time language processing are rare. This is partly because the technology needed for such studies (e.g., portable computers with considerable storage and processing capacity) has only recently become available. Moreover, as examples below will illustrate, implementing these experiments with child subjects is demanding.

The virtues described above are not the only reason to study children's real-time application of linguistic knowledge. Many theoretical objectives also motivate research on the developing parser and its relation to the developing grammar. For a lucid presentation of such motivations, see Tyler and Marslen-Wilson 1981; it is one of the earliest studies of children's real-time language processing and lays out a rationale strongly aimed toward explaining language acquisition.

9.2 Overview

This section describes two broad categories of on-line methods that can be used with children, examples of which focus on comprehension. This does not mean that on-line studies cannot also examine production processes; it simply reflects the fact that these methods have been applied to comprehension more often than to production, in both child and adult studies. This section only illustrates the potential richness of real-time data; it is not an exhaustive review of research on children's language processing. The two subsections briefly describe some neuroimaging methods and reaction-time measures, citing representative studies and mentioning advantages and disadvantages of each method.

9.2.1 Neuroimaging

It is now technically possible to study syntactic development with various neuroimaging methods. However, basic syntactic distinctions that are easily supported by other data (e.g., judgments) are still being explored with these methods, and basic psychometrics particular to each neuroimaging technique are still hotly debated. Several such measures are being used in psycholinguistic studies with adults; among these are positron emission tomography (PET), functional magnetic resonance imaging (fMRI), and event-related brain potential (ERP). To exemplify one technique likely to be fruitfully applied to syntactic development, I will focus briefly on ERP investigations.

Psycholinguistic studies measuring ERPs typically require subjects to read lists of words or sentences, but other modes of presentation are also possible (see Kutas, Neville, and Holcomb 1987, and Neville, Mills, and Lawson 1992, for work on American Sign Language). While the subject processes these stimuli, his or her brain's electrical activity is recorded by electrodes distributed across the scalp. Crucially, the brain's EEG patterns are time-locked to psycholinguistic events. A pattern is described in terms of three major features: the polarity of the response (e.g., a negative wave), its distribution over the scalp (e.g., bilateral posterior), and its latency (e.g., 400 milliseconds after the onset of the stimulus). The combination just described is the N400 component, a pattern that has been linked to semantic effects in many studies on language. (For details on ERP analyses and on specific components, see Kutas and Van Petten 1994; for a review of syntactic ERP studies, see Garrett 1995.) Some advantages of ERP research are obvious: An ERP study can generate a lot of data from tasks as easy as listening to sentences. The technique is noninvasive, and responses are automatic. Indeed, the simplicity of a subject's task and the possibility of auditory presentation of linguistic stimuli make developmental ERP research seem promising. However, disadvantages for young subjects are also clear: Many items are needed for the averaging analyses, and it is hard to get children to be still enough (e.g., not even moving their eyes) long enough (e.g., for about a hundred sentences). Moreover, questions of interpretation regarding the functional and anatomical source of various ERP components are especially vexing in the study of brains as plastic as those of children.

Despite such difficulties, some studies suggest that children's syntactic processes can be investigated with ERP measures. First, the range of syntactic phenomena being studied with ERPs is growing (e.g., Neville et al. 1991; Osterhout and Holcomb 1992; Hagoort, Brown, and Groothusen 1993). Second, a number of ERP studies have examined processing of speech in normally developing children. (For nonsense syllables, see Molfese and Hess 1978; Molfese 1980; Molfese and Wetzel 1992. For words, see Mills, Coffey-Corina, and Neville 1993; Molfese 1989, 1990. For sentences, see Holcomb, Coffey, and Neville 1992.)

To appreciate the feasibility of ERP research on syntactic development, consider Holcomb, Coffey, and Neville 1992. This study measured ERPs to final words of sentences heard and/or read by subjects aged 5 to 26 (the mode of presentation depending on the subject's literacy). These words were semantically either appropriate or inappropriate to their sentence context. For both adults and children, the N400 to anomalous words was larger. The size of the contextual effects correlated negatively with age, leading Holcomb, Coffey, and Neville to ask whether younger children rely more on contextual factors in sentence processing (both in auditory and in visual modalities) than older children and adults do. They also found that asymmetries in the hemispheres' response to semantic anomaly were most pronounced in subjects over 13. Such findings are intriguing when considered in light of evidence that human neurological development continues into the midteen years. Holcomb, Coffey, and Neville suggested that the complexity of sentence processing might be related to neural systems whose functional specialization occurs relatively late in development.

9.2.2 Reaction-Time Measures

In general, reaction-time measures are based on the assumption that different mental processes take different amounts of time. Experiments that measure processing time for linguistic stimuli systematically vary a hypothesized processing load while keeping other factors equivalent. Reaction-time (RT) differences that correspond to the hypothesized processing differences are then interpreted as indirectly reflecting those processes.[1] Although children's RTs are (usually) slower and more varied than adults', stable patterns can be found in them. Several methods exploit this fact to investigate children's language processing. Before we proceed to three examples of RT measures, it is important to note that RTs alone are not sufficient to indicate on-line sentence processing. RT tasks can vary along a continuum, from an immediate measure during a sentence to one that comes right after the sentence to one that is considerably delayed.

9.2.2.1 Monitoring Tasks Experiments in which subjects monitor linguistic stimuli for a particular target typically measure the time between the target's occurrence and a subject's response to that target. The response, usually vocal or a button press, signals that the subject has noted the target's occurrence. Subjects know the target before hearing where it might appear. The target might be a word, as in Tyler and Marslen-Wilson's (1981) comparison of linguistic and nonlinguistic influences on sentence comprehension in 5-, 7-, and 10-year-olds; or it might be a speech sound, as in Tyler's (1983) use of a mispronunciation detection task with 5-, 7-, and 10-year-olds to study reference in discourse.

A children's TV show popular in the United States in the late 1980s used the following task: a special word was designated at the beginning of each episode; for the rest of the episode, the show's cast and audience would scream wildly whenever that word was said. That this was easily (and joyfully) managed by children under 2 illustrates one advantage of monitoring tasks: the demands on the subject are relatively simple. The timed decision is also simple: it is merely a presence/absence choice. A disadvantage of monitoring tasks is that the possible relations between the target and its host material are fairly limited. For example, neither sound nor word monitoring would allow an experimenter to test coreference relations in sentences with varying noun phrases. Related to this limitation, subjects might be able to predict when the target is going to occur.

9.2.2.2 Probe Latency Tasks Probe latency tasks also measure the time it takes a subject to react to the presence of a target in linguistic stimuli. In this case, however, the subject is given the target after its occurrence and asked to decide whether it occurred previously. Note that while a subject's response is quite immediate with respect to the memory trace of the target being probed, the response itself does not occur as the sentence or phrase unfolds. An example of this task comes from Mazuka's (1990) study of children's processing of right-branching and left-branching structures in English and Japanese. Following Townsend, Ottaviano, and Bever (1979), Mazuka probed word targets with children as young as 4. After they listened to sentences like "Mary moved the box onto the big truck," children responded (yes/no) to probes about particular words in the sentences. Mazuka found evidence in the relative speed of children's responses, suggesting that their processing of sentences is facilitated in structures branching in the direction predominant in their target language.

9.2.2.3 Priming Tasks Another RT measure relies on priming effects. The term *priming* will be used here to refer to an increase in the speed of the subject's response to one element because of prior exposure to a related element. (See Fischler and Goodman 1978; Neely 1977; Swinney et al. 1979. These lexical decision experiments compared RTs to printed words, some of which followed a semantically related item.) Adult subjects typically respond to visual targets; if stimuli are presented across modalities, these targets might appear just after a particular word or phrase in sentences that the subjects are listening to. RTs to target words appearing at the same point in a sentence are then compared. The comparison of interest involves items which are matched in length and frequency but which differ in hypothesized relations to the host sentences. Faster RTs to a related target, as compared to an unrelated target, are then interpreted to reflect the speeded activation of a primed element. Because young children are not yet proficient readers, they respond to pictures rather than printed stimuli and they thus make something other than a lexical decision. Nonetheless, similar priming relations among words and pictures can be tested.

An excellent early example of this approach is Swinney and Prather's (1989) breakthrough study of children's lexical access. This experiment recalled Swinney's (1979) evidence that different meanings for an ambiguous word form are initially accessed and that the context-appropriate meaning is selected less than a second after access. Swinney and Prather found similar results with their older child subjects. In their cross-modal priming paradigm, children made a timed judgment about a picture displayed by a slide projector with a tachistoscopic shutter while they listened to a sentence. Swinney and Prather's experimental pictures contrasted food or drink items with inedibles, and their subjects made an edibility decision. As an example, Swinney and Prather used pictures of a drinking glass and of a pair of eyeglasses to probe the word *glasses* in sentences that biased the interpretation of that word (one mentioning a thirsty girl, another mentioning a nearsighted girl). The relation between sentence and picture was manipulated, and RTs reflected these manipulations. Children's RTs to pictures that were related to lexical ambiguities in the experimental sentences showed that, like adults, they access both the context-appropriate and the context-*in*appropriate meaning for a word form.

One virtue of Swinney and Prather's method is that associations among many different words can be tested. That is, each experimental sentence might include a different target. This task is also indirect; in other words, a child is not asked to interpret words as in an act-out task. A disadvantage of the cross-modal priming task is its complexity. As described here, it is challenging for children under 4. Another problem, probably partly related to the task complexity, is the great variation in subjects' RTs.

9.3 A Recipe for the Cross-Modal Priming Task

In this section I examine in detail the task just described. The example study is McKee, Nicol, and McDaniel's (1993) investigation of children's knowledge of syntactically constrained coreference. (I will henceforth refer to the study as MNM.) This example should illustrate general points regarding on-line methods and provide some how-to information that is rarely found in a journal article.

To clarify the example, I will first summarize MNM. One goal of this study was to find out if children, like adults, apply their knowledge of binding in real time. We thus needed a measure of sentence processing that would probe children's *immediate*, as opposed to postsentence, interpretation of noun phrases (NPs). A cross-modal presentation of stimuli let us measure subjects' reactions to pictures of possible referents (e.g., an alligator) while they heard sentences containing various NPs (e.g., *himself*). The relation allowed between these referents and NPs was reflected in subjects' RTs: as Nicol (1988) had done with adults, we took children's faster RTs to mean that coreference between a pictured referent and the NP being heard simultaneously was grammatical. The experiment thus relied on priming. We hypothesized that an NP understood as a particular referent would speed reaction to a picture of that referent. This measure thus offered an indirect, and child-friendly, probe of on-line NP interpretation.

It was important to elicit RTs to the same picture in different linguistic contexts, that is, after a reflexive like *himself*, after a pronoun like *him*, and after a full referring expression (R-expression) like *the alligator*. But because one cannot assume subject homogeneity with children as one might with adults, it was also important to elicit each such set of RTs from individual children (in a within-subjects design). We did this by distributing our materials over three sessions; this had the additional virtue of keeping each child's period in our test booth to about 20 minutes. We were thus able to evaluate our group of children as a whole, and also to examine individual performance with respect to each binding principle. Briefly, MNM showed that children do apply their knowledge of binding *during* sentence processing: our subjects' on-line performance corresponded with what they did in an off-line experiment probing the same syntactic knowledge.

9.3.1 A Subject's Tasks

A cross-modal presentation requires attention to both auditory and visual stimuli; that is, subjects look at pictures while listening to sentences. Each picture is related to a sentence and appears at a critical point during the sentence. Subjects make a decision about the picture and signal their decision by pressing a response button. The time between the appearance of the picture and the pushing of the button is measured. Every few items, subjects' understanding of the sentences they have heard might be directly probed. It is important to note that the processing of the auditory stimuli is the primary task, and what subjects do with the visual stimuli is a secondary task that indirectly reflects their language processing.

Example: Because the proforms *him* and *himself* were of particular interest in MNM, our experimental probes pictured animate entities. Subjects listened to sentences like (1) over headphones while judging pictures displayed on a computer screen in front of them. We contrasted pictures of animals with pictures of objects; the subject's decision was whether the depicted item was typically *alive* or *not alive*.[2]

(1) The reindeer knows that the alligator with gigantic teeth is looking at himself in an old shiny mirror.

To ensure that subjects were attending to the materials, we queried a few items during the experiment. After the response button was pushed on such an item, a bell signaled children to tell the previous "story." Whenever a response was vague, an experimenter (who shared the test booth with the child) asked about the sentence. As an example, the item in (1) was followed by questions like "Who was in that story?", "What did the alligator do?", "Did the alligator have big teeth or little teeth?" Such comprehension questions indicated how well the children attended to the sentences. Their responses, in addition to our observations of their behavior throughout the experiment, were taken into account in our judgment of the suitability of individual children as subjects. Importantly, these question breaks also gave the children a rest and the experimenter a chance to reemphasize the particulars of the task. After 40 seconds, a second bell signaled the return of the sentences and pictures.

9.3.2 Experimental Design

Many aspects of an experiment's design (e.g., conditions, number of items per condition, distribution of the items across subjects) are constrained by the materials. Thus, a first step in research on syntactic processing involves the linguistic stimuli and the theoretical questions they test. However, creation of the stimuli forces a compromise among competing requirements. On one hand, many instances of each sentence type are needed in order to get stable averages from child subjects (whose RTs vary greatly). On the other hand, we must avoid tiring, frustrating, or boring our subjects. The latter requirement reduces the number of items in the experiment, which in turn affects the number of conditions one can compare.

I recommend a within-subjects design, that is, a distribution of the items across subjects that has each subject respond to all items. There are at least two reasons for this, and they are both related to RT pitfalls. First, on-line experiments can easily probe the wrong spot. To put it another way, we must always consider the possibility—when we face negative results—that the process our experiment aimed at did occur, but occurred later (or maybe earlier) than the probe point. Second, individuals vary in the time they take to execute mental processes. Where that variation is great or where its limits are still unknown, an experimental probe that is fixed to a particular point in a series of complex and interrelated processes is at greater risk of missing the critical mark. Collecting RT data on exactly the same set of items from all of one's child subjects minimizes these risks somewhat.

Another factor affecting the experimental design is the balancing of the materials. One reason balance matters is that it affects the targeted response. Consider what speed and accuracy would mean in an experiment requiring 90% YES and 10% NO responses. In that situation, a response might be made before the lexical entries of the auditorily presented words were activated. But if the response types are balanced, it is more likely that subjects who pass an accuracy threshold have actually accessed the words immediately preceding the pictures. Now suppose one's primary analysis examines RTs of one type. The pictures eliciting these responses should be similar in complexity so that different RTs reflect the linguistic stimuli rather than picture-parse demands. Likewise, the nouns with which pictures are associated should be roughly similar in frequency and length so that RTs reflect syntactic processes rather than lexical access time.[3]

Example: To evaluate hypothesized differences among types of NPs, a sentence frame into which reflexives, pronouns, and R-expressions can rotate would be ideal. Consideration of such frames was the first step in the design of MNM. Our three conditions corresponded to these three NP types: the same 30 sentences appeared in a reflexive condition, a pronoun condition, and an R-expression condition. The sentence frame in (1) thus had the three versions shown in (2).

(2) The reindeer knows that the alligator with gigantic teeth is looking

at $\left\{ \begin{array}{l} \textit{pronoun} \\ \textit{reflexive} \\ \textit{R-expression} \end{array} \right\} \ldots$

Regardless of what condition an experimental sentence frame was in, the picture presented with it showed the same animal. All that varied across the three presentations of each sentence and its picture was the linguistic context immediately preceding the picture (e.g., each subject judged an alligator to be alive in all three presentations of (2)—after a reflexive and after a pronoun and after an R-expression). RTs elicited by the same picture and at the same point in the sentence could thus be compared. Because the more general analysis collapsed across all the items predicted to elicit a YES (or alive) response, it was important to ensure that subjects were actually making the aliveness decision rather than merely hitting the YES button as soon as any picture appeared. An equivalent number of NO-eliciting filler items was thus included.

Alert readers will probably be muttering now about the number of items our patient subjects were asked to consider. Three conditions by 30 sentence frames gives 90 experimental sentences. Attending to these plus a similar number of fillers would be demanding for anyone. There is, moreover, the problem of the repetition of items. One alligator picture would prime another alligator picture. That is, RTs would become faster with each exposure (Forster and Davis 1984), and effects of the linguistic factors might be hidden by effects of repetition. MNM handled these problems in two ways. First, sentences were counterbalanced across three presentation tapes, such that each tape contained only one version of each sentence, and each experimental condition had equal numbers of sentences. Second, the on-line experiment was conducted in three sessions, with intervals of about two weeks between the sessions. Each child was tested with each of the three tapes, one per session. Thus, all factors were within-subjects factors.

9.3.3 Materials

Two basic kinds of linguistic materials need to be constructed: the experimental items to test hypotheses, and the filler items to mask regularities in the experimental items. These materials then determine the visually presented materials. The latter indirectly probe the former by virtue of their being precisely synchronized. As in all psycholinguistic experiments, the linguistic materials are constructed to respond to theoretical questions. But practical constraints like laboratory facilities and subjects' abilities conspire against an ideal approach to theoretical hypotheses. The experimenter is limited to about 20 minutes of audiotape in any one session (roughly 50–60 sentences). Test sentences are relatively long, as compared to typical materials, so that subjects will continue to process each sentence normally during the decision task.

The linguistic materials and the decisions that subjects will make obviously constrain the visually presented materials. Sets from which to select images can be gotten from a variety of sources, keeping in mind that the pictures must eventually be displayed on a computer screen. The slowest option is either to draw these pictures or to find them in print (e.g., Snodgrass and Vanderwort 1980), and then scan them into computer-readable files. Fortunately, software packages of royalty-free, color clipart images are now available (ranging from the affordable PC Paintbrush ClipArt Library to the expensive CorelDRAW). One must proceed with caution in the selection of the pictures too. For one thing, the complexity of the images has consequences for the computer program that will eventually display them in synchrony with the linguistic materials. (Such issues will be discussed further in section 9.3.6, where I will briefly describe the display program used in MNM.) All pictures, no matter their source, should be extensively pilot-tested with the relevant age group. Simple recognition, naming, and categorization tests can be done with large sets of pictures. The best subset (containing more items than are ultimately required) should be further tested with children seeing them on-screen. These can then be edited in response to pilot subjects' suggestions. All this is not excessive because minute details can affect RTs. (For similarly careful attention paid to the coordinated timing of video frames, see chapter 5, this volume.)

Example: MNM associated specific interpretations with particular NPs in the experimental sentences. Each experimental sentence had three main NPs and two main verbs in two clauses: [NP1 verb1 [that [NP2 verb2 NP3 ...]]], as illustrated by (1). The NP whose type was manipulated always occupied NP3's position. A sentence's picture was always of NP2 and was always presented immediately after NP3. Filler sentences were paired with pictures of inanimate objects, which occurred at various points within the sentences. Some fillers contained proforms and were similar in structure to the experimental sentences; such pseudoexperimental sentences undermined a strict correlation between sentence and response type. The other fillers varied in structure. In all, each presentation tape included 60 sentences: 30 experimental, 24 filler (of which 10 were pseudoexperimental), and 6 practice; 33 sentences were paired with a YES response, and 27 with a NO response. In the examples in (3), the picture accompanying a sentence is in brackets at the point in the sentence where it appeared on-screen.

(3) a. *Experimental*
    The alligator knows that the leopard with green eyes is patting him [LEOPARD] on the head with a soft pillow.

   b. *Fillers*
    The pencils are for sale in [PENCIL] the elephant's favorite store, so he's going to go there early tomorrow morning.
    The guinea pig thinks that the seal with the balloon is buying himself [BALLOON] a beautiful toy to play with.

MNM's 30 animal names were counterbalanced as follows: Each occurred once in NP1 and once in NP2. Since NP2 was always depicted and there were only 30 experimental sentences, each animal picture was probed only once per condition. Each R-expression was mentioned only once per presentation list. The R-expressions referred to nonanimals that are typically female (e.g., nurse, princess) in order to maximally differentiate them from other characters in the sentences. The verbs were also balanced across the experimental and pseudoexperimental sentences. Each experimental sentence included a phrase modifying the embedded subject noun. This was to avoid the problem of tapping into residual activation of the matrix subject (NP1) while probing at NP3. In addition, a "padding" phrase of at least seven syllables followed NP3.

It might be useful to know how we pretested these materials. After selecting a subset of the Snodgrass and Vanderwort pictures (minus those that might have been ambiguous in an aliveness judgment; see note 2), we asked children to name and categorize them. We thus found a set of items that children easily recognized the names of; this eliminated all insects and most birds for YES responses in experimental items. We also identified animals that children judged to be female (e.g., cows, kangaroos, and cats). Since our sentences used masculine proforms these female animals were used in fillers and practice items. Finally, two children made aliveness judgments (with, and without, the accompanying stories) on the computerized versions of the pictures. We interviewed these children about the appearance of each picture on-screen and then adjusted several items to their recommendations. We also pretested all our sentences with children aged 2 to 6. To determine whether the sentences were understandable and enjoyable, we asked children to answer comprehension questions about them, or to repeat the items, or to choose their favorites from subsets of the items. After compiling the entire set of materials, we repeated this process on a smaller scale with different children to recheck all of the items.

9.3.4 Procedures

A cross-modal priming experiment includes both experimental and training procedures. Two main aspects of the experimental procedures need to be emphasized during training: first, the decision to be made and how the subject will communicate it; second, how to listen to the tape and answer comprehension questions on some items. This training, especially with younger subjects, might require a whole session.

Each experimental session should begin with a verbal review of the subject's tasks, and a short practice set to illustrate the steps in the experimental procedures. As in all such work, checking on the subjects' interest in participating after they are quite sure of what they're getting into is just as important as checking on their understanding of the experimental procedures. In addition to the procedures involved in listening to sentences and judging pictures, subjects' understanding of what they hear needs to be probed. This can be accomplished by questioning their comprehension of the sentences. Another important aspect of the procedures is the discussion with child subjects and their parents of each step in the various tasks the children will be doing. Finally, writing and later reviewing notes regarding subjects' behavior during the sessions should also be part of the regular experimental procedures.

Example: As mentioned above, each child subject in MNM participated in three experimental sessions. These were preceded by a training session, during which several activities took place. Families were first given a tour of the laboratory, which included a stop in the experiment booth to show them the computer, response buttons, and headphones. All procedures were discussed, and an off-line pretest was given to each child. (Our focus was on whether children's on-line processing is influenced by their knowledge of particular constraints. Thus, the subjects whose performance we were most interested in showed knowledge of the relevant grammatical principles in the off-line pretest.) The on-line task was then taught to the children.

The training sequence for the components of this task was determined by pilot-testing a variety of sequences. The following proved to be most successful for teaching it: First, the aliveness decision was introduced with a series of 10 pictures of animals and objects, using only the YES button.[4] Subjects were told to make the aliveness decision and press the response button as quickly, and as accurately, as possible. The same series of 10 pictures was then repeated using both the YES and NO buttons. Next, children were given time to become comfortable with the headphones. They then performed the aliveness decision during the auditory presentation of a series of practice sentences. They were asked about one of these sentences, in order to demonstrate a comprehension check. Each of the three experimental sessions began with a verbal review of the task, and a repetition of the six-sentence practice list.

9.3.5 Analyses

Many analyses of data crucially depend on specific theoretical questions, which possibilities this subsection cannot cover (see chapter 14, this volume). A few general points about RTs and accuracy scores, as well as some pitfalls to avoid, are thus emphasized here.

First, one should consider general indicators of children's performance as subjects. If pretests are not discriminating, accuracy scores and experimenter notes on children's behavior might identify those whose RTs will be examined. The need for this can be exemplified if we imagine an instance in which RTs from a group of young children strongly resemble those of adults. Comparison of their data to adult RTs would be relatively easy because explanations for children's slow RTs other than those of theoretical interest (e.g., their slower motor responses) would not necessarily apply. However, if our hypothetical group's accuracy scores were not much better than chance, we could not take their speedy RTs to reflect sentence processing. And our easy comparison to adult data could not go through. It is thus crucial to plan independent indicators of subjects' performance, through which one filters the RT data.

Second, one must eliminate as many spurious contributions to decision time as possible so that only the language processing under investigation is reflected in RT differences. For example, RT differences that reflect the ease of integration of a target into a sentence might compromise some kinds of research (e.g., so-called filler-gap experiments). A related problem, also to be dealt with at the analysis stage, is the considerable variation in children's RTs. One way to address such problems would be to compare each child's RTs to her own baseline (a move that would entail modifications in the materials and design of MNM, as described in this chapter), so that the mental and physical subcomponents of an individual's responses might be separately examined. This could take the form of a button-pushing task without experimental materials (e.g., responding to right and left arrows or to taps on the child's hands).

Third, one must average and compare the RTs themselves. That on-line processes are reflected in them might well be challenged if responses much over a second are included. (Software for running the cross-modal priming experiment might, for example, replace all RTs longer than a certain time with a cutoff value for each subject, taking into account their overall speed and variability.) Once the data set is clean, one can proceed to whatever statistical analyses are appropriate to one's design. This is one place where extensive pilot-testing and a good design prove their worth. Tortuous statistics can be avoided if items of a type elicit similar performance, and if there are enough items per condition to justify confidence in that pattern of performance. Unlike the study of individuals' utterances or judgments, the interpretation of an individual's RTs is of dubious value (unless perhaps it was based on hundreds of observations). What we hope for in this kind of research is groups of children showing similar patterns, patterns that shift in systematic relation to the experiment's conditions.

Example: Before examining children's RTs in MNM, we evaluated both their general behavior and their responses to comprehension questions (as recorded in tapes of the experimental sessions and in our lab notes). RTs from the one child who was thus shown to be consistently inattentive were eliminated from any consideration. We then tested for subject and item effects in the RT data, and finally we looked for effects of type of sentence frame (reflexive, pronoun, and R-expression). Since all items tested an intraclausal referent, we expected children who apply adult knowledge of binding on-line to respond most rapidly in the reflexive condition; further, such children should show no statistically significant difference in mean RTs in the pronoun and R-expression conditions. We thus analyzed differences in means from the experimental items (YES responses) in three pairwise comparisons: reflexives to pronouns, reflexives to R-expressions, and pronouns to R-expressions.

9.3.6 Hardware and Software

The focus here is on what is needed for the presentation of experimental materials. The preparation of materials (both audio and visual) requires facilities that few syntax research labs are likely to have. My recommendation is to get help preparing these materials from speech and vision labs.

Most of the equipment needed for running this type of experiment can be found in electronics shops. The less expensive items are response buttons and headphones. For some time, researchers have used stereo tape players for playing the sentences to subjects. For that approach, wiring and connections are needed for sending one of the tape's channels (with a tone on it) to a computer and the other (with the sentences on it) to the subject's headphones. But because sound cards are now routinely included in personal computers, it is possible to use a computer (386 or faster) to handle both the auditory and the visual materials. Coordinating the visual with the auditory materials before the experiment, and presenting them in synchrony during the experiment, can thus be accomplished with only one machine. The computer will also record RTs and sort data. Finally, a quiet spot is needed for the experiment, preferably a sound-attenuated booth without distractions.

The software needed for a cross-modal priming experiment should be able to precisely coordinate the display of text, graphics, and sound. A display program for the cross-modal priming experiment must synchronize graphic images with both the speech signal and the computer screen's refresh cycle.[5] The program I recommend for this is the DMASTR system.[6] This system is extremely fast if one uses two-color pictures, such as the Snodgrass and Vanderwort (1980) set. DMASTR can also display 16-color pictures, but the loading of such images into video memory is slower. This program gives the experimenter direct control of many details of the computer's actions; it permits one to vary the length of time that images are displayed, how they are removed from the display, and so on. DMASTR can also sort and analyze the data in a number of ways.

Example: I will begin by giving a few details on the preparation of materials for MNM, to show some of what was involved at that stage. Our sentences were recorded on a Technics cassette recorder; they were read by a woman speaking at a slightly slower than normal rate, with enhanced intonation. The sentences were digitized at a sampling frequency of 16K, and a waveform editing system (BLISS) was used to identify and then label the point in each sentence at which the picture was to appear. In the experimental and pseudoexperimental sentences, the label was placed at the offset of NP3. The labels were then converted to pulses and stored in a separate file. The sentence file and pulse file were then recorded simultaneously onto an audiotape, with the sentences on the right channel and the pulses on the left. Our pictures were first scanned by a Hewlett-Packard Scanjet; the scanned images were then converted into a format compatible with the DMASTR display system, and edited if they did not reproduce well.

We tested a variety of headphones, ranging from a Roland RHS-200 headset to $3 Walkman replacement sets. The latter were comfortable but did not block out ambient noise. The headphones we finally selected, which we also used with our adult subjects, were not optimal. Although they effectively filtered ambient noise, they were slightly too large and heavy for the children. A few children found them uncomfortable, wanting to remove them during the question breaks. Since MNM was conducted, I have found that the Sennheiser HD 320 headphones are more comfortable for children and meet my experimental requirements.

Another technical choice concerned our response buttons. Although 2- and 3-year-olds managed a one-button response for the alive cases, they produced many false positive errors. A two-button response took more practice for everyone and was very hard for children under 4, but it produced fewer errors. Opting for greater accuracy, we chose a two-button response. To minimize confusion about the buttons, we had a response box especially designed. The buttons were the same size but they differed in color and shape; they were spaced close to the edge of the button box to accommodate small hands. We tested our button box with a large number of easily nameable pictures, having children practice the aliveness judgment under time pressure.

Sentences were presented to subjects over headphones. Subjects heard stereo presentation of only the right track of the audiotape. The left track, containing only pulses, was connected to a trigger that signaled the DMASTR system both to display the appropriate visual target (for 1 second) on a computer screen, and to start a timer. The subjects' button press stopped this timer.

9.4 Conclusion

Studies of children's on-line language processing are so difficult that the relation between the language learner's developing parser and grammar is still vastly underexplored. Nonetheless, the research done to date does suggest that 4- to 6-year-olds—like adults—apply their grammatical knowledge in real time. MNM, for example, uncovered no dissociation of children's on-line and off-line performance. For the purposes of this chapter, one of the most important points we demonstrated is that Swinney and Prather's (1989) method could be extended to investigate syntactic, as well as lexical, processing in young children. Although children's average RTs were longer than those typically observed for adults, several of our children's RT means and error rates fell into the adult range for this type of experiment. The children were clearly attending to the sentences, as shown by their responses to our comprehension questions. We also showed, as Swinney and Prather did, that decisions about pictures can give results as decisions about words do. The results of such studies therefore encourage a different type of research for investigating language development. On-line methods can be used to study many aspects of grammatical competence, as well as dynamic processes. And when designs permit systematic comparison of on-line and off-line performance, researchers' ability to assign children's success or failure to appropriate sources is also enhanced.

Notes

I am grateful to Helen Cairns, Ken Forster, Merrill Garrett, Dana McDaniel, and Janet Nicol for their help with this chapter. The language acquisition study emphasized here was completed with support from the Cognitive Science Program at the University of Arizona.

1. This chapter necessarily simplifies a great many aspects of RTs and cannot therefore warn of every possible pitfall in this kind of research. As an example, RTs are affected by (at least) the current state of the system and by the nature of the task. The current state of the system cannot be known ahead of time, when the researcher is deciding where in the linguistic stream to dip his or her hook. Continuing the analogy, the existence of individual differences stirs the waters up no end. It is too easy to miss the occurrence of some step in the process by measuring at the wrong moment. If that were not enough, the nature of the experimental task contributes more difficulties. Tasks measuring RTs can vary in the directness of the relation between the RT measure itself and the target process. That is, experiments can vary, and RTs can reflect, a primary or a secondary processing load. This has a number of implications whose discussion unfortu-

nately goes beyond the scope of this chapter. Readers are warned that there are many extremely important issues to understand before proceeding with research that will elicit and then interpret children's RTs.

2. This note describes pilot work behind our aliveness decision to show how we arrived at this choice. Although the category of people offers excellent referents for testing proform interpretation, we discarded it because many young children lack the vocabulary for the necessary variety of items (e.g., waiter, chef, doctor). Switching to animals as referents, we first tried an animal/not-animal decision. But children's responses varied too much. For example, some younger children insisted that household pets were called "dogs" and "cats" rather than "animals." (See Markman 1989, for a review of children's use of superordinate terms.) The best exemplars of animals seemed to be large, zoo or circus creatures like elephants, giraffes, and hippos. These, along with familiar pets, were the animals that children named most accurately. Trying an aliveness decision next, we asked children to choose all the items that were alive from an array of pictures. They never failed to choose (alive) animals even when unable to name them. When asked how they knew that something was alive, they most frequently said that it had to be able to move. So we presented flowers and trees, pointing out that they did not move to children who agreed that these were alive. We also presented cars and trucks, pointing out that they did move to children who agreed that these were not alive. Even though these children's judgments of vehicles and plants remained remarkably accurate, we ended up excluding them from our materials because they are rarely referred to with animate proforms in English. We then tested our response buttons with a large number of easily nameable pictures, having children practice the aliveness judgment under time pressure.

3. Of course, a study of lexical processing might do otherwise. There, the frequency of a word's occurrence is precisely the kind of factor one manipulates. Word frequency refers to the number of times some form appears in the language, as indicated by a corpus like that of Francis and Kucera (1982). The question of how word frequency should be determined for children is debatable. Many researchers use Carroll, Davies, and Richman's (1971) corpus because it sampled children's books. But I prefer Francis and Kucera's corpus because its words are listed by grammatical class. This seems a safe decision given research suggesting that something like these same frequencies are reflected in children's input (e.g., Huttenlocher et al. 1991).

4. As many children spontaneously responded aloud to the nonalive pictures, we considered timing vocal responses. The speed of vocal responses suggests that they bypass some contributions to decision time (e.g., the time a child takes to choose which hand to use for pressing a button). However, we were unable to find a voice trigger for the quietest children that would not also respond to ambient sound. Another obstacle was getting children to speak only at certain points (a goal somewhat like getting them to keep their eyes still in ERP studies).

5. The refresh cycle is the time it takes the scanning device (the raster) to go down the screen. An image is not displayed as soon as it is loaded into video memory;

instead, it is displayed the next time the screen is refreshed. This is why display programs for these kinds of experiments refer to multiples of the screen refresh time.

6. DMASTR (for DOS machines) was developed by Kenneth Forster, Rod Dickinson, and others, at Monash University; it was modified at the University of Arizona by Jonathan Forster to handle graphics and sound. The DMASTR system, as well as the Snodgrass and Vanderwort images, is available through FTP. (Contact Kenneth Forster (*kforster@u.arizona.edu* for details.) As I am not experienced with programs other than DMASTR, I cannot vouch for them. But here are some options: A commercially available DOS program is MEL. Programs for Mac computers include PsyScope (available by anonymous FTP on *poppy.psy.cmu.edu*), PsychLab, and its update SuperLab. Generally, such programs require the user to write a "script" for the experiment, and they vary in the degree to which they abstract away from technical details. Unfortunately, how user-friendly a program is affects how manipulable it is at the level of what one's computer is actually doing. As an example, DMASTR is relatively hard to understand, but this is because it gives the experimenter a great deal of choice in manipulating experimental details. A useful technical resource is the journal *Behavioral Research Methods, Instruments, and Computers*. The Info-Psyling list is another useful resource for people wanting to learn more about these kinds of methodological details. (Contact *psyling@psy.gla.ac.uk* about joining.)

PART III

Judgment Data

Chapter 10

The Truth-Value Judgment Task	Peter Gordon

10.1 The Nature and History of the Truth-Value Judgment Task

The truth-value judgment (TVJ) task has proved to be one of the most illuminating methods of assessing children's linguistic competence developed in recent years. The fundamental property of this task is that it requires the child simply to make a bipolar judgment about whether a statement accurately describes a particular situation alluded to in some context or preamble. The success of the task clearly resides in the simplicity of the child's response and the significant amount of information that can be gathered about the child's understanding of complex constructions. With this method, it is possible to evaluate the child's understanding of complex constructions that might have seemed untestable only a few years ago.

In this chapter I will describe two kinds of TVJ tasks: *yes/no tasks* where the child responds either "yes" or "no" to a question regarding a situation and *reward/punishment tasks* where the child either rewards a puppet for making a true statement or punishes it for making a false statement about a situation.

The yes/no type TVJ task was first seen in child language studies in Abrams et al. 1978. In the study reported there, the authors asked children yes/no questions using passive and cleft constructions and examined the validity of their responses as a measure of their comprehension of those constructions. After a relatively long hibernation, the method emerged again when Gordon and Chafetz (1986) used it to examine the acquisition of actional versus nonactional passives. More recently, Stephen Crain and several others have extensively used the reward/ punishment version of the task to evaluate children's knowledge of complex syntactic principles and quantification (Crain 1991).

Of course, the psycholinguistics literature contains numerous studies that require subjects to respond either "yes" or "no" to a particular question or display such as in a lexical decision task. A key difference is that unlike the TVJ tasks, such tasks tend to be inherently metalinguistic in nature, asking subjects to judge whether a string is a word or not, whether a word belongs to a particular category, and so on. Other studies such as sentence verification tasks are less metalinguistic, and subjects directly answer questions about situations (e.g., Clark 1974).

A major difference in the aims of language acquisition studies and those of adult studies is that the latter tend to test for performance variables where reaction times are used to make inferences about the structure of and access to existing knowledge. In acquisition studies one is generally interested in determining whether that knowledge exists at all. Of course, there is always the possibility that the apparent lack of linguistic competence could be due to performance factors in any particular case. The TVJ task generally minimizes this possibility—if constructed properly—and may act as a demonstration that knowledge exists in the child or is perhaps structured in some transitional manner.

Other tasks used in language acquisition studies have been equally simple in terms of requiring only a bipolar response. A classic method is the grammaticality judgment task, where the child hears a sentence and is asked whether it was "good" or "silly," or "right" or "wrong" (see chapter 11, this volume), or where the child is told to reward a puppet who "said it right" (Gordon 1981, 1982; Hochberg 1986). Both of these methods superficially resemble a TVJ task. However, there is a fundamental difference.

In grammaticality judgment tasks and other metalinguistic tasks, there is an implicit assumption that the child understands the notion of a sentence being "good"/"right" or "silly"/"wrong" as relating to intuitions about grammaticality. The TVJ task, on the other hand, makes no such assumptions. Rather, it assumes only that the child has some conception of the notion of truth in the sense of a correspondence between what is said and the situation referred to. Crucially, this requires the child to have an idea of what was said—that is, to construct a valid interpretation of the sentence via the parsing mechanisms, grammar, pragmatic assumptions, semantic entailments, and so on, that are available to her at that point in development. The advantage is that the task does not require the child to bring any of these processes to consciousness in any explicit way.

10.2   Design Issues

Let me begin by describing the two kinds of TVJ tasks with illustrations from the literature. First, consider the yes/no version. In this task the experimenter is attempting to obtain a measure of the child's competence with regard to a particular construction. For example, Gordon and Chafetz (1986) were interested in children's understanding of actional and nonactional passives. This interest arose from an intriguing effect originally noticed by Maratsos et al. (1979), namely, that children appeared to perform worse on nonactional passives than on actional passives. Gordon and Chafetz (1986) wanted to study whether this deficit with nonactional passives could be due to a simple function of input frequencies for these two kinds of passives. Since children hear fewer nonactional passives, it is possible that, to some extent, they might have difficulty with nonactional passives because they initially learn passives verb by verb, rather than as a general rule. Gordon and Chafetz reasoned that if verb-by-verb learning was indeed taking place, then children should perform consistently over a test-retest of the same verbs.

Previous tests of the passive (de Villiers 1984; de Villiers, Phinney, and Avery 1982; Maratsos et al. 1979; Maratsos et al. 1985; Sudhalter and Braine 1985) had employed either picture identification tasks or agent identification tasks. In the former task children have to choose which of two pictures correctly depicts the passive sentence being spoken by the experimenter. Clearly, depicting states such as knowing and liking is problematic. In the agent identification task the child hears a passive sentence such as "Mickey was kicked by Goofy" and is then asked, "Who did it?" or "Who kicked the other one?" Although this paradigm works well for action verbs such as *kick*, it also encounters serious problems with nonaction verbs such as *know* and *like*, where it is not clear that anyone is actually "doing" anything, since no strict agent role is associated with these verbs. In addition, there is evidence that children are less likely to remember the arguments of nonaction verbs than those of action verbs, even when these verbs are in the active voice (Lempert and Kinsbourne 1981). It could therefore be the case that differences in children's performance on actional and nonactional passives are simply an effect of memory and hence one of performance rather than competence.

The TVJ task is ideal in this situation, since it eliminates these problems. In this task the child is presented with a short story describing the events in a picture—for example, a story about a boy called John, waking up and hearing music on the radio. The child is then asked two questions like those in (1) and (2).

(1) Was the music heard by John?

(2) Was John heard by the music?

Let us consider the demands of this task. First, comprehension of the passive construction is revealed through the appropriate choice of argument order. This turns out to be equally natural for both action and nonaction verbs. The task involves no pragmatic anomalies associated with attempting to distinguish agency within nonactional states. Second, the task requires that the child does in fact understand the passive construction in order to answer correctly.

On the other hand, the task requires no more memory load than that required for everyday discourse processing where some semantic evaluation of a sentence is required. That is, the child can evaluate the truth of the sentences directly against the real-world situation, without having to store in memory the arguments associated with the verbs. In addition, this task allows use of nonreversible passives, where switching of arguments results in an anomaly and there is therefore no possibility that the child can get confused about who is doing what in the task. In other tasks, such as picture identification or toy-moving tasks, nonreversible passives allow the child to get the answer right by using semantic/pragmatic principles without necessarily knowing the passive construction itself (Bever 1970). Since this is not possible in the TVJ task, researchers using it can take advantage of the reduction in memory demands allowed by nonreversible constructions.

Given the design of Gordon and Chafetz's study, it was possible to examine children's consistency from one week to the next in their understanding of passives of particular verbs. The results indeed showed a high degree of verb-by-verb consistency, thus supporting the idea that the effects of actionality could be explained in terms of input frequencies and lexical learning strategies.

Next, let us consider the reward/punishment version of the TVJ task. As an example, Crain and McKee (1985) were interested in examining children's understanding of backward anaphora in light of claims by Solan (1983) and Tavakolian (1977) that children initially show a failure to allow such processes. Backward anaphora is the process whereby a pronoun or other anaphoric element precedes its antecedent, normally a full noun phrase or referring expression (R-expression) such as *John* or *the dog*. If children do disallow such coreference simply on the basis of word order, then this fact would suggest that they employ linear rather than structural principles in formulating grammatical rules. Such a finding would suggest that at least some of children's early grammatical inductions are not structurally dependent, contradicting Chomsky (1965) and Crain and Nakayama (1987).

In Tavakolian's (1977) task, children were asked to act out a sentence like (3).

(3) For HIM to kiss the LION would make the DUCK happy.

The majority of 3- to 5-year-olds acted out this task by having a third animal, not mentioned in the sentence, be the referent for the pronoun. In this case both the third animal and the duck are possible antecedents for *him* in the adult grammar. Therefore, the children's responses indicate only a preference for an extrasentential coreferent, not a prohibition against backward anaphora per se.

The TVJ task allows the researcher to obtain responses that are less ambiguous than those elicited by Tavakolian's task. This can be done by narrowing the possible interpretations and making the task as simple as possible for the child. Crain and McKee (1985) tested children as young as 2 years of age on a task in which they saw an event occur while an experimenter described it. Kermit the Frog then made a statement about the event. Children were told that if what Kermit said was true, they were to feed him a cookie. If not, they were to feed him a rag. Clearly, the humor is a crucial element of this design since it engages the children, making both the positive and negative responses enjoyable for the child without the negative connotations normally associated with a negative response.

Using this task, Crain and McKee (1985) were able to produce unambiguous evidence that 2- to 5-year-old children were quite willing to allow backward anaphora in sentences, but only in cases where this was allowed by the structural principles of grammar (Principle C of Chomsky 1981). Thus, they rewarded Kermit for statements such as (4), where *the lion* is coreferential with, but is not c-commanded by, the pronoun *he*. On the other hand, they gave Kermit the rag for sentences like (5), where *the Smurf* is coreferential with the pronoun, which c-commands *the Smurf*, violating Principle C.

(4) When HE stole the chickens, the LION was inside the box.

(5) *HE ate the hamburger when the SMURF was inside the fence.

This ingenious study provides powerful evidence that children use structural rather than linear principles in grammar formation and that, in this case, the principle they use appears to be the correct adult form that is unlikely to have been learned through modeling or instruction (see Crain 1991).

10.2.1 The Role of Context and Plausible Denial

Crain et al. (to appear) have recently made strong methodological arguments about the design of the TVJ task and the kind of context that should be provided. They carried out a series of studies in response to reports that children misinterpret sentences containing universal quantifiers such as *every* (Philip 1991, 1992; Roeper and de Villiers 1991; Takahashi 1991). In one of these tasks, children are shown a picture of three farmers each feeding a donkey, plus one donkey not being fed. They are then asked the question in (6). Children typically respond "no," pointing out that one of the donkeys is not being fed by a farmer. Similarly, when the picture shows three donkeys and four farmers, they respond negatively to the question in (7).

(6) Is every farmer feeding a donkey?

(7) Is a farmer feeding every donkey?

One explanation of this error is what Philip (1991, 1992) calls the "symmetrical interpretation." This account states that in universally quantified sentences children require that the elements be in one-to-one correspondence regardless of the position and scope of the quantifier.

Crain et al. (to appear) point out that in Philip's procedure—and in other studies on this topic—there is a pragmatic problem with the task. That is, when children see an "extra element" in the picture, either a donkey or a farmer, there is a pragmatic bias to suspect that this extra element is there for some reason, and if children do take the existence of the extra element to be relevant, they can only indicate this by responding negatively. Crain et al. suggest that although children may be grammatically competent, they may override this competence in favor of pragmatic strategies. They also point out that denial in this context can only be interpreted within the symmetrical account.

Crain et al. devised a set of stories that again contained an extra element; however, this element was generated within the context of the story, not as a ruse by the experimenter to fool the child. For example, one story went as follows:

A mother and her two children go skiing, and come to the ski lodge afterwards for a drink. There are cups of hot apple cider and bottles of soda set out on a table. The mother takes a cup of apple cider, but the children are tempted by the sodas. The mother persuades the children to drink the apple cider instead because it will warm them up. The children each have a cup of apple cider. (p. 33)

Kermit the Frog then described the situation:

(8) Every skier drank a cup of hot apple cider.

Children rewarded or punished Kermit according to whether they thought what he said was true or not.

What is crucial in this scenario is that when the children in the story took their apple cider, there were extra cups of cider left on the table. This is functionally equivalent to the extra elements in the donkey studies. What was different about these two scenarios? Crain et al. explain that the difference is that the cider story provides a so-called context of plausible denial: "... if circumstances had been different in an obvious way it would be appropriate to deny the test sentence" (p. 19). For example, if there had not been enough cider cups, then the child could deny that every skier was drinking cider.[1] Crain et al. propose that if the contexts are set up with sufficient detail to allow a plausible denial, then children will not resort to pragmatic strategies in attempting to account for the extra elements in the story.

Within the set of studies that Crain et al. describe, the notion of plausible denial is supported by the fact that the manipulation worked, and children who had previously shown a symmetrical interpretation in the donkey task now showed the correct adult interpretation. Unfortunately, it is not known whether this change was due to the existence of plausible denial, as Crain et al. suggest, or to a host of other differences between these two tasks. For example, it could be hypothesized that the reason that children ignored the extra cups of cider in the latter study is simply that the cups were backgrounded and did not figure significantly in the story. On the other hand, when the extra donkeys or farmers are presented statically within the donkey pictures, they are foregrounded and likely to distract the child into thinking that they are relevant.

Although this explanation does not deny the child's competence in quantification as demonstrated by Crain et al.'s method, it does pose a question about the source of the superior performance on the cider task as compared with the donkey task. This is significant in the present context because it raises another question, namely, whether the notion of plausible denial should necessarily be incorporated into a prescription for the design of TVJ experiments. At present I remain agnostic on this issue in the absence of confirming evidence. For example, if a researcher using Crain et al.'s procedure were to point out the undrunk cups of cider to the child subjects, would the results be the same? Similarly, if in the donkey task the extra elements were somehow backgrounded, would children still deny the questions in (2) and (3)?

Since it is not possible to state which factor (plausible denial or backgrounding) is crucial here, the design of experiments should take both factors into account until empirical support for one position is available. If the aim of a study is to determine maximal competence in children, then, like Crain et al., the experimenter should both create situations that provide plausible denial and not include elements within a task that serve only to distract the child from a correct interpretation.

On the other hand, the fact that children are so easily distracted by irrelevant information — of the type in the donkey-farmer pictures—is interesting in itself. In choosing whether to include irrelevant or distracting elements in a task, the experimenter must be clear about what questions are being asked. If the study is investigating children's maximal competence, then extraneous elements should be minimized and backgrounded. If the focus is on processing or pragmatic differences between adults and children, then it is legitimate to include such elements, though conclusions should be drawn cautiously. In other words, having distracted children into making an invalid response, the experimenter should not then claim that children therefore lack grammatical principles, even though they may fail to show evidence of them within that particular task.

10.2.2 Choosing a Truth-Value Judgment Task

Another issue raised by Crain et al. (to appear) is that Philip's (1991, 1992) method is not well suited to revealing competence in that it uses only static pictures that cannot provide the necessary context to allow for plausible denial. By contrast, in Crain et al.'s study toys were used to act out the preamble to the TVJ task. The latter procedure not only allows a full development of the preamble, but also is very useful in holding the child's attention.

In the past the use of static pictures has generally been associated with the yes/no task, and the use of extensive stories with props has generally been associated with the reward/punishment design. However, these tasks and contexts are not necessarily linked. A yes/no question could easily follow an extensive preamble acted out with toys and props, and a true or false statement could easily be made by a puppet describing a static picture.

Of course, the experimenter should decide which format is most appropriate for the task at hand. In a particular case, for example, constructing a yes/no question out of the relevant structure might be thought to add extra processing demands on the child, and therefore it might be more prudent to use the reward/punishment method. Probably, if there are going to be any such limitations, they are more likely to show up in the yes/no task; the reward/punishment task is more adaptable in this regard. On the other hand, it is often harder for a single experimenter to carry out the reward/punishment task, since usually in this design one person manipulates the toys and tells the story and another person works the puppet. Although it is probably possible for a single experimenter to carry out this task, an experimenter faced with working alone might favor the yes/no task for simplicity's sake.

Of course, the choice between formats will also be determined by the kind of construction being tested and the relationships of various elements within the task. Thus, in a study like Gordon and Chafetz's (1986), where extraneous elements do not play a role, it is quite satisfactory and much simpler to use pictures rather than having extended story lines acted out with toys.

On a recent field trip to the Kadiweu tribe in southern Brazil I became aware of other problems that can arise in choosing a TVJ design. Filomena Sandalo and I were interested in studying the acquisition of binding in this language because it admits structures that appear to violate Principle C. Thus, a sentence such as *HE-said that JOHN washed the dishes* allows the pronominal element (a verbal affix) to corefer with the R-expression, *John* (Sandalo 1995). We started by using a puppet with the reward/punishment design. Unfortunately, the children had never encountered puppets before and reacted with a mixture of curiosity and fear that often led to tears before we changed the design. To add further problems, we could not resort to a yes/no design because Kadiweu has no words for *yes* and *no* and therefore does not allow yes/no questions. We ended up asking the children, "Who said it?" for the above sentence, which worked more satisfactorily. For those who venture beyond familiar borders, it is advisable to consider such factors before leaving.

10.3 Construction of the Truth-Value Judgment Task

Having outlined some of the basic issues relating to TVJ tasks, I will now discuss the actual construction of a TVJ task for any hypothetical structure.

10.3.1 Training

Training for the TVJ task, although not demanded, is often desirable. For example, there is a general tendency for adult subjects to have a positive bias in verification tasks, being faster and more accurate to respond to true rather than false statements (Wason 1961). It seems plausible that children might also have such a disposition to favor encoding the truth of a statement relative to a situation rather than its falsity. The reward/ punishment paradigm fosters the likelihood that giving each type of response will be equally attractive to the child by making the negative response funny (e.g., feeding a rag to Kermit). Unfortunately, it is not clear that in such cases the negative response might not become too attractive and tip the balance. In cases of doubt, data from a training study could provide evidence about whether such biases exist in the task. Such training could also encourage children to produce a balance of positive and negative responses rather than perseverating with a single type of response. Crain and Thornton (1990) report that in order to prevent this kind of pattern, they included many trials, some for which the appropriate response was negative and others for which it was positive. However, there is some advantage to getting this pattern established prior to rather than during the main phase of the experiment.

Gordon and Chafetz (1986) included a training phase in their study of passives for reasons having to do with the design of the experiment. In that study, they required that children answer both true and false versions of the yes/no question (see (1) and (2)). This was done in an attempt to eliminate some of the random responses that children might be making because of inattention. That is, if a child is not paying attention to the passive structure and is responding somewhat randomly to a question, then he will have a 50% chance of responding correctly on any single trial. On the other hand, anticipating that there will be a second item where the structure is reversed, the child may focus on the details of the construction more carefully.

Prior to testing, children were told that they would be asked two questions about a story and picture, and that they were to respond "yes" to one and "no" to the other. In the training phase, a simple construction was tested: children were shown a picture of, say, a box on a table and were asked, "Is the box on the table?" and "Is the table on the box?" With these simple items, it was possible to get children to think in terms of responding "yes" to one question and "no" to the other. In addition, if a child failed to differentiate responses, it was possible to correct this problem during the training phase rather than during the main test and thereby to avoid losing data.

10.3.2 Context/Preamble

In all TVJ tasks the function of the preamble is to set up a situation in which production of the construction being tested is natural and comprehensible, and violates no pragmatic constraints or felicity conditions. In addition, the preamble should be constructed in such a way that at least two viable interpretations of the test construction are possible. Although one of these may be the only correct interpretation, it is crucial that, were the child to have an incorrect grammar, the situation make available an interpretation that is consistent with that incorrect grammar, and that the appropriate response—given the incorrect grammar—be the opposite of the response arising from the correct grammar. In addition, it is desirable that the situation depicted in the preamble make each of these interpretations equally salient, independent of the actual test sentence.

Of course, this begs the question of how to equate for salience. It is sometimes impossible to do this within a single context, since it may be that the correct response is to reward the puppet for a statement that correctly describes the scene as in the backward anaphora study of Crain and McKee (1985). In order to show backward anaphora, the child must accept Kermit's statement about the situation in (4), which is perhaps more salient than rejecting it, given a bias toward positivity. In such a case, it is crucial that the positive responses be counterbalanced with equally salient negative responses, as in (5). In this case, then, it is the pattern of both positive and negative responses rather than a single response type that supports the hypothesis.

An example showing where it is possible to equate for salience within the preamble comes from a study investigating the Strong Crossover Constraint (Crain 1991). In this study, children were told the following story using toy figures:

This is a *Sesame Street* story with Big Bird, Bert, and Grover. In this story they are all going for a walk with RoboCop and this Ghostbuster just before dark. The problem was that mosquitos came out at dark, and bit everyone except for RoboCop and the Ghostbuster because they have metal suits on. Big Bird got the most bites, and is having trouble scratching them. RoboCop and the Ghostbuster say, "We'll help you. We don't have any bites." Bert says, "I don't need RoboCop and the Ghostbuster to help me. I can reach my bites." And Grover says, "Me neither. I don't need RoboCop and the Ghostbuster to help me."

Kermit then commented:

(9) I know who THEY scratched. BERT and GROVER.

If children obey the Strong Crossover Constraint, they should reject this sentence. Notice that there are two equally salient antecedents for *they* in this context. On one interpretation, *they* refers to RoboCop and the Ghostbuster; this antecedent is false within the context of the story and thus should lead to rag feeding. On the other interpretation, *they* refers to Bert and Grover; however, this antecedent violates Strong Crossover and should not be entertained by children who adhere to this constraint. It is possible to determine more exactly whether children in fact do entertain only the first interpretation by asking them to correct Kermit's statement.

Notice that the preamble includes a strong context for interpretation within an incorrect grammar, namely, a context where Bert and Grover are the antecedents for *they*. Since many grammatical principles are negative (i.e., stated in the form of constraints), one is often interested in constructions that violate them. If children obey the constraints, then they will fail to make the interpretation under which the principle is violated and thus reject the sentence. One can provide strong evidence for the existence of a principle if children consistently show evidence for the interpretation that does not violate the principle. This can be achieved by asking a follow-up question to verify that the child did in fact make only one of the possible interpretations. For example, one can ask the child to correct Kermit, or one can probe the child about certain elements in the story. In fact, follow-up questions are recommended in any study, since they can provide more data on the child's knowledge. The only drawback is that the follow-up question might cause the child to think that the original response was incorrect and should therefore be changed on this or future items. Therefore, such follow-up questions should be positive in tone and seem like a natural continuation of the preceding discourse.

There is no strict formula for determining how much context should be provided for a particular task. This needs to be determined on the basis of the construction being evaluated and careful consideration of the demand characteristics of the task itself. These considerations should include the following elements:

1. There should be a plausible context in which it would be "natural" for a puppet to be using that construction.
2. The story should provide possible states of affairs that could support both positive and negative responses to the question.
3. Processing demands on the child should be minimized.
4. Caution should be exercised when including "distractor" elements in the task. These are elements that are superfluous to the correct interpretation of the sentence. A child who attends to those elements in responding might have only a tenuous control over grammatical principles but not necessarily lack those principles altogether.

These kinds of issues are by no means unique to the design of TVJ tasks. What is perhaps unusual is that with TVJ tasks it is possible to be very careful in dealing with many of these concerns by providing the right kind of context. For example, one of the most important means of reducing processing load is to provide a very vivid display with toys and props that can act as a support for memory demands. If the context is available in front of the child and can be accessed without memory demands, then it is less likely that such performance factors will play a role in the child's response. Attentional demands are also a consideration. Making the stories as entertaining as possible, using familiar figures from current child culture, and making the response as entertaining as possible crucially maintains the child's attention and reduces the possibility that performance factors will intrude on the responses.

The same basic principles apply if the stimuli are limited to pictures. These should be bright and colorful, but not too "busy" (i.e., they should not include too many elements that are irrelevant to the story and that the child might pick up on inadvertently). Of course, if the aim is to distract the child with such elements, then, as mentioned previously, one must be careful to limit the interpretation of the results with regard to children's true competence. I might also note, on this topic, that quite subtle changes in the design of a picture can radically affect the way children construe the situation being depicted. For example, Lempert (1984) has shown that children are more likely to use passives to describe pictures where the patient is colored in and the agent is not. Presumably, use of the passive indicates some kind of perspective shift toward a foregrounding of the patient over the agent. One can imagine other foregrounding and back-grounding cues such as proximity, relative size, animacy, and potency, which could affect the way that children construe the relationships within the picture and might in turn affect their responses. If possible, such asymmetries should be avoided unless they are a manipulation of the study.

10.3.3 Problems and Pitfalls

What problems might arise in designing a TVJ task? One type of problem pervasive in psychology is the so-called Clever Hans effect, where the experimenter unwittingly cues subjects into producing the correct answer and thereby overestimates their competence. Such cues can be extremely subtle, in the form of facial expressions, gaze, tone of voice, fluency differences, and a whole host of related forms of body language. Unlike researchers working in laboratory settings, researchers working with children in natural settings do not usually have the luxury of isolating the experimenter from the subject or being blind to the conditions. Attempts to restrict contamination in this way are likely to arouse feelings of anonymity, boredom, and fear in the child and therefore lead to inattention. Such concerns appear to be no more prominent in the TVJ task than other methods of studying language acquisition. However, since the TVJ task might require the experimenter to produce an ungrammatical, inappropriate, or infelicitous statement in relation to the context, it would be well to practice making such statements in a fluent manner so they are indistinguishable from statements that do not violate any of these standards (see chapter 6, this volume). In addition, if there are several possible interpretations for a particular construction, it is advisable to keep one's eyes fixed on the child and averted from the display while waiting for the child's response. This will help avoid providing subtle cues to the child. Since students who help in conducting experiments are often relatively inexperienced, they should certainly be made aware of such possible effects and be trained to avoid telegraphing correct answers.

Underestimating competence is also a concern. Underestimation can result from several factors alluded to earlier. Primarily, though, it is crucial that the preamble not be made overly complex so that the child loses track of the participants and their actions. It should include as many participants and events as are necessary to set up the target construction, but no more. In addition, the target construction should be designed to be as simple as possible while still requiring the child's knowledge of the appropriate grammatical construction.

10.3.4 Design Issues and Data Analysis

Since statistical issues are dealt with in detail in chapter 14 of this volume, here I will simply outline the major kinds of analyses resulting from the TVJ task and suggest the appropriate kinds of tests. In general, unless the results are completely categorical (e.g., all responses were as predicted), it is advisable to produce standard statistical analyses to support one's conclusions.

In designing an experiment, it is generally advisable to prepare as many items as are practical for testing; and, if possible, the number of test and control items should be equal. In the TVJ task this might amount to preparing equal numbers of positive and negative items. The limits on how many items one should use are dictated by factors such as not wanting to bore the child with repetitious procedures or make the procedure so long that the child cannot attend well by the end of the task.

One must also consider whether the task will be between subjects or within subjects. Within-subjects designs allow more powerful statistical analyses, but are subject to possible contamination effects between conditions. If one is concerned that the response to a particular construction might affect the child's response to another construction, one might consider having separate groups of children participate in these two conditions, matched as closely as possible for factors like age and sex. Alternatively, one could stick to a within-subjects design and order the two conditions so that children receive one type of item on the first half of the test and the other type of item on the second half of the test, with both orders being represented across subject groups. One can then test for contamination by looking at group differences for each order. If there are differences, then one might consider analyzing only the first half of the items for each child, using between-subjects analyses.

A typical TVJ task results in several data points for each child. Usually, the number of items for which the correct answer is positive and the number for which the correct answer is negative should be equal. Given this scenario, the analyses are relatively straightforward. One can first carry out a t test comparing the number of "yes" or reward responses to the target positive items with the number of "yes" or reward responses to the target negative items. Alternatively, one might be comparing different kinds of items and therefore be interested in the number of correct responses across conditions. For example, in comparing action with nonaction passives, Gordon and Chafetz (1986) analyzed the number of correct responses per condition (action vs. nonaction). In this case there was no positive or negative target; rather, the pattern of "yes" and "no" responses over the two questions indicated whether the child's response was correct or not. In this case the analyses are basically the same: numbers of correct response patterns are compared across conditions using the t test.

The choice of a related or independent t test will depend on whether the study uses a within-subjects or between-subjects design, respectively. If the experimenter wishes to look at multiple factors and interactions such Condition × Age, then the relevant analyses of variance should be used (see chapter 14, this volume). If the study uses a within-subjects design, then a repeated measures analysis of variance should be used. This is sometimes found in the multivariate analysis-of-variance programs of statistical packages such as SPSS. Analyses should ideally be carried out on both subjects and items. This is to ensure that the results are generalizable not only to other subjects, but also to other sets of items of the same kind. H. H. Clark (1973) recommends computing the Min F', which is a composite of these two analyses and is somewhat more stringent. However, separate subject and item analyses are usually considered adequate for making inferences about the generalization of results.

As an example, let us look at the backward anaphora study of Crain and McKee (1985). In this design the experimenter presents the child with several sentences like (4) where backward anaphora is allowed (*When HE stole the chickens, the LION was inside the box*); such sentences are target positive items. In target negative items backward anaphora is disallowed, as in (5) (*HE ate the hamburger when the SMURF was inside the fence*).

Assuming that children only reward or punish Kermit and complete all of the items, the experimenter can use the raw number of reward responses for each condition, which is the same as considering the number of punishment responses. Since children receive both kinds of items, this is then a within-subjects design utilizing the related t test. If the numbers of target positive items and target negative items differ (which should be avoided in any event), then the proportion of reward responses to each of these conditions should be used instead of the raw scores.

Some children may produce irrelevant responses such as feeding Kermit both the cookie and the rag, or they may not respond at all. In such cases irrelevant responses should be discounted and scores calculated as a proportion of the usable responses from that child. If the number of usable responses becomes less than about 75% of the items, then the experimenter should probably consider dropping that subject from the analysis and noting in the results that the subject had been dropped. A similar principle would hold for children who leave the experiment early, but again complete at least 75% of the task. An exception might be made if several children showed a pattern of irrelevant responses associated with one particular kind of structure. In such a case, rather than discarding these children's data, the experimenter might consider performing a test comparing the proportion of irrelevant responses for that structure compared to other structures tested in the experiment.

Giving children proper training before the main test is one way to avoid such problems, ensuring that they understand what is required in the task. Running a few pilot trials is also useful in ensuring that the task runs smoothly and that the experimenters are fluent and fluid in presenting the context associated with the task, manipulating puppets, and so on.

To avoid having subjects leave prematurely, one should not overload them with items; yet one should not underestimate their capacity, either. The number of items to be presented will depend on several factors such as the age of the children, the length of time it takes to present the context, the amount of training required, and the availability of the candidate items in the language. For example, one might be looking at a particular kind of lexical item that is simply not very frequent in the language, such as irregular plurals.

Given an average preamble a few sentences long, most 3- to 5-year-olds should be able to handle up to about 20 test items plus training items. If the preamble is longer or the task appears repetitive, it is possible to halve this number for two conditions and still obtain a satisfactory number of responses for analysis. For 2-year-olds and younger 3-year-olds, who might be less able to maintain attention, the number might be limited to about 8 to 10 items. Again, pilot testing can be very useful in determining a usable number of items. If the number becomes very small, then one might consider using a between-subjects design so that each child subject provides a useful number of data points for the condition that he or she represents.

If it turns out that only a few items can be included in the design—say, three or fewer per condition—there is a concern that the data might violate assumptions about underlying normal distributions required by the t test. Although parametric tests, which make such assumptions, do tend to be fairly robust against violations of normality, one might consider using a nonparametric test such as the Mann-Whitney for between-subjects designs or the Wilcoxon for within-subjects designs. In these tests the scores for each subject are ranked ordinally against each other, and the sums of those ranks are used as the basis for determining differences.

Besides the comparison of target positive and negative items, separate analyses should be carried out for both the target positive and target negative items to determine whether the responses were significantly different from chance. The procedure here is the standard t test against what would be expected from chance responding. Normally, since there are only two possible responses, the expected chance value would be 50% for both positive and negative responses. However, the task must be carefully examined to be sure that this is indeed the case. It is possible that there is more than one way to arrive at a particular response. In this case, if chance is considered to occur at the point of choice rather than the point of response, the expected chance value might not be 50% if there are more than two choices.

For example, suppose an experimenter, testing for adherence to Principle X, sets up a situation in which the correct interpretation of the test sentence requires coreference between an anaphoric element and animal A. The alternative interpretation, which violates Principle X, can be constructed through coreference with animal B, C, or D. For example, the sentence *The dog said that the monkey is washing himself* (with a cat and squirrel looking on) requires that only the monkey can be the coreferent of *himself*. If a child pays no attention to the context and just randomly gives one of the two available response choices—"yes"/reward or "no"/punishment—then chance occurs at the point of response and responses should be evenly divided between positive and negative. On the other hand, a child who pays attention to the context, but does not know which animal should be the coreferent, might pick any animal randomly—at the point of choice—and respond appropriately according to the interpretation in which the randomly chosen animal is the coreferent of the anaphoric element. In this case the child would have a 25% chance of responding correctly and a 75% chance of responding incorrectly.

The same caution applies in cases where a construction could be many ways ambiguous for the child who does not have the correct adult grammar. If there are two possible incorrect interpretations and only one correct interpretation, then again the probabilities should be adjusted to 67% and 33%, respectively. Ideally, the study should be designed in such a way that these problems do not arise. However, sometimes they are unavoidable and must be taken into account.

It is also sometimes useful to look at individual differences. That is, different groups of children appear to be at different developmental stages, or to have different kinds of grammars, and thus may show clusters of response patterns over different sets of items or over a series of experiments. For example, in their study of universal quantifiers, Crain et al. (to appear) first identified children who gave incorrect responses on the donkey task and then selected them for further testing on follow-up tasks such as the cider task outlined earlier. This kind of selectivity is one method of using individual differences to further probe linguistic competence. In using this method, however, one should always bear in mind that it involves selecting a subgroup of children and that any conclusions should not refer to "children" universally.

Sometimes one is looking for evidence of a pattern of abilities whereby competence on one construction is associated with competence on another construction (and likewise for the lack thereof). This can be demonstrated by creating a 2×2 matrix where columns represent construction A (pass versus fail) and rows represent construction B (pass versus fail). Each child's pattern of responses to constructions A and B will put the child into one of the four cells of the matrix (pass-pass, pass-fail, fail-pass, fail-fail). A chi-square test will show that the two constructions are significantly associated if there are more subjects on the consistent diagonal (pass-pass or fail-fail) than would be expected by chance. It is important to remember that, in the chi-square analysis, no child can contribute more than one data point to the matrix.

10.4   Appropriate Uses for the Truth-Value Judgment Task

For which populations is the TVJ task most appropriate, and which kinds of issues is it best suited to investigate? The TVJ task is adaptable for children of almost any age, so long as they are able to either answer a yes/no question or feed a puppet according to the experimenter's instructions. Of course, this does not mean that children of any age will necessarily demonstrate competence. With very young children it may be advisable to include a pretest/training phase, on the basis of which children can be selected who are able to respond appropriately when tested using the simplest of constructions. Children as young as 2 years of age can participate in TVJ tasks (Crain and McKee 1985), and certainly by 3 years of age they should be quite comfortable with the procedure. In the other direction, there appears to be no principled limit on how old subjects can be, and it is possible that a version of the procedure might even be useful for testing adults, perhaps incorporating reaction times into the procedure. For older children, the stories should be adapted so they are age-appropriate, although the usual cast of *Sesame Street* and comic book characters are probably good for several years.

One very promising new direction is the use of the TVJ task with language-impaired populations. Early evidence of the task's utility for these populations comes from a study by Franks and Connell (in press). They report on a procedure called the video multiple interpretation task in which children are presented with videotapes of stories and are then asked yes/no questions about the events in the videos. With this procedure, Franks and Connell successfully tested children with specific language impairment on their knowledge of complex constraints on binding. One might speculate that the TVJ task would be well suited for studying any kind of population for which the experimenter wants to minimize demands on the subject in areas such as production. Adult aphasics and language-impaired children could be tested for underlying competence that might be hidden by evaluations based on spoken language or other comprehension tasks. The task might also be adapted for second language learners whose lack of spoken competence may hide greater grammatical knowledge than is immediately evident.

The TVJ task appears to be extremely adaptable for testing many kinds of constructions, and in many cases is the best choice. In a few cases it is less appropriate however; I will consider these first. Primarily, the TVJ task tests a child's interpretation of constructions relative to that child's current grammar. It cannot actually test the child's judgment about the grammaticality of that construction, nor should a correct answer be taken to indicate such a judgment. In addition, the TVJ task cannot test for production, since the child is not required to produce anything more complex than a "yes" or "no" response, or the action of feeding a puppet. On the other hand, it is possible to follow up the task with a correction by the child. Thus, if Kermit is fed the rag, he may ask the child to tell him what he should have said, or to elaborate on elements of the story, and thereby elicit the appropriate construction under consideration.

The TVJ task is limited to testing constructions that are embedded within statements rather than questions. This may seem odd since one version of the task relies on yes/no questions. However, within the TVJ task the yes/no questions are questions about the statements embedded within those questions. Thus, *Was John heard by the music?* is a question about the truth of the underlying statement *John was heard by the music*; it is not a test of the question form itself.

Much of current linguistic theory focuses on the allowability of *wh*-movement in complex structures. To test the child's knowledge of the principles that license or prohibit such movement requires that the child respond in some way in relation to the question qua question. Since *wh*-questions do not have truth-values, it is difficult to study them using the TVJ task. Perhaps the only way to do this is to embed the appropriate *wh*-question within a matrix statement—for example, in a report of what some other character in the story had asked about. For example, Kermit might say something like, "Grover knows who the lion kissed before eating." In this case the story might relate that one animal ate fruit and another was eaten by the lion, that both were kissed first, and that Grover witnessed only one of the kissing episodes. Although this could work, it seems cumbersome and the construction might be more easily tested by other methods. McDaniel and McKee (1992) report on use of a task examining the Strong Crossover Constraint. In this case Kermit was asked a question and answered it, and the child rewarded or punished him based on the validity of his answer.

With these few reservations, the TVJ task is an invaluable tool for testing children's knowledge of language. It can be used to study all aspects of grammar and is particularly suited for testing syntax and sentence-based semantics. The task lends itself well to constructions that involve statements but is more cumbersome for constructions like *wh*-questions. The heart of the design of TVJ tasks lies in the context provided for the test sentence. Although the experimenter must be very careful in constructing these contexts, they can set up a test that provides crucial information concerning the child's linguistic competence in many populations. This relatively new technique is fast becoming the method of choice for testing many kinds of linguistic constructions in children. Given the task's many advantages, this trend should continue.

Note

1. Notice that this definition of plausible denial differs from the traditional notion where negative constructions are used only if the affirmative is the default assumption (Wason 1965).

Chapter 11

Eliciting Judgments of Grammaticality and Reference

Dana McDaniel and
Helen Smith Cairns

11.1 Background

In the generative grammar tradition, syntactic data have most often consisted of native speaker judgments. Syntacticians who study adult grammars, however, tend not to approach the task of eliciting data as an experiment. Instead, they informally ask themselves, colleagues, and native speaker friends for judgments about sentences as the need arises. The technique we describe in this chapter is one that approaches the elicitation of judgments as an experiment. Although we focus here on children, similar techniques can be used with adult subjects. (See Cowart 1994, forthcoming, for a discussion of experiments designed to elicit judgments from adults.) Much of what we say therefore applies to adult, as well as child, subjects.

Acquisitionists have only recently begun to investigate children's grammars through elicitation of judgments. There are several reasons for this. One is that the informal method of data collection used by syntacticians was simply not considered by acquisitionists to be a basis for experimental research. Another was the belief that young children would be unable to give grammaticality judgments. This view was reinforced by research on the development of metalinguistic skills that supported the hypothesis that children must be in the concrete operational stage of cognitive development (having acquired the ability to decenter and, thus, conserve) before they can make the distinctions between form and content necessary to give reliable well-formedness judgments (Hakes 1980; van Kleeck 1982). Two kinds of work have called this belief into question, however. De Villiers and de Villiers (1974) elicited well-formedness judgments from 4-year-olds, who are generally believed to be too young to conserve.

Schlisselberg (1988) compared the ability to give well-formedness judgments to conservation ability in people aged 3;6 to 6;6. She found that some of her youngest subjects were able to give reliable well-formedness judgments, although they were unable to conserve by standard measures. The notion that the ability to conserve is necessary for a person to have metalinguistic judgments has been further called into question by a series of experiments (Donaldson 1982; Gelman 1982) that conclude that standard conservation measures place considerable metalinguistic demands upon subjects. Although we have never explicitly tested the conservation skills of our subjects, we have demonstrated that people as young as 3 or 4 are able to think and talk about language in much the same way that adult informants do. For the past 10 years, together with a number of collaborators, we have been conducting studies on children's syntax using grammaticality judgments. Other researchers, such as Stromswold (1990b) and Smith-Lock (1993), have begun using this type of task as well. We described our procedure in McDaniel and Cairns 1990 and have been fine-tuning it since then.

A grammaticality judgment task can be used to investigate almost any area of syntax. The judgments can be either well-formedness judgments or judgments about interpretation, such as those involving reference possibilities. These two types of judgments are illustrated in (1), where (1a) is a well-formedness judgment and (1b) is a judgment about reference.

(1) a. *Who did you see Bill and* is a poorly formed sentence.
    b. In the sentence *Mary likes herself*, *herself* must refer to Mary.

The latter becomes a well-formedness judgment if referential information is referred to in the judgment, as shown in (2).

(2) *Mary likes herself* is a poorly formed sentence, if *herself* refers to someone other than Mary. *Mary likes herself* is a well-formed sentence, if *herself* refers to Mary.

The areas of syntax that have been investigated using grammaticality judgment tasks include binding theory (McDaniel, Cairns, and Hsu 1990; McDaniel and Maxfield 1992b); control theory and pronominal reference (McDaniel, Cairns, and Hsu 1991; Cairns et al. 1994); Subjacency, the Empty Category Principle, *wh*-movement types, multiple questions, and relative clause constructions (McDaniel, Chiu, and Maxfield 1995; Maxfield and McDaniel 1991; McDaniel and McKee 1995); subject-auxiliary inversion (Stromswold 1990b); and parasitic gaps and resumptive pronouns (Maxfield and McDaniel 1991; McDaniel and Maxfield 1992a).

11.2 Procedure

There are many possible ways of conducting a grammaticality judgment task. In the following description, we focus on the approaches we have taken and make suggestions based on our experience. An example protocol from such a task is given in (3).

(3) *Experimenter* If there are two boys and Grover is talking to this one [enacts with props], does it sound right or wrong to say, "This [holds out boy Grover talked to] is the boy what Grover talked to"?
Subject Wrong.

Before we present the experimental sentences to subjects, we give them training and practice, followed by a pretest. In this section we first present a detailed description of our training session, which we believe is crucial to the success of the task. We then discuss the pretest and the elicitation of judgments of the experimental sentences, both judgments of grammaticality and judgments of reference. Finally, we turn to issues involving materials, subjects, and scoring.

11.2.1 Training and Practice Session
As with most procedures, it is best to give subjects some kind of introduction and training before beginning the actual experiment. In the case of eliciting grammaticality judgments, the training session often plays the crucial role of establishing language as the topic of interest. Many of the subjects are preliterate, and this is likely to be their first experience of a conversation about language. If it is not clear to them that language is the topic, they may focus on content rather than form; that is, they may mistakenly think that the experimenter is interested in their opinions of various scenarios. There are many ways to establish language as a topic. If the subjects are likely to have had some exposure to more than one language (around the neighborhood or on television), then discussion of different languages is an excellent topic to begin with. Interactions usually go something like the (hypothetical) one illustrated in (4).

(4) *Experimenter*   The language we're speaking is called "English."
Have you ever heard anyone speaking another language?
Subject   My father knows Hebrew. / I heard Spanish on *Sesame Street.*
Experimenter   Do you know how other languages work? Let me show you. How do we say this in English? [points to an object—say, a shoe]
Subject   "Shoe."
Experimenter   That's right. In other languages, you say something different, but it means the same thing. Like in French, you say "chaussure" when you're talking about this thing.

This type of interaction establishes language as a topic, while also emphasizing the form/content distinction (since the same thing has different names depending on the language). However, in parts of the country where children have not been exposed much to other languages, this approach tends to be unsuccessful. Another topic, which could replace the first or be pursued in addition to it, is language acquisition itself. This has the advantage of giving the subjects an idea of what we are studying. Interactions on this topic tend to go as in (5).

(5) *Experimenter*   Do you know anyone who can't speak any language at all or who doesn't understand anything?
Subject   Babies. / Deaf people. / Dogs. / No.
Experimenter   That's right! / But deaf people know a language—it just has signs rather than spoken words. / But I mean people, not animals ... I was thinking of babies. When you were born, you couldn't understand anything or say anything—and neither could I. And now you know how to talk. You know English. Do you remember how you learned to talk?
Subject   No. / I just got bigger. / From my parents.
Experimenter   We really don't know how people learn to talk. That's what I'm trying to figure out. I'm a linguist. A linguist is a kind of scientist who studies language. For this project, I'm going around asking all different people for their opinions about English. I write down what they say and then I go home and try to figure out stuff about language and about how people learn language.

A variant on (5), which works especially well with school-aged children, is to begin by explaining what a linguist is, as in (6).

(6) *Experimenter* Before I tell you what we'll be doing, I'll explain why we're doing it. It's because we're linguists. You've probably never heard of a linguist before, but it's a kind of scientist. You've probably heard of scientists, right? What kinds of scientists have you learned about? [after discussing these] Well, a linguist is a kind of scientist that studies language. When I'm talking right now, my brain is doing something to make the words come out of my mouth just right, and your brain is doing something too. Your brain is putting my words together so you can understand what I'm saying. But we don't really know how our brains do that, and that's what linguists are trying to find out. We're also trying to find out how people learn language. [discussion similar to (5)]

As long as language is established as the topic, any introduction seems effective. We only avoid telling children that their grammars may be different from those of adults, since although we want them to understand the general purpose of the studies, we don't want them to worry about right versus wrong answers.

Once the experimenter and the subject have engaged in a conversation about language, the task itself can be introduced. We usually introduce it as shown in (7).

(7) *Experimenter* I'm going to ask you what you think of a bunch of sentences in English. I'm going to say something and you tell me whether it sounds like I'm talking right or whether it sounds like I'm talking wrong. The best way to do this is if we pretend that I don't know English very well and you're going to help me learn it. I'll sometimes say things the right way and sometimes the wrong way. If I say it right, you say, "That's right!", but if I say it wrong, you say, "No, that's wrong; that sounds funny."

Some experimenters (de Villiers and de Villiers 1974; Stromswold 1990b) have a puppet present the sentences. This responds to the concern that children might be uncomfortable telling adults that they are wrong. We have encountered this problem only rarely, however. When it occurs, we address it simply by asking the child to say "wrong," as illustrated in (8).

(8) *Experimenter* [to child who appears not to want to reject anything] When I say something wrong, you need to say "wrong," OK? Can you say "wrong"? [child doesn't say anything] Say "wrong."
    Child Wrong.

Experimenter   Good! You say "wrong" like that every time I say something that sounds wrong or funny to you, OK?

Surprisingly, having the child say "wrong" this way has solved the problem in most cases. We prefer this over using a puppet, since we worry that a puppet could distract the subject from the task. In any case, it is important to pay particular attention to ensuring that the subject will reject ungrammatical sentences. This is because in the judgment task, as in many others, many people have a bias to answer "yes," so there is a greater danger of spurious acceptances than rejections.

In presenting the task initially, we start with words rather than with sentences. We point to a prop—say, a strawberry—and ask the subject whether the right word to describe it is *chair*. Most subjects catch on right away and say "no." We then remind the subject that we will also say things the right way sometimes, and we name another object correctly. We go through as many single words as the subject needs to catch on, but few subjects have needed more than the initial two words. At that point we tell the subject that we are going to ask about whole sentences, rather than just single words. We do not worry about whether subjects understand the word *sentence*, since they can grasp the concept through the examples. We remind them of the task and then act out a whole scenario, while narrating it. We then ask whether the scenario can be described using a certain sentence. This is illustrated in (9).

(9) *Experimenter*   Suppose that this lion goes to this water and starts drinking it, like this. Suppose that I want to *say* what's happening. I'm going to try to say it and you tell me if I'm saying it the right way or the wrong way. "The lion water drinking is."

Many subjects understand the task right away and say that the sentence ("The lion water drinking is") sounds wrong. For these subjects, we go on to a grammatical example and then present a few more practice sentences. Other subjects need some prompting. In the practice session we give as much prompting and feedback as seems necessary. There are many different ways the interaction can proceed if the subject says that the sentence sounds good. An example is given in (10).

(10) *Experimenter*   Are you sure? Listen again to the way I'm talking: "The lion water drinking is."
   Subject   Yes.

Experimenter   Can you say it? You say what's happening. What's happening? What's the lion doing?
Subject   Drinking water.
Experimenter   Ah, so you would say, "The lion is drinking water"?
Subject   Yes.
Experimenter   But that's not what I said. I didn't say, "The lion is drinking water." I said, "The lion water drinking is." Doesn't my way sound funny?
Subject   Yes.
Experimenter   So my way was wrong. The words were all jumbled up, right? When I say something wrong like that, you need to say "wrong," OK?

In a case like this we usually give another ungrammatical example similar to the first, which the subjects generally reject. We then go on to other practice sentences. Most subjects do not need more than a few practice sentences to be completely comfortable with the task (but we give more detail on subjects in section 11.2.6).

In the practice session it is important to ensure that the subject is judging form and not content. The inclusion of a context with each sentence already does a lot to preclude this type of error, since the context is presupposed. To emphasize further the distinction between form and content, we include grammatical sentences that convey undesirable meanings, such as a character breaking something, and ungrammatical sentences that convey desirable actions, such as hugging. If the subject's responses to such sentences indicate judgments of content, rather than form, the experimenter explains that the event itself doesn't matter, just how the event is described.

It is advisable that the grammaticality distinctions used for the practice session be varied and involve phenomena that are thought to be acquired early. They should be varied so that subjects do not think that we are interested in only one type of ungrammaticality, such as incorrect word order. They should be acquired early because the experimenter needs to know how subjects will judge the sentences if they understand the task. This is, of course, tricky, because there is no way to be sure of the subject's grammar beforehand. We have based our practice materials on previous observations about children of the age we are testing. For example, since children appear to master word order early, we use word order violations as ungrammatical examples. In our own work we have found that just about all 4-year-olds correctly reject violations involving the distribution of reflexives; sentences like (11a–b) are therefore good practice for 4-year-old subjects (as long as the experiment is not about reflexives).

(11) a. *Himself went to the store.
     b. *Grover hurt herself. (meaning either that Grover hurt Grover or that Grover hurt a female character)

Gender seems to be mastered even earlier, so that a sentence like (11b) matched with a context where Grover hurt himself could be used with younger subjects. By age 3, most people will reject some types of subject-verb agreement violations. In our experience, person is mastered earlier than number, so that sentences like (12) work the best for the practice session.

(12) *The zebra am jumping.

(With respect to number agreement, we have found that young children have an easier time rejecting *are* with a singular subject than *is* with a plural subject.) Other types of sentences that have worked well with 3-year-olds and older 2-year-olds are those with extra or missing function words, as in (13).

(13) a. *The zebra jumped on the a the chair.
     b. *The zebra jumped chair.

In training, if an individual consistently gives an unexpected response, such as accepting (12), and yet also rejects other sentences, it can be assumed that the subject's grammar really does allow that sentence type. In such a case, a note should be made about the nonadult judgment.

If the experimental items include judgments of reference or judgments of interrogatives, these need to be introduced in the practice session. Eliciting judgments on interrogatives and judgments of reference requires items to be presented somewhat differently than when eliciting grammaticality judgments of declaratives. The differences will be discussed in sections 11.2.3 and 11.2.4. For now, we simply point out that in spite of the differences, we suggest starting the practice session with grammaticality judgments of declaratives, if the experimental items involve declaratives as well as interrogatives or judgments of reference. Furthermore, it is probably best to start with declaratives even if all the experimental items are interrogatives, since judging declaratives seems easier and therefore provides a simpler introduction to the task. If including practice on more than one type of judgment makes the practice session too long, it can be divided into two sessions.

As in the case of declaratives, the grammaticality distinctions used for judgments of reference and judgments of interrogatives should involve phenomena that are acquired early. In the case of interrogatives, the same aspects of grammar can be manipulated as in the declaratives. The sentences in (14), for example, are good for practice.

(14) a. *Where go you yesterday?
     b. *Who ate the a the cheese?

A good construction with which to introduce judgments of reference is one with a pronoun as the subject, as in (15).

(15) She went to the store.

As long as it is made clear that the sentence is uttered in a context where some character is already under discussion, even very young children correctly report that *she* can refer to any female character, but not to a male character. In training for judgments of reference, it is also a good idea to include grammatical sentences paired with a nonmatching context. An example is a passive sentence with an active interpretation, such as (16).

(16) The girl is being chased by the dog. [to describe a girl chasing a dog]

Since some subjects may need more practice than others, it is wise to prepare a relatively long list of sentences that includes a few backup sentences for each item. For a subject who catches on right away (meeting some criterion, such as giving five correct judgments in a row), the practice session could contain as few as 6 practice sentences, whereas subjects who have more difficulty might judge as many as 15 sentences in the practice session before they reach the same level of proficiency as those who catch on faster.

11.2.2 Pretest

Following the practice session (perhaps on a different day, if it is long), it is advisable to give a pretest to screen out subjects who have not understood the task. In a longitudinal study, such a pretest may be given at every session to ensure that subjects remember the task (which, in our experience, they almost always do). The sentence types that made up the practice session (sentences with similar structures but different lexical items) can be used again as pretest items. Recall that in some cases subjects' judgments on the practice items are consistently nonadult. In these cases the nonadult judgment is considered the "correct" response (since it is consistent) for the pretest items. We usually use six sentence types (three grammatical and three ungrammatical) from the practice session to make up the pretest. In order to pass the pretest, the subject must reject all three ungrammatical sentences and accept at least two of the three grammatical sentences.

11.2.3 Eliciting Judgments of Grammaticality
In this section we describe some of the ways we have presented sentences for judgment. One way to elicit judgments is simply to present a sentence to the subject and ask how it sounds. There are several ways to pose the question and several ways to make use of props. The question can be posed in (at least) the ways given in (17).

(17) a. Does it sound right or wrong to say ...
    b. Does this sentence sound good or bad ...
    c. Is this the right way or the wrong way to say it in English ...
    d. How about ...
    e. Is it OK to say ...
    f. Can I say ...

We usually begin with (17a) (see above discussion of the training session), but once the subject has understood the task, the phrasing of the question doesn't seem to matter. We only suggest avoiding "Can you say ..." (the formula frequently used by linguists) because some subjects interpret it as a request for repetition. One other word of caution: though all the phrases in (17) are beginnings of interrogatives, it is important to avoid putting interrogative intonation on the sentence to be judged (unless it is also interrogative).

In order to judge a sentence, one must imagine possible contexts that the sentence would fit. Props play the role of making this task easier for subjects, or even of removing it entirely. One way to use props is simply to have them provide a reference for the lexical items in the sentences. The experimenter can hold them or point to them while presenting the sentences. We have conducted several studies using props in this way. More recently we have used props to provide a context, as described in the discussion of the training session. We give another example in (18).

(18) Suppose Bert is eating some cookies [make Bert eat cookies], or at least that's what Grover thinks [hold out Grover]. Is this the right way to say it?: "Grover thinks that Bert is eating some cookies."

As just mentioned, this use of props enables the subject to consider the grammaticality of the sentence without having to think up possible contexts for it. We have found that the task tends to run more smoothly this way with adult, as well as child, informants.

The only difficult part of providing a context is determining the narration that accompanies it. The narration should be minimal, so that subjects do not perceive it as a "story," which could divert them from the sentence and direct their attention to the content rather than the form. Some narration is necessary, since subjects will not necessarily interpret the enactment in the intended way. In (18), for example, it would not be possible to enact Grover thinking something about Bert without the accompanying narration. Even with a simpler sentence, like "Bert is hugging Grover," without a narration a subject might think that Bert was pulling Grover, for example, and therefore reject the sentence. For this reason, the narration should include all the lexical items in the sentence. On the other hand, for the experimental items, it is best not to use the construction of interest. In (18), for example, if the study is investigating whether children allow *that* at the beginning of an embedded clause, the narration should not include the sentence "Grover thinks that Bert is eating some cookies," or any sentence containing the sequence "Grover thinks that ..." It is also important to avoid the alternative without *that* ("Grover thinks Bert is ..."), since this might also influence the subject's judgment of *that*. These considerations sometimes result in rather awkward wording in the narration, which is not a problem; however, ungrammatical sentences should be avoided. In investigating the distribution of reflexives, one might want to include a sentence like "Grover is hitting himself," for example. The first two narrations shown in (19) are both inadvisable.

(19) a. Suppose that Grover is hitting himself, like this. [shows Grover hitting himself]

b. Suppose that Grover is hitting Grover, like this. [shows Grover hitting himself]

c. Suppose that Grover is doing some hitting, like this. [shows Grover hitting himself]

d. Suppose that Grover is doing this: hit, hit, hit. [making Grover hit himself]

(19a) uses the same wording as the sentence, and (19b) is ungrammatical. (19c) and (19d) are preferable, since they avoid both of these problems.

The same procedure can be used for investigating interrogatives (as in McDaniel, Chiu, and Maxfield 1995). The only complication that arises is the possible confusion between the answer to the question itself and the answer to the question of its grammaticality. We have found that the best way to keep the subject focused on the latter is to use a puppet as a prop. The puppet (which should be controlled by a second experimenter) serves as a character to whom the questions can be addressed. (Using a puppet *as a prop* is distinct from using a puppet to present sentences for judgment, which was mentioned earlier.) An example is given in (20), where *Nelly* is the puppet's name.

(20) Suppose Nelly likes someone, but I don't know who. Is this the right way to ask her?: "Nelly, who do you like?"

Since the question is addressed to Nelly, subjects are not tempted to answer it. Generally, the puppet does not answer any questions either, since the questions are never actually posed. (The puppet might converse with subjects between items, however.) In the event that a subject does try to answer a question or guess the answer, it is best to respond, perhaps through an interaction with the puppet, and then start the item again from the beginning, reminding the subject of the grammaticality issue.

11.2.4 Eliciting Judgments of Reference

The task of eliciting judgments of reference is actually quite similar to the interview technique developed by Chomsky (1969) and to the truth-value judgment task (chapter 10, this volume). Like grammaticality judgments, judgments of reference can be elicited with or without an accompanying context.

If a context is provided, each sentence-interpretation pair becomes a separate item to judge, and the procedure is identical to the judgment procedure described in section 11.2.3, except that the same sentence is given more than once with different contexts, as in (21).

(21) *Experimenter*   Suppose we have Grover and Bert, and Grover is doing some patting, like this. [makes Grover pat Bert] Does this sound right or wrong?: "Grover is patting him."
Subject   Right.
Experimenter   How about if Grover's doing this? [makes Grover pat himself] Does it sound right or wrong now to say, "Grover is patting him"?

Since each sentence-interpretation pair is a separate item to judge, the items with the same sentence, such as the two items in (21), do not have to be presented consecutively. In the studies we have conducted on control theory (sentences like "Grover patted Bert before jumping over the fence"), we have found it easier to present all the possible jumpers (Grover, Bert, and a sentence-external character) consecutively. This enables the subject to focus on all the possible interpretations of that sentence. One final comment on the version of the procedure with a context is that we have also presented the contexts using pictures instead of enactments (Cairns et al. 1995). The use of pictures, which are also presented consecutively, makes it easier to vary the order of presentation of different contexts across subjects in a systematic way.

If a context is not provided, the experimenter asks about the interpretation by asking which characters could be performing or receiving the action. For example, for the sentence "Grover is patting him," the experimenter might ask about the reference possibilities for *him* as shown in (22).

(22) *Experimenter*   If I say, "Grover is patting him," who could it mean that Grover's patting?
Subject   Bert.
Experimenter   So it could mean this. [makes Grover pat Bert]
Could it also mean this if I say, "Grover's patting him"? [makes Grover pat himself]

Note that in asking for alternative interpretations, it is important to keep repeating the sentence, so that the subject does not forget it or unknowingly alter it. (See chapter 7, this volume, for discussion of this issue.)

A variant on the above protocol is to have the subject first enact the sentence with the props. Once the subject has acted it out one way, the experimenter asks about the other possibilities as in (22). These variants are close enough that they can be used together in the same experiment, the choice of protocol depending on whether an individual subject wants to act out the sentences.

In some cases it is advisable to elicit grammaticality judgments on sentences before asking about the possible interpretations. This is especially important if there is any doubt about the grammatical status of the sentences for the subjects. For example, Chomsky (1969) found that many children misinterpreted control sentences containing the verb *promise* as object-controlled instead of subject-controlled (e.g., "Joe promised Tam to leave" would mean that Joe promised Tam that *Tam* could leave). However, many English speakers simply find this construction ungrammatical. In a case like this it would be important to ask subjects to judge the sentence for its grammaticality before asking about reference possibilities.

11.2.5 Materials

In this section we discuss a variety of issues involving materials: number of items per session, number of tokens per type, ordering of items, and use of fillers.

The number of sentences that can be judged in one session depends on the informant and on the sentences. In our experience, if the sentences are complex (e.g., two-clause control structures with multiple interpretations or two-clause interrogatives), subjects begin to tire after 10 to 15 sentences.

Syntacticians often present adult informants with only one sentence of a particular type. This is inadvisable (for adult and child informants), since all kinds of nonlinguistic factors can influence an informant at a particular moment. On the other hand, presenting each sentence type just once allows the linguist to spend more time on each; in some cases one sentence turns into a mini-interview on its own. With a large number of tokens of each type, the informant is more likely to tire, and little time can be spent on each sentence. We suggest using a small number of tokens of each type, probably no more than three or four. Another possibility is to use just one or two tokens if the subject's judgment is clear, but to add extra tokens of the same type to the end of the session in cases where the subject is unsure. A more systematic variant on this design consists of presenting three tokens of each type, two of which are given to all subjects, on two separate days. A third token is given only to subjects whose judgments on the first and second days were not consistent. In any case, the different tokens of a type should differ only in lexical items that most likely do not play a role in the grammatical status of the sentence type. The most obvious type of modification is the interchanging of characters (Bert for Ernie, etc.). In general, it seems safer to interchange nouns than verbs. In interchanging verbs, care should be taken to keep the verb class constant, since verb classes can affect acceptability.

In many cases the experimental items will include sets of similar sentences. For example, a study on *wh*-movement might include the pair in (23) (cases of the Left Branch Constraint, according to which extraction from a left branch is blocked).

(23) a.   Whose book did you read?
     b.   *Whose did you read book?

One possibility is to separate these, so that subjects will judge each one independently from the other. This is the approach used in many experimental designs, in which the purpose of subjects' responses is often concealed from them. Instead, they are told that they are doing something else, such as helping a puppet in some way. In such cases it is usually important to separate the experimental items, so that subjects won't "guess" what the experiment is about. On the other hand, judgment tasks differ from those others in that the subjects are aware of the goal, which is to judge sentences to inform a linguist. Since this is the case, it may actually be better to keep similar items together. It could be confusing to be asked to judge an item like (23a) a few sentences before or after judging (23b). Informants can more easily focus on the part of the sentence in question if they are given the two together. Another advantage to presenting such items together is that the scenario can be given just once for both sentences, which makes the session run faster and more smoothly. As mentioned earlier, with judgments of reference, we have found that keeping similar items together works much better than separating them.

However the above issue is resolved, another one arises—namely, how to order sets of similar sentences (like (23a) and (23b)) with respect to each other. The answer to this question depends largely on the types of sentences being judged. Our only general suggestion is that the order should vary across items, so that no pattern emerges. For example, the grammatical version of grammatical/ungrammatical pairs should sometimes precede and sometimes follow the ungrammatical version. In judgments of reference, the order of different types of interpretations, such as external versus internal reference, should vary. (Of course, the possibility of systematic variation is limited in the protocol where the subject enacts the sentence first.)

A final issue concerning materials is fillers. Fillers serve a number of purposes: breaking a pattern in the materials, breaking a response pattern, giving the subject a rest, checking if the subject is paying attention. It is a good idea to use variants of the practice/pretest materials as fillers. This enables the experimenter to know whether the informant is paying attention, while changing the presentation pattern for the subjects. If a subject gets a filler wrong, the session can be stopped and continued on a different day, or a few more fillers adapted from the pretest can be inserted at that point to ensure that the subject is paying attention again. In order for the fillers to serve to break a sequence of "yes" or "no" responses, a grammatical and an ungrammatical version of each filler can be prepared. If the last two responses the informant has given were both "no" responses, the "yes" filler can be used, and otherwise the "no" filler. In addition to preventing the informant from developing a "yes" or "no" response pattern, this ensures that the subject will give both "yes" and "no" responses. Since the subjects' judgments on the experimental items are not known in advance, yes/no patterns cannot be preplanned.

11.2.6 Subjects

Though it has been claimed that people younger than 6 or 7 years old are not metalinguistically aware, we have successfully elicited grammaticality judgments from people as young as 3 and have even worked with a few 2-year-old subjects (2;9–2;11). However, people younger than 3 (and some 3-year-olds) often seem unable to understand the task. It is generally the case that people aged 4 and older can perform the task, though there is a great deal of individual variation (among children as well as adults). It is our impression that after age 3 or 4, the ability to perform the task does not improve with age, but is a function of whatever factors make some people better informants than others.

During the training session, it usually becomes clear if a subject is an especially good or poor informant. Most subjects are somewhere in between and, with practice, become quite good at the task. Exceptionally good informants tend to think hard about each sentence, sometimes offer additional information, and greatly enjoy the task. Exceptionally poor informants have trouble understanding or focusing on the task. One solution is to give such people several training sessions on different days. Sometimes it happens that the task "sinks in" between the first training session and the second. For some difficult subjects, it helps to keep the props completely out of sight (in a bag) except as they are needed for each item. Other subjects can focus more easily on the task if they can choose some of the lexical items (i.e., the experimenter can ask, at least for the fillers, "Who do you want this next one to be about?"). Some subjects spontaneously correct the ungrammatical sentences and/or try to provide explanations for the ungrammaticality. Explanations (provided by adults, as well as children) are often content-based, even though the initial judgment is based on form. For example, a subject might explain that the sentence "The elephant are jumping" is bad because elephants can't jump, but say that "The elephant is jumping" is a good sentence. We do not consider such explanations to be problematic and we simply disregard them. Some subjects have no trouble giving judgments, but are not able to deal with more than four or five sentences at a time. For such subjects, the session can be broken down. Sometimes these subjects can handle several short sessions in the same day (so that the experimenter can work with a few other subjects and then call the first one back). Subjects who really cannot handle the task must of course be excluded. In our experience, we lose approximately 10% to 25% of 3- to 5-year-old subjects for this reason.

A final note concerning subjects is that, in our view, it is essential to include an adult control group in every experiment. The adult control group serves two purposes. The first is to test the extent to which the task reflects grammatical knowledge. If many adults accept an ungrammatical sentence, for example, it may be because the sentence or the context was not presented well or involved some type of ambiguity. The second reason to include an adult control group is to verify the judgments of the community, which presumably represents the children's target dialect. Usually, the judgments are as expected, but occasionally they are surprising. McDaniel and McKee (1995), for example, found many adults who accepted resumptive pronouns in sentences like "That's the girl that Grover likes her dog." Similarly, in cases where syntacticians have reported dialect variation, an adult control group can indicate which dialect is most common for the area. Ideally, the adult control group would be as big as the child subject group, and we suggest making the adult control group at least the size of one of the child subgroups (such as one age group). It is important to use the same protocol with the adult control group that is used with the child subjects.

11.2.7 General Considerations

People who have been trained in experimental procedures often have some concerns about the judgment methodology that we believe are unwarranted. One relates to the fact that some children may require more practice and feedback than others to become proficient at the task. This contradicts the rigid rule (taught in experimental psychology classes) that every subject should be treated exactly the same. We feel that the true desideratum should be that every subject should give, as nearly as possible, equally reliable data. Although this goal can never be completely achieved, allowing differential practice to some prespecified level of proficiency comes as close as is reasonable to expect in any experimental task. Schlisselberg (1988) specifically tested response reliability over two sessions and found it to be quite high.

Unequal treatment of subjects may also legitimately arise if an informant has given a particularly interesting pattern of responses and the experimenter wants to explore the informant's grammar beyond the prepared set of experimental materials. Such extra questions are perfectly appropriate, as long as they are saved until the end of the interview so they will not influence the experimental protocol.

Another concern is that the interactive nature of the task can lead to an unacceptable loss of objectivity, allowing experimenter bias to creep into the situation. This could manifest itself in the experimenter's unconsciously influencing the subject's responses, the "Clever Hans effect." It has usually been our experience that child informants are quite confident and persistent in their judgments. Once they understand the task, they are not concerned with seeking assistance from the experimenter. For subjects who seem unsure of themselves, however, it is a good idea for the experimenter to look away immediately after presenting each item. This can be done unobtrusively by simply looking at the props or the response sheet rather than making eye contact with the subject. The very fact that our experiments have yielded quite clear yet unexpected results makes us confident that we have not unconsciously influenced our subjects.

Experimenter bias could also manifest itself in the experimenter's interpretation of the subjects' responses. This is usually not a problem, since most subjects give very definite verbal responses, or nonverbal ones in the form of head nodding or shaking. Sometimes, however, informants (child or adult) may be uncertain about particular judgments. These uncertain responses should be coded as such. It can frequently be informative to note which constructions produce less clear judgments, for children or adults.

11.2.8 Scoring

Responses should be carefully recorded on a response sheet during the session, by a second experimenter if possible. An audio recording can capture interesting remarks as well as verbal responses but will not, of course, record nonverbal responses. Data from the initial response sheet are then transferred to another data sheet on which sentence tokens are organized by type. What happens next depends upon the type of analysis being undertaken.

If the study is one that compares group data, every response can simply be counted for each subject. For instance, in a study comparing judgments from 3-, 4-, and 5-year-olds of the grammaticality of "Grover hit himself" in a context in which Grover is hitting Ernie (which is a violation of Principle A of binding theory), one would simply count the numbers of acceptances (or rejections) of the sentence for each subject at each age level and perform some group test like an analysis of variance, followed by a post hoc test of differences among the means, assuming a main effect of age.

If, as is more usually the case, the study analyzes individual children with respect to particular aspects of grammar, decisions must be made. How many responses to tokens of a particular sentence type will be required to characterize the subject's response? Suppose, given the example above, that an individual subject rejected three tokens of a Principle A violation, but accepted one. Fortunately, this kind of decision does not have to be made often, because judgments are usually quite consistent across tokens of a single type. Furthermore, some kinds of inconsistency can signal that a child is in a transitional period with respect to some aspect of grammar. Individual decisions must be made based on the particular hypothesis being tested and the analyses being performed. In some cases one might want to argue that three responses out of four indicates obedience to Principle A; in others, one might want to distinguish all children whose responses include even a single Principle A violation. (See Crain and Wexler, to appear, for a detailed discussion of these issues.) In any case, the decision criteria must be clearly described and defended when the study is reported.

11.3   Advantages and Disadvantages

In this section we will discuss the main advantages and disadvantages of the judgment methodology. In order to end on a positive note, we begin with the disadvantages.

11.3.1   Disadvantages

Most of the disadvantages of this procedure hold for naive informants of any age, not just child informants, and have to do with the relatively subjective nature of the task and variation in individual subjects. It is essential that the linguist relate well to the informants and be able to sense when they are losing concentration, have questions, and so on. Another problem is that some informants tire easily and get confused, especially with a large number of sentences. Finally, many informants exhibit a "yes" response bias. As discussed earlier, this response bias can be addressed in the training session and through fillers.

The interpretation of individual responses may present a problem. If the subject is consistent, it is natural to assume that the judgments reflect the subject's grammar. However, one can never be completely sure about why a subject rejects a certain sentence. Asking subjects does not help much, since they themselves may not know. (In fact, if they reject a sentence based on their tacit knowledge of grammar, they certainly do not know.) Since a subject presumably must parse a sentence before being able to render a judgment about its well-formedness, it is reasonable to wonder how parsing difficulty affects grammaticality judgments. It could be that a subject will reject an unparsable sentence as ill formed; or the presence of a "yes" bias could lead the subject to accept such a sentence. Common sense suggests that parsing difficulties will produce responses that are less confident and consistent than are responses to easily parsable sentences. However, little is actually known about the interaction of parsing and judgments. A careful researcher will attempt to construct experimental sentences to minimize parsing complexity. When unrelated to the grammaticality issues under investigation, grammatical relations should be in canonical order, clause boundaries should be marked, clauses should be on a right branch rather than center-embedded, sentence subjects should be animate, and sentences should describe plausible events. Another approach, used by Stromswold (1990b), is to construct the materials in pairs, so that each item has an equivalent that differs from it only in the syntactic structure under investigation (e.g., "Why is Joe running?" and "Why Joe is running?" in a study of subject-auxiliary inversion). If a subject rejects one member of the pair and accepts the other one, it can be assumed that the rejection is due to the syntax.

Another problem, discussed in section 11.2, is that the sentences used in practice must be sentences for which subjects' judgments are relatively certain. This means that the practice sentences are often simple, whereas the experimental sentences may be complex. This problem can be addressed by including practice sentences that are long but contain little embedding or that contain more than one instance of one type of simple embedding (such as "Grover's dog's bowl . . . ").

Finally, two problems are specific to child subjects. First, very young people usually cannot be tested. Data from people under 2, which are not only relevant but crucial to acquisition theory, generally cannot be obtained using this procedure. Second, testing a group of, say, 4-year-olds differs from testing a group of adult speakers in that the latter population can be assumed to be more or less homogeneous with respect to grammar. In the case of 4-year-olds, it is theoretically possible that each one has a different grammar. It is therefore unclear whether a response pattern that is consistent but idiosyncratic is of theoretical interest. The responses could represent an individual's grammar, which should be accounted for, or they could simply constitute noise in the data. How this issue is resolved depends on a variety of factors, but in any case researchers should be on the alert for subjects with response patterns similar to idiosyncratic patterns found in past research.

11.3.2   Advantages
As in the case of the disadvantages, the advantages of using the judgment task with children are largely the same as those of using it with adult informants. In fact, it is the procedure of choice for syntacticians who study adult grammars.

This leads to the advantage that, in comparing children's and adults' grammars, it is possible to use the same procedure with both groups of subjects. Almost all facts about adult grammars have been determined using a version of the grammaticality judgment procedure.

By asking informants for judgments, the researcher can fairly directly evaluate hypotheses about their grammars. In the case of judgments of reference, it is possible to determine all the possible interpretations of a sentence allowed by a subject's grammar. In the case of judgments of grammaticality, an advantage that this task has over many others is that the materials can include sentences that are ungrammatical for adults. Ungrammatical sentences have been used with very young children in picture selection tasks (Gerken and McIntosh 1993b; chapter 6, this volume), but most other procedures do not lend themselves to the inclusion of ungrammatical materials. Finally, the grammaticality judgment task not only allows us to find out whether sentences that are ungrammatical for adults are grammatical for children but also allow us to find out whether sentences that are grammatical for adults are ungrammatical for children.

Another advantage of this task is that the subject is not distracted by a game. Although one might think that only a game can hold a subject's interest, we have not found this to be true (in most cases). Subjects tend to be interested in helping a scientist and able to focus directly on the task that actually concerns us.

A final advantage has to do with materials. Several different types of phenomena can be investigated in a single study. One could include sentence types as different as, for example, *wh*-questions and declaratives containing control structures. The possibility of variation in materials facilitates the investigation of correlations among different phenomena. For example, McDaniel and Maxfield (1992a) included in their materials such varied constructions as illicit parasitic gap constructions (e.g., "That's the girl that hugged the zebra before Cookie Monster talked to"), Principle C violations (e.g., "He said that Grover is hungry," where *he* refers to Grover), and Subjacency violations (e.g., "Who did you hug Bert before you patted?"). They found a correlation between judgments on illicit parasitic gap constructions and judgments on Principle C violations, but found no correlation between judgments on the parasitic gap cases and judgments on Subjacency violations.

11.4 Conclusion

In this chapter we have presented our procedures for obtaining judgments of grammaticality and reference. Our goal has been to combine the best features of standard experimental procedure with the linguist's informal method of obtaining linguistic intuitions. Both have demonstrated their potential, in the service of creative scholars, to reveal critical information about human linguistic systems. By the same token, we feel that our interview technique promises to provide insight into the grammars of children.

Note

We are grateful to Cecile McKee for commenting on earlier versions of this chapter.

PART IV
General Issues

Chapter 12

Crosslinguistic Investigation   Celia Jakubowicz

12.1 Introduction

Although the idea of resorting to comparative data has existed from early times, only recently has crosslinguistic investigation come to be used as a research paradigm for studying the acquisition of syntax. Anchored in the linguistic research program inaugurated by the theory of generative grammar (Chomsky 1955, 1957, 1965), the actual concept of crosslinguistic investigation of language acquisition is founded on the Principles and Parameters model (Chomsky 1981, 1986b, 1993, 1994; Chomsky and Lasnik 1993), and it involves a deliberate attempt to isolate one or several properties of specific language grammars from other factors that may affect what can be revealed of children's grammatical competence in any given task. If certain acquisition effects replicate across language grammars that share a specific grammatical property, and not across those that do not, the property and how it arises during language acquisition can be characterized precisely.

This chapter has two main goals: to illustrate different forms that a crosslinguistic project may adopt, and to discuss why and how each step of a crosslinguistic design must be systematically controlled across the languages included in the research project. These two topics, presented in sections 12.4 through 12.6, are preceded by a historical outline that contrasts the goals of comparative acquisition work carried out before the emergence of the generative grammar program with those that emanate from this framework (section 12.2), and by a brief characterization of the Principles and Parameters framework and its impact on language acquisition research (section 12.3).

12.2   A Historical Outline

For centuries thinkers have been puzzled by how children are able to learn
any language to which they are exposed even though languages differ
from one another. Many questions have been raised by philosophers, and
by psychologists, linguists, biologists, and educators. For example: What
are the relations between nature and nurture in the acquisition of language? Are children's linguistic capacities biased toward one particular
language, say, Hebrew rather than Phrygian? Which is the common an-
cestor of related languages? During the 19th century scholars considered
that a way to answer these and related queries was to determine developmental patterns both of children exposed to language under different
conditions and of children acquiring different languages. The idea of
having recourse to comparative data can be found in many 19th-century
books and articles concerned with language learning, such as those by
Perez (1878), Egger (1879), and Compayré (1899) in France; Preyer
(1882), Franke (1899), and Ament (1899) in Germany; and Pollock (1878)
and Sully (1896) in England. In 1907 the classic volume *Die Kindersprache*
was published by Clara and William Stern; the authors presented detailed
observations of their own three children and compared their studies with
those previously reported in the literature. As McCarthy (1946; see also
Leopold 1971) remarks, all these studies were based on diary reports, and
most were concerned chiefly with the acquisition of vocabulary from the
appearance of the first word up to the fourth or fifth year. During this era
psychologists and educators sought general principles of language learning beyond individual languages; philosophers, linguists, and biologists
considered that comparative child language data might provide an answer
to questions raised by evolutionary theories and historical linguistics. If,
as claimed by Gramont (1902, 61), "toutes les modifications phonétiques,
morphologiques et syntaxiques qui caractérisent la vie des langues appa-
raîssent dans le parler des enfants" ('Every phonetic, morphological, or
syntactic change that takes part in language evolution shows up in the
speech of children'), children's productions could be used as a tool to
investigate the origin of language and its diachronic changes.

   During the first half of the 20th century, in parallel with the development of structural linguistics, the number of descriptive studies rose
quickly and steeply. Children's speech was tape-recorded, transcribed,
and analyzed in order to evaluate how many vocabulary items children
master at particular ages, which parts of speech children produce most

frequently, and when the first word combinations occur. Word frequency counts and studies on the amount and rate of talking (without reference to the quality of the expression or to the complexity of sentence structure) were also common. Statistical analyses and tables comparing patterns of acquisition within and between languages were provided, as McCarthy's (1946) review illustrates. The linguistic vocabulary employed in such work was borrowed from traditional grammar, and little or no attempt was made to explain the specificity of the process of language acquisition. Particularly throughout the latter part of this period, under the influence of behaviorism and especially in the United States, mainstream psychology considered language development as a process of complex habit formation occurring under the shaping effect of the environment.

This state of affairs changed radically with the birth of generative grammar (Chomsky 1955, 1957). Chomsky's conception of the language faculty, supplemented by his in-depth criticism of behaviorist theories (Chomsky 1959), opened the way for development of a different approach to first language acquisition, one that focuses attention on how the child comes to master the rules that constitute the mature system of language knowledge along the lines suggested by linguistic theory.

In the early 1960s several investigators found that early word combinations occurring in recorded speech samples of children acquiring English were not random (Braine 1963; Brown and Fraser 1963; Miller and Ervin 1964). In order to account for the regularities of word choice and word order in children's productions, these researchers proposed simple generative grammars, which became known as the "pivot-open class distinction" or the "pivot grammar" (McNeill 1966a,b). Other authors presented a transformational grammar account, along the lines suggested by Chomsky (1957, 1965), to represent the child's knowledge of language structure.[1] Furthermore, at the end of this decade numerous studies of speech samples of children learning languages other than English became available (see, e.g., Kernan 1969, on Samoan; Blount 1969, on Luo; and McNeill 1966a and McNeill and McNeill 1966b, on Japanese).[2]

It was in this context that Bowerman (1970, published in 1973) presented her doctoral dissertation on children's early syntactic development, which can be considered as the first modern crosslinguistic study of language acquisition. In this study Bowerman compared the speech of two Finnish children with that of American, Luo, and Samoan children, at their earliest period of language development. Bowerman had two goals. First, she wanted to determine whether there are similarities in the way all children acquire language, regardless of the particularities of the language to which they are exposed. If such regularities were to be found, they could be attributed to the operation of general principles of language acquisition rather than to the exposure to specific languages. Second, she wanted to determine whether or not two different hypotheses about Universal Grammar (UG; transformational grammar (Chomsky 1965) and case grammar (Fillmore 1968)) and the account of the beginning of syntactic development in terms of a pivot grammar (McNeill 1966a,b) provide an accurate representation of children's early linguistic competence.

Although a discussion of Bowerman 1973 is beyond the scope of this chapter (for such a discussion, see Atkinson 1975, 1982), I would like to mention the reasons why it can be considered a pioneering work in the domain of modern crosslinguistic research. First, Bowerman was aware that in order to make comparison possible, her Finnish samples (the primary data for her investigation) should be collected, selected, and prepared for analysis according to the criteria used with the already existing samples from English-speaking children. Second, although Bowerman focused more on the semantic and syntactic commonalities of children's utterances than on their structural differences, the analysis of acquisition data from languages with different properties allowed her to make observations about the influence that the constraints of children's native language exert on their early speech. Certain of these observations allowed Bowerman to challenge McNeill's (1966a,b) hypothesis that children's early linguistic knowledge can be represented by rules of the base component (of a transformational grammar) only, and Fodor's (1966) suggestion that the acquisition of (transformational) reordering rules depends upon the presence of inflections in children's speech.

Bowerman concluded that the representations of children's early linguistic competence provided by the three different frameworks she considered were all unsatisfactory, each in different respects.[3] Actually, children's speech did not fit naturally into the theories of grammar then available. Moreover, by the mid-1970s Chomsky's theories of rule systems had changed, and a radically different theory, Generative Semantics, appeared. These developments led researchers to feel that studying children's grammar was impossible. Indeed, during much of the 1970s, virtually no language acquisition research was guided by theory. Psycholinguists turned to topics insulated from any theoretical principles, such as mother-child interaction, the order of acquisition of morphemes, the use of heuristics in the interpretation of different types of constructions, and gestures and use of language in the classroom and other social situations.

In the 1980s things changed once again. In the late 1960s it became clear that the Standard Theory (Chomsky 1965) faced extremely serious problems with respect to explanatory adequacy: namely, if UG permitted rule systems of considerable complexity (like those assumed in this framework), then too many rule systems would be available to the mind/brain and the correct one could never be selected on the basis of the primary linguistic data.[4] Several general principles were successively formulated and attributed to UG. In the late 1970s these and other developments leading to reduction in the variety and freedom of application of possible rules coincided with a renewed interest in comparative syntax. Analysis of various syntactic domains, especially in the Romance and Germanic languages, provided the basis for seriously addressing the issue of syntactic variation across languages within the general theory itself and thus turning away from previous accounts in which linguistic variation resulted from differences between language-particular rules. This line of research culminated in the Principles and Parameters theory, which constitutes the current framework for research in comparative grammar and language acquisition in the generative tradition. This model was given its first systematic formulation by Chomsky in his 1979 Pisa Lectures, a modified version of which appeared in 1981. In the following section I present the basic assumptions of this theory, focusing on its effects on crosslinguistic acquisition research.

12.3   The Theory of Principles and Parameters

The Principles and Parameters theory can be conceived as a modular structure, the components of which are defined by two types of entities: principles and parameters. The principles represent the properties and operations that are invariant across the grammars of all natural languages, such as Move α, X-bar theory, the Extended Projection Principle, the binding principles; the principles that govern the distribution of overt NPs and empty categories, those that determine why certain processes can apply only within a limited domain, and so forth (Chomsky 1981, 1986a; Chomsky and Lasnik 1993). The parameters characterize specific options or values that each of the principles can adopt across languages; that is, parameters define the limited space of possible linguistic variation.

Chomsky argues that knowledge of a specific I(nternalized)-language—that is, knowledge of a core grammar—is nothing more than an array of choices of the various parameters, selected in accord with the options permitted by UG. Within this framework, language acquisition can be characterized as the process whereby the child, genetically endowed with the principles and parameters, fixes the values of the parameters on the basis of evidence and thus derives a specific instance of UG, namely, the grammar of the language to which she is exposed. According to Chomsky, language acquisition is not something the child does; rather, it is something that happens to the child placed in a linguistic environment, which determines how the options left open by UG are fixed, yielding different languages.

For illustration, let us look at the principles that determine the organization of words into phrases. Consider the following constructions:

(1) a. VP: eat the cake
    b. NP: destruction of the city
    c. AP: full of dust
    d. PP: from Paris

Each of these phrases consists of a head and its complement. The head of the verbal phrase (VP) is the verb *eat*, the head of the noun phrase (NP) is the noun *destruction*; the head of the adjective phrase (AP) is the adjective *full*; and the head of the prepositional phrase (PP) is the preposition *from*. In each of these examples the complement is an NP. One fact about these constructions is that in each, the head precedes its complements. The same is true of certain other languages, for example, French. Still other languages are different. In Japanese and Miskito, for example, the head follows the complement in each case. An example of a Japanese VP is given in (2).

(2) ouchi-o   kaita no
    house-ACC drew
    'drew a house'

Order aside, the general structure illustrated in (1) can be represented by the principle in (3), where X and Y stand for any of the lexical categories V, N, A, or P.

(3) XP = X – YP

This formula means that for each choice of X (V, N, A, or P) there is a phrase XP (VP, NP, AP, PP), with the lexical category X as its head and the phrase YP as its complement (where YP is some projection of Y in accordance with (3)). Principle (3) belongs to the part of the grammar regulating the structure of phrases that has come to be known as X-bar theory. Although it is assumed that this principle is universal, as we have seen, the order of complements with respect to the head varies crosslinguistically: either the head is first as in English (each lexical head precedes its complement), or the head is final as in Japanese (each lexical head follows its complement). This variation can be accounted for by associating principle (3) of X-bar theory with a head parameter involving two specific options: "head-initial" and "head-final." Simplifying somewhat, if the relevant parameter can have only two values, the child's task will be reduced to selecting the value appropriate for the language being acquired, on the basis of the speech input received. Thus, a child exposed to utterances of English will fix the value of the head parameter as "head-initial" and will know that the language is consistently head-initial. Similarly, a child exposed to simple Japanese sentences will fix the value as "head-final" and will therefore know that this language is consistently head-final.[5]

This view of language acquisition in terms of parameter setting led to the formulation of a research program involving three interdependent tasks: (1) to study the domain of variation of a given principle of UG in order to identify the parameter with which it is associated; (2) to study the linguistic development of children acquiring languages that adopt similar or different parametric values regarding this UG principle; and (3) to provide a plausible account of how a parameter is set.

The development of this research program brought under consideration data from numerous different languages. For example, children's obedience to the binding principles has been studied in a variety of languages with differing distribution of reflexive and nonreflexive pronouns, such as English (Chien and Wexler 1990; Jakubowicz 1984; Kaufman 1988; Otsu 1981; Solan 1987; Wexler and Chien, 1985), Spanish (Jakubowicz, in preparation; Padilla-Rivera 1990), Dutch (Deutsch, Koster, and Koster 1986; Koster 1993, 1995), Korean (Lee and Wexler 1987), Chinese (Chien and Wexler 1987), French (Jakubowicz 1989a,b, 1991, 1993, 1994a,b), Danish (Jakubowicz 1994b; Jakubowicz and Olsen 1988; Olsen 1992), Italian (McKee 1992), Russian (Avrutin and Wexler 1992; Bailyn 1992), Icelandic (Sigurjónsdóttir and Hyams 1992), and Japanese (Mazuka and Lust 1994).[6]

Other research has focused on the use of subjects by children acquiring languages such as Italian and English that differ according to whether or not they allow a pronominal subject to be left unexpressed in a tensed clause (e.g., Bloom 1990, 1993; Hyams 1986, 1992; Mazuka et al. 1995; Valian 1991, 1994).[7]

Other researchers have studied the acquisition of interrogative constructions in languages that differ with respect to both the number of question words available and their position within the sentence (see, e.g., Roeper and de Villiers 1992, for English; Roeper and de Villiers 1994 and Weissenborn, Roeper, and de Villiers 1995, for a comparative study of English, German, and French; Pérez-Leroux 1991, for Spanish; Penner 1992, for a comparison of Bernese Swiss German and Standard German; and Goodluck, Kudra, and Saah 1994 and Saah and Goodluck, to appear, for a comparison of English, Akan, and Serbo-Croatian).

Another topic that has been and still is extensively studied is how early and through what steps children determine the sentential position of the verb in languages that differ in this respect (see, e.g., Boser et al. 1992, Clahsen 1986, and Whitman 1994, for German; Déprez and Pierce 1993, for a comparative study of English and French; and Meisel and Mueller 1992 and Weissenborn 1994, for a comparison between French and German).

This and other research opened up vast areas of novel facts and provided a number of alternative accounts regarding what types of parameters are involved in particular linguistic variations and how the proposed parameters are set by children.

In the following sections I turn to suggestions concerning the forms that a crosslinguistic project can adopt and the factors that must be controlled in a crosslinguistic design.

12.4 Paradigms for Crosslinguistic Studies

A crosslinguistic project may involve two (or more) language grammars that are either similar or different with respect to the linguistic property being investigated. Although stronger support for a specific hypothesis may come from a comparison of children's linguistic behavior in two languages that differ with regard to the theoretical question the investigation attempts to answer, the former approach should not be dismissed. Even if two specific language grammars function alike with respect to the property being investigated, they may still differ with respect to other linguistic properties. If the prediction tested by this type of study is not disconfirmed by the data, not only will the hypothesis from which the prediction is derived be supported, but so will the abstract linguistic property at the basis of the study.

For the sake of illustrating these points concretely, I present three examples. One is a hypothetical crosslinguistic study involving two language grammars that do not differ with respect to the linguistic property being investigated; the other two are drawn from a real crosslinguistic study involving two languages that do differ with respect to the property being investigated.

12.4.1 Research across Two Languages That Do Not Differ with Respect to the Property Being Investigated

Suppose an investigator is interested in the acquisition of pronouns. A review of the literature shows that several authors have attempted to explain the linguistic behavior of pronouns across languages (e.g., Corver and Delfitto 1993; Haegeman 1994; Holmberg 1986; Kayne 1975, 1983; Jakubowicz 1994a; Rizzi 1986). Although the accounts differ from one another, they all indicate that pronouns fall into three classes that display different morphosyntactic properties: strong pronouns, weak pronouns, and genuine syntactic clitics. Roughly speaking, strong pronouns behave like regular NPs: they may be stressed, used to answer a question, coordinated, topicalized, and clefted. None of these processes is available for genuine syntactic clitics; these are heads overtly incorporated into their verbal host, with which they form a morphological constituent. Weak pronouns are in general unstressed elements, cliticized at the phonological level to a host with which they form a prosodic unity.

The investigator adopts the proposal that these three classes of pronouns display different degrees of morphological deficiency: namely, that weak pronouns occupy an intermediate status between the morphologically least deficient forms—strong pronouns—and the most deficient ones—genuine syntactic clitics (Cardinaletti and Starke 1994). The investigator decides to conduct a crosslinguistic study to test the hypothesis that morphologically less deficient pronouns are acquired before more deficient ones. The investigator chooses (or has the opportunity) to carry out this study on Danish and German. Now, although these two languages differ with respect to a number of syntactic processes, they are alike with respect to the following property: in both languages subject (personal) pronouns are strong pronouns and object pronouns qualify as either weak or strong depending on stress. Excluding stressed object pronouns from this project, under the hypothesis just mentioned the investigator expects that acquisition of object pronouns should be delayed with respect to acquisition of subject pronouns in both languages. If the prediction of this hypothetical study is not disconfirmed, the investigator may conclude that the data are consistent with the hypothesis that morphologically less deficient pronouns are acquired before more deficient ones. Of course, the same conclusion could be drawn from studying only one of the two languages, say, Danish. What does the crosslinguistic study add? Demonstrating that similar effects are obtained in two languages that differ with respect to other linguistic properties, the investigator supports the hypothesis that the property at the basis of the study—the distinction between different types of pronouns—is legitimate.

12.4.2 Research across Two Languages That Differ with Respect to the Property Being Investigated

Now suppose that a second investigator, being interested in the same topic, addresses the same theoretical question as the first—namely, whether or not morphologically less deficient pronouns are acquired before more deficient ones. The second investigator believes that a most comprehensive test of the hypothesis will be provided by a crosslinguistic study involving two languages in which subject and object pronouns are different morphosyntactic entities both within and between the two languages. Two such languages are German and French. In German, subject (personal) pronouns are strong and unstressed object pronouns are weak. In contrast, in French, with the exception of first and second person plural forms, subject pronouns are weak pronouns and object pronouns are genuine syntactic clitics. Now note that although these two languages differ with respect to the type of pronoun occurring in subject and object position, according to the hierarchy of morphological deficiency, in both languages subject pronouns (whether strong as in German, or weak as in French) are morphologically less deficient than object pronouns (weak pronouns in German and genuine syntactic clitics in French). Thus, under the hypothesis that morphologically less deficient pronouns are acquired before more deficient ones, it is expected that the order "subject pronouns > object pronouns" should be observed both by children acquiring German and by those acquiring French. Indeed, the results of a study currently being carried out (Jakubowicz et al., in press) appear to support this prediction. The analysis of 2;2- to 2;6-year-old children's productions, obtained in two different data collection settings (free interactions and an elicited production task), shows that in both French and German object pronouns appear to be delayed with respect to subject pronouns. The demonstration that the subject/object asymmetry is observed regardless of whether subject pronouns are strong or weak, and regardless of whether object pronouns are weak or genuine clitics, supports the hypothesis that less deficient pronouns are acquired before more deficient ones. Moreover, the result suggests that children abide by the hierarchy of morphological deficiency according to the classes of pronouns available in the language to which they are exposed.

Note now that although the study just discussed provides stronger support for the hypothesis than does the previous one, in order to reject an alternative account of the observed subject/object asymmetry, a further step seems necessary. Such an alternative hypothesis can, for example, state that regardless of their morphosyntactic properties, the acquisition of pronouns in object position is delayed universally with respect to the acquisition of pronouns in subject position.

Now, from the point of view of the hierarchy of morphological deficiency and the acquisition hypothesis considered throughout, French and German are only superficially different from one another. Crucial evidence in support of the hypothesis that morphologically less deficient pronouns are acquired before more deficient ones will certainly come from a cross linguistic study involving two languages that differ radically with respect to the question being investigated. Such a project requires comparing children acquiring a language where subject pronouns are morphologically less deficient than object pronouns with children acquiring a language where subject and object pronouns do not differ in morphological deficiency. For concreteness, suppose that in the latter language both subject and object pronouns are strong, as for example in Russian. If the hypothesis considered so far is correct, no subject/object asymmetry should arise in this language. Thus, two different predictions are associated with the same hypothesis: object pronouns should be delayed with respect to subject pronouns in the former but not in the latter language. If these predictions are confirmed by the data, the original hypothesis is strongly supported. If it is not, that is, if the order "subject pronouns > object pronouns" is observed throughout, the hypothesis

that relates order of acquisition and morphosyntactic properties of pronouns will be rejected. Thus, a crosslinguistic study involving two languages that differ radically with respect to the linguistic property being
investigated seems to provide the strongest means for testing a specific
hypothesis.

So far we have discussed different forms that a crosslinguistic project
can adopt. Let us now consider requirements that the experimental design
must obey, regardless of the type of crosslinguistic project the investigator
decides to undertake.

12.5   Requirements

As suggested by the previous discussion, the main goal of a crosslinguistic
project is to assess whether certain acquisition effects replicate across
specific language grammars that share a certain grammatical property and
not across those that do not. Such a paradigm provides a powerful means
to test hypotheses concerning the linguistic factors involved in the acquisition effect, inasmuch as only properties of specific language grammars are
varied as an experimental variable throughout. Thus, other factors such
as length and meaning of the linguistic materials, the requirements of the
task, the procedure followed to test the children, the criteria used to
constitute the sample, and the scoring procedures and analyses must be
kept constant. Only in this manner will it be possible to claim that the
observed acquisition effects are due to the linguistic property being investigated, and not to other factors such as mediating performance variables,
which still remain poorly understood.

Let us consider why and how each step of an experimental design must
be systematically controlled across the languages being studied in the
research project. This discussion focuses mainly on experiments testing
comprehension of syntactic properties.

12.5.1   Linguistic Materials
In this section we consider a variety of issues involving materials: test
sentences, fillers, pretest sentences, and ordering of items in the experimental list.

12.5.1.1   Test Sentences   A particular difficulty in studying language acquisition comes from the fact that processing variables intervening in
language production and comprehension may also be developing. These

may affect what can be revealed of a child's grammatical competence, when the child is presented with linguistic materials in any given task. As is well known, younger children have a lower mean length of utterance than older children, a smaller vocabulary, a lower capacity to pay attention, and perhaps also a more limited memory workspace. The influence of these factors is complex and still poorly understood. Of course, it would be important to have an adequate assessment of the role these factors play in the comprehension and production of sentences by the child. For example, suppose we knew that processing constraints affecting children's comprehension of sentences containing a main and a subordinate clause are the same regardless of whether the embedded verb is finite or not. In such a case it would not matter whether the test sentences used to assess children's knowledge of a specific linguistic property contained a finite embedded clause in one of the languages to be compared and an infinitival one in the other. If we do not know whether or not the sentence frame affects the child's interpretation of the linguistic property being investigated, the best way to solve this potential source of difficulty is to construct test sentences of the same structure in both languages. Suppose we decide to use sentences with finite embedded clauses. Although we do not know how these sentences are processed, under the assumption that they fall under particular processing constraints, these will certainly be the same in the two languages. Thus, if any variance is observed between the results from the two languages, the hypothesis that this variance might come from the structure of the test sentences will be discarded.

Taking care with the sentence frame of the test sentences is a necessary but not sufficient condition to achieve uniformity regarding the test sentences used in a crosslinguistic study. Length and lexical content should also be controlled. If they are, another possible source of variation is canceled.

What I have said so far may have given the impression that the experimenter is completely free to choose the sentence frame, the length, and the lexical content of the test sentences, subject only to the condition that these should be exactly the same in the two languages to be compared. However, this condition cannot always be fulfilled. It may well happen that a specific instantiation of the experimental variable requires a particular sentence frame and/or particular lexical content in one of the languages but not in the other. In this case, to ensure uniformity both within and between languages, the experimenter will be obliged to construct the test sentences on the basis of the constructions where this instantiation of the experimental variable is legitimate.

Example: An example drawn from a crosslinguistic study on the comprehension and production of reflexive and nonreflexive pronouns in French and Danish (Jakubowicz 1994a,b; Jakubowicz and Olsen 1988; Olsen 1992) illustrates this last point. In this study we wanted to know whether or not children's knowledge of syntactically constrained coreference relations involving reflexive and nonreflexive pronouns appears at the same time in French and Danish. These two languages were interesting to compare because, as shown by the literature and by our own study of the linguistic behavior of these expressions, reflexive and nonreflexive pronouns are different morphosyntactic entities in French and Danish. Furthermore, Danish, but not French, allows one of its reflexive expressions (*sig*) to be referentially dependent on the subject of the matrix clause, that is, outside the domain of the subject of its own clause (henceforth: long-distance binding). Although a full description of these two types of pronouns is beyond the scope of this chapter, a brief overview of their distribution will be useful to understand the rationale underlying the construction of test sentences.

First, consider French, where reflexive and nonreflexive clitic pronouns are in complementary distribution. As illustrated below, the reflexive *se* must be referentially dependent upon the subject of its own clause (henceforth: local binding), and the nonreflexive *le* must be disjoint in reference from its local subject. Furthermore, because *le* cannot be used ostensively, in the absence of a linguistic context it corefers with the matrix subject.

(4) Pierre$_j$ croit   que Jean$_i$ se$_{i/*j}$ déteste.
     Pierre believes that Jean REFL hates
     'Pierre believes that Jean hates himself.'

(5) Pierre$_j$ croit que Jean$_i$ le$_{j/*i}$ déteste.
     'Pierre believes that Jean hates him.'

In Danish the situation is different. The strong complex reflexive *sig selv* must be locally bound to the subject of its own clause, like *se* in French. In contrast, the weak reflexive *sig* may or must be long-distance-bound, depending on lexical and tense properties of its governing verb. Thus, in modern Danish, local binding of *sig* is legitimate if its governor is an affectedness verb (e.g., *wash, brush, cover, defend, protect*) and can be long-distance-bound if and only if it occurs in the context of a nonfinite nonaffectedness verb (e.g., *criticize, respect, love, talk to, point to, aim at*).[8] These two properties are illustrated below. The examples in (6) show that *sig* can or cannot have *Ida* as antecedent, depending on the lexical properties of the verb. The examples in (7) illustrate that long-distance binding of *sig* is possible if and only if the expression occurs in the context of a nonfinite nonaffectedness verb.

(6) a. Ida$_i$ vasker/børster/forsvarer sig$_i$.
        Ida washes/brushes/defends REFL
        'Ida washes/brushes/defends herself.'

  b. *Ida$_i$ kritiserer/elsker/taler om   sig$_i$.
        Ida criticizes/loves/talks about REFL
        'Ida criticizes/loves/talks about herself.'

(7) a. Jens$_i$ bad   mig om at kritisere/tale om   sig$_i$.
        Jens asked me   to criticize/talk about REFL
        'Jens asked me to criticize/talk about him (= Jens).'

  b. *Jens$_i$ siger at Jeg kritiserer/taler om sig$_i$.
        'Jens says that I criticize/talk about him (= Jens).'

Finally, like its French counterpart, the Danish nonreflexive pronoun *ham/hende* must be disjoint in reference from the subject of its own clause.

This brief overview indicates that *se* and *le/la* in French, as well as *sig selv* and *ham/hende* in Danish, may occur with any type of verb in any sentence frame. In contrast, the occurrence of *sig* is constrained: it requires an affectedness verb to be interpreted as locally bound, and it must occur in a nonfinite embedded clause with a nonaffectedness verb to be interpreted as long-distance-bound.

Taking this information into account, let us turn to the construction of test sentences for the comprehension task. First, it was necessary to determine the sentence frame in which reflexive and nonreflexive pronouns would be tested in both languages. In order to satisfy interpretive constraints on nonreflexive pronouns and on long-distance binding of *sig*, it was clear that all test sentences should be two-clause sentences, containing a main and a subordinate clause. Moreover, because long-distance binding is disallowed when *sig* occurs in a finite embedded clause (see (7b)), in order to make within- and between-language comparisons possible, we were forced to couch the expressions to be tested in sentences where the embedded clause was infinitival and the empty embedded subject (PRO) was coreferential with the matrix object. Thus, test sentences were object control sentences, similar in structure to (7a). Second, the fact that obligatory long-distance binding is possible if and only if *sig* is governed by a nonaffectedness verb compelled us to use sentences where besides being infinitival, the embedded verb belongs to the class of nonaffectedness predicates.

Furthermore, as in any other off-line experiment, at least four instances of each test condition are needed to have a reliable mean score of responses from subjects whose attention or willingness to respond may fluctuate. Accordingly, four different nonaffectedness predicates, likely to be known by young children and able to be pictured (see below), were selected: *arroser/sprøjte på* 'spray at', *éclairer/lyse på* 'shine [the light] at', *viser/sigte på* 'aim at', and *montrer du doigt/pege på* 'point at'. Each verb was used in each test condition. As a result, each test sentence appeared in both a reflexive condition and a nonreflexive pronoun condition in both languages, and in a long-distance binding condition in Danish. The matrix verb was the same in all test sentences, and the NPs in subject and object position, although not exactly the same in the two languages, referred to characters well known by French and Danish children. Examples are given in (8) and (9).

(8) Kiki demande à Nounours   de *se/le*   viser.
     Kiki asks   Teddy Bear to REFL/him aim

(9) Bamse   beder om Anders And   om at sigte på
     Teddy Bear asks   Donald Duck to   aim at
     sig selv/ham/sig.
     REFL-self/him/REFL

Example (9) indicates that children's interpretation of sentences in which *sig* must be locally bound was not tested in this study. Had we included this condition, the number of test sentences would have been twice as large in Danish as in French (16 vs. 8). Worse, because locally bound *sig* can occur only in the context of an affectedness predicate, the comparison with French would have been biased unless French reflexive and nonreflexive pronouns were tested also in the context of an affectedness verb. Of course, we could have decided to test all the expressions but long-distance-bound *sig* in sentences where the verb governing the expression was an affectedness verb. In such a case, if different results had been obtained for long-distance-bound *sig* than for *sig selv* in Danish and *se* in French, we would not have known whether the observed difference was due to the condition "long-distance binding" or to the condition "verb type." In order to make both within- and between-language comparisons possible, we could also have considered including sentences where the expressions *sig selv* and *ham/hende* in Danish and *se* and *le/la* in French occurred with both affectedness and nonaffectedness predicates, while locally bound *sig* and long-distance-bound *sig* occurred in the context of an affectedness and a nonaffectedness predicate, respectively. Considering that at least four repetitions of each condition are needed, in this case we would have obtained 16 test sentences in French and 24 in Danish. Since besides test sentences, an experimental list includes filler items and pretest items (see below), too many sentences would have to have been presented to each child in this case, and more than one session per child would have been needed. For practical reasons, we wanted to avoid testing children over two sessions. Thus, we limited this study to the expressions *sig selv*, *ham/ hende*, and long-distance-bound *sig* in Danish and *se* and *le/la* in French.

12.5.1.2 Filler Sentences Filler sentences, also called distractors, have a threefold purpose: (1) to mask regularities in the test sentences, (2) to break the sequence of similar test trials/response types, and (3) to avoid tiring or boring the child through presentation of materials that are similar in structure and lexical content, as in the example discussed above. Ideally, the same number of filler sentences should be presented in each language, and these sentences should display the same structure and lexical content (these being distinct, of course, from those involved in the test sentences). Several factors may work against this ideal approach, however.

Example: In our Danish/French study, three conditions per sentence were tested in the former language, but only two in the latter. Thus, each of the four sentence frames was presented one more time in Danish than in French, giving rise to 12 and 8 test sentences, respectively. Although in our study we included the same number of fillers, four in each language, a better decision would have been to include six fillers in Danish and four in French. Because fillers are interposed between test sentences, this option would have allowed us to insert a filler after the same number of successive test trials in both languages. As a result, the experimental lists would have been equalized with respect to the type and number of test trials that followed each other without a break.

However, including more fillers in one language than in the other has a potential disadvantage: it enlarges the experimental list still further in the language where test items are already more numerous. In cases like this, the researcher will need to decide whether the two languages should be made uniform with respect to the length of the experimental list or with respect to the organization of test sentences and fillers within each list. I believe that within certain limits—for example, when the linguistic materials involve no more than 24 items (pretest sentences, test sentences, and fillers counted together)—uniformity with respect to the organization of items within the list should be preferred.

12.5.1.3 Pretest Sentences Depending on the theoretical question being investigated and the procedure, pretest sentences may be used for training purposes before beginning the actual experiment, that is, to familiarize the child with the task. They may also be used for sampling purposes, particularly when the investigator does not know whether the youngest children to be tested (e.g., 2- or 3-year-old children) are able to process and/or understand apparently complex syntactic configurations involved in the test sentences. Whichever purpose the training session serves, a crosslinguistic study requires that the number, structure, and meaning of pretest sentences be as similar as possible in the languages that are compared.

Example: In our French/Danish study, pretest sentences were used both to familiarize the child with the picture selection task and for sampling purposes. Two types of test sentences were created. The first type consisted of two finite one-clause sentences with either a reflexive or a nonreflexive pronoun.

(10) Mickey et Donald jouent au coiffeur. Montres-moi l'image où tu vois: Donald le coiffe.
'Mickey and Donald are playing at hairdressing. Show me the picture where you see: Donald is combing him.'

The second type consisted of four two-clause object control constructions. These were similar in structure to the test sentences but contained different verbs and a referential expression instead of a reflexive or a nonreflexive pronoun.

(11) Minnie demande à Chaperon Rouge de brosser le chat.
'Minnie asks Little Red Riding Hood to brush the cat.'

Children who failed on more than one of these object control sentences were not included in the sample.

12.5.1.4 The Experimental List In most studies the experimental items include sets of similar sentences. They are similar because although with different lexical content, each test condition is repeated at least four times, and because all test conditions rotate in the same sentence (as in (8) and (9)). The experimenter must decide how to order sets of similar sentences with respect to each other within the experimental list. This decision depends largely on the types of sentences required by the study. In general, I suggest that the order should vary across items, so that no pattern emerges. For example, one test condition should sometimes precede another, and sometimes follow it. Furthermore, two instantiations of the same test condition may sometimes occur together. Finally, as mentioned earlier, filler materials should be inserted at specific positions within the list. The pseudorandom order of items thereby obtained should be as similar as possible across the languages involved in the study. If there exists an effect of test-item presentation order (e.g., if a response to a given test item is influenced by the preceding trial), the effect would presumably be the same in both languages. In that manner, if any variance is observed between the results of the languages being compared, it will be possible to discard the hypothesis that the observed variance may come from the organization of items within the experimental list.

Clearly, it is easy to ensure strict similarity across the lists of the languages being compared when the number of test conditions, and hence the number of test sentences, is the same in both languages. When it is not, following criteria such as those just mentioned will ensure similarity at least with respect to the organization of items across the two lists.

Example: To ensure variation across items, the following criteria were used in the French/Danish study to order test sentences and fillers within each language list.

First, two successive sentences should involve different pairs of characters and different lexical content. In our study, for example, if a given sentence referred to *Teddy Bear* and *Donald* and the embedded verb was *to aim at*, the following sentence referred to two other characters (e.g., *Minnie* and *Little Red Riding Hood*) and the embedded verb was different (e.g., *to spray at*).

Second, two instances of a given test condition, or two different test conditions giving rise to the same type of response, should be presented in succession at least once in the list. For example, in the French list two test sentences with the nonreflexive pronoun (*le/la*) occurred in succession, and in the Danish list a test sentence with the nonreflexive pronoun *hende* followed a sentence with *sig* and a masculine NP in matrix subject position.

Third, two or three successive test sentences should involve different test conditions, and their order should vary after a filler sentence. For example, in the French list a test sentence with the reflexive *se* preceded one with the nonreflexive pronoun *le*, which preceded a filler sentence; after that filler came a test sentence with the nonreflexive pronoun *la*, followed by one with the reflexive *se*. In the Danish list a sentence with the locally bound reflexive *sig selv* preceded one with the nonreflexive pronoun *ham* before a filler, and followed a sentence with *sig* after that filler.

Needless to say, although the order of test sentences and fillers was created according to these criteria, the lists themselves were not exactly the same in both languages. One inherent difference arose from the fact that three conditions were tested in Danish, but only two in French. Another was linked to the fact that we kept to the same number of distractors in both languages. As suggested above, if we had used more fillers in Danish than in French (six and four, respectively), the two lists would have matched better with respect to ordering of items.

12.5.2 The Experimental Task

As previous chapters have shown, various methods are now available to evaluate children's knowledge of syntax. Although these methods differ, they share the unavoidable property of assessing language knowledge through measurement and analysis of various modes of language behavior like speaking and understanding. In other words, because there is no direct empirical access to grammatical competence, all evidence of language knowledge or of the nature of the processing systems that implement this knowledge must derive from the analysis of linguistic performance manifested in the course of a specific task.

Now, different tasks vary with respect to the mode of behavior they address, for example, production versus comprehension. These are subjected to different processing constraints that affect what can be revealed of grammatical competence in any given task (see chapter 9, this volume). Furthermore, even when addressing the same mode of behavior—for example, comprehension—two different tasks, like picture selection and act-out, may vary in the directness of their mapping between the mental representation of the stimulus, which involves grammatical competence, and the behavior reflecting this representation. As argued by different authors (Crain and Fodor 1987; Lust, Chien, and Flynn 1987), one of two tasks calling for the same mode of behavior may involve memory, attention, and other intervening performance variables to a greater degree than the other.

As also shown in previous chapters, it is usually the case that the experimenter adapts any given method to the theoretical question he or she addresses, and to his or her own convictions concerning different aspects of the task. For example, Gerken and Shady (chapter 6) show that the picture selection task may vary with respect to the presentation of the linguistic stimuli (before or together with the presentation of the pictures), the nature of the pictures (color, size), the number of pictures (two, four), the experimenter's way of handling unusual responses, and so on.

These considerations suggest that in order to neutralize the role of variables mediating the mapping between grammatical knowledge and performance, the same task, applied under the same conditions, should be used across languages in a crosslinguistic study. Assuming that the effects of a given task will be the same in the languages being compared, if different acquisition effects are found it will not be possible to impute the observed differences to task factors.

Example: To test children's comprehension of sentences with either a reflexive or a nonreflexive pronoun in French and Danish, we used a picture selection task. As shown in figure 12.1, accompanying each sentence was a set of three colored pictures placed at the angles of an imaginary triangle. The representation of the events referred to by the sentence and the position of the characters in each picture were the same in the French and Danish picture arrays. Similar criteria were used to the effect that in both languages, appropriate and inappropriate pictures should occupy one of the three positions in an array the same number of times. On the test trials, two of the three pictures showed a self-oriented and a non-self-oriented action involving the two characters mentioned in the test sentence (pictures (a) and (b) in figure 12.1). These pictures corresponded to a correct response for a reflexive and for a nonreflexive pronoun, respectively. Note that the picture showing a non-self-oriented action (picture (b)) was also the correct response for long-distance binding in Danish. For test sentences with a reflexive, in half of the trials the third picture showed a self-oriented action realized by the character in matrix subject position (picture (c1)), and in the other half the third picture showed the character mentioned in the embedded clause performing a self-oriented action and a character not mentioned in the test sentence (instead of the character mentioned in the matrix clause) standing

Figure 12.1
Schematic representation of the picture arrays

alongside (picture (c2)). For a test sentence with a nonreflexive pronoun in both languages and for a sentence with long-distance-bound *sig* in Danish, in half of the trials the third picture showed a non-self-oriented action involving the two characters mentioned in the test sentence, with inverted grammatical roles (i.e., the matrix subject was exchanged for the embedded subject and vice versa) (picture (c3)); in the other half the third picture showed the character mentioned in the embedded clause performing a non-self-oriented action and a character not mentioned in the test sentence (instead of the character mentioned in the matrix clause) standing alongside (picture (c4)). Thus, each array accompanying a test trial contained one picture that matched the test sentence and two that did not. The latter depicted three possible incorrect interpretations of any given test condition: a binding error, a grammatical relation error, or a negligence or memory error concerning the character mentioned in the matrix clause. Pictures accompanying filler trials and pretest sentences without pronouns were constructed according to the same criteria, and these were the same in both languages.

12.5.3 Procedure

A crosslinguistic study must be administered under standardized conditions. These concern the procedure followed in both the training and the test section of the experiment. Thus, whichever instructions the investigator uses to familiarize the children with the stimuli and the task, they should be the same for all the languages considered in the study. The investigator must also decide in advance whether the child will or will not be corrected during the training session, whether stimuli will be presented once or twice before the child is asked to provide an answer, what to do when the child does not answer on a particular trial or the experimenter feels that the child has responded incorrectly because of being inattentive during that trial, and so on. For example, the investigator may decide to repeat the stimulus right away, repeat it at the end of the experimental list, or not repeat it at all. One or another of these options may differently affect children's behavior on the remaining items of the list. Making the procedure uniform across the languages being tested will dismiss the possibility that different response patterns in these languages derive from the way the task was administered.

Example: In the French/Danish study, to familiarize the children with the linguistic materials, the picture arrays, and the task, we first presented the copy book containing the picture arrays to small groups of children in their kindergarten classroom. The children were asked to give the names of the characters represented in the pictures, identify the events, and find the appropriate picture for a couple of sentences not included in the linguistic materials. After this collective familiarization session, children were tested individually.

As mentioned earlier, this study involved both a comprehension task and an elicited production task. Both were carried out using the picture arrays. The procedure was as follows. The experimenter presented the child with an array of three pictures. For two of these three pictures the experimenter then asked the child to answer one question of the form "What is X doing?" and one of the form "What is X doing to Y?", X and Y being the names of the characters represented in the two pictures. For the picture arrays accompanying test sentences, the first question was asked when pointing to a picture where a self-oriented action was represented, and the second question was asked when pointing to one where a non-self-oriented action was represented. These two questions were intended to obtain productions with reflexive and nonreflexive pronouns, respectively. To elicit utterances with long-distance-bound *sig*, the question "What does X ask Y to do?" was presented. For the third picture in each array, the experimenter either provided a commentary or asked the child to name the characters in the picture. After that, the child received the following instruction: "Show me the picture where you see" followed by a sentence. The same procedure was used for pretest sentences, test sentences, and fillers. Questions and sentences were presented only once. If, for a particular trial, the child did not answer, the question and/or the sentence was repeated at the end of the pretest list for the training session and at the end of the experimental list for test sentences and fillers.

12.5.4 Subjects

Anderson (1946) points out that although an investigator is always concerned with a finite population, for scientific purposes the subjects studied in any investigation become the representatives of an infinite population. For example, if an experimenter studies the comprehension of interrogative sentences by 30 3-year-old children attending the first grade of a day care center, these children become the representatives of the children in first day care center grades in our society. However, it is usually the case in our society that human beings belong to different strata based on income, educational level, cultural background, and a variety of related factors. Because these strata differ markedly in the facilities and opportunities they offer children, questions like "Of what population is this group a sample?" and "Is it a good sample?" are of great importance. Thus, in any research project care must be taken to define precisely the criteria underlying the inclusion of subjects in a given sample. These criteria concern the educational or socioeconomic level of the parents, the age and sex of the children, their mean-length-of-utterance values, particularly for young children, whether or not they attend a nursery school, day care center, or kindergarten, their capacity or willingness to participate in a given task, and the sample size.

With respect to crosslinguistic investigation, sampling is another factor that needs to be held constant, so that the characteristics of the sample do not affect the main factor under observation, namely, the specific-language-grammar property being studied. Thus, ideally, samples should be as uniform as possible with respect to the criteria mentioned here. For example, the problem of age sampling is solved by using the same number of children at each age level (e.g., 48 at 2 years, 48 at 3 years, and so on), both within each language and across the languages being tested. Age stratification can be further controlled by testing children on their birthdays, or within one month of their birthdate. When for practical reasons this procedure cannot be followed, the investigator may, for both languages, select a constant number of children born in each month, so that, for example, 4 children are tested at 2 years and 0 months, 4 are tested at 2 years and 1 month, and so on. As Anderson (1946) notes, selecting the same number of children at each age level not only improves sampling; it also simplifies calculations and the determination of various statistical constants.

12.5.5 Scoring and Analysis of Data

The last factors that must be kept constant in a crosslinguistic study concern the procedures followed for scoring and analyzing the data. To the extent that subject responses have been recorded in a systematic and similar fashion for the languages being compared (i.e., to the extent that the same kind of information is available for the samples being compared), it will be possible to apply the same criteria when scoring the data.

If the study is one that compares groups by age data, the investigator may simply count the number of correct (or incorrect) responses in each test condition for each subject at each age level. To this end, the investigator will decide in advance whether or not only the first response should be taken into account for a test trial that has been repeated. An investigator who is interested in the nature of incorrect responses, based on the particular hypothesis being tested, will count the number of specific and previously defined types of errors for each child at each age level; error categories should of course be the same across the languages being compared. If the investigator is analyzing individual patterns of responses— for example, to determine how many children within each age group show consistent responses across the repetitions of test condition(s)—again, similar scoring procedures should be followed. Finally, correct (or incorrect) scores for age groups should be subjected to the same type of statistical analysis and be similarly expressed, say, in terms of percentages or in terms of mean number of responses per condition.

Example: In the French/Danish study, children's verbal and nonverbal responses were recorded by the investigator on a previously prepared response sheet. For the comprehension data obtained through picture selection, a diagram reproducing each picture array in a codified form appeared to the right of each sentence included in the materials. The experimenter's task was to circle the number in this diagram corresponding to the child's choice. Thus, for each test sentence the experimenter recorded whether the child gave a correct response (coded as 1) and whether the response involved a binding error, a grammatical function error, or a matrix subject error (coded as 2, 3a, and 3b, respectively). Because this system of notation was used for both languages, it was possible to apply the same scoring procedure and the same type of analysis for both. Specifically, we counted the number of correct responses and the number of different types of errors made by each child at each age level in each test condition. These data were submitted to an analysis of variance using subjects and expression types as main factors.

Children's responses to the questions designed to elicit utterances with either a reflexive or a nonreflexive pronoun in both languages, and long-distance-bound *sig* in Danish, were recorded to the right of each question written on the response sheet. For each question type, responses were included in one of the following categories: (1) expected pronoun type, (2) incorrect pronoun type (e.g., a reflexive instead of a nonreflexive pronoun), (3) lexical NP, and (4) object of the verb not expressed (dropped). Then we counted for each question type how many times each child in each age group produced responses falling into one or another of the above categories. These data were submitted to an analysis of variance using subjects and question types as main factors in both languages.

12.6   Final Thoughts

Any scientific inquiry involves a deliberate attempt to isolate certain phenomena and replicate them under controlled conditions in order to determine their characteristic relations. In crosslinguistic investigation, the main experimental factor is one or several properties of specific language grammars. Determining this property's nature and effects becomes possible by holding other factors constant so that they do not affect the particular phenomena under observation. When linguistic materials, the task, its administration, the selection of subjects, and the scoring and analysis of data are standardized and held constant across the languages being compared, the crosslinguistic approach provides a reliable and valid method for testing hypotheses regarding grammatical properties in the emergence of language knowledge.

Although we have focused on experimental methods, it is clear that crosslinguistic studies based on corpus data or intended to assess syntax in clinical settings should also proceed along the lines described here. For example, investigators working on spontaneous production data can establish in advance the conditions under which data will be collected, transcribed, quantified, analyzed, and presented in the languages being compared (see chapters 1 and 2, this volume). When, as usually happens, the study is based on already existing records and these have not been collected under similar conditions, uniformity across the languages might be ensured if at least the remaining aspects are systematically controlled.

As understanding of the effects of different factors on children's language behavior increases, it will be possible, at least for certain factors, to relax the strict matching of conditions called for here. For example, if independent evidence shows that two different comprehension or production tasks give rise to similar results, or that sentences involving either a finite or an infinitival embedded clause are equally well understood by the children being tested, it will not matter whether children learning the languages being compared are presented with the same or different tasks, or whether test conditions are couched in the same or different sentence frames. Inasmuch as understanding of these questions is still limited, choices regarding each step of the research should be explicitly formulated, standardized, and kept constant across the languages being studied. The test should be administered by experimenters trained along similar lines, and children's responses should be recorded by well-trained observers. By meticulously controlling all factors but the grammatical property being studied, the investigator will be able to provide a precise characterization of the property's effects on acquisition, and to allow replications by other investigators with new samples of children learning the same or different languages.

As mentioned in section 12.3, an important body of research is now available regarding children's knowledge of specific grammatical properties in different languages. Much of this work has been independently carried out by different investigators, using different tasks, different linguistic materials, different sampling criteria, and so on. The question arises whether or not it is legitimate or interesting to use the results obtained by these investigators for comparative purposes, that is, in order to assess whether certain acquisition effects replicate across language grammars that share a certain grammatical property and not across those that do not share this property. Common sense indicates that because results like these arise from different testing conditions, they must be cautiously interpreted but not disregarded. In language acquisition, as in any other discipline, a distinction can be made among (1) facts and generalizations regarding the specific property with which the investigator is concerned, (2) the methods, or the techniques and procedures, by means of which these facts are obtained, and (3) the theory or the framework of assumptions on which the hypotheses regarding these facts are based. Anderson (1946) remarks that a science is composed of many parts that grow at different rates and mature at different times. In the beginning, little concern with methods is shown. As the significant problems are more clearly perceived and formulated, designed experiments replace simple observations. Theory-guided research on language acquisition has now reached the point where it can critically examine its methods and results, and deliberately design new controlled studies either to test new hypotheses or to retest those addressed in previous research. All things considered, the suggestions advocated in sections 12.4 and 12.5 on how to conduct crosslinguistic investigation may be seen as tools that are used, modified, and improved as new problems are met.

Today's language acquisition investigators have a great advantage over yesterday's; the advantage lies not in their interest or ability to do research, but in the concepts and tools that have been forged in the intervening period.

Notes

1. See Atkinson 1982 for references and for a critical review of these proposals.

2. Blount's and Kernan's dissertations, as well as several other University of California at Berkeley dissertations on the acquisition of various native languages, emerged from *A Field Manual for Cross-cultural Study of the Acquisition of Communicative Competence*, edited by Dan Slobin in 1967. Slobin suggested that in addition to looking for universal stages of acquisition, researchers could use crosslinguistic data to determine both conceptual starting points for linguistic forms and children's strategies for constructing morphosyntactic systems. On the basis of the crosslinguistic evidence available in the early 1970s, he proposed a set of "operating principles" for the construction of language (Slobin 1973); once the database of his still ongoing crosslinguistic project became broader, he both modified and extended them (Slobin 1985b). A characteristic of the research done in this framework is that it proceeds inductively, without reference to any current theory of linguistic knowledge; the details of children's spontaneous speech at successive phases of development in different languages is examined in order to infer general principles that could give rise to the observed patterns. A compendium of surveys of the acquisition of numerous different language types is presented in Slobin 1985b.

3. As pointed out by Pinker (1984, 2), the problem of determining which grammar best fits a corpus of child speech was nearly impossible to solve, "... specially since the rules in the grammars proposed often contained arbitrary mixtures of adult syntactic categories, semantic features, phonological features and specific words," often bearing a shallow relationship to the rule systems proposed in linguistic theory.

4. According to the model of acquisition assumed in the Standard Theory and the Extended Standard Theory, the child determined the grammar of his language by writing rules in the rule-writing system, under the constraints that the rules must be compatible with the data and that the grammar must be the most highly valued by the evaluation metric (see Williams 1987).

5. It is now known that matters are not so simple as presented in the text; indeed, a number of different analyses of X-bar theory and word order effects have been proposed, first within the Principles and Parameters framework and more recently within the Minimalist Program approach to linguistic theory (Chomsky 1993, 1994), to deal with a wider range of cases. (See, among other works, Kayne 1994, Koopman 1984, and Travis 1984.) In any case, the precise grammatical characterizations of X-bar theory and of the parameter accounting for word order variation are irrelevant for the present discussion.

6. Binding principles govern necessary or possible anaphoric relations between different types of NPs: anaphors (reciprocals and reflexive pronouns like *each other* and *himself*, respectively), nonreflexive pronouns (like *him/her*), and R(eferential)-expressions (like *John, the table*).

7. Consider the following examples:

(i) a. Come como un animal.
        El/Ella come como un animal.
    b. *Mange comme une bête.
        Il/Elle mange comme une bête.
    c. *Eats like an animal.
        He/She eats like an animal.

These examples show that as in Italian, in Spanish (ia) the subject pronoun may be left unexpressed, whereas in French (ib) and English (ic) the corresponding sentence is ungrammatical if the subject pronoun is not expressed. Languages that allow a pronominal subject to be left unexpressed are called pro-drop languages; they "drop" the subject pronoun. Italian and Spanish are pro-drop languages; English and French are not. This crosslinguistic variation is referred to as the pro-drop parameter.

8. According to Anderson (1979), an affected object undergoes a physical or abstract change of state or location through the event denoted by the verb. Tenny (1987) proposes a characterization of affectedness in aspectual terms.

Chapter 13

Assessing Morphosyntax in Clinical Settings

Laurence B. Leonard

13.1 Introduction

Although most children acquire language effortlessly and in a relatively brief span of time, some are not so fortunate. Approximately 5% of all 5-year-olds have a specific language impairment (SLI) (Tomblin 1993). These children have normal hearing, show age-appropriate scores on non-verbal tests of intelligence, and present no clear evidence of neurological impairment, yet their language ability is strikingly poor.

Another 3% of all children have mental retardation. At least half of the children who are mildly mentally retarded and almost all children with moderate to severe retardation have language disorders (NIH, NINDS 1988). This seems to be true whether the retardation is due to genetic irregularities, as in Down syndrome and Fragile X syndrome, or to some as yet unknown factor.

Smaller numbers of children are diagnosed as autistic. These children exhibit a striking disturbance in their interactions with others, and all show deficits in language ability to some degree. Finally, there are children who begin life normally but incur brain injury through trauma or stroke that leaves them impaired in their ability to produce or comprehend language.

At least for the most prevalent of these conditions—SLI and mental retardation—morphosyntax is one of the prominent areas of language difficulty (see reviews in Chapman 1995; Fowler 1990; Johnston 1988; Rice 1991; Rondal 1993; Rosenberg and Abbeduto 1993). For example, children with SLI not only are slow in their development of morphosyntax relative to same-age peers but also show more limited abilities in these areas than one would expect given their vocabulary abilities and even the length of their utterances. These extraordinary problems with morphosyntax take the form of limited use of a range of grammatical morphemes (e.g., Johnston and Schery 1976; Steckol and Leonard 1979), less frequent use of certain types of complementation, negative particles, and auxiliary movement (e.g., Johnston and Kamhi 1984), and a greater tendency to omit obligatory arguments (e.g., King and Fletcher 1993).

Many children with mental retardation are likewise especially deficient in their morphosyntactic ability. For example, children with Down syndrome exhibit lexical abilities that are more limited than their tested mental ages, yet their scores on measures of morphosyntax are lower still (Miller 1988). Studies showing lower-than-mental-age morphosyntactic comprehension (e.g., Bartel, Bryen, and Keehn 1973) and production (e.g., Fowler, Gelman, and Gleitman 1994; Lovell and Bradbury 1967) are relatively common in the literature on mental retardation.

These children's special problems in the area of morphosyntax have two important implications. First, and most obviously, it is unlikely that a comprehensive understanding of SLI and mental retardation will be possible without a firm grasp of the morphosyntactic deficits in these children. Because such deficits are so striking in these groups of children, it seems improbable that they are simply an ancillary part of the overall condition. Second, groups of children with extraordinary problems in morphosyntax may represent excellent test cases of current theories of grammatical organization or development. For example, it might prove to be the case that some component of the grammar that is assumed to be a separate module can be shown to be selectively disrupted, or spared, in some subgroup of children with language disorders. Alternatively, it could be that a disruption of some aspect of grammar assumed to be a prerequisite for other key attainments can be shown to be sufficient to steer the child's grammatical development off course.

Theories that invoke maturational principles or critical periods are also obvious ones to be applied to children with language disorders. One of the hallmarks of language disorders in children is a slow rate of language development. It is natural to inquire, then, whether there are certain later-developing principles or parametric variations that remain inaccessible to these children.

The purpose of this chapter is to discuss the assessment of morphosyntax in children with language disorders. Methods of examining these children's morphosyntax will be reviewed, obstacles to interpretation will be identified, and several solutions to the problems identified will be proposed. Included in the latter will be a discussion of the different means of isolating the morphosyntactic abilities of these children from other factors that might interact with morphosyntax. Let us begin with a few facts about children with language disorders that serve as preliminaries to the assessment of these children's morphosyntactic abilities.

13.2 Some Characteristics of Children with Language Disorders

13.2.1 Heterogeneity within Clinical Subgroups

Unfortunately, the classification of children into different clinical subgroups such as SLI, Down syndrome, and autism does not lead to homogeneous clusters of children. Even within these subgroups, considerable heterogeneity exists. Some of this heterogeneity is attributable to individual differences in language ability, including morphosyntactic abilities. In other cases, the variability lies in some other area. Even in these instances, the assessment of morphosyntax can be affected.

One source of variability is the relationship between the comprehension and the production of language by these children. Some children's production seems to be roughly comparable to their comprehension, whereas other children show production abilities that lag well behind their comprehension abilities. The ramifications of such differences between children are probably clear; morphosyntactic measures based on production might be appropriate for the first type of child but might grossly underestimate the abilities of the second.

Another source of variability is phonological ability. Phonology is an area of vulnerability in many children with language disorders, but abilities can vary considerably. Some children in a subgroup may be less accomplished in achieving the appropriate output form of morphosyntactic elements, such as grammatical inflections (requiring word-final consonants, in the case of English) and free-standing closed-class morphemes (often requiring the use of weak syllables). For such children, production measures of morphosyntax must be administered with great care.

Lexical knowledge also varies. Among children with SLI and those with certain types of mental retardation, there are children whose lexical development appears to outpace their morphosyntactic development. In such cases, casually constructed measures of a child's ability to understand sentences might give the impression of the comprehension of morphosyntactic details that were instead apprehended by lexical means.

Weaknesses in lexical ability can also be found. Within particular subgroups such as the SLI population, there are children who exhibit

word-finding problems. These children sometimes have difficulty producing words that they apparently comprehend; even on simple single-word
naming tasks they may err, or, if correct, show significantly slower response times than would be expected given their comprehension ability.
Production measures of morphosyntax can obviously be problematic in
these cases, unless a means of conveying the requisite vocabulary to the
child is found.

13.2.2 Processing Limitations

In the past decade the language acquisition literature has provided a
number of examples in which a grammatical principle previously assumed
to be acquired rather late is shown to be well established in children at a
much younger age (e.g., Crain 1991). The reason these principles appeared
to be later attainments was that the method of assessment originally
employed placed significant demands on the children's processing capacities. Once these demands were reduced, children appeared to have command of the principles.

The issue of processing limitations looms large in the study of children
with language disorders. Even the subgroup assumed to be most capable
outside of language—children with SLI—has been shown to perform at
subpar levels on a wide range of tasks, some having little to do with
language. These tasks have included the discrimination and sequencing of
complex tones (Tallal and Piercy 1973), judgments of whether or not two
geometric shapes presented at different angles were the same (Johnston
and Ellis Weismer 1983), and even simple button pressing in response
to a signal (Hughes and Sussman 1983). This is not to deny that these
children may have highly specific deficits in morphosyntax that are independent of processing problems. However, it appears that many of these
children also have a subtle but general processing limitation that can
easily interfere with the assessment of their morphosyntax and give the
appearance of certain types of deficits that are not actually there.

13.2.3 Gaps between World Knowledge and Language Ability

Most children with language disorders know more about the world than
they can possibly express (or comprehend) through language. This is
because the most prevalent clinical subgroups (including many children
with mental retardation) possess nonverbal cognitive abilities that exceed
their abilities with language. Furthermore, many of these children com-

municate with others in a manner that displays a knowledge of sharing information and turn-taking that greatly outstrips their skill in expressing or fully comprehending sentences.

This disparity between knowledge of the physical and social world on the one hand and the means to express this knowledge through language on the other can pose problems for assessment. Specifically, this discrepancy practically invites the invention of compensatory strategies by children with language disorders. Care must be taken to ensure that a peculiar response pattern is not due to some extralinguistic solution created by the child.

13.2.4   Inactive and Passive Conversationalists
Unfortunately, along with children whose communicative intents outpace their ability to express them, there are also children with language disorders who are conversational underachievers. What little they may know about language is not put to good communicative use (e.g., Craig 1991; Fey and Leonard 1983). Fey (1986) identified two such groups as inactive conversationalists and passive conversationalists. The first type of child is neither as assertive nor as responsive to social partners as expected; the second type is responsive, but rarely makes substantive contributions to the conversation. Inactive conversationalists constitute a major challenge to assessment, for both comprehension and production measures require the child to participate. Passive conversationalists present problems only for certain types of assessment. In particular, the number of utterances obtained in spontaneous speech samples may be quite meager. It is probably no coincidence that investigators have discovered that the total number of words (and, presumably, utterances) spoken per unit of time is an important diagnostic indicator (Miller 1991).

13.3   Examining the Morphosyntax of Children with Language Disorders

The study of morphosyntax in children with language disorders is not especially new. Work of this type began at least 30 years ago, much of it within the framework of then-current linguistic theory (e.g., Lackner 1968; Menyuk 1964). Although research interest in the morphosyntax of children with language disorders waned in the late 1970s and early 1980s, interest in this area has been rekindled. Much of the recent work has been couched in the Principles and Parameters framework (Chomsky 1986a). Research has focused on the use of passives (Smith-Lock 1992), auxiliary movement (Hadley 1993), the determiner system (Leonard 1994), nominative case (Loeb and Leonard 1991), the control of tense and agreement (Rice and Oetting 1993; Rice, Wexler, and Cleave, in press), and knowledge of binding (Franks and Connell, in press), among other areas. For example, Loeb and Leonard (1991) reported that children with SLI often fail to mark nominative case in their preverbal pronoun use (producing instead utterances such as "Him go home") and likewise show only limited use of tense and agreement inflections. This finding prompted Loeb and Leonard to suggest that a significant part of these children's morphosyntactic difficulties may reflect problems with INFL. Smith-Lock (1992) examined the use of passives by children with SLI and concluded that these children's difficulty centers on the inflectional morphology required in this construction; details of the passive pertaining to principles of Universal Grammar, such as argument chains, do not seem to be problematic.

Since at least the early 1970s, the assessment of morphosyntax has been a main fixture of clinical work. Most clinical measures of morphosyntax used today are based on descriptive frameworks that are rather generic in nature. Although this renders them less than ideal for testing current theories of grammatical organization and grammatical development, their emphasis on representative and frequently occurring morphosyntactic forms ensures that only the most circumscribed of morphosyntactic deficits could go undetected.

In the clinical setting, a distinction is often made between standardized tests of language ability and nonstandardized measures. The former are commercially available instruments that were developed through the testing of groups of children at different ages. Ideally, psychometric criteria (e.g., test-retest and interexaminer reliability, concurrent validity) have been met. However, reviews of the available instruments reveal that tests vary widely in this regard (see McCauley and Swisher 1984; Plante and Vance 1994).

Standardized tests vary in their focus. Many are comprehensive, dealing with phonology and semantics as well as morphosyntax. An example of such a test is the Test of Language Development: Primary 2 (Newcomer and Hammill 1988). Others are more narrowly focused. There are many tests that are concerned primarily with morphosyntax. These include the Carrow Elicited Language Inventory (Carrow 1974), the Northwestern Syntax Screening Test (Lee 1971), the Structured Photographic Expressive Language Test–II (Werner and Kresheck 1983), the CID Grammatical Analysis of Elicited Language (Moog and Geers 1979), the Patterned

Elicitation Syntax Test (Young and Perachio 1981), the Test for Auditory Comprehension of Language—Revised (Carrow-Woolfolk 1985), and the Test for Examining Expressive Morphology (Shipley, Stone, and Sue 1983). Standardized tests typically provide a single score or set of scores that indicates how the child performed relative to children of the same age in the standardization sample.

It is paradoxical that the factors that make a standardized test psychometrically suitable are the same ones that limit its value as a tool for linguistic investigation. Standardized tests are designed to document how a child stands relative to same-age peers within some broad domain of ability. Such tests must be capable of reliably and validly distinguishing groups of "average" children who differ by as little as six months in age. To accomplish this, the tests must be sensitive only to those differences in ability that quite consistently distinguish children in the two age groups. This means that if particular structures with theoretical or even clinical importance are produced or understood with considerable variability across adjacent age groups, they might not be included in the final, published version of the test. For this reason, standardized tests should probably be used primarily to document a child's general level of linguistic functioning relative to same-age peers. The work of discovering the details of a child's morphosyntactic system should be left to in-depth probes that do not carry the burden of meeting particular psychometric criteria.

In many clinical settings, nonstandardized measures are used to supplement (and, in some cases, even replace) standardized tests. These measures can be used for a variety of purposes (Leonard et al. 1978). They are typically constructed by the practitioner to examine more closely some narrower aspect of the child's semantic, phonological, or morphosyntactic comprehension or production. Nonstandardized measures are essentially experimental tasks, and would be called by this name if constructed by a researcher. They make up an important part of a skilled practitioner's clinical repertoire. Typically they are constructed because available standardized tests provide little or no information regarding a child's production or comprehension of certain morphosyntactic elements judged to be of diagnostic or therapeutic importance.

13.3.1 Tasks Used in Assessing Morphosyntax in Children with Language Disorders

The tasks employed in both standardized tests and nonstandardized measures largely come from the language acquisition literature. Although existing tasks are sometimes modified to meet clinical needs, there is no separate regimen of tasks specific to the clinical enterprise. For example, a sentence imitation task is used in the Carrow Elicited Language Inventory, a picture selection task in the Test for Auditory Comprehension of Language–Revised, and a sentence completion task in the Test for Examining Expressive Morphology. Act-out tasks and grammaticality judgment tasks are not as commonly used in standardized tests; however, items involving these tasks can be found in the Vocabulary Comprehension Scale (Bangs 1975) and the Bankson Language Test–2 (Bankson 1990), respectively. Elicited production tasks are employed in a number of standardized tests, such as the Formulated Sentences subtest of the Clinical Evaluation of Language Fundamentals–Revised (Semel, Wiig, and Secord 1987). However, those designed to constrain the morphosyntax of the child's response (e.g., "Ask him where the girl is going") seem to be confined to nonstandardized measures (e.g., Wilcox and Leonard 1978).

Modifications of common tasks are also found in standardized tests. For example, two types of delayed as opposed to immediate imitation have been used. In the version used in the Patterned Elicitation Syntax Test, the examiner points to three consecutive pictures, provides the appropriate sentence description for each, and then asks the child to describe the pictures. In the version used in the Northwestern Syntax Screening Test, the examiner provides appropriate sentence descriptions for each of two pictures, but without pointing to the picture that corresponds to each sentence. The child is then asked to provide the sentence that matches the picture indicated by the examiner.

In the CID Grammatical Analysis of Elicited Language, a variation one step further removed from immediate imitation is employed. In this test the examiner initiates an activity (e.g., placing a toy boy in a red chair and a toy girl in a yellow chair) and models a particular sentence construction (e.g., describing the objects with Noun + copula *be* + Preposition Phrase constructions such as "The boy is in the red chair"). The child is then asked to describe the remaining objects (e.g., "The girl is in the yellow chair").

Paraphrase tasks have also been employed, in which the child hears a brief story and is asked to retell it to another listener. The assumption is that the story is too long to be remembered verbatim, and thus in the child's attempt to paraphrase it, it will be conveyed in a manner more in keeping with the child's grammar.

Of course, morphosyntactic measures computed from spontaneous speech samples also form an important part of assessment. Some of these measures, such as Developmental Sentence Scoring (Lee 1974), have been standardized, whereas others, such as the Language Assessment, Remediation and Screening Procedure (LARSP) (Crystal, Fletcher, and Garman 1976), are primarily descriptive. Computer analysis programs have been developed for these and other measures of spontaneous speech (e.g., Long and Fey 1989; Miller and Chapman 1991).

Because nonstandardized measures constitute such a significant part of clinical assessment, the work illustrated in the preceding chapters of this volume is highly applicable. This is true not only because of the care taken by the authors to ensure that the target forms are highly felicitous, but also because many of these morphosyntactic forms are only just beginning to receive clinical attention.

13.3.2 Comparisons with Normally Developing Children

To the extent that data obtained from children with language disorders are to be compared with data from normally developing children on the same task, the question arises as to which group of normally developing children constitutes the most appropriate comparison group. The answer depends a great deal on the conceptual and attentional demands of the task as well as the linguistic requirements for appropriate responding, apart from the structure of interest.

The most obvious type of matching is matching for chronological age. However, there are limits to its utility. Children with language disorders are weaker than same-age peers on almost every metric of language that can be devised. Therefore, the interpretation of data from a focused investigation of some morphosyntactic form will be significantly hampered. It might be that the form under investigation is an especially important one to examine in children with language disorders. However, it would be difficult to argue that a finding of a significant deficit in this area relative to age controls was due to the particular factors assumed to be operative and not some more global factor.

Chronological age matching is even more problematic when children with mental retardation serve as the focus of investigation. In this case, nonverbal cognitive deficits as well as more global deficits of language might be responsible for the findings. A common strategy employed by researchers is to use younger normally developing children matched according to mental age as the comparison group.

Along with using a chronological- or mental-age-matched comparison group, most studies also use a group of younger normally developing children matched to the children with language disorders on some measure of language ability. The most frequently employed measure is mean length of utterance (MLU). This measure is especially appropriate when the study focuses on the production of morphosyntactic forms that require some minimum utterance length. In this way, a finding of a difference between children with language disorders and a group of MLU control children on, say, the use of passives with *by* clauses cannot be attributed to differences in the children's ability to produce utterances of sufficient length.

There are instances in which a control for language production other than MLU is in order. For example, if the focus of study is on the use of grammatical morphology, a researcher is taking a risk in adopting MLU as the basis for matching groups of children. That is, because MLU is affected by a child's use of grammatical morphemes, any failure to find a difference between groups of children might be due to the use of a matching technique that equates the children on one of the very variables of experimental interest. To guard against this possibility, some investigators have employed the mean number of arguments expressed per utterance or the mean number of open-class words used per utterance as the basis for matching groups of children.

Measures of phonology can also serve as useful matching criteria. Assume again that an investigator wishes to examine the use of grammatical morphology by children with language disorders, and the language of interest is English. To ensure that any limited use of grammatical morphemes by the children with language disorders is not due to a more general problem with unstressed syllables or word-final consonants, a comparison group might be employed that consists of younger normally developing children matched with the children with language disorders on their ability to produce unstressed syllables and word-final consonants in monomorphemic contexts (e.g., *ba*nana, be*d*).

Another production measure that can serve as a matching criterion is expressive vocabulary. One question that might be pursued is whether children with language disorders remain at a point of using only one word at a time for protracted periods. To explore such a question, children with language disorders who are limited to single-word utterances might be compared with a group of younger normally developing children matched with the first group according to the number of different words in their expressive vocabularies. The question of interest in this case is whether the normally developing children—unlike the children with language disorders—produce multiword utterances.

Of course, the questions of interest to investigators are not limited to matters of production; children's understanding of particular morphosyntactic forms can also be important. In studies of this type, a production measure such as MLU is probably inappropriate as a basis for matching subject groups because children with language disorders often exhibit poorer production than comprehension. The use of a production measure, then, might result in a significant mismatch in general language comprehension that favors the children with language disorders. For this reason, some measure of language comprehension might serve as a more appropriate basis for matching groups. For example, if the experiment were concerned with children's ability to comprehend relative clauses, children with language disorders and younger normally developing children might be matched on a measure that assesses comprehension of sentences whose lengths are similar to those in which relative clauses appear. One such candidate might be the Token Test for Children (DiSimoni 1978), a test in which the child must comply with requests such as "Touch the small yellow circle and the large green square."

13.4 Interpreting Differences between Normally Developing Children and Children with Language Disorders

In the earlier literature, the pattern of morphosyntactic use exhibited by children with language disorders relative to normally developing children was often described as reflecting either a "delay" or a "deviance." Unfortunately, this dichotomy was as misleading as it was helpful. A delay might be taken to mean that the child's pattern replicated that of children a few years younger, and that in time the child would attain age-appropriate ability. A deviance, in contrast, seemed to imply some pattern that bordered on the bizarre.

In fact, neither of these descriptions accurately characterizes the pattern seen most frequently in children with language disorders. Most often these children do make the same errors of omission and commission that are reported for younger normally developing children. What makes language disorders in children something other than a simple delay is the fact that many children show uneven profiles; they may resemble normally developing children two years younger in the use of one element of morphosyntax, and children three years younger in the use of another element. Thus, it can be said that the morphosyntactic profiles of most children with language disorders are unlike those seen in normally developing children at any single age. Furthermore, even though many children with language disorders eventually control structures typically associated with the preschool ages, the degree to which they control some of the more advanced details of language is often in doubt.

It was noted earlier that the most appropriate comparison group in studies of children with language disorders is often a group of younger normally developing children who are comparable to the children with language disorders on some language measure. It was argued that this type of subject group matching can serve as an important control for some ability that, left unchecked, could interfere with the interpretation of the data of interest. However, it is probably also clear at this point that such matching strategies lend themselves rather well to research questions that take as their premise that children with language disorders are not simply delayed in their morphosyntactic development. If a researcher matches a group of children with language disorders and a group of younger normally developing children on the basis of, say, the mean number of arguments expressed in their utterances and then compares the two groups on the use of elements associated with a functional category such as INFL, for example, it is clear that the researcher is testing a hypothesis that children with language disorders exhibit uneven profiles. That is, even though the children with language disorders might resemble the younger normally developing group in one respect (by virtue of their being matched on this dimension of language), they will not resemble this group in another respect. If, on the other hand, the two groups matched according to mean number of arguments were also found to be highly similar in their use of INFL elements, something more akin to a delay might be assumed.

13.5   The Crosslinguistic Study of Children with Language Disorders

Crosslinguistic studies of children with language disorders can be extremely valuable. For example, there are several competing accounts of the morphosyntactic problems seen in children with SLI (e.g., Gopnik and Crago 1991; Leonard 1989; Loeb and Leonard 1991; Rice and Oetting 1993; Rice, Wexler, and Cleave, in press). Although these accounts vary considerably in the particular factors assumed to be responsible for the morphosyntactic deficits, the available data from English-speaking children with SLI are compatible with most of them.

Fortunately, given the diversity of factors assumed to be operative in these accounts, the study of children with SLI acquiring other languages can produce results that are more consistent with some of these accounts than others. For example, some accounts attribute much of the difficulty to the paucity of grammatical morphemes in the input or the phonetic properties of these morphemes (e.g., Leonard 1989), whereas other accounts assume that the difficulty rests in an underlying grammar that treats tense and agreement as optional (e.g., Rice Wexler, and Cleave, in press). Given these assumptions, it would seem that if the first type of account were correct, children with SLI who are acquiring a language in which grammatical morphology is abundant and salient should have less difficulty with this domain of language. In contrast, if the second type of account were correct, significant difficulties with grammatical morphology should be seen in this morphologically rich language as well.

In recent years, studies of the morphosyntax of children with SLI acquiring Dutch (e.g., Bol and de Jong 1992; Leemans 1994), German (e.g., Clahsen 1989; Lindner and Johnston 1992), Hebrew (e.g., Dromi, Leonard, and Shteiman 1993; Leonard and Dromi 1994), Italian (e.g., Leonard et al. 1992; Leonard et al. 1987), and Swedish (e.g., Hansson and Nettelbladt 1995) have appeared, among others. As a result of this work, weaknesses in most of the available accounts of morphosyntactic deficits in these children have been identified. Several accounts have been revised, and others abandoned.

Investigators pursuing crosslinguistic research must always overcome obstacles. In the case of research that focuses on children with language disorders, a few additional problems emerge. First, researchers must probably restrict their study to languages spoken in cultures that recognize some children as having a language disorder. Second, there probably needs to be a clinical profession within the culture to help ensure that the children identified as potential subjects are in fact those children with a disorder. The availability of clinical assessment instruments in the culture —preferably standardized tests—is also important. Given the heterogeneity even among children within the same clinical subgroup, some uniformity in the clinical protocol is beneficial for the sake of subject description and replication. Finally, some familiarity with the clinical terminology used in the culture is necessary. For example, whereas *developmental dysphasia* is often viewed as an alternative term for SLI, in Italy the term is usually restricted to the most seriously affected children with SLI. Great care must be taken to ensure that the same types of children are being included in comparisons of children with language disorders from two different language groups.

Even with these safeguards, all problems of interpretation are not removed. For example, among developed countries, significant differences exist in the age at which children are identified as being at risk for language disorders and the age at which intervention is offered. The result is that in some countries it is difficult to find a 4-year-old with a language disorder who has not already begun receiving services, whereas in other countries many children with problems have not yet been brought to the attention of health and education providers. Given this state of affairs, it is clear that the degree of morphosyntactic deficit shown by, say, two 5-year-olds with SLI from different language groups could look vastly different, not because of the particular language being acquired, but because one child has benefited from up to two years of intervention whereas the other has only just been diagnosed.

An especially strong design in crosslinguistic research with language disorders is one in which comparisons are made between normally developing children and children with language disorders within and between languages. Furthermore, it would be ideal to use, in each language, a younger normally developing group matched with the children with language disorders on some general measure of language ability in addition to a chronological- or mental-age-matched comparison group.

Finding a uniform measure of language ability to serve as a basis for matching across different languages may not be possible. In these cases, it might be necessary to match children on the basis of standard scores on standardized tests of language that purport to measure the same domain of language. For example, children with language disorders who speak two different languages might be matched on the basis of scoring between 1.5 and 2 standard deviations below the mean for their age on some test (different in the two languages) of morphosyntactic comprehension. In each language, younger normally developing children might be selected who earned the same raw scores on the test as the children with language disorders, and whose scores were within 1 standard deviation of the mean for their age.

For certain crosslinguistic comparisons, the same language measure might serve as the basis for matching. For example, although MLU computed in morphemes could not serve as a reasonable basis for matching

English- and Italian-speaking children, MLU computed in words seems less problematic. This is not to deny the important differences that hold between the two languages in the morphological richness of free-standing closed-class morphemes (e.g., Italian articles are marked for number and gender as well as definiteness). However, a high degree of comparability might be seen across the two languages, these differences notwithstanding.

Among the tests of comparability that might be used to assess the adequancy of MLU in words for crosslinguistic comparisons are whether (1) the MLU control children in each language are significantly younger than the children with language disorders; (2) the age controls in each language have significantly higher MLUs than the children with language disorders; and (3) the MLU control children and the age control children in one language are similar in age and MLU, respectively, to their counterparts in the other language.

13.6 Summary

Morphosyntax often constitutes a serious problem for children with language disorders. A clearer picture of why this area of language is so difficult for these children may shed light on the nature of language impairment itself. The study of morphosyntactic problems in these children might have the additional benefit of providing test cases for current theories of grammatical organization and development.

Meaningful research on the morphosyntactic problems of children with language disorders requires an understanding of the factors that may interfere with interpretation of the data. These include linguistic factors such as phonological, lexical, and general language comprehension ability, as well as factors such as degree of world knowledge, limitations in processing capacity, and conversational reticence.

Clinical work makes use of both standardized language tests and practitioner-devised nonstandardized measures. The tasks themselves are borrowed from the language acquisition literature. Modifications are occasionally made in these tasks to suit clinical needs; however, manipulation of characters and events to meet felicity conditions may not always be made with great precision. The clinical enterprise could benefit from the methodological refinements seen in recent language acquisition research.

There are many morphosyntactic structures discussed in the literature that have yet to be examined carefully in children with language disorders. However, to facilitate interpretation of the results, careful attention must be paid to the comparison groups employed. Along with the more customary age-matched control group, normally developing children matched with the children with language disorders on MLU, argument structure, lexical development, phonological ability, or overall language comprehension level might be selected, depending on the research question posed. Comparisons that make use of such groups should permit a determination of whether children with language disorders have more difficulty with the morphosyntactic structures under study than their production or comprehension of other features of language would lead one to expect. If differences are observed, then the conclusion that these children are unlike normally developing children at any single stage of development seems warranted.

The crosslinguistic study of children with language disorders can be very useful in evaluating the relative adequacy of competing accounts of morphosyntactic deficits in these children. However, such research brings with it its own requirements for selecting appropriate measures on which children within and between languages should be matched.

The study of children with language disorders is replete with unanswered questions. However, through the thoughtful selection and creative testing of crucial morphosyntactic structures, important steps toward answering many of these questions can be taken.

Chapter 14

Issues in Designing Research and Evaluating Data Pertaining to Children's Syntactic Knowledge

Jennifer Ryan Hsu and
Louis Michael Hsu

14.1 Introduction

Although many research and quantitative methods are available to scientists studying human behavior, only some of these methods have application to research on first language acquisition. This is due, in part, to the types of questions that are asked. It is also related to the nature of the subjects and limitations in the types of tasks that can be used with such a population. In this chapter we will discuss some of the research designs and data analysis methods that are commonly used in the study of first language acquisition. Our purpose in writing this chapter is to introduce some of the basic concepts of experimental design and hypothesis testing that are relevant to research on the acquisition of syntactic knowledge. The chapter is designed to foster an appreciation of the relations among research questions, research designs, and methods of data analysis.

There are three general questions that are most often addressed in research on the acquisition of syntactic knowledge. First, what do children know about the structure of language? Studies addressing this question may examine the nature of particular rules and/or principles operating within children's grammars. For example, they may investigate the types of sentences children produce, how children interpret various constructions, and the kinds of errors they make across different types of sentences. Second, how does the child's knowledge system change over time? Answers to this question require comparing the performance of children from different age groups and/or comparing the performance of the same children at several points in time. Third, how is the knowledge system acquired and why does it change over time? This question may be examined in studies investigating the role of maturation, universals, parameter setting, and other types of processing or learning mechanisms. It may also be addressed in studies that investigate the role of environmental variables such as characteristics of "motherese" and the relationship between linguistic input and the child's developing knowledge system.

14.2   Research Designs: Objectives, Terminology, Classification, and Data Analysis

Myers and Well (1991) note that the objective of research is to determine whether, how, and to what extent variables of interest are related. For example, studies investigating how children's grammars change over time may examine the relationship between specific linguistic variables and age, mean length of utterance (MLU), or some other measure of developmental change. Myers and Well also note that the more specific goal of many studies is to determine *causal* relations between two sets of variables. This goal applies to studies addressing explanatory questions. In studies that are concerned with causal relations, it is useful to distinguish three categories of variables: *independent*, *dependent*, and *nuisance* variables. The (presumed) causal variables are often called the independent variables or factors, the (presumed) caused variables are called the dependent variables, and other variables that can pose threats to the validity of inferences about causal relations between independent and dependent variables are called the nuisance variables. (Nuisance variables are sometimes called extraneous variables, covariates, or confounding variables.) It should be noted that in many studies in which this terminology (viz., independent and dependent variables) is used, causal relationships are implied rather than explicitly stated. Independent, dependent, and nuisance variables can be *nominal*, *ordinal*, *interval*, or *ratio* scaled. The distinctions among nominal, ordinal, interval, and ratio scales involve information that scale scores carry concerning the attribute that the scale is intended to measure. *Nominal* "measurements" carry information about membership in categories of the attribute so that individuals with the same "measurement" belong to the same category. For example, if the attribute is gender, a code or scale value of "1" might be used to designate "male," and a code or scale value of "2" might designate "female." *Ordinal* measurements carry information about rank order of individuals with respect to the attribute. The rank order of the ordinal measurements must correspond to the rank order of individuals with respect to that attribute. In addition to information about rank ordering, *interval* measurements also carry information about distances between individuals on an attribute continuum. Equal differences between measurements must correspond to equal differences in the attribute. Added to information carried by interval measurements, *ratio* measurements carry information about relative amounts of the attribute possessed by two individuals. The ratio of two measurements must yield ratio information about the attribute. The Stanford-Binet IQ scale is generally considered to have properties of an ordinal scale of the construct of "intelligence" since it permits rank ordering of children in terms of intelligence. However, no one would claim that if one child has an IQ that is twice that of another, the first child is twice as "intelligent" as the second. Thus, no one would claim that the Stanford Binet is a ratio scale. It is important to note that some scales (including IQ scales and MLU as discussed below) are considered to fall somewhere between ordinal and interval scales. Interval and ratio scales are sometimes called *metric* scales (Kennedy 1992).

The classification of a scale depends on the construct that the scale is intended to measure. For example, if MLU is used only as a measure of "length of an utterance," then it could be considered a ratio scale of this construct. Note that in this case the construct "length of an utterance" is in effect identified with the operation of measuring MLU. However, if MLU is used as an index of the construct "level of grammatical development," then it would have properties of an ordinal or interval scale depending on whether it is considered to yield only ordinal or ordinal and interval information about complexity. Uses of MLU in the literature suggest that many researchers believe MLU to have or to approximate interval scale properties. However, no one would argue that MLU is a ratio scale for the construct "level of grammatical development." The levels of measurement of the variables included in a study have important implications for (1) choices of data analysis models (see sections 14.3.3.3 and 14.4) and (2) interpretation of results.

The general plan of a study is called the *research design*. It includes specifying the independent variables and the points in time when data are collected as well as the methods of selecting and assigning subjects to levels (or values) of the independent variable(s). One way of classifying research designs is in terms of whether levels (or values) of the independent variable vary across or within subjects. If they vary across subjects (i.e., different subjects are at different levels of an independent variable), the design is called a *between-subjects design*. A between-subjects design can include more than one factor (e.g., gender and age). If levels of an independent variable vary within subjects (i.e., levels of each independent variable occur in or are presented to each subject), the design is called a *within-subjects design*. An experimental design can include more than one within-subjects factor. If levels of some independent variables vary between subjects, and levels of other independent variables vary within subjects, then the design is called a *mixed design*.

A study conducted by Strohner and Nelson (1974) illustrates some of these basic concepts. The study, which used an act-out task involving puppets, demonstrated how children's interpretations of sentences were influenced by three independent variables: age, grammatical voice, and sentence type. The dependent variable was the number of correct responses. Among the independent variables, age was a between-subjects variable. Participants were 45 children who were classified into three age groups: 3;1 to 3;7, 4;1 to 4;6, and 5;0 to 5;6. Thus, the between-subjects variable, age, had three levels. A between-subjects variable necessarily implies that different levels contain different groups of subjects. Voice and sentence type constituted within-subjects variables: all combinations of levels of these variables were presented to each subject. Strohner and Nelson investigated the effects of active and passive voice, yielding two levels of voice, and the effects of probable, improbable, and reversible sentences, yielding three levels of the variable termed "sentence type." Two tokens of each construction were included, for a total of 12 sentences. Thus, all 12 sentences were presented to each subject. Table 14.1 shows the layout of the design of Strohner and Nelson's study. It is often convenient to use columns to represent levels or combinations of levels of the within-subjects factor(s) and rows to represent levels or combinations of levels of the between-subjects factor(s). As illustrated in table 14.1,

Table 14.1
Strohner and Nelson's (1974) study of the effects of age, voice, and sentence type on children's interpretation of sentences. (*Pro* = probable, *Impr* = improbable, *Rev* = reversible)

| Between-subjects factor | Levels of two within-subjects factors | | | | | |
| | Active | | | Passive | | |
Age groups	Pro	Impr	Rev	Pro	Impr	Rev
1. 3;1–3;7						
2. 4;1–4;6						
3. 5;0–5;6						

Strohner and Nelson's study combines a between-subjects factor and two within-subjects factors. Thus, it is an example of a mixed design.

When age is the independent variable and performance differences between age groups are expected to reflect developmental changes, a between-subjects design may also be called a *cross-sectional design* and a within-subjects design may also be called a *longitudinal design.* A cross-sectional design may be used to compare the performance of different children from various age groups observed at one time point; a longitudinal design compares the performance of the same children at several time points. In these designs, the performance measure is the dependent variable, and age is the independent variable. Strohner and Nelson's study illustrated in table 14.1 is an example of a cross-sectional design involving three age groups. In a longitudinal design, age would be described as a within-subjects variable because different levels of age occur within (rather than across) subjects.

Distinctions among research designs that are based on the number of within- and between-subjects factors have implications concerning research questions that can be addressed, data analysis models, methods of controlling effects of nuisance variables, and validity of causal inferences. Some of these implications will be discussed in the context of each of these major categories of experimental designs.

14.3   Between-Subjects Designs

Part of a study by Hsu et al. (1991) may be used to illustrate some characteristics of between-subjects designs. One aspect of this study examined the effects of children's ages on their interpretations of pronominal sentences. Restricted backward pronominal sentences such as *The zebra tells him that the deer will jump over the fence* were presented to children in an enactment task. The animals that the children selected as antecedents of the pronoun, *him*, were classified as either manifestations of external reference (i.e., animals not mentioned in the sentence) or internal coreference (i.e., either *the zebra* or *the deer* was selected). As illustrated in table 14.2, the independent between-subjects variable was age, which had five levels, and the dependent variable was the number of external reference responses on restricted backward pronominal sentences. One hypothesis examined within the context of this design was that the number of external reference responses would increase with age. This hypothesis was supported. (Note that the study did include other types of pronominal

Table 14.2
A between-subjects design with one independent variable, age, and one dependent variable, number of external reference responses on restricted backward pronominal sentences

Between-subjects variable: age groups	Dependent variable: number of external reference responses on restricted backward pronominal sentences
1. 3;0–3;11	
2. 4;0–4;11	
3. 5;0–5;11	
4. 6;0–6;11	
5. 7;0–8;0	

sentences, and it was also observed that the patterns of pronominal interpretation across the types varied among children from the different age groups.)

14.3.1   Using Response Patterns to Define Independent Variables in Between-Subjects Designs

Cross-sectional studies in which age is the independent variable illustrate one type of between-subjects design. Another type that has been found useful in research on the acquisition of syntactic knowledge uses theoretically meaningful response patterns as levels of the independent variable. Group statistics sometimes hide important information regarding the response patterns of individual children. For example, in Hsu et al.'s (1991) cross-sectional study illustrated in table 14.2, the average number of external responses for each age group masked the fact that some children manifested all external responses, others none, and still others a combination of external and internal responses. In Strohner and Nelson's (1974) study, averages for the active and passive sentences provide no information on how individual children performed on both types. Some children may have manifested correct responses on both, others incorrect responses on both, and still others correct responses on one but not the other. However, defining levels of independent variables in between-subjects designs in terms of meaningful response patterns and relating them to some dependent variable can provide information regarding the nature of individual children's grammatical systems.

A response pattern can be viewed as a category defined in terms of performance on two or more variables. In the simplest case, the variables could be dichotomous. For example, each variable might be the performance (correct, incorrect) of children on a certain sentence type. Given two types of sentences, four response patterns might be defined: correct on both, incorrect on both, correct on the first and incorrect on the second, and incorrect on the first and correct on the second. Alternatively, the last two patterns could be combined into one, namely, one correct response. Categories other than correct versus incorrect may also be used. A priori criteria of theoretical meaningfulness or practical usefulness can guide the definition of the patterns. Once the patterns have been defined, they may then be used to define levels of the independent variable. This approach is illustrated in a study conducted by Hsu, Cairns, and Fiengo (1985) in which they developed a set of categories termed "grammar types" that classified children on the basis of their interpretation of a set of sentences. The categories were defined in terms of the particular characters (i.e., the subject or object noun phrase) in the main clause that were selected to carry out actions specified in a dependent clause. The classification system revealed that individual children were consistent in the types of responses they manifested across a number of sentence types, a fact that was not evident in the averages reported for each sentence. The classification system also revealed some types of patterns that could not be identified on the basis of the averages alone.

The prediction that the grammar types represented a developmental sequence was examined in a between-subjects design in which the category "grammar type" was the independent variable and age, the dependent variable. (See Hsu, et al. 1989 for a follow-up study that employed a similar design.) As illustrated in table 14.3, this is a single-factor between-subjects design. It is similar to the between-subjects design illustrated in table 14.2 except that subjects are grouped according to grammar type rather than age. Furthermore, age is now used as a dependent, metric variable (rather than a categorical variable). (Recall that section 14.2 defines "metric" as an interval or ratio scale.)

It is important to note that although the categories, grammar types, are defined in terms of response patterns across sentence types, this is not a within-subjects design. The categories are a between-subjects variable that is defined in terms of patterns of performance across a set of sentences. The hypothesis that the grammar types represent a developmental progression resulted in the prediction (which was confirmed) that (1) there

Table 14.3

A between-subjects design with one independent variable, grammar type, and one dependent variable, age

Independent between-subjects-variable: grammar types	Dependent variable: age
1. Grammar type 1	
2. Grammar type 2	
3. Grammar type 3	
4. Grammar type 4	
5. Grammar type 5	

would be a significant difference in the ages of the children classified according to grammar type and (2) there would be a specific ordering of the age means. The developmental hypothesis could also be investigated by determining whether children classified in the various categories manifested differences on other developmental measures such as MLU and developmental sentence scoring (DSS) scores. (See Lee 1974 and Hughes, Fey, and Long 1992, for a discussion of DSS scores, and see Hsu, Cairns, and Fiengo 1985, for an example of how DSS scores confirmed the hypothesis regarding the developmental progression of grammar types.)

Questions addressing explanatory issues may also be investigated using classification systems based on individual response patterns. Studies of this type examine the relationship between the response patterns and one or more dependent variables that provide information about the child's knowledge system. One type of explanatory question concerns the nature of the knowledge system that underlies the response profile. The design described in table 14.3 may be used to examine this type of question. For example, Hsu, Cairns, and Fiengo (1985) examined the nature of the grammatical systems characterizing the "grammar types" by examining the effect of a semantic bias on children's acceptability judgments. They argued that resistance to a semantic bias would provide evidence that children have assigned a structural analysis to the sentences; susceptibility to such a bias would provide evidence that interpretations were based on the operation of a strategy. Their study followed the structure outlined in table 14.3 except that the dependent variable was the number of "silly" judgments on semantically biased sentences. Confirmation of predictions regarding group differences in the number of "silly" judgments supported the structural account.

Hsu et al. (1989) also employed the design illustrated in table 14.3. Using an enactment task, they demonstrated that a relationship exists between children's interpretation of sentences involving control and those involving forward coreference. The "grammar types," which were based on children's interpretation of a set of sentences involving control, were used as the independent variable. However, in this study the dependent variable was the number of subject coreference responses on forward pronominal sentences such as *The lion kissed the tiger after he jumped over the fence.* That is, the dependent variable was the number of responses in which the main clause subject noun phrase, *the lion*, was selected as the antecedent of the pronoun, *he*.

14.3.2 Limitations of Designs with Nonmanipulable Independent Variables

In some studies the independent variable can be manipulated in the sense that subjects can be randomly assigned to its levels. Such studies are generally described as pure or true experiments. In developmental studies, subjects cannot be randomly assigned to levels of variables such as age, MLU, DSS scores, IQ, and gender. Furthermore, categories such as grammar types cannot be assigned to subjects. These variables are all inherent characteristics of the subjects. The major advantage of random assignment of subjects to levels of the independent variable is that it virtually ensures (provided samples are reasonably large (Hsu 1989)) that groups assigned to different levels will not differ in any practically important ways on variables such as socioeconomic level, age, gender, racial composition, and MLU. Note that random assignment does not eliminate effects of nuisance variables. That is, the nuisance variables will still influence the dependent variable for each individual. However, by equating groups with respect to these variables, randomization tends to rule out the possibility that differences (or lack of differences) in group statistics computed on the dependent variable were caused by group differences on the nuisance variables.

The researcher need not even have measures of nuisance variables and need not even know of their existence or importance in order to achieve equivalence of groups with random assignment. Equivalence of groups on preexisting variables is important in ruling out possible biasing effect of these variables on estimates of effects of the independent variable on the dependent variable. In this context the expression "biasing effects" means overestimation or underestimation of effects of the independent variable on the dependent variable. In studies with nonmanipulable variables, it is possible that obtained differences (or the absence of differences) may be attributable to initial preexisting differences in gender composition, age, socioeconomic level, and so on, of the groups rather than to effects of the independent variable on the dependent variable. Darlington (1990) provides a thoughtful discussion of advantages and limitations of random assignment. Additional methods for controlling the effects of nuisance variables are discussed in sections 14.5.4 and 14.6.2.1.

14.3.3   Data Analysis Issues

Data analysis issues in research designs differ in terms of their generality. Certain issues are relevant to all experimental designs; others are relevant only to some designs. In this section we focus on some of the more general issues as well as some issues that are relevant specifically to between-subjects designs. Four general data analysis issues are the choice between descriptive and inferential methods, the choice among methods of controlling risks of drawing incorrect inferences, the choice between parametric and nonparametric models, and the choice among methods of increasing statistical power.

14.3.3.1   Descriptive versus Inferential Data Analysis Methods   Descriptive, and especially graphical, methods of data analysis have been used instead of inferential methods primarily in single-subject designs or designs involving a very small number of subjects. Kazdin (1982) summarizes some of the major drawbacks of the exclusive use of descriptive methods. First, such methods lack specific decision rules for the identifying reliable effects. Second, these methods tend to encourage subjective and inconsistent evaluation of effects. Third, many factors contribute to judgments about the data, and the manner in which these factors are integrated in making a decision is unclear. Fourth, dramatic effects are generally needed for consistency of interpretation across judges. Although the exclusive use of descriptive methods is generally not recommended, their use in conjunction with hypothesis testing (one type of inferential method) is at times extremely helpful. This is particularly the case in studies that focus on interaction effects (see section 14.5).

Hypothesis testing is one way of drawing statistical inferences. The logic of hypothesis testing can be illustrated in the context of a hypothetical two-independent-groups design concerned with whether there is a difference in complexity of language (as measured by MLU) among very young children who have been classified as either "referential" (i.e., children whose early lexicons are dominated by nominals) or "expressive" (i.e., children whose early lexicons contain fewer object words but more pronouns and functions words than observed in the lexicons of referential speakers). (Note that the expectation that there might be a difference could be based on Nelson's (1973) observation that children manifesting the expressive style exhibited a more gradual transition into combinatorial utterances than those manifesting the referential style.) With respect to our hypothetical investigation, it is assumed that the object of such a study is not limited to describing the observed data but that the researcher is primarily interested in drawing inferences about the differences in the MLUs of referential and expressive children in the general population of 2-year-olds. The researcher's hypothesis might be that the mean MLU of referential children will be greater than that of expressive children.

More generally, it is characteristics of the populations, such as means, variances, overlap of distributions, and effect sizes (standardized differences between population means), that are primarily of interest. These characteristics are called *parameters*. Corresponding characteristics (means, variances, etc.) of the observed samples are called *statistics*. The problem is one of drawing inferences about the unobserved parameters of interest from knowledge of the observed statistics. If the samples included in the study can be viewed as random samples from the populations of interest, then it is possible to develop reasonable rules for drawing these inferences. Investigators are primarily interested in whether the data support their research hypotheses. In the example regarding the MLUs of referential and expressive children, the investigator is interested in whether any obtained sample mean difference reflects a difference in the population means. Hypothesis testing addresses this question in an indirect way, by determining whether the difference between the sample means can (or cannot) reasonably be attributed to random sampling from populations with identical means. If it can, then the hypothesis of equality of population means (generally called the *null hypothesis*) cannot be ruled out, and one cannot safely conclude that the population means differ. That is, one cannot safely reject the null hypothesis. On the other hand, if the difference between the sample means is "exceptionally large," where "exceptionally large" has been defined so that if the null hypothesis is true, differences of that size have a very small probability of occurrence, then one may feel reasonably sure that the null hypothesis is not true and therefore that the population means differ. In that case the null hypothesis is rejected, and the alternative to this hypothesis (viz., that the population means differ) is accepted. The results would be considered to support the *research hypothesis*. The probability that the null hypothesis will be rejected when it is in fact true is called the *significance level* of the test. The rejection of a true null hypothesis is called a *type I error*. Thus, the significance level can also be described as the *risk* of a type I error. As implied above, this risk is related to an a priori definition of what is to be viewed as an "exceptionally large" difference between sample means. Conventionally acceptable risks of type I errors are .05, .01, and .001. If the null hypothesis is rejected when population means do differ, then a correct decision has been made. The probability that such a decision will be made is called the *power* of the test.

The most popular test of the difference between means of two independent samples is called the *pooled variance t test*. In the case of this test, hypothesis testing involves comparing a model that restricts the means of the two populations that the groups come from to the same value, with another model that does not make this restriction. The restriction implies that the former model is simpler than the latter, in the sense that it involves fewer parameters. There is only one population mean to be estimated in the former model, whereas there are two in the latter. The statistical null hypothesis for the pooled variance *t* test usually states that the two population means are equal. In other words, this hypothesis coincides with the restriction that differentiates the two models. The statistical alternative hypothesis is, in effect, a statement that two mean parameters are needed to account for the data, rather than one. In most applications of the pooled variance *t* test, the researcher's prediction (substantive hypothesis, expectation, hope, belief) is associated with the alternative statistical hypothesis and therefore with the more complex model. That is, the researcher generally believes (expects, predicts, hopes) that two (rather than one) population means are needed to account for the data. This is the case in the above example regarding predicted differences in MLUs of very young referential and expressive children. Rejection of the null hypothesis indicates that the more complex model has significantly greater explanatory power than the simpler model. Failure to reject the null hypothesis indicates that there is no scientifically acceptable evidence that the more complex model has more explanatory power.

Hypothesis testing can generally be considered to involve comparison of a more complex model with a simpler model (Maxwell and Delaney 1990), and it is restrictions on parameters of the more complex model (e.g., the restriction that the two population means be equal in the case of the pooled variance t test) that define the simpler model, differentiate the two models, and define the null hypothesis. In many traditional applications of hypothesis testing, the researcher's substantive hypothesis (expectation) is associated with the more complex (unrestricted) model. But it should be noted that there are circumstances in which the researcher's expectation (prediction, substantive hypothesis, hope, belief) is associated with the less complex of the two models that are compared in the hypothesis test. This frequently occurs in branches of statistics called path analysis and structural equation modeling. It also occurs in more traditional types of statistical analyses such as when a researcher expects that relatively simple analysis-of-covariance models (see sections 14.3.3.4 and 14.5.4 for more information on these models) will satisfactorily account for the data, rather than more complex models that allow for interaction of covariates with independent variables. There are also instances in which researchers include effects of nuisance variables in analysis-of-variance models but do not expect these effects to be significant (e.g., see the discussion in section 5.4 of Lust and Clifford 1986; Cairns et al. 1994; Cairns et al. 1995). Identification of a researcher's substantive hypothesis with the null hypothesis (simpler model) also occurs when researchers use the somewhat controversial strategy of "model trimming." Model trimming usually involves hypothesis testing following data-suggested modification of models (see Cairns et al. 1994 and Cairns et al. 1995, for an illustration, and Myers and Well 1991, for information about conditions under which model trimming is justified).

14.3.3.2   Testing Contrasts and Controlling Type I Error Rates   The hypothetical example regarding expected differences in the MLUs of referential and expressive children illustrates a study involving two independent groups. This type of study is a special case of the single-factor between-subjects design illustrated in tables 14.2 and 14.3 that involve two or more independent groups of subjects. In the two-group case, predictions regarding expected mean differences in performance of the groups on a response measure are most often evaluated with a conventional pooled variance t test.

In single-factor between-subjects designs involving three or more groups, predictions regarding expected differences in performance on the response measure are most often evaluated with *omnibus analysis-of-variance F tests* followed by tests of contrasts of means. The *omnibus F test* is a test of the null hypothesis that all population means are equal. Tests of contrast of means are tests of hypotheses that the difference between the means of two subsets of population means has some fixed value (usually zero). When each subset includes only one mean, the test of the contrast is simply a test of a hypothesis about the value of the difference between two population means.

This type of analysis is illustrated in Hsu, Cairns, and Fiengo's (1985) evaluation of the predictions regarding the relationship between the five grammar types and age or DSS scores. It is also illustrated in Hsu et al.'s (1989) evaluation of the relationship between grammar types and the number of subject responses on forward pronominal sentences and Hsu et al.'s (1991) analysis of the relationship between age and the number of external responses on restricted backward pronominal sentences. For example, Hsu et al. (1991) reported that children classified according to five age groups differed significantly with respect to the number of external responses on restricted backward pronominal sentences. The omnibus F test led to rejection of the null hypothesis that all population means were equal; thus, the mean response measure is not constant across populations from which the age groups included in the study are considered to be random samples. However, this F ratio does not provide any information about which pairs of population means differ. For example, do children from age groups 1 and 2 differ significantly with respect to number of external responses or do children from age groups 2 and 3, 2 and 4, or 2 and 5, and so on, differ significantly with respect to the number of external responses? Questions of this type, described as questions about *pairwise contrasts* of means, can be addressed with tests of statistical significance of these contrasts. The null hypothesis usually states that a difference between two population means is zero. Rejection of the null hypothesis indicates that the population means differ. Most often, researchers are interested in a "family" of contrast hypotheses (e.g., all pairwise contrasts). In general, the more tests that are included in a family, the larger the risk that at least one type I error will occur if each test of significance is carried out at one of the conventional significance levels. Thus, it is desirable to control the risk of at least one type I error when there are many contrasts in the "family."

In addition to the number of tests in a family of tests that are of interest to the researcher, and the significance level per test, factors that influence the choice of method of controlling type I errors include whether the tests were planned (a priori) or not (post mortem, a posteriori, post hoc), whether the family of tests consists exclusively of pairwise contrast tests or includes all possible contrasts, and whether the tests are independent or not. Some of the most popular methods of controlling the risk of at least one type I error, in families of tests, include the Bonferroni *t* tests, Tukey's HSD tests, Scheffe's *F* tests, and Dunnett's test (see Kirk 1982; Myers and Well 1991).

14.3.3.3   Parametric versus Nonparametric Analysis-of-Variance Models for a Design with One Between-Subjects Factor   All of the tests described in section 14.3.3.2 are examples of what are called *parametric* tests. Hypothesis tests that are based on fewer and/or less restrictive assumptions than those of parametric tests are generally called *nonparametric* tests. In spite of their more restrictive assumptions, parametric tests are more popular than nonparametric tests. Four reasons for their popularity are that (1) parametric analysis-of-variance models are more flexible in the sense that they have been derived for a greater variety of experimental designs and can be used to address a greater variety of questions than their nonparametric analogues, (2) when the assumptions of parametric models are tenable, the parametric models are usually more powerful than their nonparametric analogues (i.e., effects of the independent variable(s) on the dependent variable(s) are more likely to be detected with these parametric models than with their nonparametric analogues), (3) parametric tests are better known than nonparametric tests, and (4) more statistical software is available for parametric than for nonparametric models. Excellent texts concerned primarily with parametric analysis-of-variance models and related designs include Myers and Well 1991 and Kirk 1982. Excellent nonparametric analysis texts include Marascuilo and McSweeney 1977 and Lehmann 1975.

Nominal, ordinal, and dichotomous response measures are often encountered in linguistic research. Several nonparametric alternatives to parametric tests are available to test hypotheses about these response measures. Some popular tests are chi-square tests of independence and homogeneity, binomial tests, probit analysis, logistic regression, and log-linear models. Only two nonparametric tests that have applications in research on the acquisition of syntactic knowledge will be described and illustrated here: the chi-square tests of independence and the binomial tests. These were selected because of their popularity and simplicity. Their simplicity allows a closer examination of the logic of hypothesis testing.

Chi-Square Test of Independence   In general, the chi-square test of independence is used to determine whether or not two or more categorical variables are related. In the case of two categorical variables, evidence that they are related consists of evidence that they are not "independent." Therefore, explanation of the concept of "independence" implies the type of relation among variables that this test is meant to detect. Note that the logic of the chi-square test is similar to that of the *t* test (discussed above) in the sense that support for the researcher's usual prediction (dependence, difference between means) consists of evidence against acceptability of the simpler (null hypothesis) model (independence, no difference between means).

Consider what might be meant by the statement that the appearance of two-word combinations is unrelated to, or independent of, achievement of Piaget's final stage of sensorimotor development. A reasonable interpretation would be that attainment of the final stage of sensorimotor development does not increase the probability of appearance of two-word combinations. If this were the case, then it might be expected that the proportion of children who manifest two-word combinations should be the same among those who have attained the final stage of sensorimotor development as among those who have not yet attained that stage. This proportion would then have to equal the proportion of all children who manifest two-word combinations. Now suppose that we draw a random sample of 1000 children from some population that is of interest to the researcher and classify them as illustrated in table 14.4. The above discussion implies that if the classification variables are independent (unrelated), then $(100/1000)(200) = 20$ final-stage children, and $(100/1000)(800) = 80$ below-final-stage children, would be expected to manifest two-word

Table 14.4
Two-word combinations and attainment of the final stage of sensorimotor development: marginal frequencies of a contingency table for a chi-square test of independence

Final stage attained		Two-word combinations		
		Absent	Present	Total
Yes				200
No				800
	Total	900	100	1000

combinations. Since the number of final-stage children is 200, then $(200 - 20) = 180$ of them would be expected not to manifest two-word combinations. Similarly, $(800 - 80) = 720$ of the below-final-stage children would be expected not to manifest two-word combinations. Note how the expected number of children in any cell of the 2×2 table (table 14.4) can be viewed as the product of the marginal relative frequencies, multiplied by the total number of children in the table, if the two classification variables are independent. The chi-square test of independence involves a comparison of the frequencies actually observed in the four cells of tables of this type with the frequencies expected under the hypothesis of independence. This size of the chi-square statistic computed from this information will increase with an increase in the discrepancies between these observed and expected frequencies. Clearly, if a much larger proportion of final-stage children than of below-final-stage children manifest two-word combinations (and chi-square is therefore very large), then the independence (unrelated) hypothesis would be considered untenable.

Table 14.4 illustrates the cross-classification of data on two categorical variables, each of which has two levels (present-absent; yes-no). This type of table is called a 2×2 contingency table. More generally, contingency tables can be constructed for more than two categorical variables, and each of these variables can have two or more levels. The concept of independence, introduced above, generalizes to any contingency table. For example, given three categorical variables, with $i = 1, 2, \ldots, r$ levels of the first variable, $j = 1, 2, \ldots, c$ levels of the second variable, and $k = 1, 2, \ldots, m$ levels of the third variable, the expected number of cases in cell (i, j, k), given independence, would be the product of the marginal relative frequencies corresponding to this cell, times the sample size.

Applications of the chi-square test of independence to a 3×3 contingency table may be illustrated using McDaniel and Maxfield's (1992b) study. As illustrated in table 14.5, their study included a 3×3 contingency table that cross-classified 35 children in terms of their knowledge of Principles B and C. The Pearson chi-square statistic calculated for this table suggests that knowledge of Principle B is related to knowledge of Principle C (chi-square $= 15.55$, $p < .004$). The expression $p < .004$ means that if the null hypothesis of independence were true, the probability of obtaining a chi-square statistic of 15.55 or more would be less than .004. It is called the p-level, or p-value, of the test. However, it should be noted that obtained p-values of the Pearson chi-square test are suspect when a large number of cells of the contingency table have small expected

Table 14.5
A 3 × 3 contingency table cross-classifying children according to responses indicating knowledge of Principle B and knowledge of Principle C violations on two sentences. ("+" = presence of knowledge; "−" = absence of knowledge; *Mixed* = partial knowledge)

Knowledge of Principle B	Responses indicating knowledge of Principle C violations on two sentences		
	Reject both	Reject one	Accept both
+B	16	1	0
Mixed B	3	4	0
−B	6	2	3

frequencies. This was the case for table 14.5. Good statistical software packages (such as SYSTAT) detect problems of this type and provide warnings to the user.

Binomial Test   A binomial experiment may be defined as an experiment consisting of N trials, each of which has two outcomes. In general, one of these two outcomes can be called a "success" and the other a "failure" (where these terms need not have their usual connotations). For example, the N trials might be five tosses of a die. A success could be defined as an ace (one point shows up), and a failure could be defined as a non-ace (more than one point shows up). The number of successes that occur in the N trials is described as the binomial random variable X. In the die-tossing experiment this variable could take on values $X = 0$, $X = 1$, $X = 2$, $X = 3$, $X = 4$, and $X = 5$. If the probability of obtaining a success is the same across trials (call this constant probability Pi), and if the outcomes of the trials are independent, then it can be shown that the probability, $P(X = x)$, that the binomial variable will take on the value $X = x$ (where x designates a specific numerical value of this variable) will be

$$P(X = x) = N!/[x!(N - x)!]Pi^x[1 - Pi]^{(N-x)},$$

where $N! = N(N - 1)(N - 2) \ldots (3)(2)(1)$, $x!$ and $(N - x)!$ are similarly defined, and where $0! = 1$ (by definition).

For example, in the die-tossing illustration, if $Pi = 1/6 = .17$ (given a perfectly symmetrical and balanced six-sided die), the probability of obtaining 4 successes (4 aces) in the five-toss experiment would be

$P(X = 4) = 5!/[4!(5 - 1)!](.17)^4(1 - .17)^1$

$$= .0035.$$

Similarly, the $P(X = 5)$ can be shown to be .0001.

As an illustration, consider an enactment task that is used to determine children's knowledge of some aspect of grammar. In such a task, children are often presented with several choices of response, only one of which suggests that they have this knowledge. For example, consider a study involving an enactment task in which it is of interest to determine which animal children select to carry out the action specified in a subordinate clause. Imagine further that a particular child is asked to select one from a set of six animals. Suppose that the child is presented with five trials, each of which involves a choice among six possible responses (six animals), and that all five trials are designed to provide information about the same aspect of grammar. The child's "score" can be defined as the number of trials on which she gave the correct response (i.e., the number of correct animals selected). It is desirable to determine whether the score the child obtained is sufficiently high to conclude (beyond a reasonable doubt) that the child knows the aspect of syntax under study.

If the child did not have the knowledge and was guessing on each trial, it might be reasonable to assume that she would have a probability of $1/6 = .17$ of obtaining the correct response (correct animal) on any given trial. It might also be reasonable to assume that this child's responses are independent from trial to trial: that is, the probability of a correct response on any given trial is not affected by outcomes of the other trials. Given these assumptions, this child's score could be viewed as a binomial random variable, for an $N = 5$ trial binomial experiment with $Pi = .17$. Therefore, the probability that this child would obtain a score of at least 4 correct responses would be (as in the die-tossing experiment) .0035 + .0001 = .0036. In other words, if a child lacks knowledge of the aspect of grammar under study and is merely guessing, that child would have an extremely small chance of obtaining a score of 4 or more correct responses. On the basis of this information the researcher might feel reasonably confident that children who obtain scores of at least 4 are not responding at random and presumably have knowledge of that aspect of syntax. Note that if there were four animals to choose from, in response to each of the five sentences, the logic described above implies that a child would have a probability of .0156 of picking at least four correct animals, if this child was responding at random. If there were only two animals per trial and five trials, the child would have a probability of .1875 of getting at least 4 correct responses.

Stromswold's (1995b) investigation of children's acquisition of subject and object *wh*-questions illustrates another application of the binomial test. She reports that, in a sample of 12 children, (1) 8 acquired *what* object questions before *what* subject questions, (2) 4 acquired *what* object and subject questions at the same time, and (3) no children began asking *what* subject questions before they began asking *what* object questions. If "success" is defined as the acquisition of *what* object questions prior to or at the same time as *what* subject questions and "failure" is defined as the acquisition of *what* subject questions prior to *what* object questions, and if the null hypothesis states that the probabilities of success and failure are equal, then the probability of observing 12 successes and 0 failures under the null hypothesis is < .01. On the basis of this result, the binomial test was interpreted as indicating that *what* object questions are acquired before or at the same time as, rather than after, *what* subject questions. This version of the binomial test is sometimes called the *sign test*.

The chi-square test of independence and the binomial test are two of the oldest and most popular statistical tests. In the case of chi-square tests of independence for tables larger than 2×2, researchers are generally interested in asking more focused questions than questions about presence of absence of independence in the entire table. Excellent sources on this topic include Marascuilo and McSweeney 1977 and Bishop, Fienberg, and Holland 1975.

14.3.3.4 Methods of Increasing the Statistical Power of Tests of Significance

The final general issue regarding data analysis in between-subjects designs concerns the statistical power of tests of hypotheses. Recall that power refers to the probability that the test will lead to rejection of the null hypothesis when the alternative (to the null) hypothesis is true. Assuming that the researcher's hypothesis is identified with the statistical alternative hypothesis, the power of the test is the probability that the researcher's prediction will be confirmed if this alternative is true. Several factors influence this probability. One factor is the choice of statistical test. A researcher could choose between parametric and nonparametric tests as well as among each type of test to test hypotheses about differences in locations or other characteristics of distributions of scores. In general, as noted above, parametric tests are more powerful than nonparametric tests provided the assumptions of the parametric tests are tenable. For example, in pre- and posttest designs, in which response measures are obtained before as well as after administration of the levels of the between-subjects independent variable, some of the major choices among parametric statistical tests of effects of this independent variable include (1) analysis of variance of postscores, (2) analysis of variance of gain or change scores, and (3) analysis of covariance of postscores, partialing out effects of prescores (see Cook and Campbell 1979, for a nice introduction to analysis of covariance). The powers of the tests associated with (1), (2), and (3) can vary greatly. However, it should be noted that the hypotheses tested and therefore the substantive questions addressed depend on the choice of (1), (2), or (3), even though all of these hypotheses are concerned with effects of this independent variable on means. More specifically, the null hypotheses are respectively that (1) the mean of postscores is identical across levels of this independent variable, (2) means of pre- and postscore differences are equal across levels of the independent variable, and (3) postscore means corresponding to any fixed prescore are identical across levels of the between-subjects independent variable. A second factor that affects statistical power is the number of subjects included in the study. In general, the larger the total sample size, the greater the power (other things being equal). The third factor is the degree of imbalance of the design. For any fixed total sample size, maximum power for omnibus hypotheses tests occurs with equal numbers of subjects assigned to levels or combinations of levels of the independent variable(s). The fourth factor is actual degree of separation of population means. Measures of separation of population means are examples of *effect size* parameters. The larger the separation of these means (the larger the effect sizes), the greater will be the power of tests of hypotheses about means. Reliability and sensitivity of the response measures are also factors. Unreliability of response measures adds to the residual or error variance in a design. Such increases in error variance generally lead to decreases in statistical power. Unreliability can also have other harmful effects, especially in analyses of covariance. In addition, some response measures may be sensitive to effects of the independent variable(s), whereas others may not. Finally, lack of uniformity of conditions under which independent variables are administered adds to the residual variance and therefore generally reduces power.

14.4   Within-Subjects Designs: Repeated Measure Designs

14.4.1   Nominal versus Metric Independent Variables

Now let us turn to within-subjects designs. Imagine a hypothetical study investigating the effects of two play contexts (e.g., role playing without objects vs. play involving the manipulation of objects) on the complexity of children's language, and consider that each child will be exposed to both contexts. In this study, complexity is measured by the MLU of a spontaneous language sample taken while the children are participating in each of the play contexts. The study would involve comparing the MLU scores across contexts to determine if the two play contexts had different effects. This type of study involves multiple measurements on the same subjects and for this reason is called a *within-subjects* or *repeated measures design*. In this example, there are only two levels of one within-subjects independent variable. More generally, within-subjects designs may include several independent variables, each of which can have two or more levels. The repeated measures of these designs are commensurable, which means that they are expressed in comparable units. From the perspective of types of questions addressed and relevant statistical tests, it is convenient to distinguish two categories of repeated measures designs in terms of whether or not the within-subjects factors are metric variables (see section 14.2).

Category 1. In category 1 designs, the within-subjects factor is measured on less than an interval scale. Several examples are given to illustrate the types of questions the design can be used to address. The first is the hypothetical study on the effect of play context described above. The within-subjects factor, play context, has two levels that are levels of a nominal variable. The MLU measures are commensurable dependent variables. In this example, the question of interest is whether the two play contexts have different effects on MLU.

The second example, a study by Grodzinsky and Kave (1993/1994), illustrates a design involving three levels of a within-subjects factor. This study, which investigated children's knowledge of Principle A in Hebrew, presented the same sentence in three different picture contexts: a picture that matched the meaning, and two mismatching conditions in which two types of incorrect meanings were depicted. A truth-value task was used, and the dependent variable involved the number of the children's "yes" decisions, indicating that the sentence correctly described the pictures. Knowledge of Principle A was revealed by "yes" responses to the "match-

Table 14.6
Grodzinsky and Kave's (1993/1994) study illustrating a repeated measures design with one within-subjects variable, picture context

	Levels of the within-subjects variable		
Subjects	Match	Mismatch type 1	Mismatch type 2
1			
2			
3			
.			
.			
.			
k			

ing" condition. The layout of this example is illustrated in table 14.6. The research question focused on whether there would be differences in the number of "yes" responses across the three conditions. The results indicated that young Hebrew-speaking children know Principle A.

Each age group in Strohner and Nelson's (1974) study (see table 14.1) illustrates a third type of category 1 design. Recall that these researchers manipulated two within-subjects variables called voice (i.e., actives and passives) and type (i.e., probable, improbable, and reversible). The purpose of this study was to investigate the effects of manipulating these characteristics of sentences on children's act-out performance. This example differs from the two just discussed in that the research question was investigated by manipulating construction types rather than the nonlinguistic context.

Category 2. In category 2 designs the within-subjects factor is measured on an interval or ratio scale. The most popular version of this design in research on the acquisition of syntactic knowledge involves the use of Age or Time as a within-subjects factor and a single response or performance measure as the repeatedly observed dependent variable. Repeated administration of a set of sentences to one group of subjects for the purpose of determining how their responses to these sentences change over time illustrates a category 2 design. If the intervening period is relatively short (i.e., one or two days), and if real changes in syntactic knowledge are not expected to occur in such a short interval, then the study would be concerned with test-retest reliability. As noted in section 14.3, when the time span covers a range in which developmental changes are expected to occur, this kind of repeated measures design is called a *longitudinal design*. Changes in the within-subjects scores over time provide information about rates of development, growth, maturation, changes in classifications, and so on.

14.4.2 Some Data Analysis Issues in Repeated Measures Designs

Both parametric and nonparametric analysis-of-variance models may be used to test hypotheses in single-factor repeated measures designs. In these designs, there is no between-subjects factor, and each subject in a single group is measured at each level of the within-subjects factor. Most often, the researcher predicts or expects differences in means of the response measure at different levels of the within-subjects factor in both categories of designs. Consider the first example, which predicted that the MLUs of language samples from children exposed to the different play contexts would differ. *Correlated t-tests* (*t* tests applicable to within-subjects designs) might be used to determine if the obtained difference is significant. When there are more than two levels of the within-subjects factor, omnibus parametric *F* tests can be used to address the researcher's predictions regarding expected differences by assessing the tenability of the null hypothesis of equality of the means associated with all levels of the independent variable. *F* tests of contrasts between means are usually of interest in both category 1 and category 2 designs. Methods of controlling type I errors in these designs are discussed in Kirk 1982.

Category 2 designs may also be used to estimate and test hypotheses about functional relations of response measures to the within-subjects factor. For example, when the within-subjects factor is age of subjects, *F* tests can be used to determine if there is evidence of significant linear (i.e., performance improves at a constant rate with age), quadratic (the growth rate changes in one direction with time), cubic (the growth rate changes in one direction, and then in the other, with the passage of time), and so forth, components to the developmental trend observed in the group. Both univariate and multivariate parametric models may be used to test hypotheses in repeated measures designs. In general, the multivariate tests are based on fewer or less restrictive assumptions than the corresponding univariate tests.

As was the case with between-subjects designs, nonparametric analogues are available for most parametric models. An important criterion for choosing between parametric and nonparametric tests in repeated measures designs is the level of measurement of the response scales. With dichotomous or ordinal measurements, nonparametric omnibus, contrast, and trend tests are generally preferable to parametric tests. For example, Friedman's nonparametric chi-square test may be used to test the omnibus null hypothesis of a single within-subjects factor design when the response measure has ordinal scale properties (within subjects). The Wilcoxon Signed Ranks test may be used to test hypotheses about contrasts in this type of design. The Cochran Q test may be used to test omnibus as well as contrast hypotheses in single-factor repeated measures designs when the response measure is dichotomous (e.g., correct, incorrect). Myers and Well (1991) and Lehmann (1975) provide excellent descriptions of these tests. Lehmann (1975) also presents many other nonparametric alternatives to parametric tests. Both parametric and nonparametric models for repeated measures designs differ from parametric and nonparametric models for between-subjects designs insofar as they take into account the lack of independence of measures obtained on the same subject.

14.5 Multifactor Designs

14.5.1 Terminology
As noted above, studies may involve more than one independent variable. There may be two or more within-subjects factors, and/or two or more between-subjects factors. Each factor (independent variable) may in turn have two or more levels. Designs that have two or more factors are called *factorial designs*. The design is sometimes described in terms of numbers of levels of its factors. For example, a $2 \times 4 \times 5$ design would be a three-factor factorial design with two levels for the first factor, four for the second, and five for the third. Experimental designs can also be described in terms of the number of within- and between-subjects factors. For example, an experimental design may be described as a 3-within- and 1-between-subjects factor design. As noted in section 14.2, an experimental design that has both within- and between-subjects factors can be described as a *mixed design* (Myers and Well 1991). In section 14.2 we also noted that Strohner and Nelson's (1974) study, which has one between-subjects factor and two within-subjects factors, is an example of a mixed design. Recall that there were three levels of the between-subjects factor, Age. There were also two within-subjects factors: Voice, with two levels (active and passive), and Sentence Type, with three levels (probable,

Table 14.7
A mixed design with one between-subjects factor, gender, and one within-subjects factor, screen type

	Levels of the within-subjects factor	
Between-subjects factor: gender	Match	Nonmatch
1. Male		
2. Female		

improbable, and reversible). Thus, Strohner and Nelson's study could be described as a $3 \times 2 \times 3$ factorial design.

A study by Golinkoff et al. (1987) illustrates a simple mixed design. They used the intermodal preferential looking paradigm to investigate young children's comprehension of nouns, verbs, and word order. The first experiment in this study involved only nouns. As illustrated in table 14.7, Golinkoff et al. (1987) used a mixed design with one between-subjects factor, Gender, and one within-subjects factor, Screen Type (i.e., a screen that matched or did not match a noun presented auditorily). Total visual fixation time was the dependent variable. It was predicted that children would look longer at the matching screen than at the non-matching screen. This prediction was confirmed.

14.5.2 Interactions

14.5.2.1 Estimation and Testing of Interaction Effects Single-factor designs address questions about equality or inequality of means of dependent variables at different levels of the single factor. These are called *main effects* questions, and their tests of statistical significance are called *main effects tests*. For example, Hsu et al. (1991) examined the effect of age on the number of external responses to restricted backward pronominal sentences in a single-factor, between-subjects design. The omnibus F test of the "main effects" of age would be a test of the null hypothesis that the dependent variable means are equal across levels of the factor. In two-factor designs, questions about main effects of a factor can be tested, averaging over levels of the second factor, as well as within each level of the second factor. The former types of tests are called *main effects tests* and the latter are called *simple main effects tests*. In Golinkoff et al.'s (1987) study illustrated in table 14.7, one could test the main effects of matching versus nonmatching screen averaging over genders, or one could test the simple main effects hypothesis for matching versus nonmatching screen within each level of gender. If the simple main effects of matching versus nonmatching screen are the same at both levels of gender, then the main effects of screen will coincide with the simple main effects of screen at each level of gender. However, there is no assurance that this will be the case. When it is not the case, *interaction* of the two factors is said to be present. For example, girls might look longer at the matching screen than the nonmatching screen whereas boys might not. This could result in significant overall main effects for screen but a significant simple main effect of screen only for girls. This would be an example of an interaction effect since the effect of screen varies across levels of the second factor, Gender. Figure 14.1 illustrates some possible results that may be obtained in a factorial design such as Golinkoff et al.'s study. Example (1) in figure 14.1 illustrates the case of overall main effects for screen but simple main effects of screen only for girls. Thus, interaction effects are present. Example (2) illustrates the presence of interaction effects in the absence of overall main effects for screen or gender, and example (3) illustrates the presence of a main effect of screen and gender in the absence of any interaction effects. With respect to the part of Golinkoff et al.'s (1987) study that investigated nouns (experiment 1), only a main effect of screen was reported. There were no significant main effects for gender or significant interaction effects in experiment 1.

One major objective of using experimental designs with more than one factor is to obtain information about *interaction effects*. This is the case whether the design includes only within-subjects factors, only between-subjects factors, or a combination of within- and between-subjects factors. For example, in the case of two-factor designs, the simple main effect of one of the two factors (either one) may change across levels of the other, and it may be the detection of this change that is the principal concern of the study. Note that the concept of an interaction effect requires that the dependent variable be measured on a metric scale.

14.5.2.2 Ordinal and Disordinal Interactions Cronbach and Snow (1981) distinguish between *ordinal* and *disordinal interactions*. Disordinal interaction occurs when the simple main effects of one factor change in direction, across levels of the second factor. Thus, in Golinkoff et al.'s (1987) study, if girls looked longer at the matching screen than the nonmatching screen but boys looked longer at the nonmatching screen, then

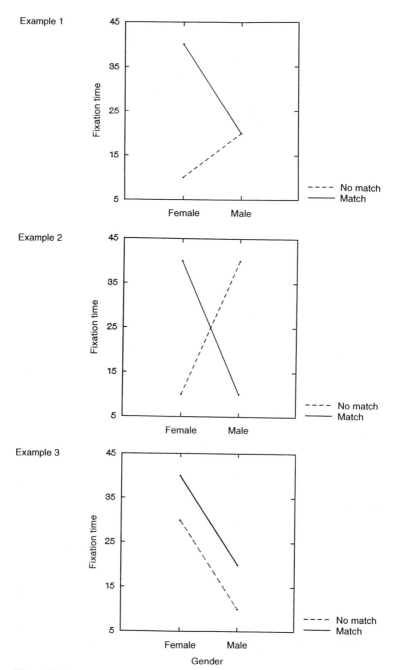

Figure 14.1
Schematic drawings illustrating some possible results that may be obtained from
a two-factor study

the gender by screen interaction would be disordinal. With ordinal interaction, on the other hand, although simple main effects of one factor change over levels of the other, there is no reversal of the direction of effects. For example, both boys and girls might look longer at the matching screen than the nonmatching screen but the difference manifested by girls might be greater than that manifested by boys. Statistical models for multifactor designs can provide tests of significance of interaction effects. The null hypothesis usually states that these effects are absent. Its rejection then implies that interaction is present: that is, that the effect of one factor changes significantly (in the statistical sense) across levels of the second.

When significant interaction of two factors is found, it must be realized that main effects of one factor, which can be viewed as averages of corresponding simple main effects, can be misleading, since main effects are not equal to corresponding simple main effects in the presence of interaction. With disordinal interactions it is even possible to have complete absence of main effects of a factor even though highly significant simple main effects of this factor are present (see figure 14.1, example 2).

14.5.3 Higher-Order Interactions

Interactions of two factors are called *first-order* interactions or two-factor interactions. When three factors are present, *second-order* interaction effects can occur. A second-order interaction means that the interaction of two factors changes across levels of the third factor. Interaction of two factors (say, A and B) at one level of a third factor (say, C) is called *simple interaction* of these factors (A, B) at that level of the third factor (C). Thus, second-order interaction would occur if the simple AB interaction at one level of C differed from the simple AB interaction at another level of C. For example, consider Strohner and Nelson's (1974) study, which has one between-subjects factor (Age) and two within-subjects factors (Voice: Actives vs. Passives; and Sentence Type: Probable, Improbable, and Reversible). A second-order interaction would be present if an ordinal simple interaction of Age and Voice occurred in Reversible sentences and no simple interaction of Age and Voice occurred in either the Probable or the Improbable sentences. A second-order interaction would also be present if a simple ordinal interaction of Age and Voice occurred for Reversible sentences, but simple disordinal interactions of Age and Voice occurred for the Probable and Improbable sentences, or if opposite simple ordinal interactions of Age and Voice occurred at any of the three levels of the Sentence Type factor. Definitions of interactions involving more than three factors can be generalized from the previous discussion. Thus, four-factor (third-order) interaction effects mean that three-factor interaction effects change across levels of a fourth factor; five-factor interaction effects mean that four-factor interaction effects change across levels of a fifth factor, and so on.

14.5.4 Interaction Effects in Mixed Designs: Possible Research Questions and Design Issues

Factors in multifactor designs may be independent variables whose effects on the dependent variable are of interest, or nuisance variables whose effects need to be estimated and controlled in order to draw valid inferences about relations of independent and dependent variables. Nuisance variables may be called blocking variables when they are included as factors in the design. A block usually consists of a group of individuals who are homogeneous with respect to the nuisance variable(s). The nuisance variable may be one or a combination of several demographic characteristics. It may also be a manipulated variable such as some characteristic of the stimuli to which subjects have been exposed. Blocking permits isolation of effects of the nuisance variable. In multifactor designs, interactions among independent variables as well as interactions of independent and nuisance variables may be of interest. The following examples illustrate some of these ideas.

Mixed designs frequently involve cross-sectional components. In these mixed designs, interactions of between-subjects factors, within-subjects factors, and between- with within-subjects factors may be investigated. A typical example is one in which the between-subjects variable involves age groups and the within-subjects variable involves sentence types. Many of these studies are concerned not only with questions regarding changes across age groups but also with some explanatory or theoretical issues. A general approach to investigating theoretical issues involves manipulation of the within-subjects variable, sentence types, along some critical dimension. Lust and her colleagues have conducted a number of studies (Lust and Clifford 1986; Lust, Solan, et al. 1986; Sherman and Lust 1986) that have used this type of mixed design. For example, using an imitation task, Lust and Clifford (1986) investigated the effect of one between-subjects variable, age, with nine levels, and three within-subjects factors, each with two levels. The within-subjects variables were type of pronoun (forward or backward), degree of embedding (+ or − depth), and distance of pronoun from the antecedent ($+$ or $-$ distance). The three within-subjects factors were selected to examine the effects of directionality, sensitivity to dominance relations, and distance of the pronoun from the antecedent within the sentence. Whereas the first two factors were related to theoretical issues, the third was viewed as a nuisance factor. An analysis of variance revealed a significant main effect for age but no interaction between this variable and the three within-subjects variables. This finding was expected. There were also main effects for direction and depth as well as interaction effects between these two variables. Finally, tests of interactions of distance with the independent variables revealed no significant effects; this finding was also expected. Thus, in addition to illustrating how interaction effects may be related to the central research questions, this study demonstrates how variability associated with a nuisance variable, in this case a within-subjects factor, and the interaction of this variable with the independent variables may be explicitly estimated and partialed out in multifactor designs.

Studies using categories based on individual response patterns may also be incorporated into mixed designs. Cairns et al. (1994, 1995) conducted a study in which the between-subjects variable of interest was a category reflecting whether or not children obey a pronominal coreference requirement (PCR) in interpreting forward pronominal sentences. The study, which involved a mixed design, employed two between- and two within-subjects factors to evaluate a theoretical question regarding the nature of the PCR. In particular, Cairns et al. were interested in determining whether the PCR is a pragmatic or grammatical rule. The question was addressed by investigating the effect of a contextual bias on children's interpretation of three types of sentences. To control for possible nuisance variables related to the ordering of nouns in the sentences, three separate sets of stimuli were created, each with a different ordering of the nouns mentioned in the sentences. Different sets were administered to different groups so that order of presentation was a between-subjects blocking factor. Since there were no significant main effects or interactions involving this nuisance variable, it was eliminated from further analyses (cf. the discussion of model trimming in section 14.3.3.1). As illustrated in table 14.8, children were classified according to whether or not they manifested the PCR, the between-subjects factor of primary interest. One within-subjects factor, sentence types, had three levels; the other, story context, had two. The response measure involved a picture selection task that revealed the child's judgments regarding the possible antecedents for

Table 14.8

A mixed design involving one between-subjects factor, pronoun coreference requirement (PCR), and two within-subjects factors, sentence type and story context. (" − " = without the story context; " + " = with the story context)

	Levels of two within-subjects factors					
			Sentence type			
	1		2		3	
			Story context			
Between-subjects factor: PCR	−	+	−	+	−	+
1. Children with the PCR						
2. Children without the PCR						

either pronouns or PRO depending on the sentence type. The number of responses indicating selection of an external referent was the dependent variable. This design permitted testing for the main effects of the PCR category, sentence type, and context as well as for interactions of these variables. The results revealed main effects for PCR and story context but not for sentence type. A critical aspect of the study was whether there would be a difference in the effect of story context for children without the PCR as compared to those with the PCR and further, whether the effect would be similar for both PRO and pronouns. Results regarding the presence or absence of interaction effects were critical for answering these questions. No significant interaction effects were obtained. This study provides another illustration of how the presence or absence of interaction effects may be central to the research questions under investigation.

14.6   Reliability, Validity of Causal Inferences, and Generalizability

The basic goal of research investigating children's syntactic knowledge is to obtain unambiguous answers to specific research questions. Several approaches to reducing or eliminating ambiguity can be distinguished. The first approach (illustrated above) involves fitting realistic and appropriate models to data. For example, an analysis-of-covariance model, or a blocking analysis-of-variance model, whose assumptions are tenable, can yield (relatively) unambiguous conclusions about the relation of an independent variable to a dependent variable by allowing the researcher to estimate and partial out effects of one or more nuisance variables by *statistical modeling* of these effects. A second approach consists of identifying and selecting dependent variables with satisfactory *psychometric* characteristics. Good *reliability* is generally necessary for lack of ambiguity. A third approach to reducing or eliminating ambiguity involves *experimental design* aspects of the research. Experimental design can be used to increase both the validity of causal inferences (*internal validity*) and the generalizability of the conclusions (*external validity*). This section focuses on some *psychometric* and *experimental design* issues relevant to ambiguity reduction.

14.6.1 Reliability Issues

Reliability requires consistency in the measurement of the elicited behaviors. Two types of reliability are particularly important in acquisition studies: *test-retest* and *interrater*. Test-retest reliability refers to the temporal stability of a child's performance on a task. The task may involve the same sentences or alternative forms of the same sentence type. Although it is generally assumed that children's responses represent stable patterns that will change only as a function of changes in the underlying grammatical system, few studies have reported reliability statistics. As noted in section 14.4, category 2 designs may be used to determine the stability of children's response patterns (see Allen and Yen 1979 for additional information about test-retest reliability).

Interrater reliability refers to the extent to which raters agree on the scoring of identical responses. For many tasks, the actual tabulation of the responses is straightforward and the assumption of high interrater agreement does not need to be examined. However, this type of reliability needs to be established for those tasks in which the classification of a child's response involves subjective rater judgments. For example, in the intermodal preferential looking paradigm, it is important to determine the extent of agreement in judgments that the child actually looked at a particular screen (see chapter 5, this volume). In production tasks, it is important to determine whether there is agreement on the transcription of the child's utterances. In act-out tasks, it is important to determine whether there is agreement on which objects were selected, the relative timing of the actions (e.g., whether objects are used simultaneously or sequentially), and the nature of the actions. These examples are not exhaustive but are mentioned to illustrate how many of the tasks involve subjective judgments. The most popular measure of interrater agreement is the Kappa coefficient (see Fleiss 1981). One reason for the popularity of

Kappa is that (unlike many other interrater agreement indices) it attempts to adjust for chance agreement.

14.6.2 Internal and External Validity Issues

14.6.2.1 Internal Validity Cook and Campbell (1979) discuss two types of validity: *internal* and *external validity*. Internal validity refers to the extent to which a causal relationship between two variables can be inferred. External validity refers to the extent to which "the presumed causal relationship can be generalized to and across alternate measures of the cause and effect and across different types of persons, settings and times" (Cook and Campbell 1979, 37).

With respect to internal validity, an important aspect of research design involves methods for controlling the operation of *extraneous* or *confounding* variables (the terms *nuisance variables* and *covariates* may also be used). These variables would be described in the terminology of Cook and Campbell (1979) as *threats to internal validity*. They threaten the validity of causal inferences if the experimental design and/or the statistical model fitted to the data do not satisfactorily partial out their effects. Sections 14.3.3.1 and 14.5.4 introduced statistical methods (blocking and analysis of covariance) for controlling effects of nuisance variables. Many chapters in this book provide a detailed discussion of possible nuisance variables that constitute threats to the internal validity of each of the procedures used to investigate children's syntactic knowledge. These chapters also present various methods for controlling the operation of the nuisance variables.

Several variables that may lead to spurious conclusions or failure to detect a relationship between the independent and dependent variables, and experimental (as opposed to statistical) methods of controlling their effects, deserve additional comment. A number of possible nuisance variables are associated with the vocabulary used in the experimental sentences. One is semantic bias. The vocabulary items used to construct the experimental sentences may result in response biases that mask the effect of the structural features that are being investigated. These response biases may be associated with semantic features such as gender and role distinctions. For example, regardless of the syntactic structure of the sentence, some children may limit the actions associated with some lexical nouns (i.e., only mothers can feed a baby). Two other variables are familiarity of the vocabulary items and phonological characteristics. Both of these variables can increase the difficulty of processing a sentence, irrespective of syntactic structure. Thus, it is important to ensure that the vocabulary in the experimental sentences does not differ in any systematic way with respect to all of these features. There are, however, several additional experimental procedures that may be employed to control for the possible systematic effects of vocabulary items. One procedure involves the use of vocabulary pretests. In general, participation in most studies is contingent on the child's demonstrating knowledge of all the vocabulary used in constructing the experimental sentences. In addition to vocabulary pretests, designs may include counterbalancing or random assignment of the critical lexical items to the experimental sentences. One method of counterbalancing for lexical items can be illustrated with a hypothetical study examining children's interpretation of active and passive sentences. Matching pairs of active and passive sentences could be created using the same lexical items. For example:

Set A
Active: The boy kissed the girl.
Passive: The girl was kissed by the boy.

Set B
Active: The girl kissed the boy.
Passive: The boy was kissed by the girl.

Notice that the vocabulary is balanced in the active and passive pairs as well as in sets A and B. Within each age group, one group of children would receive set A and another group, set B. All children would receive an equal number of actives and passives, and assignment to sets would be random. The counterbalancing would then create two groups of subjects (those exposed to set A and those exposed to set B). Sets A and B could then be viewed as levels of a between-subjects factor. Methods for analyzing the data are discussed in section 14.5.4. A second example of counterbalancing vocabulary consists of ensuring that specific words occur with equal frequency in all possible positions within a sentence. For example, the nouns used to construct the experimental sentences would occur with equal frequency in subject and object positions, or the verbs used to construct sentences would occur with equal frequency across all the construction types used in the study. In this way, any possible response biases related to specific vocabulary items would be balanced so that systematic effects are canceled out. Alternatively, randomly generating combinations of lexical items from the set of vocabulary items to be used in the study also controls the influence of systematic response biases associated with specific words.

The nonmanipulated structural features of the experimental sentences may also influence a child's responses irrespective of the particular aspect of syntax under study. For example, Goodluck and Tavakolian (1982) demonstrated that the number of animate NPs in a sentence increased the difficulty of relative clause sentences. Thus, to the extent possible, the number of animate NPs in a sentence needs to be controlled. The number must also be constant across all construction types. Otherwise, differences in the child's performance may be due to the number of animate NPs and not attributable to the variable of interest. In addition, some experimental variables may result in sentences that differ in length or differ in other ways that may influence a child's responses. In addition to the statistical methods of controlling these variables (e.g., see section 14.5.4), the experimental method of including filler sentences (nonexperimental control sentences) may be used. The fillers can be constructed in such a way as to isolate the effects of 'the variable of interest. For example, if they are equivalent in length but less complex than the experimental sentences, then they can reveal whether length or complexity is the variable influencing a child's performance.

The number and complexity of the experimental sentences included in a research study is also an important consideration. Although it is desirable from the point of view of reliability to include a number of tokens of each construction type, fatigue factors and limited attention spans constrain the length of testing sessions. This is especially true for experiments involving younger children. In addition to ensuring that the sessions are an appropriate length, it is important either to counterbalance the order of presentation of sentences across subjects or to randomize the order of presentation to control for possible fatigue and/or attention effects. Inclusion of filler sentences also provides important controls for detecting such effects. Furthermore, including some "easy" filler sentences may ensure that the child does not become overwhelmed by the difficulty of the task. It is important to remember that children quickly lose interest when they are not experiencing success, even when the experimenter is giving the usual encouragement.

Another threat to internal validity is primarily related to tasks focusing on comprehension. Hamburger and Crain (1982) report results indicating that children's ability to correctly interpret relative clauses is influenced by whether the context meets the felicity conditions required by the construction. These results suggest that the contexts connected with the experimental sentences should be constructed to be consistent with any semantic and/or pragmatic requirements related to the construction.

Response biases that may be related to specific tasks constitute another class of threats. For example, in tasks requiring a "yes" or "no," children may differ in their tendency to respond affirmatively rather than negatively. This tendency is sometimes called the "acquiescence response set." In truth-value tasks, some children may prefer to stuff rags into the mouth of an animal rather than to offer a reward; in the intermodal preferential looking paradigm, some may prefer to look to the right screen rather than the left. In act-out tasks, some children may exhibit biases in the manipulation of objects, especially in the enactment of complex sentences. Many task effects may be controlled by including filler sentences. Counterbalancing the sentences or presentation of the experimental stimuli (as in the case of the intermodal preferential looking paradigm) is also recommended. Within the context of psychological research, Kline (1986) discusses the acquiescence response set as well as several other response sets and methods for controlling their effects.

Another type of response bias is related to children's assumptions regarding acceptable responses. Children may assume that some types of responses are not allowed unless they receive training that identifies the range of acceptable responses. For example, in acting out the antecedents of pronomial sentences, children may not manifest selection of NPs not mentioned in the sentence unless they are trained that such responses are acceptable. In general, it is important to provide sufficient *preexperimental training* to ensure that children (1) are capable of performing the task and (2) will manifest responses that reflect their knowledge of the constructions under study.

Studies that classify children on some categorical variable may be subject to an additional threat to internal validity that has been termed *statistical regression* (Cook and Campbell 1979). This refers to the tendency of individuals selected on the basis of extreme scores on a pretest to manifest scores on subsequent tests that are more toward the center of the distribution of scores in the population. Individuals selected on the basis of low scores are likely to manifest higher scores on retesting, and those selected on the basis of high scores are likely to manifest lower scores on retesting. As Cook and Campbell (1979, 53) point out, the magnitude of the regression in cases in which the regression is associated with measurement errors "depends both on the test-retest reliability of a measure and on the difference between the mean of a deliberately selected subgroup and the mean of the population from which the subgroup was chosen. The higher the reliability and the smaller the difference, the less will be the regression." This problem is relevant to studies in which children are classified on the basis of their responses to a subset of sentences and are later tested on a second set of sentences. Some problems and methods of controlling effects of measurement-error-caused regression toward the mean are discussed by Hsu (1995). Rogosa (1988) provides a critical and comprehensive discussion of these and related topics.

A final issue concerns the validity of assumptions regarding response patterns that are assumed to reflect adult linguistic competence. A variety of studies (Hsu, Cairns, and Bialo 1987; Hsu et al. 1989; Hsu et al. 1991; Sigurjónsdóttir and Hyams 1992; McDaniel and Maxfield 1992b) have demonstrated that adults cannot be assumed to manifest perfect performance on some types of sentences and some experimental tasks. In addition, assumptions about the nature of adult intuitions for specific constructions may not necessarily be correct for the entire population. As a result, it is essential to include adequate adult control groups in acquisition studies to empirically determine the response patterns that truly represent adult linguistic competence. The data from the adult subjects may be included in the statistical analyses of the results or they may be presented descriptively to document claims regarding adult levels of performance.

14.6.2.2 External Validity   The issue of external validity (i.e., the generalizability of findings across various kinds of persons, settings, and times) is particularly important in studies of the acquisition of syntax. Because of the young age of the population and the types of tasks, the studies must involve individual testing during short time periods. Further, the studies typically involve small sample sizes, nonrandom subject selection, and high attrition rates. Subject selection is frequently a result of whether permission can be obtained to conduct the study and whether parents are willing to grant permission for their children to be tested. It is also a function of whether a child is able or willing to perform the task. These factors tend to result in samples that differ in systematic ways from the population of interest. High attrition rates may also bias the characteristics of the sample. For these reasons, the results typically cannot be generalized to various racial, social, or geographical groups. (See also chapter 1 of this volume for a discussion of how issues regarding the quality of the data may ultimately limit the generalizability of the findings.) Our basic recommendation regarding external validity is to include a detailed description of the subjects (i.e., race, social class, geographical distribution, parental educational level, number of siblings, birth order, etc.) who are included in the study and to limit generalizations accordingly.

14.7 Conclusions

In this chapter we have presented some of the basic concepts of experimental design, statistical analysis, and psychometrics that are relevant to research on children's acquisition of syntactic knowledge. We have described published and hypothetical studies to illustrate many of these concepts as well as the types of research questions that may be addressed. We would recommend the following sources for more intensive and extensive coverage of experimental design, statistical analysis, and psychometric topics that are relevant to research on the acquisition of syntactic knowledge. Two of the best sources of information about experimental designs and parametric analysis-of-variance models are Myers and Well 1991 and Kirk 1982. Cook and Campbell 1979, Huitema 1980, and Maxwell and Delaney 1990 provide insightful discussions of analysis-of-covariance models and the problems of using these models in empirical studies. Excellent discussions of internal and external validity as well as related experimental and statistical methods have appeared in Cook and Campbell 1979 and Kazdin 1992. Two of the most useful texts on nonparametric statistics are Marascuilo and McSweeney 1977 and Lehmann 1975. Both texts provide numerous worked-out examples. The discussion of interactions in Cronbach and Snow 1981 is outstanding. A valuable source of information about psychometric theory is Lord and Novick 1968. However, this book assumes more statistical background on the part of the reader than other sources listed here.

Note
This chapter is dedicated to our daughter, Lily Ting Hsu, who has enriched our lives in innumerable ways.

References

Abney, S. 1987. The English noun phrase in its sentential aspect. Doctoral dissertation, MIT.

Abrams, K. H., C. Chiarello, K. Cress, S. Green, and N. Ellelt. 1978. The relation between mother-to-child speech and word-order comprehension strategies in children. In R. N. Campbell and P. T. Smith, eds., *Recent advances in the psychology of language*. Vol. 4a, *Language development and mother-child interaction*. New York: Plenum Press.

Allen, M. J., and W. M. Yen 1979. *Introduction to measurement theory*. Monterey, Calif.: Brooks/Cole.

Allen, S. 1994. Acquisition of some mechanisms of transitivity alternation in arctic Quebec Inuktitut. Doctoral dissertation, McGill University.

Allen, S., and M. Crago. 1993. Early acquisition of passive morphology in Inuktitut. In E. Clark, ed., *Proceedings of the Twenty-Fourth Annual Child Language Research Forum*. Stanford, Calif.: CSLI Publications. Distributed by Cambridge University Press.

Ament, W. 1899. *Die Entwicklung von Sprechen und Denken beim Kinde*. Leipzig.

Anderson, J. E. 1946. Methods of child psychology. In L. Carmichael, ed., *Manual of child psychology*. New York: Wiley.

Anderson, M. 1979. Noun phrase structure. Doctoral dissertation, University of Connecticut.

Armidon, A., and P. Carey. 1972. Why five year olds cannot understand *before* and *after*. *Journal of Verbal Learning and Verbal Behavior* 11, 417–423.

Atkinson, M. 1975. Review of Bowerman. *Journal of Linguistics* 11, 87–101.

Atkinson, M. 1982. *Explanations in the study of child language development*. Cambridge: Cambridge University Press.

Avrutin, S., and K. Wexler. 1992. Development of Principle B in Russian: Coindexation at LF and coreference. *Language Acquisition* 2, 259–306.

Bailyn, J. F. 1992. LF movement of anaphors and the acquisition of embedded clauses in Russian. *Language Acquisition* 2, 307–336.

Bangs, T. 1975. *Vocabulary Comprehension Scale*. Boston: Teaching Resources.

Bankson, N. 1990. *Bankson Language Test–2*. Austin, Tex.: Pro-Ed.

Barbier, I. 1995. The structure of VP and IP: A study of word order in early childhood Dutch. Doctoral dissertation, Cornell University.

Bartel, N., D. Bryen, and S. Keehn. 1973. Language comprehension in the mentally retarded child. *Exceptional Children* 39, 375–382.

Barton, D. 1980. Phonemic perception in children. In G. H. Yeni-Komshian, J. F. Kavanagh, and G. A. Ferguson, eds., *Child phonology*. Vol. 2, *Perception*. New York: Academic Press.

Bates, E. 1993. Comprehension and production in early language development. *Monographs of the Society for Research in Child Development* 58 (2–4, Serial No. 233), 222–242.

Beilin, H., and B. Lust. 1975. A study in the development of logical and linguistic connectives. In H. Beilin, ed., *Studies in the cognitive basis of language development*. New York: Academic Press.

Bellugi, U. 1967. The acquisition of negation. Doctoral dissertation, Harvard University.

Bellugi, U. 1971. Simplification in children's language. In R. Huxley and E. Ingram, eds., *Language acquisition: Models and methods*. New York: Academic Press.

Berko, J. 1958. The child's learning of English morphology. *Word* 14, 150–177.

Bever, T. 1970. The cognitive basis for linguistic structure. In J. R. Hayes, ed., *Cognition and the development of language*. New York: Wiley.

Bever, T. 1975. Psychologically real grammar emerges because of its role in language acquisition. In D. P. Dato, ed., *Developmental psycholinguistics: Theory and applications*. Washington, D. C.: Georgetown University Press.

Bishop, Y. M. M., S. E. Fienberg, and P. W. Holland. 1975. *Discrete multivariate analysis*. Cambridge, Mass.: MIT Press.

Bloom, L. 1970. *Language development: Form and function in emerging grammars*. Cambridge, Mass.: MIT Press.

Bloom, L. 1973. *One word at a time: The use of single word utterances before syntax*. The Hague: Mouton.

Bloom, L., L. Hood, and P. Lightbown. 1974. Imitation in language development: If, when and why. *Cognitive Psychology* 6, 380–420.

Bloom, L., and M. Lahey. 1978. *Language development and language disorders*. New York: Wiley.

Bloom, L., M. Lahey, M. Hood, K. Lifter, and K. Fiess. 1980. Complex sentences: Acquisition of syntactic connectives and the semantic relations they encode. *Journal of Child Language* 7, 235–261.

Bloom, P. 1990. Subjectless sentences in child language. *Linguistic Inquiry* 21, 491–504.

Bloom, P. 1993. Grammatical continuity in language development: The case of subjectless sentences. *Linguistic Inquiry* 24, 721–734.

Blount, B. G. 1969. Acquisition of language by Luo children. Doctoral dissertation, University of California, Berkeley.

Bol, G., and J. de Jong. 1992. Auxiliary verbs in Dutch language-impaired children. *Scandinavian Journal of Logopedics and Phoniatrics* 17, 17–21.

Borer, H., and K. Wexler. 1987. The maturation of syntax. In T. Roeper and E. Williams, eds., *Parameter setting*. Dordrecht: Reidel.

Borer, H., and K. Wexler. 1992. Bi-unique relations and the maturation of grammatical principles. *Natural Language & Linguistic Theory* 10, 147–189.

Boser, K. 1989. The first language acquisition of German word order. Bachelor's honors thesis, Cornell University.

Boser, K., B. Lust, L. Santelmann, and J. Whitman. 1992. The syntax of CP and V-2 in early child German: The strong continuity hypothesis. In K. Broderick, ed., *NELS 22*. GLSA, University of Massachusetts, Amherst.

Bowerman, M. 1973. *Early syntactic development: A cross-linguistic study with special reference to Finnish*. Cambridge: Cambridge University Press.

Bowerman, M. 1974. Learning the structure of causative verbs: A study in the relationship of cognitive, semantic and syntactic development. *Papers and Reports on Child Language Development* 8, 142–178.

Bowerman, M. 1982. Reorganizational processes in lexical and syntactic development. In E. Wanner and L. Gleitman, eds., *Language acquisition: The state of the art*. Cambridge: Cambridge University Press.

Braine, M. D. S. 1963. The ontogeny of English phrase structure: The first phase. *Language* 39, 1–14.

Bresnan, J. 1978. Contraction and the transformational cycle in English. Indiana University Linguistics Club, Bloomington.

Brown, R. 1968. The development of *wh*-questions in child speech. *Journal of Verbal Learning and Verbal Behavior* 7, 279–290.

Brown, R. 1973. *A first language: The early stages*. Cambridge, Mass.: Harvard University Press.

Brown, R., and C. Fraser. 1963. The acquisition of syntax. In C. N. Cofer and B. S. Musgrave, eds., *Verbal behavior and learning: Problems and processes*. New York: McGraw-Hill.

Brown, R., and C. Hanlon. 1970. Derivational complexity and order of acquisition in child speech. In J. R. Hayes, ed., *Cognition and the development of language*. New York: Wiley.

Cairns, H. S., J. R. Hsu, D. McDaniel, S. Parsons, and D. Konstantyn. 1994. Referents for PRO and overt pronouns: Effects of grammar and discourse bias. Paper presented at the 18th Annual Boston University Conference on Language Development, Boston, January.

Cairns, H. S., D. McDaniel, J. R. Hsu, S. Parsons, and D. Konstantyn. 1995. Grammatical and discourse principles in children's grammars: The pronoun coreference requirement. In E. Fernandez, ed., *CUNYForum* 19. Ph.D. Program in Linguistics, City University of New York.

Cairns, H. S., D. McDaniel, J. R. Hsu, and M. Rapp. 1994. A longitudinal study of control types and the adverbial coreference requirement in young children. *Language* 70, 260–288.

Cambon, J., and H. Sinclair. 1974. Relations between syntax and semantics: Are they "easy to see"? *British Journal of Psychology* 65, 133–140.

Cardinaletti, A., and M. Starke. 1994. The typology of structural deficiency. On the "Three grammatical classes." Ms., University of Venice and University of Geneva.

Carroll, J., P. Davies, and B. Richman, eds. 1971. *The American Heritage word frequency book*. Boston: Houghton Mifflin.

Carrow, E. 1974. *Carrow Elicited Language Inventory*. Austin, Tex.: Learning Concepts.

Carrow-Woolfolk, E. 1985. *Test of Auditory Comprehension of Language–Revised*. Allen, Tex.: DLM Teaching Resources.

Chapman, R. 1995. Language development in children and adolescents with Down syndrome. In P. Fletcher and B. MacWhinney, eds., *Handbook of child language*. Oxford: Blackwell.

Chien, Y.-C. 1983. Topic-comment structure and grammatical structure in first language acquisition of Mandarin Chinese. Doctoral dissertation, Cornell University.

Chien, Y.-C., and B. Lust. 1985. The concepts of topic and subject in first language acquisition of Mandarin Chinese. *Child Development* 56, 1359–1375.

Chien, Y.-C., and K. Wexler. 1987. Children's acquisition of the locality condition for reflexives and pronouns. *Papers and Reports on Child Language Development* 26, 30–39.

Chien, Y.-C., and K. Wexler. 1990. Children's knowledge of locality conditions in binding as evidence for the modularity of syntax and pragmatics. *Language Acquisition* 1, 225–295.

Chomsky, C. 1969. *The acquisition of syntax in children from 5 to 10*. Cambridge, Mass.: MIT Press.

Chomsky, N. 1955. *The logical structure of linguistic theory*. New York: Plenum (1975).

Chomsky, N. 1957. *Syntactic structures*. The Hague: Mouton.

Chomsky, N. 1959. Review of B. F. Skinner's *Verbal behavior*. *Language* 35, 26–58.

Chomsky, N. 1964. Formal discussion. In U. Bellugi and R. Brown, eds., The acquisition of language. *Monographs of the Society for Research in Child Development* 29 (1, Serial No. 92).

Chomsky, N. 1965. *Aspects of the theory of syntax*. Cambridge, Mass.: MIT Press.

Chomsky, N. 1976. Conditions on rules of grammar. *Linguistic Analysis* 2, 303–351.

Chomsky, N. 1981. *Lectures on government and binding*. Dordrecht: Foris.

Chomsky, N. 1986a. *Barriers*. Cambridge, Mass.: MIT Press.

Chomsky, N. 1986b. *Knowledge of language: Its nature, origin, and use*. New York: Praeger.

Chomsky, N. 1991. Some notes on the economy of derivation and representation. In R. Freidin, ed., *Principles and parameters in comparative grammar*. Cambridge, Mass.: MIT Press.

Chomsky, N. 1993. A minimalist program for linguistic theory. In K. Hale and S. J. Keyser, eds., *The view from Building 20: Essays in linguistics in honor of Sylvain Bromberger*. Cambridge, Mass.: MIT Press.

Chomsky, N. 1994. Bare phrase structure MIT Occasional Papers in Linguistics 5. MITWPL, Department of Linguistics and Philosophy, MIT.

Chomsky, N., and H. Lasnik. 1993. The theory of principles and parameters. In J. Jacobs, A. von Stechow, W. Sternefeld, and T. Venneman, eds., *Syntax: An international handbook of contemporary research*. Berlin: de Gruyter.

Cinque, G. 1990. *Types of $\bar{A}$-dependencies*. Cambridge, Mass.: MIT Press.

Clahsen, H. 1986. Verb inflections in German child language: Acquisition of agreement markers and the functions they encode. *Linguistics* 24, 79–121.

Clahsen, H. 1989. The grammatical characterization of developmental dysphasia. *Linguistics* 27, 897–920.

Clahsen, H., M. Rothweiler, A. Woest, and G. F. Marcus. 1992. Regular and irregular inflection in the acquisition of German noun plurals. *Cognition* 45, 225–255.

Clark, E. 1973. On the acquisition of the meaning of *before* and *after*. *Journal of Verbal Learning and Verbal Behavior* 10, 266–275.

Clark, E. 1978. Strategies for communicating. *Child Development* 49, 953–959.

Clark, H. H. 1973. The language-as-fixed-effect fallacy: A critique of language statistics in psychological research. *Journal of Verbal Learning and Verbal Behavior* 12, 335–359.

Clark, H. H. 1974. Semantics and comprehension. In T. A. Sebeok, ed., *Linguistics and adjacent arts and sciences*. The Hague: Mouton.

Clark, R. 1982. Theory and method in child-language research: Are we assuming too much? In S. Kuczaj, ed., *Language development*. Vol. 1, *Syntax and semantics*. Hillsdale, N.J.: Lawrence Erlbaum.

Cocking R. R., and S. McHale. 1981. A comparative study of the use of pictures and objects in assessing children's receptive and productive language. *Journal of Child Language* 8, 1–13.

Cohen, L. B., J. DeLoache, and M. S. Strauss. 1979. Infant visual perception. In J. Osofsky, ed., *Handbook of infant development*. New York: Wiley.

Cohen, L. B., and L. M. Oakes. 1993. How infants perceive a simple causal event. *Developmental Psychology* 29, 421–433.

Cohen Sherman, J. 1983. The acquisition of control in complement sentences: The role of structural and lexical factors. Doctoral dissertation, Cornell University.

Cohen Sherman, J., and B. Lust. 1993. Children are in control. *Cognition* 46, 1–51.

Compayré, G. 1899. *L'évolution intellectuelle et morale de l'enfant*. Paris.

Cook, T. D., and D. T. Campbell. 1979. *Quasiexperimentation: Design analysis issues for field settings*. Boston: Houghton Mifflin.

Cooper, R. P., and R. N. Aslin. 1990. Preference for infant-directed speech in the first month after birth. *Child Development* 61, 1584–1595.

Corver, N., and D. Delfitto. 1993. Feature asymmetry and the nature of pronoun movement. Ms., Tilburg University and University of Utrecht.

Cowart, W. 1994. Anchoring and grammar effects in judgments of sentence acceptability. *Perceptual and Motor Skills* 79, 1171–1182.

Cowart, W. Forthcoming. *Survey methods in syntactic research*. Thousand Oaks, Calif.: Sage Publications.

Crago, M. B. 1988. Cultural context in communicative interaction of Inuit children. Doctoral dissertation, McGill University.

Craig, H. 1991. Pragmatic characteristics of the child with specific language impairment: An interactionist perspective. In T. Gallagher, ed., *Pragmatics of language*. San Diego, Calif.: Singular Publishing.

Crain, S. 1982. Temporal terms: Mastery by age five. *Papers and Reports on Child Language Development* 21, 33–38.

Crain, S. 1991. Language acquisition in the absence of experience. *Behavioral and Brain Sciences* 14, 597–612.

Crain, S., and J. D. Fodor. 1987. Competence and performance in child language. In *Haskins Laboratories status report on speech research*, SR 99/100. Haskins Laboratories, New Haven, Conn.

Crain, S., and C. McKee. 1985. The acquisition of structural restrictions on anaphora. In S. Berman, J.-W. Choe, and J. McDonough, eds., *Proceedings of NELS 16*. GLSA, University of Massachusetts, Amherst.

Crain, S., C. McKee, and M. Emiliani. 1990. Visiting relatives in Italy. In L. Frazier and J. G. de Villiers, eds., *Language processing and language acquisition*. Dordrecht: Kluwer.

Crain, S., and M. Nakayama. 1987. Structure dependence in grammar formation. *Language* 63, 522–543.

Crain, S., and R. Thornton. 1990. Levels of representation in child grammar. Paper presented at the 13th GLOW Colloquium, Cambridge.

Crain, S., and R. Thornton. 1991. Recharting the course of language acquisition: Studies in elicited production. In N. Krasnegor et al., eds., *Biological and behavioral determinants of language development*. Hillsdale, N.J.: Lawrence Erlbaum.

Crain, S., R. Thornton, C. Boster, L. Conway, D. Lillo-Martin, and E. Woodams. To appear. Quantification without qualification. *Language Acquisition*.

Crain, S., R. Thornton, and K. Murasugi. 1987. Capturing the evasive passive. Paper presented at the 12th Annual Boston University Conference on Language Development, Boston.

Crain, S., and K. Wexler. To appear. Methodology in the study of language acquisition: A minimalist/modular approach. In W. C. Ritchie and T. K. Bhatia, eds., *Handbook of first language acquisition*. San Diego, Calif.: Academic Press.

Cromer, R. F. 1970. Children are nice to understand: Surface structure clues for the recovery of deep structure. *British Journal of Psychology* 61, 367–408.

Cromer, R. F. 1987. Language growth with experience without feedback. *Journal of Psycholinguistic Research* 16, 223–232.

Cromer, R. F. 1983. A longitudinal study of the acquisition of word knowledge: Evidence against gradual learning. *British Journal of Developmental Psychology* 61, 307–316.

Cronbach, L. J., and R. E. Snow. 1981. *Aptitudes and instructional methods: A handbook for research on interactions*. New York: Irvington.

Crystal, D., P. Fletcher, and M. Garman. 1976. *The grammatical analysis of language disability*. London: Edward Arnold.

Dale, P. S., E. Bates, S. J. Reznick, and C. Morisset. 1989. The validity of a parent report instrument of child language at 20 months. *Journal of Child Language* 16, 239–250.

Darlington, R. B. 1990. *Regression and linear models*. New York: McGraw-Hill.

Darwin, C. 1877. A bibliographical sketch of an infant. *Mind* 2, 285–294.

Demuth, K. 1984. Aspects of Sesotho language acquisition. Indiana University Linguistics Club, Bloomington.

Demuth, K. 1989. Maturation and the acquisition of Sesotho passive. *Language* 65, 56–80.

Demuth, K. 1990. Subject, topic and the Sesotho passive. *Journal of Child Language* 17, 67–84.

Demuth, K. 1992. The acquisition of Sesotho. In D. I. Slobin, ed., *The crosslinguistic study of language acquisition*. Vol. 3. Hillsdale, N.J.: Lawrence Erlbaum.

Demuth, K. 1993. Issues in the acquisition of the Sesotho tonal system. *Journal of Child Language* 20, 275–301.

Demuth, K. 1995. Questions, relatives, and minimal projection. *Language Acquisition* 4, 49–71.

Demuth, K. 1996. The prosodic structure of early words. In J. Morgan and K. Demuth, eds., *Signal to syntax: Bootstrapping from speech to grammar in early acquisition*. Hillsdale, N.J.: Lawrence Erlbaum.

Déprez, V., and A. Pierce. 1993. Negation and functional projections in early grammar. *Linguistic Inquiry* 24, 25–67.

Deutsch, W. C., C. Koster, and J. Koster. 1986. What can we learn from children's errors in understanding anaphora? *Linguistics* 24, 203–225.

de Villiers, J. G. 1984. Learning the passive from models: Some contradictory data. Paper presented at the 9th Annual Boston University Conference on Language Development, Boston, October.

de Villiers, J. G. 1991. Why questions? In T. L. Maxfield and B. Plunkett, eds., *Papers in the acquisition of wh*. GLSA, University of Massachusetts, Amherst.

de Villiers, J. G. 1995. Questioning minds and answering machines. In D. Mac-Laughlin and S. McEwen, eds., *Proceedings of the 19th Annual Boston University Conference on Language Development*. Somerville, Mass.: Cascadilla Press.

de Villiers, J. G., and P. A. de Villiers. 1973. Development of the use of word order in comprehension. *Journal of Psycholinguistic Research* 2, 331–341.

de Villiers, J. G., and P. A. de Villiers. 1974. Competence and performance in child language: Are children really competent to judge? *Journal of Child Language* 1, 11–22.

de Villiers, J. G., M. Phinney, and A. Avery. 1982. Understanding passives with non-action verbs. Paper presented at the 7th Annual Boston University Conference on Language Development, Boston, October.

de Villiers, J. G., and T. Roeper. 1991. Introduction. In T. L. Maxfield and B. Plunkett, eds., *Papers in the acquisition of wh*. GLSA, University of Massachusetts, Amherst.

de Villiers, J. G., and T. Roeper. 1995. Relative clauses are barriers to *wh*-movement for young children. *Journal of Child Language* 22, 389–404.

de Villiers, J. G., T. Roeper, and A. Vainikka. 1990. The acquisition of long-distance rules. In L. Frazier and J. G. de Villiers, eds., *Language processing and language acquisition*. Dordrecht: Kluwer.

de Villiers, J. G., H. Tager-Flusberg, K. Hakuta, and M. Cohen. 1979. Children's comprehension of relative clauses. *Journal of Psycholinguistic Research* 8, 499–518.

de Villiers, P. A., and J. G. de Villiers. 1979. Form and function in the development of sentence negation. *Papers and Reports on Child Language Development* 17, 56–64.

DiSimoni, F. 1978. *Token Test for Children*. Allen, Tex.: DLM Teaching Resources.

Donaldson, M. 1982. Conservation: What is the question? *British Journal of Psychology* 73, 199–207.

Dromi, E., and R. Berman. 1982. A morphemic measure of early language development: Data from modern Hebrew. *Journal of Child Language* 9, 403–424.

Dromi, E., L. Leonard, and M. Shteiman. 1993. The grammatical morphology of Hebrew-speaking children with specific language impairment: Some competing hypotheses. *Journal of Speech and Hearing Research* 36, 760–771.

Duhem, P. 1906. *La théorie physique: Son objet, sa structure.* Paris: Rivière.

Edwards, J. 1992. Computer methods in child language research: Four principles for the use of archived data. *Journal of Child Language* 19, 435–458.

Edwards, J. 1993. Perfecting research techniques in an imperfect world: Response to MacWhinney and Snow. *Journal of Child Language* 20, 209–216.

Edwards, J., and M. Lampert. 1993. *Talking data: Transcription and coding in discourse research.* Hillsdale, N.J.: Lawrence Erlbaum.

Egger, E. 1879. *Observations et réflexions sur le développement de l'intelligence et du langage chez les enfants.* Paris.

Eisele, J., and B. Lust. To appear. Knowledge about pronouns: A developmental study using a truth-value judgment task. *Child Development.*

Eisenberg, S., and H. S. Cairns. 1994. The development of infinitives from three to five. *Journal of Child Language* 21, 713–734.

Epstein, W. 1961. The influence of syntactical structure on learning. *American Journal of Psychology* 74, 80–85.

Erreich, S. 1984. Learning how to ask: Patterns of inversion in yes/no and *wh*-questions. *Journal of Child Language* 11, 579–592.

Fay, D. 1978. Transformations as mental operations: A reply to Kuczaj. *Journal of Child Language* 5, 143–149.

Fenson, L., P. S. Dale, J. S. Reznick, E. Bates, D. Thal, and S. J. Pethick. 1994. Variability in early communicative development. *Monographs of the Society for Research in Child Development* 59 (5, Serial No. 242).

Fernald, A. 1985. Four-month-old infants prefer to listen to motherese. *Infant Behavior and Development* 8, 181–195.

Fernald, A., G. McRoberts, and C. Herrera. In press. Effects of prosody and word position on lexical comprehension in infants. *Experimental Psychology.*

Fey, M. 1986. *Language intervention with young children.* San Diego, Calif.: College-Hill Press.

Fey, M., and L. Leonard. 1983. Pragmatic skills of children with specific language impairment. In T. Gallagher and C. Prutting, eds., *Pragmatic assessment and intervention issues in language.* San Diego, Calif.: College-Hill Press.

Fillmore, C. J. 1968. The case for case. In E. Bach and R. T. Harms, eds., *Universals in linguistic theory.* New York: Holt, Rinehart and Winston.

Finney, M. 1994. The effects of gap position and discourse information in the acquisition of purpose clause constructions by second language learners. Doctoral dissertation, University of Ottawa.

Fischler, I., and G. O. Goodman. 1978. Latency of associative activation in memory. *Journal of Experimental Psychology: Human Perception and Performance* 4, 455–470.

Fitzgerald, G. F. 1895. The ether and earth's atmosphere. *Science* 13, 390.

Fleiss, J. L. 1981. *Statistical methods for rates and proportions.* New York: Wiley.

Flynn, S. 1987. *A parameter-setting model of L2 acquisition: Experimental studies in anaphora.* Dordrecht: Reidel.

Flynn, S., and S. Epstein. In preparation. Processing vs. grammatical deficits: A test of native speakers. Ms., MIT and Harvard University.

Flynn, S., and B. Lust. 1981. Acquisition of relative clauses: Developmental changes in their heads. In W. Harbert and J. Herschensohn, eds., *Cornell working papers in linguistics.* Department of Modern Languages and Linguistics, Cornell University.

Fodor, J. A. 1966. Comments in the general discussion on the Slobin presentation. In F. Smith and G. A. Miller, eds., *The genesis of language: A psycholinguistic approach.* Cambridge, Mass.: MIT Press.

Foley, C. In preparation. Operator-variable binding in the initial state: Evidence from the acquisition of French and English. Doctoral dissertation, Cornell University.

Forster, K. I. 1979. Levels of processing and the structure of the language processor. In W. E. Cooper and E. C. T. Walker, eds., *Sentence processing.* Hillsdale, N.J.: Lawrence Erlbaum.

Forster, K. I. 1989. On knowing how many entries. In D. S. Gorfein, ed., *Resolving semantic ambiguity.* Berlin: Springer-Verlag.

Forster, K. I., and C. Davis. 1984. Repetition priming and frequency attenuation in lexical access. *Journal of Experimental Psychology: General* 112, 309–346.

Fortescue, M. D. 1985. Learning to speak Greenlandic: A case study of a two-year-old's morphology in a polysynthetic language. *First Language* 5, 101–114.

Fortescue, M. D., and L. Lennert Olsen. 1992. The acquisition of West Greenlandic. In D. I. Slobin, ed., *The crosslinguistic study of language acquisition.* Vol. 3. Hillsdale, N.J.: Lawrence Erlbaum.

Fowler, C. 1990. Language abilities in children with Down syndrome: Evidence for a specific syntactic delay. In D. Cicchetti and M. Beeghly, eds., *Children with Down syndrome: A developmental perspective.* Cambridge: Cambridge University Press.

Fowler, C., R. Gelman, and L. Gleitman. 1994. The course of language learning in children with Down syndrome: Longitudinal and language level comparisons with young normally developing children. In H. Tager-Flusberg, ed., *Constraints on language acquisition.* Hillsdale, N.J.: Lawrence Erlbaum.

Francis, N., and H. Kucera. 1982. *Frequency analysis of English usage: Lexicon and grammar.* Boston: Houghton Mifflin.

Franke, C. 1899. Sprachentwicklung der Kinder und der Menschheit. In W. Rein, ed., *Handbuch der Pädagogik*, VI.

Franks, S., and P. Connell. In press. Knowledge of binding in normal and SLI children. *Journal of Child Language*.

Fraser, C., U. Bellugi, and R. Brown. 1963. Control of grammar in imitation, comprehension, and production. *Journal of Verbal Learning and Verbal Behavior* 2, 121–135.

Frazier, L. 1987. Sentence processing: A tutorial review. In M. Coltheart, ed., *Attention and performance*. Vol. 12. Hillsdale, N.J.: Lawrence Erlbaum.

Friedman, S., and M. Stevenson. 1975. Developmental changes in the understanding of implied motion in two-dimensional pictures. *Child Development* 46, 773–778.

Gair, J., B. Lust, L. Sumangala, and M. Rodrigo. To appear. Acquisition of null subjects and control in some Sinhala adverbial clauses. In J. Gair, ed., *Studies in South Asian linguistics*. Oxford: Oxford University Press.

Gardner, M. 1985. *Receptive One-Word Picture Vocabulary Test*. Novato, Calif.: Academic Therapy Publications.

Garrett, M. F. 1980. Levels of processing in sentence production. In B. Butterworth, ed., *Language production*. Vol. 1, *Speech and talk*. London: Academic Press.

Garrett, M. F. 1990. Sentence processing. In D. Osherson and H. Lasnik, eds., *Language: An invitation to cognitive science, vol. 1*. Cambridge, Mass.: MIT Press.

Garrett, M. F. 1995. The structure of language processing: Neuropsychological evidence. In M. Gazzaniga, ed., *Cognitive neuroscience*. Cambridge, Mass.: MIT Press.

Gelman, R. 1982. Accessing one-to-one correspondence: Still another paper about conservation. *British Journal of Psychology* 73, 209–220.

Gelman, S. A., and M. Taylor. 1984. How two-year-old children interpret proper and common names for unfamiliar objects. *Child Development* 55, 1535–1540.

Gerken, L. A. 1982. The effect of clause segmentation on coreference interpretations in children. Master's thesis, Columbia University.

Gerken, L. A. 1991. The metrical basis for children's subjectless sentences. *Journal of Memory and Language* 30, 431–451.

Gerken, L. A. 1993. Young children's representation of prosodic phonology: Evidence from English-speakers' weak syllable omissions. *Journal of Memory and Language* 33, 19–38.

Gerken, L. A. 1994. Sentential processes in early child language: Evidence from the perception and production of function morphemes. In J. Goodman and H. C. Nusbaum, eds., *The development of speech perception: The transition from speech sounds to spoken words*. Cambridge, Mass.: MIT Press.

Gerken, L. A., and B. McIntosh. 1993a. Function morphemes in the sentence comprehension of normally developing and language delayed children. Ms., State University of New York, Buffalo.

Gerken, L. A., and B. McIntosh. 1993b. Interplay of function morphemes and prosody in early language. *Developmental Psychology* 29, 448–457.

Gerken, L. A., B. Landau, and R. Remez. 1990. Function morphemes in young children's speech perception and production. *Developmental Psychology* 26, 204–216.

Gleitman, L., H. Gleitman, B. Landau, and E. Wanner. 1988. Where learning begins: Initial representations for language learning. In F. Newmeyer, ed., *The Cambridge linguistic survey*. New York: Cambridge University Press.

Gleitman, L., and E. Wanner. 1982. The state of the state of the art. In E. Wanner and L. Gleitman, eds., *Language acquisition: The state of the art*. Cambridge: Cambridge University Press.

Golinkoff, R. M., A. Alioto, K. Hirsh-Pasek, and D. Kaufman. 1992. Infants learn lexical items better in infant-directed than in adult-directed speech. Paper presented at the 17th Annual Boston University Conference on Language Development, Boston, October.

Golinkoff, R. M., and K. Hirsh-Pasek. 1981. A new approach to language comprehension. Unpublished grant proposal, University of Delaware and Temple University.

Golinkoff, R. M., K. Hirsh-Pasek, K. M. Cauley, and L. Gordon. 1987. The eyes have it: Lexical and syntactic comprehension in a new paradigm. *Journal of Child Language* 14, 23–45.

Goodluck, H. 1981. Children's grammar of complement subject interpretation. In S. Tavakolian, ed., *Language acquisition and linguistic theory*. Cambridge, Mass.: MIT Press.

Goodluck, H. 1987. Children's interpretation of pronouns and null NPs: An alternative view. In B. Lust, ed., *Studies in the acquisition of anaphora*. Vol. 2, *Applying the constraints*. Dordrecht: Reidel.

Goodluck, H. 1990. Knowledge integration in processing and acquisition: Comments on Grimshaw and Rosen. In L. Frazier and J. G. de Villiers, eds., *Language processing and language acquisition*. Dordrecht: Kluwer.

Goodluck, H., and D. Behne. 1992. Development in control and extraction. In J. Weissenborn, H. Goodluck, and T. Roeper, eds., *Theoretical issues in language acquisition*. Hillsdale, N.J.: Lawrence Erlbaum.

Goodluck, H., D. Kudra, and K. K. Saah. 1994. On the default mechanism for interrogative binding. Ms., University of Ottawa and University of Ghana.

Goodluck, H., J. Sedivy, and M. Foley. 1989. *Wh*-questions and extraction from temporal adjuncts: A case for movement. *Papers and Reports on Child Language Development* 28, 123–130.

Goodluck, H., and L. Solan. 1979. A reevaluation of the basic operations hypothesis. *Cognition* 7, 85–91.

Goodluck, H., and L. Solan. 1995. C-command and Principle C in children's grammar: A replication study. *Cahiers linguistiques d'Ottawa* 23, *Supplément*, 43–52.

Goodluck, H., and S. Tavakolian. 1982. Competence and processing in children's grammar of relative clauses. *Cognition* 11, 1–27.

Goodluck, H., and A. Terzi. 1995. Controlled PRO and the acquisition of Greek. Paper presented at the 20th Annual Boston University Conference on Language Development, Boston, November.

Gopnik, M., and M. Crago. 1991. Familial aggregation of a developmental language disorder. *Cognition* 39, 1–58.

Gordon, P. 1981. Syntactic acquisition of the count/mass distinction. *Papers and Reports on Child Language Development* 20, 70–77.

Gordon, P. 1982. The acquisition of syntactic categories: The case of the count/mass distinction. Doctoral dissertation, Department of Psychology, MIT.

Gordon, P., and J. Chafetz. 1986. Lexical learning and generalization in the passive acquisition. Paper presented at the 11th Annual Boston University Conference on Language Development, Boston, October.

Gramont, M. 1902. Observations sur le language des enfants. In *Mélanges linguistiques offerts à M. Antoine Meillet*. Paris.

Grégoire, A. 1937. *L'apprentissage du language: Les deux premières années*. Liège/Paris.

Grégoire, A. 1947. *L'apprentissage du langage. La troisième année et les années suivantes*. N.p.

Grieve, R., R. Hoogenraad, and D. Murray. 1977. On the young child's use of lexis and syntax in understanding locative instructions. *Cognition* 5, 235–250.

Grimshaw, J. 1981. Form, function, and the language acquisition device. In C. L. Baker and J. J. McCarthy, eds., *The logical problem of language acquisition*. Cambridge, Mass.: MIT Press.

Grodzinsky, Y., and G. Kave. 1993/1994. Do children really know Condition A? *Language Acquisition* 3, 41–54.

Gropen, J., S. Pinker, M. Hollander, and R. Goldberg. 1991. Affectedness and direct objects: The role of lexical semantics in the acquisition of verb argument structure. *Cognition* 41, 153–195.

Gropen, J., S. Pinker, M. Hollander, R. Goldberg, and R. Wilson. 1989. The learnability and acquisition of the dative alternation in English. *Language* 65, 203–257.

Guasti, M. T. In press. Acquisition of Italian interrogatives. In H. Clahsen, ed., *Generative studies of the acquisition of case and agreement*. Amsterdam: John Benjamins.

Guasti, M. T., and U. Shlonsky. In press. The acquisition of French relative clauses reconsidered. *Language Acquisition.*

Guasti, M. T., R. Thornton, and K. Wexler. 1995. Negation in children's questions: The case of English. In D. MacLaughlin and S. McEwen, eds., *Proceedings of the 19th Annual Boston University Conference on Language Development.* Somerville, Mass.: Cascadilla Press.

Hadley, P. 1993. A longitudinal investigation of the auxiliary system in children with specific language impairment. Doctoral dissertation, University of Kansas, Lawrence.

Haegeman, L. 1994. Root infinitives, tenses and truncated structures. Ms., University of Geneva.

Hagoort, P., C. Brown, and J. Groothusen. 1993. The syntactic positive shift (SPS) as an ERP-measure of syntactic processing. *Language and Cognitive Processes* 8, 439–483.

Hakes, D. T. 1980. *The development of metalinguistic abilities in children.* Berlin: Springer-Verlag.

Hamburger, H. 1980. A deletion ahead of its time. *Cognition* 8, 389–416.

Hamburger, H., and S. Crain. 1982. Relative acquisition. In S. Kuczaj, ed., *Language development.* Vol. 1, *Syntax and semantics.* Hillsdale, N.J.: Lawrence Erlbaum.

Hamburger, H., and S. Crain. 1987. Plans and semantics in human processing of language. *Cognitive Science* 11, 101–136.

Hansson, K., and U. Nettelbladt. 1995. Grammatical characteristics of Swedish children with SLI. *Journal of Speech and Hearing Research* 38, 589–598.

Hirsh-Pasek, K., and R. M. Golinkoff. 1996. *The origins of grammar: Evidence from early language comprehension.* Cambridge, Mass.: MIT Press.

Hirsh-Pasek, K., R. M. Golinkoff, G. Hermon, and D. Kaufman. 1995. Evidence from comprehension for the early knowledge of pronouns. In E. Clark, ed., *Proceedings of the Twenty-Sixth Annual Child Language Research Forum.* Stanford, Calif.: CSLI Publications. Distributed by Cambridge University Press.

Hirsh-Pasek, K., R. M. Golinkoff, and L. Naigles. 1996. Young children's ability to use syntactic frames to derive meaning. In *The origins of grammar: Evidence from early language comprehension.* Cambridge, Mass.: MIT Press.

Hochberg, J. 1986. Children's judgments of transitivity errors. *Journal of Child Language* 13, 317–334.

Hoekstra, T., and B. Schwartz. 1994. *Language acquisition studies in generative grammar.* Amsterdam: John Benjamins.

Holcomb, P., S. Coffey, and H. Neville. 1992. Auditory and visual sentence processing: A developmental analysis using event-related potentials. *Developmental Neuropsychology* 5, 235–253.

Holmberg, A. 1986. Word order and syntactic features. Doctoral dissertation, University of Stockholm.

Hsu, J. R., H. S. Cairns, and N. Bialo. 1987. *When*-questions: A study of how children linguistically encode temporal information. *Journal of Psycholinguistic Research* 16, 241–255.

Hsu, J. R., H. S. Cairns, and R. W. Fiengo. 1985. The development of grammars underlying children's interpretation of complex sentences. *Cognition* 20, 25–48.

Hsu, J. R., H. S. Cairns, S. Eisenberg, and G. Schlisselberg. 1989. Control and coreference in early childhood. *Journal of Child Language* 16, 599–622.

Hsu, J. R., H. S. Cairns, S. Eisenberg, and G. Schlisselberg. 1991. When do children avoid backwards coreference? *Journal of Child Language* 18, 339–353.

Hsu, L. M. 1989. Random sampling, randomization and equivalence of contrasted groups in psychotherapy outcome research. *Journal of Consulting and Clinical Psychology* 57, 131–137.

Hsu, L. M. 1995. Regression toward the mean associated with measurement error and the identification of improvement and deterioration in psychotherapy. *Journal of Consulting and Clinical Psychology* 63, 141–144.

Hughes, D. L., M. E. Fey, and S. H. Long. 1992. Developmental sentence scoring: Still useful after all these years. *Topics in Language Disorders* 12, 1–12.

Hughes, M., and H. Sussman. 1983. An assessment of cerebral dominance in language-disordered children via a time-sharing paradigm. *Brain and Language* 19, 48–64.

Huitema, B. E. 1980. *The analysis of covariance and alternatives.* New York: Wiley.

Hurford, J. 1975. A child and the English question formation rule. *Journal of Child Language* 2, 299–301.

Huttenlocher, J., W. Haight, A. Bryk, M. Seltzer, and T. Lyons. 1991. Early vocabulary growth: Relation to language input and gender. *Developmental Psychology* 27, 236–248.

Hyams, N. 1986. *Language acquisition and the theory of parameters.* Dordrecht: Reidel.

Hyams, N. 1992. A reanalysis of null subjects in child language. In J. Weissenborn, H. Goodluck, and T. Roeper, eds., *Theoretical issues in language acquisition.* Hillsdale, N.J.: Lawrence Erlbaum.

Jakubowicz, C. 1984. Markedness and binding principles. In C. Jones and P. Sells, eds., *Proceedings of NELS 14.* GLSA, University of Massachusetts, Amherst.

Jakubowicz, C. 1989a. Invariance of Universal Grammar principles in the acquisition of reflexive and nonreflexive pronouns, passive, *promise* and raising constructions in French. Paper presented at the 14th Annual Boston University Conference on Language Development, Boston, October.

Jakubowicz, C. 1989b. Maturation or invariance of Universal Grammar principles in language acquisition. *Probus* 3, 283–340.

Jakubowicz, C. 1991. L'acquisition des anaphores et des pronoms lexicaux en français. In J. Guéron and J.-Y. Pollock, eds., *Grammaire générative et syntaxe comparée*. Paris: Editions du CNRS.

Jakubowicz, C. 1993. Linguistic theory and language acquisition facts: Reformulation, maturation or invariance of binding principles. In E. Reuland and W. Abraham, eds., *Knowledge and language: Issues in representation and acquisition*. Boston: Kluwer.

Jakubowicz, C. 1994a. On the morphological specification of reflexives: Implications for acquisition. In M. Gonzalez, ed., *NELS 24*. Vol. 1. GLSA, University of Massachusetts, Amherst.

Jakubowicz, C. 1994b. Reflexives in French and Danish: Morphology, syntax and acquisition. In B. Lust, G. Hermon, and J. Kornfilt, eds., *Syntactic theory and first language acquisition: Cross-linguistic perspectives*. Vol. 2, *Binding, dependencies, and learnability*. Hillsdale, N.J.: Lawrence Erlbaum.

Jakubowicz, C. In preparation. Comprehension and production of complement clitics by Spanish-speaking children. Ms., Laboratoire de Psychologie Expérimentale, CNRS, Université de Paris V.

Jakubowicz, C., N. Mueller, O.-K. Kang, C. Rigaut, and B. Riemer. 1995. On the acquisition of the pronominal system in French and German. In M. Bernstein, ed., *Proceedings of the 20th Annual Boston University Conference on Language Development*. Somerville, Mass.: Cascadilla Press.

Jakubowicz, C., and L. Olsen. 1988. Reflexive anaphors and pronouns in Danish. Paper presented at the 13th Annual Boston University Conference on Language Development, Boston, October.

Johnson, H. 1975. The meaning of *before* and *after* for preschool children. *Journal of Experimental Child Psychology* 19, 88–99.

Johnston, J. 1988. Specific language disorders in the child. In N. Lass, J. Northern, L. McReynolds, and D. Yoder, eds., *Handbook of speech-language pathology and audiology*. Philadelphia: B. C. Decker.

Johnston, J., and S. Ellis Weismer. 1983. Mental rotation abilities in language-disordered children. *Journal of Speech and Hearing Disorders* 26, 397–403.

Johnston, J., and A. Kamhi. 1984. Syntactic and semantic aspects of the utterances of language-impaired children: The same can be less. *Merrill-Palmer Quarterly* 30, 65–85.

Johnston, J., and T. Schery. 1976. The use of grammatical morphemes by children with communication disorders. In D. Morehead and A. Morehead, eds., *Normal and deficient child language*. Baltimore, Md.: University Park Press.

Katz, B., G. Baker, and J. McNamara. 1974. What's in a name? On the child's acquisition of proper and common nouns. *Child Development* 45, 269–273.

Kaufman, D. 1988. Grammatical and cognitive interactions in the study of children's knowledge of binding theory and reference relations. Doctoral dissertation, Temple University.

Kay, D. A., and J. M. Anglin. 1982. Overextension and underextension in the child's expressive and receptive speech. *Journal of Child Language* 9, 83–98.

Kayne, R. 1975. *French syntax.* Cambridge, Mass.: MIT Press.

Kayne, R. 1983. *Connectedness and binary branching.* Dordrecht: Foris.

Kayne, R. 1994. *The antisymmetry of syntax.* Cambridge, Mass.: MIT Press.

Kazdin, A. L. 1982. *Single-case research designs: Methods for clinical and applied settings.* New York: Oxford University Press.

Kazdin, A. L. 1992. *Research design in clinical psychology.* Boston: Allyn and Bacon.

Kemler Nelson, D. G., K. Hirsh-Pasek, P. W. Juscyzk, and K. Wright Cassidy. 1989. How the prosodic cues in motherese might assist language learning. *Journal of Child Language* 16, 53–68.

Kennedy, J. J. 1992. *Analyzing qualitative data.* New York: Praeger.

Kernan, K. T. 1969. The acquisition of language by Samoan children. Doctoral dissertation, University of California, Berkeley.

King, G., and P. Fletcher. 1993. Grammatical problems in school-age children with specific language impairment. *Clinical Linguistics and Phonetics* 7, 339–352.

Kirk, R. E. 1982. *Experimental design: Procedures for the behavioral sciences.* 2nd ed. Monterey, Calif.: Brooks/Cole.

Klima, E., and U. Bellugi. 1966. Syntactic regularities in the speech of children. In J. Lyons and R. J. Wales, eds., *Psycholinguistic papers.* Edinburgh: Edinburgh University Press.

Kline, P. 1986. *A handbook of test construction: Introduction to psychometric design.* London: Methuen.

Koopman, H. 1984. *The syntax of verbs.* Dordrecht: Foris.

Koster, C. 1993. Errors in anaphora acquisition. Doctoral dissertation, OTS, Utrecht University.

Koster, C. 1995. Le destin de la théorie du liage réformulée. In C. Jakubowicz, ed., *Grammaire universelle et acquisition du langage. Recherches linguistiques de Vincennes* 24, 103–124.

Kuczaj, S. 1976. *-ing, -s* and *-ed:* A study of the acquisition of certain verb inflections. Doctoral dissertation, University of Minnesota.

Kudra, D., H. Goodluck, and L. Progovac. 1994. The acquisition of long distance binding in Serbo-Croatian. Paper presented at the annual meeting of the Linguistic Society of America, Boston, January.

Kuhl, P. K. 1985. Methods in the study of infant speech perception. In G. Gottlieb and N. A. Krasnegor, eds., *Measurement of audition and vision in the first year of postnatal life: A methodological overview.* Norwood, N.J.: Ablex.

Kuhl, P. K., and A. N. Meltzoff. 1982. The bimodal perception of speech in infancy. *Science* 218, 1138–1141.

Kutas, M., H. Neville, and P. Holcomb. 1987. A preliminary comparison of the N400 response to semantic anomalies during reading, listening, and signing. *Electroencephalography and Clinical Neurophysiology, Supplement 39*, 325–330.

Kutas, M., and C. Van Petten. 1994. Psycholinguistics electrified: Event-related brain potential investigations. In M. Gernsbacher, ed., *Handbook of psycholinguistics*. San Diego, Calif.: Academic Press.

Labelle, M. 1990. Predication, *wh*-movement and the development of relative clauses. *Language Acquisition* 1, 95–119.

Lackner, J. 1968. A developmental study of language behavior in retarded children. *Neuropsychologia* 6, 301–320.

Lasnik, H., and S. Crain. 1985. On the acquisition of pronominal reference. Review of L. Solan, *Pronominal reference: Child language and the theory of grammar. Lingua* 65, 135–154.

Lasnik, H., and J. Uriagereka. 1988. *A course in GB syntax: Lectures on binding and empty categories.* Cambridge, Mass.: MIT Press.

Lebeaux, D. 1988. Language acquisition and the form of the grammar. Doctoral dissertation, University of Massachusetts, Amherst.

Lee, H., and K. Wexler. 1987. The acquisition of reflexives and pronouns in Korean: From a cross-linguistic perspective. Paper presented at the 12th Annual Boston University Conference on Language Development, Boston, October.

Lee, L. 1971. *Northwestern Syntax Screening Test.* Evanston, Ill.: Northwestern University Press.

Lee, L. 1974. *Developmental sentence analysis.* Evanston, Ill.: Northwestern University Press.

Lee, L. L. 1970. A screening test for syntax development. *Journal of Speech and Hearing Disorders* 35, 103–112.

Leemans, G. 1994. The acquisition of verb placement in Dutch SLI children. Paper presented at the European Symposium on Child Language Disorders, Garderen, The Netherlands, May.

Leftheri, K. 1991. Learning to interpret *wh*-questions in Greek. Honors thesis, Smith College.

Legum, S. 1975. Strategies in the acquisition of relative clauses. *Southwest Regional Laboratory Technical Note*, TN 2-75-10.

Lehmann, E. L. 1975. *Nonparametrics: Statistical methods based on ranks.* New York: McGraw-Hill.

Lempert, H. 1984. Topic as starting point in syntax. *Monographs of the Society for Research in Child Development* 49 (5, Serial No. 208).

Lempert, H., and M. Kinsbourne. 1981. How young children represent sentences: Evidence from the superiority of noun recall from action as compared to stative sequences. *Journal of Psycholinguistic Research* 10, 155–166.

Leonard, L. 1989. Language learnability and specific language impairment in children. *Applied Psycholinguistics* 10, 179–202.

Leonard, L. 1994. Functional categories in the grammars of children with specific language impairment. Ms., Purdue University.

Leonard, L., U. Bortolini, M. C. Caselli, K. McGregor, and L. Sabbadini. 1992. Morphological deficits in children with specific language impairment: The status of features in the underlying grammar. *Language Acquisition* 2, 151–179.

Leonard, L., and E. Dromi. 1994. The use of Hebrew verb morphology by children with specific language impairment and children developing normally. *First Language* 14, 283–304.

Leonard, L., C. Prutting, J. Perozzi, and R. Berkley. 1978. Nonstandardized approaches to the assessment of language behaviors. *Asha* 20, 371–379.

Leonard, L., L. Sabbadini, J. Leonard, and V. Volterra. 1987. Specific language impairment in children: A crosslinguistic study. *Brain and Language* 32, 233–252.

Leopold, W. F. 1971. The study of child language and infant bilingualism. In A. Bar-Adon and W. F. Leopold, eds., *Child language: A book of readings.* Englewood Cliffs, N.J.: Prentice-Hall.

Lightfoot, D. 1976. Trace theory and twice-moved NPs. *Linguistic Inquiry* 7, 559–582.

Lindner, K., and J. Johnston. 1992. Grammatical morphology in language-impaired children acquiring English or German as their first language: A functional perspective. *Applied Psycholinguistics* 13, 115–129.

Loeb, D., and L. Leonard. 1991. Subject case marking and verb morphology in normally developing and specifically language-impaired children. *Journal of Speech and Hearing Research* 34, 340–346.

Long, S., and M. Fey. 1989. *Computerized profiling* (Version 6.2). Ithaca, N.Y.: Computerized Profiling.

Lord, F. M., and M. R. Novick. 1968. *Statistical theories of mental test scores.* Reading, Mass.: Addison-Wesley.

Lorenz, H. A. 1895. *Versuch einer Theorie der elektrischen und optischen Erscheinungen in bewegten Körpern.* Leiden: Brill.

Lovell, K., and B. Bradbury. 1967. The learning of English morphology in educationally subnormal special school children. *American Journal of Mental Deficiency* 72, 609–615.

Lovell, K., and E. M. Dixon. 1967. The growth of the control of grammar in imitation, comprehension, and production. *Journal of Child Psychology and Psychiatry* 8, 31–39.

Lust, B. 1977. Conjunction reduction in child language. *Journal of Child Language* 4, 257–287.

Lust, B. 1981a. Constraint on anaphora in early child language: A prediction for a universal. In S. Tavakolian, ed., *Language acquisition and linguistic theory.* Cambridge, Mass.: MIT Press.

Lust, B. 1981b. On coordinating studies of coordination: Problems of method and theory in first language acquisition. A reply to Ardery. *Journal of Child Language* 8, 454–470.

Lust, B. 1983. On the notion "principal branching direction": A parameter of Universal Grammar. In Y. Otsu, H. van Riemsdijk, K. Inoue, A. Kamio, and N. Kawasaki, eds., *Studies in generative grammar and language acquisition*. Tokyo Hakugei University, Japan.

Lust, B., ed. 1986. *Studies in the acquisition of anaphora*. Vol. 1, *Defining the constraints*. Dordrecht, Reidel.

Lust, B., ed. 1987. *Studies in the acquisition of anaphora*. Vol. 2, *Applying the constraints*. Dordrecht: Reidel.

Lust, B. 1994. Functional projection of CP and phrase structure parameterization: An argument for the strong continuity hypothesis. In B. Lust, M. Suñer, and J. Whitman, eds., *Syntactic theory and first language acquisition: Cross-linguistic perspectives*. Vol. 1, *Heads, projection, and learnability*. Hillsdale, N.J.: Lawrence Erlbaum.

Lust, B. In preparation. *Universal Grammar and the initial state: Crosslinguistic studies of directionality*. Cambridge, Mass.: MIT Press.

Lust, B. To appear. Universal Grammar: The "strong continuity" hypothesis in first language acquisition. In W. C. Ritchie and T. K. Bhatia, eds., *Handbook of first language acquisition*. San Diego, Calif.: Academic Press.

Lust, B., T. Bhatia, J. Gair, V. Sharma, and J. Khare. To appear. Children's acquisition of Hindi anaphora: A parameter-setting approach. In V. Ghambir, ed., *Teaching and acquisition of South Asian languages*. Philadelphia: University of Pennsylvania Press.

Lust, B., and Y.-C. Chien. 1984. The structure of coordination in first language acquisition of Chinese. *Cognition* 17, 49–83.

Lust, B., Y.-C. Chien, and S. Flynn. 1987. What children know: Methods for the study of first language acquisition. In B. Lust, ed., *Studies in the acquisition of anaphora*. Vol. 2, *Applying the constraints*. Dordrecht: Reidel.

Lust, B., and T. Clifford. 1986. The 3-D study: Effects of depth, distance and directionality on children's acquisition of anaphora. In B. Lust, ed., *Studies in the acquisition of anaphora*. Vol. 1, *Defining the constraints*. Dordrecht: Reidel.

Lust, B., S. Flynn, Y.-C. Chien, and T. Clifford. 1980. Coordination: The role of syntactic, pragmatic and processing factors in first language acquisition. *Papers and Reports on Child Language Development* 19, 79–87.

Lust, B., S. Flynn, C. Foley, and Y.-C. Chien. To appear. How do we know what children know? Current advances in establishing scientific methods for the study of language acquisition and linguistic theory. In W. C. Ritchie and T. K. Bhatia, eds., *Handbook of first language acquisition*. San Diego, Calif.: Academic Press.

Lust, B., and K.-O. Lee. 1988. On the first language acquisition of Korean pronominal anaphora: The roles of configuration and linearity. In E. Baek, ed.,

Papers from the Sixth International Conference on Korean Linguistics. International Circle of Korean Linguistics and the Department of East Asian Studies, University of Toronto.

Lust, B., K. Loveland, and R. Kornet. 1980. The development of anaphora in first language: Syntactic and pragmatic constraints. *Linguistic Analysis* 6, 217–249.

Lust, B., and L. Mangione. 1983. The principal branching direction parameter in first language acquisition of anaphora. In P. Sells and C. Jones, eds., *Proceedings of NELS 13.* GLSA, University of Massachusetts, Amherst.

Lust, B., L. Mangione, and Y.-C. Chien. 1984. The determination of empty categories in first language acquisition of Chinese. In W. Harbert, ed., *Cornell University working papers in linguistics 6.* Department of Modern Languages and Linguistics, Cornell University.

Lust, B., and R. Mazuka. 1989. Cross-linguistic studies of directionality in first language acquisition: The Japanese data. *Journal of Child Language* 16, 665–684.

Lust, B., J. Eisele, and R. Mazuka. 1992. The binding theory module: Evidence from first language acquisition for Principle C. *Language* 68, 333–358.

Lust, B., and C. A. Mervis. 1980. Coordination in the natural speech of young children. *Journal of Child Language* 7, 279–304.

Lust, B., L. Solan, S. Flynn, C. Cross, and E. Schuetz. 1986. A comparison of null and pronoun anaphora in first language acquisition. In B. Lust, ed., *Studies in the acquisition of anaphora.* Vol. 1, *Defining the constraints.* Dordrecht: Reidel.

Lust, B., M. Suñer, and J. Whitman, eds. 1994. *Syntactic theory and first language acquisition: Cross-linguistic perspectives.* Vol. 1, *Heads, projections, and learnability.* Hillsdale, N.J.: Lawrence Erlbaum.

Lust, B., and T. K. Wakayama. 1979. The structure of coordination in young children's acquisition of Japanese. In F. Eckman and A. Hastings, ed., *Studies in first and second language acquisition.* Rowley, Mass.: Newbury House.

Lust, B., and T. K. Wakayama. 1981. Word order in Japanese first language acquisition. In P. Dale and D. Ingram, eds., *Child language: An international perspective.* Baltimore, Md.: University Park Press.

Lust, B., T. K. Wakayama, R. Mazuka, and W. Snyder. 1986. Distinguishing effects of parameter-setting in early syntax: A cross-linguistic study of Japanese and English. Paper presented at the Stanford University Conference on Child Language, April.

MacWhinney, B. 1991. *The CHILDES handbook: Tools for analyzing talk.* Hillsdale, N.J.: Lawrence Erlbaum.

MacWhinney, B., and C. Snow. 1985. The Child Language Data Exchange System. *Journal of Child Language* 12, 271–296.

Marascuilo, L. S., and M. McSweeney. 1977. *Nonparametric and distribution-free methods for the social sciences.* Monterey, Calif.: Brooks/Cole.

Maratsos, M. 1974a. Children who get worse at understanding the passive: A replication of Bever. *Journal of Psycholinguistic Research* 3, 65–74.

Maratsos, M. 1974b. How preschool children understand missing complement subjects. *Child Development* 45, 700–706.

Maratsos, M. 1976. *The use of definite and indefinite reference in young children: An experimental study of semantic acquisition.* Cambridge: Cambridge University Press.

Maratsos, M. 1984. Some current issues in the study of the acquisition of grammar. In J. Flavell and E. Markman, eds., *Handbook of child psychology.* Vol. 3, *Cognitive development.* 4th ed. New York: Wiley.

Maratsos, M., D. E. C. Fox, J. A. Becker, and M. Chalkley. 1985. Semantic restrictions on children's passives. *Cognition* 19, 167–191.

Maratsos, M., and S. Kuczaj. 1978. Against the transformationalist account: A simpler analysis of auxiliary overmarkings. *Journal of Child Language* 5, 337–345.

Maratsos, M., S. Kuczaj, D. E. C. Fox, and M. Chalkley. 1979. Some empirical studies in the acquisition of transformational relations: Passives, negatives, and the past tense. In W. A. Collins, ed., *Minnesota Symposium on Child Psychology.* Vol. 12. Hillsdale, N.J.: Lawrence Erlbaum.

Marcus, G. F. 1993. Negative evidence in language acquisition. *Cognition* 46, 53–85.

Marcus, G. F., S. Pinker, M. Ullman, M. Hollander, T. J. Rosen, and F. Xu. 1992. Overregularization in language acquisition. *Monographs of the Society for Research in Child Development* 57 (4, Serial No. 228).

Markman, E. 1989. *Categorization and naming in children.* Cambridge, Mass.: MIT Press.

Marks, L. E., and G. A. Miller. 1964. The role of semantic and syntactic constraints in the memorization of English sentences. *Journal of Verbal Learning and Verbal Behavior* 3, 1–5.

Maxfield, T. L., and D. McDaniel. 1991. What do children know without learning? In T. L. Maxfield and B. Plunkett, eds., *Papers in the acquisition of wh.* GLSA, University of Massachusetts, Amherst.

Maxfield, T. L., and B. Plunkett, eds. 1991. *Papers in the acquisition of wh.* GLSA, University of Massachusetts, Amherst.

Maxwell, S. E., and H. D. Delaney. 1990. *Designing experiments and analyzing data: A model comparison perspective.* Belmont, Calif.: Wadsworth.

Mayer, J. W., A. Erreich, and V. Valian. 1978. Transformations, basic operations and language acquisition. *Cognition* 6, 1–13.

Mazuka, R. 1990. Japanese and English children's processing of complex sentences: An experimental comparison. Doctoral dissertation, Cornell University.

Mazuka, R., and B. Lust. 1994. When is an anaphor not an anaphor? A study of Japanese "zibun." In B. Lust, G. Hermon, and J. Kornfilt, eds., *Syntactic theory and first language acquisition: Cross-linguistic perspectives.* Vol. 2, *Binding, dependencies, and learnability.* Hillsdale, N.J.: Lawrence Erlbaum.

Mazuka, R., B. Lust, T. Wakayama, and W. Snyder. 1995. "Null subject grammar" and phrase structure in early syntax acquisition: A cross-linguistic study of Japanese and English. In C. Jakubowicz, ed., *Grammaire universelle et acquisition du langage. Recherches linguistiques de Vincennes* 24, 55–81.

McCarthy, D. 1946. Language development in children. In L. Carmichael, ed., *Manual of child psychology*. New York: Wiley.

McCauley, R., and L. Swisher. 1984. Psychometric review of language and articulation tests for preschool children. *Journal of Speech and Hearing Disorders* 49, 338–348.

McDaniel, D., and H. S. Cairns. 1990. The child as informant: Eliciting intuitions from young children. *Journal of Psycholinguistic Research* 19, 331–344.

McDaniel, D., H. S. Cairns, and J. R. Hsu. 1990. Binding principles in the grammars of young children. *Language Acquisition* 1, 121–138.

McDaniel, D., H. S. Cairns, and J. R. Hsu. 1991. Control principles in the grammars of young children. *Language Acquisition* 1, 297–335.

McDaniel, D., B. Chiu, and T. L. Maxfield. 1995. Parameters for *wh*-movement types: Evidence from child English. *Natural Language & Linguistic Theory* 13, 709–753.

McDaniel, D., and T. L. Maxfield. 1992a. The nature of the anti-c-command requirement: Evidence from young children. *Linguistic Inquiry* 23, 667–671.

McDaniel, D., and T. L. Maxfield. 1992b. Principle B and contrastive stress. *Language Acquisition* 2, 337–358.

McDaniel, D., and C. McKee. 1992. Which children did they show obey strong crossover? In H. Goodluck and M. Rochemont, eds., *Island constraints: Theory, acquisition, and processing*. Dordrecht: Kluwer.

McDaniel, D., and C. McKee. 1995. Children's oblique relatives. Paper presented at the 20th Annual Boston University Conference on Language Development, Boston, November.

McKee, C. 1992. A comparison of pronouns and anaphors in Italian and English acquisition. *Language Acquisition* 1, 21–55.

McKee, C., J. Cripe, and M. Campos. 1995. A study of lexical factors in syntactic development. Ms., University of Arizona.

McKee, C., and M. Emiliani. 1992. Il clitico: C'e ma non si vede. *Natural Language & Linguistic Theory* 10, 415–438.

McKee, C., J. Nicol, and D. McDaniel. 1993. Children's application of binding during sentence processing. *Language and Cognitive Processes* 8, 265–290.

McNeill, D. 1966a. The creation of language by children. In J. Lyons and R. J. Wales, eds., *Psycholinguistic papers*. Edinburgh: Edinburgh University Press.

McNeill, D. 1966b. Developmental psycholinguistics. In F. Smith and G. A. Miller, eds., *The genesis of language: A psycholinguistic approach*. Cambridge, Mass.: MIT Press.

McNeill, D., and N. McNeill. 1966. What does a child mean when he says "no"? In E. Zale, ed., *Proceedings of the Conference on Language and Language Behavior.* New York: Appleton-Century-Crofts.

Meisel, J., ed. 1992. *The acquisition of verb placement: Functional categories and V2 phenomena in language development.* Dordrecht: Kluwer.

Meisel, J., and N. Mueller. 1992. Finiteness and verb placement in early child grammars: Evidence from the simultaneous acquisition of two first languages: French and German. In J. Meisel, ed., *The acquisition of verb placement: Functional categories and V2 phenomena in language development.* Dordrecht: Kluwer.

Meltzoff, A. N., and R. W. Borton. 1979. Intermodal matching by human neonates. *Nature* 282, 403–404.

Meltzoff, A. N., and K. Moore. 1985. Cognitive foundations and social functions of imitation and intermodal representation in infancy. In J. Mehler and R. Fox, eds., *Neonate cognition: Beyond the blooming buzzing confusion.* Hillsdale, N.J.: Lawrence Erlbaum.

Menyuk, P. 1964. Comparison of grammar of children with functionally deviant and normal speech. *Journal of Speech and Hearing Research* 7, 109–121.

Michelson, A. A. 1881. The relative motion of the earth and the luminiferous ether. *American Journal of Science*, series 3, vol. 22, 120–129.

Miller, G. A., and S. Isard. 1963. Some perceptual consequences of linguistic rules. *Journal of Verbal Learning and Verbal Behavior* 2, 217–228.

Miller, J. 1988. The developmental asynchrony of language development in children with Down syndrome. In L. Nadel, ed., *The psychobiology of Down syndrome.* Cambridge, Mass.: MIT Press.

Miller, J. 1991. Quantifying productive language disorders. In J. Miller, ed., *Research on child language disorders.* Austin, Tex.: Pro-Ed.

Miller, J., and R. Chapman. 1991. *SALT: Systematic Analysis of Language Transcripts.* Language Lab, University of Wisconsin.

Miller, J., and D. Yoder. 1974. Ontogenetic language teaching strategies for retarded children. In R. Schiefelbusch and L. Lloyd, eds., *Language perspectives.* Baltimore, Md.: University Park Press.

Miller, W., and S. Ervin. 1964. The development of grammar in child language. In U. Bellugi and R. Brown, eds., *The acquisition of language. Monographs of the Society for Research in Child Development* 29 (1, Serial No. 92).

Mills, D., S. Coffey-Corina, and H. Neville. 1993. Language acquisition and cerebral specialization in 20-month-old infants. *Journal of Cognitive Neuroscience* 5, 317–334.

Molfese, D. L. 1980. The phoneme and the engram: Electrophysiological evidence for the acoustic invariant in stop consonants. *Brain and Language* 9, 372–376.

Molfese, D. L. 1989. Electrophysiological correlates of word meanings in 14-month-old human infants. *Developmental Neuropsychology* 5, 70–103.

Molfese, D. L. 1990. Auditory evoked responses recorded from 16-month-old human infants to words they did and did not know. *Brain and Language* 38, 345–363.

Molfese, D. L., and T. Hess. 1978. Hemispheric specialization for VOT perception in the preschool child. *Journal of Experimental Child Psychology* 26, 71–84.

Molfese, D. L., and F. Wetzel. 1992. Short- and long-term auditory recognition memory in 14-month-old human infants: Electrophysiological correlates. *Developmental Neuropsychology* 8, 135–160.

Moog, J., and A. Geers. 1979. *CID Grammatical Analysis of Elicited Language.* St. Louis, Mo.: Central Institute for the Deaf.

Morgan, R. A. 1984. Auditory discrimination in speech-impaired and normal children. *British Journal of Disorders of Communication* 19, 89–96.

Myers, J. L., and A. D. Well. 1991. *Research design and statistical analysis.* New York: Harper-Collins.

Naigles, L. 1990. Children use syntax to learn verb meanings. *Journal of Child Language* 17, 357–374.

Naigles, L., and S. Gelman. 1995. Overextensions in comprehension and production revisited: Preferential-looking in a study of *dog, cat,* and *cow. Journal of Child Language* 22, 19–45.

Naigles, L., and E. Kako. 1993. First contact: Biases in verb learning with and without syntactic information. *Child Development* 64, 1665–1697.

Nakayama, M. 1987. Performance factors in subject-auxiliary inversion by children. *Journal of Child Language* 14, 113–125.

National Institutes of Health, National Institute on Neurological Disorders and Stroke. 1988. *Developmental speech and language disorders: Hope through research.* Bethesda, Md.: National Institutes of Health.

Neely, J. H. 1977. Semantic priming and retrieval from lexical memory: Roles of inhibitionless spreading activation and limited-capacity attention. *Journal of Experimental Psychology: General* 106, 226–254.

Nelson, K. 1973. Structure and strategy in learning to talk. *Monographs of the Society for Reasearch in Child Development* 38 (1–2, Serial No. 149).

Neville, H., D. Mills, and D. Lawson. 1992 Fractionating language: Different neural subsystems with different sensitive periods. *Cerebral Cortex* 2, 244–258.

Neville, H., J. Nicol, A. Barss, K. I. Forster, and M. F. Garrett. 1991. Syntactically based sentence processing classes: Evidence from event-related brain potentials. *Journal of Cognitive Neuropsychology* 3, 155–170.

Newcomer. P., and D. Hammill. 1977. *The Test of Language Development.* Austin, Tex.: Empire Press.

Newcomer, P., and D. Hammill. 1988. *Test of Language Development: Primary 2.* Austin, Tex.: Pro-Ed.

Nicol, J. 1988. Coreference processing during sentence understanding. Doctoral dissertation, MIT.

Nuñez del Prado, Z., C. Foley, R. Proman, and B. Lust. 1994. Subordinate CP and prodrop: Evidence for degree-n learnability from an experimental study of Spanish and English. In M. Gonzalez, ed., *NELS 24*. Vol. 2. GLSA, University of Massachusetts, Amherst.

Ochs, E. 1979. Transcription as theory. In E. Ochs and B. Schieffelin, eds., *Developmental pragmatics*. New York: Academic Press.

O'Leary, C., and S. Crain. 1994. Negative polarity items (a positive result) and positive polarity items (a negative result). Paper presented at the 18th Annual Boston University Conference on Language Development, Boston, January.

Olsen, L. 1992. Théorie linguistique et acquisition du langage: Etude contrastive des relations anaphoriques, syntaxe danoise et syntaxe comparée. Doctoral dissertation, Université de Paris 8.

O'Shea, M. V. 1907. *Linguistic development and education*. New York: Macmillan.

Osterhout, L., and P. Holcomb. 1992. Event-related brain potentials elicited by syntactic anomaly. *Journal of Memory and Language* 31, 785–806.

Otsu, Y. 1981. Universal Grammar and syntactic development in children: Toward a theory of syntactic development. Doctoral dissertation, MIT.

Padilla-Rivera, J. 1990. *On the definition of binding domains in Spanish*. Dordrecht: Kluwer.

Penner, Z. 1992. Asking questions without CPs: On the acquisition of *wh*-questions in Bernese Swiss German and Standard German. Ms., University of Bern.

Perez, B. 1878. *La psychologie de l'enfant: Les trois premières années*. Paris.

Pérez-Leroux, A. T. 1991. The acquisition of long distance movement in Caribbean Spanish. In T. L. Maxfield and B. Plunkett, eds., *Papers in the acquisition of wh*. GLSA, University of Massachusetts, Amherst.

Pérez-Leroux, A. T. 1995. Resumptives in the acquisition of relative clauses. *Language Acquisition* 4, 105–139.

Peters, A., and L. Menn. 1993. False starts and filler syllables: Ways to learn grammatical morphemes. *Language* 69, 742–778.

Petretic, P. A., and P. D. Tweney. 1977. Does comprehension precede production? The development of children's responses to telegraphic sentences of varying grammatical adequacy. *Journal of Child Language* 4, 201–209.

Philip, W. 1991. Spreading in the acquisition of universal quantifiers. In *Proceedings of the West Coast Conference on Formal Linguistics*. Stanford, Calif.: CSLI Publications. Distributed by Cambridge University Press.

Philip, W. 1992. Distributivity and logical form in the emergence of universal quantification. In *Ohio State working papers in linguistics* 40. Department of Linguistics, The Ohio State University.

Philip, W., and J. G. de Villiers. 1992. Monotonicity and the acquisition of weak *wh*-islands. In E. Clark, ed., *Proceedings of the Twenty-Fourth Annual Child Language Research Forum*. Stanford, Calif.: CSLI Publications. Distributed by Cambridge University Press.

Phinney, M. 1981. Syntactic constraints and the acquisition of embedded sentential complements. Doctoral dissertation, Universtiy of Massachusetts, Amherst.

Piaget, J. 1968. *La formation du symbole chez l'enfant*. Paris: Delachaux et Niestlé.

Pierce, A. 1992. *Language acquisition and syntactic theory: A comparative analysis of French and English child grammars*. Dordrecht: Kluwer.

Pinhas, J., and B. Lust. 1987. Principles of pronoun anaphora in the acquisition of oral language by the hearing impaired. In B. Lust, ed., *Studies in the acquisition of anaphora*. Vol. 2, *Applying the constraints*. Dordrecht: Reidel.

Pinker, S. 1982. A theory of the acquisition of lexical interpretive grammars. In J. Bresnan, ed., *The mental representation of grammatical relations*. Cambridge, Mass.: MIT Press.

Pinker, S. 1984. *Language learnability and language development*. Cambridge, Mass.: Harvard University Press.

Pinker, S. 1989. *Learnability and cognition: The acquisition of argument structure*. Cambridge, Mass.: MIT Press.

Pinker, S., D. Lebeaux, and L. A. Frost. 1987. Productivity and constraints in the acquisition of the passive. *Cognition* 26, 195–267.

Pinker, S., and A. Prince. 1988. On language and connectionism: Analysis of a parallel distributed processing model of language acquisition. *Cognition* 28, 73–193.

Plante, E., and R. Vance. 1994. Selection of preschool language tests: A data-based approach. *Language, Speech, and Hearing Services in Schools* 25, 15–24.

Pollock, F. 1878. An infant's progress in language. *Mind* 3, 392–401.

Popper, K. 1959. *The logic of scientific discovery*. London: Hutchinson.

Preyer, W. 1882. *Die Seele des Kindes*. Leipzig.

Prideaux, G. 1976. A functional analysis of English question acquisition: A response to Hurford. *Journal of Child Language* 3, 417–422.

Provonost, W., and C. Dumbleton. 1953. A picture-type speech sound discrimination test. *Journal of Speech and Hearing Disorders* 18, 258–266.

Pye, C. 1992. The acquisition of K'iche' Maya. In D. I. Slobin, ed., *The cross-linguistic study of language acquisition*. Vol. 3. Hillsdale, N.J.: Lawrence Erlbaum.

Pye, C., and P. Quixtan Poz. 1988. Precocious passives (and antipassives) in Quiche Mayan. *Papers and Reports on Child Language Development* 27, 71–80.

Quine, W. V. O. 1953. Two dogmas of empiricism. In *From a logical point of view: 9 logico-philosophical essays*. New York: Harper.

Radford, A 1990. *Syntactic theory and the acquisition of English syntax.* Oxford: Blackwell.

Radford, A. 1994. The syntax of questions in child English. *Journal of Child Language* 21, 211–236.

Reichenbach, H. 1978. Induction and probability: Remarks on Karl Popper's *The logic of scientific discovery.* In M. Reichenbach and R. S. Cohen, eds., *Hans Reichenbach: Selected writings 1909–1953.* Vol. 2. Dordecht: Reidel.

Reinhart, T. 1976. The syntactic domain of anaphora. Doctoral dissertation, MIT.

Rescorla, L. A. 1980. Overextension in language development. *Journal of Child Language* 7, 321–335.

Rescorla, L. A. 1991. Identifying expressive language delay at age 2. *Topics in Language Disorders* 11, 14–20.

Rice, M. 1991. Children with specific language impairment: Toward a model of teachability. In N. Krasnegor, D. Rumbaugh, R. Schiefelbusch, and M. Studdert-Kennedy, eds., *Biological and behavioral determinants of language development.* Hillsdale, N.J.: Lawrence Erlbaum.

Rice, M., and J. Oetting. 1993. Morphological deficits of children: Evaluation of number marking and agreement. *Journal of Speech and Hearing Research* 36, 1249–1257.

Rice, M., K. Wexler, and P. Cleave. In press. Specific language impairment as a period of extended optional infinitive. *Journal of Speech and Hearing Research.*

Rizzi, L. 1986. On the status of object clitics in Romance. In O. Jaeggli and C. Silva Corvalan, eds., *Studies in Romance linguistics.* Dordrecht: Foris.

Rizzi, L. 1990. *Relativized Minimality.* Cambridge, Mass.: MIT Press.

Roeper, T., and J. G. de Villiers. 1991. The emergence of bound variable structures. In T. L. Maxfield and B. Plunkett, eds., *Papers in the acquisition of wh.* GLSA, University of Massachusetts, Amherst.

Roeper, T., and J. G. de Villiers. 1992. Ordered decisions in the acquisition of *wh*-questions. In J. Weissenborn, H. Goodluck, and T. Roeper, eds., *Theoretical issues in language acquisition.* Hillsdale, N.J.: Lawrence Erlbaum.

Roeper, T., and J. G. de Villiers. 1994. Lexical links in the *wh*-chain. In B. Lust, G. Hermon, and J. Kornfilt, eds., *Syntactic theory and first language acquisition: Cross-linguistic perspectives.* Vol. 2, *Binding, dependencies, and learnability.* Hillsdale, N.J.: Lawrence Erlbaum.

Rogosa, D. 1988. Myths about longitudinal research. In K. W. Schaie, R. T. Campbell, W. Meredith, and S. C. Rawlings, eds., *Methodological issues in aging research.* New York: Springer-Verlag.

Rondal, J. 1993. Down's syndrome. In D. Bishop and K. Mogford, eds., *Language development in exceptional circumstances.* Hillsdale, N.J.: Lawrence Erlbaum.

Rosenberg, S., and L. Abbeduto. 1993. *Language and communication in mental retardation*. Hillsdale, N.J.: Lawrence Erlbaum.

Rota, G. C. 1964. The number of partitions of a set. *American Mathematical Monthly* 71, 498–504.

Rumelhart, D. E., and J. L. McClelland. 1986. On learning the past tenses of English verbs: Implicit rules or parallel distributed processing? In J. L. McClelland, D. E. Rumelhart, and the PDP Research Group, *Parallel distributed processing: Explorations in the microstructure of cognition*. Cambridge, Mass.: MIT Press.

Rumelhart, D. E., and J. L. McClelland. 1987. Learning the past tenses of English verbs: Implicit rules or parallel distributed processing? In B. J. MacWhinney, ed., *Mechanisms of language acquisition*. Hillsdale, N.J.: Lawrence Erlbaum.

Saah, K. K., and H. Goodluck. To appear. Island effects in parsing and grammar: Evidence from Akan. *The Linguistic Review*.

Saddy, D. 1992. Islands in an aphasic individual. In H. Goodluck and M. Rochemont, eds., *Island constraints: Theory, acquisition and processing*. Dordrecht: Kluwer.

Sandalo, F. 1995. Kadiweu as a pronominal argument language. Paper presented at the annual meeting of the Linguistic Society of America, New Orleans, January.

Sarma, J. 1991. The acquisition of *wh*-questions in English. Doctoral dissertation, University of Connecticut, Storrs.

Schlesinger, I. M. 1971. Production of utterances in language acquisition. In D. I. Slobin, ed., *The ontogenesis of grammar*. New York: Academic Press.

Schlisselberg, G. 1988. Development of selected conservation skills and the ability to judge sentence well-formedness in young children. Doctoral dissertation, City University of New York.

Semel, E., E. Wiig, and W. Secord. 1987. *CELF-R: Clinical Evaluation of Language Fundamentals – Revised*. San Antonio, Tex.: Psychological Corporation.

Seymour, H., L. Bland, T. Champion, J. G. de Villiers, and T. Roeper. 1992. Long-distance *wh*-movement in children with divergent language backgrounds. Poster presented at the Convention of the American Speech and Hearing Association, San Antonio, November.

Shady, M. E. 1994. Distributional, positional and prosodic cues in early sentence comprehension. Ms., State University of New York, Buffalo.

Shady, M. E., and L. A. Gerken. 1995. Grammatical and caregiver cues in early sentence comprehension. In E. Clark, ed., *Proceedings of the Twenty-Sixth Annual Child Research Forum*. Stanford, Calif.: CSLI Publications. Distributed by Cambridge University Press.

Shady, M. E., L. A. Gerken, and P. W. Jusczyk. 1995. Prosody serves as a marker to local co-occurrence patterns in ten-month-olds. In D. MacLaughlin and S. McEwen, eds., *Proceedings of the 19th Annual Boston University Conference on Language Development*. Somerville, Mass.: Cascadilla Press.

Shafer, V. L., L. A. Gerken, J. L. Shucard, and D. W. Shucard. 1993. "The" and the brain: An electrophysiological study of infants' sensitivity of English function morphemes. Ms., State University of New York, Buffalo.

Shatz, M. 1978. On the development of communicative understandings: An early strategy for interpreting and responding to messages. *Cognitive Psychology* 10, 271–301.

Sheldon, A. 1974. The role of parallel function in the acquisition of relative clauses in English. *Journal of Verbal Learning and Verbal Behavior* 13, 274–281.

Sherman, J. C., and B. Lust. 1986. Syntactic and lexical constraints on the acquisition of control in complement sentences. In B. Lust, ed., *Studies in the acquisition of anaphora*. Vol. 1, *Defining the constraints*. Dordrecht: Reidel.

Shipley, E. F., C. S. Smith, and L. R. Gleitman. 1969. A study in the acquisition of language: Free responses to commands. *Language* 45, 322–342.

Shipley, K., T. Stone, and M. Sue. 1983. *Test for Examining Expressive Morphology*. Tucson, Ariz.: Communication Skill Builders.

Sigurjónsdóttir, S., and N. Hyams. 1992. Reflexivization and logophoricity: Evidence from the acquisition of Icelandic. *Language Acquisition* 2, 359–413.

Slobin, D. I., ed. 1967. *A field manual for cross-cultural study of the acquisition of communicative competence*. Berkeley, Calif.: ASUC Bookstore.

Slobin, D. I. 1973. Cognitive prerequisites for the development of grammar. In C. A. Ferguson and D. I. Slobin, eds., *Studies of child language development*. New York: Holt, Rinehart and Winston.

Slobin, D. I. 1985a. Crosslinguistic evidence for the language-making capacity. In D. I. Slobin, ed., *The crosslinguistic study of language acquisition*. Vol. 2. Hillsdale, N.J.: Lawrence Erlbaum.

Slobin, D. I., ed. 1985b. *The crosslinguistic study of language acquisition*. Vols. 1 and 2. Hillsdale, N.J.: Lawrence Erlbaum.

Slobin, D. I., ed. 1992. *The crosslinguistic study of language acquisition*. Vol 3. Hillsdale, N.J.: Lawrence Erlbaum.

Slobin, D. I., and C. Welsh. 1973. Elicited imitation as a research tool in developmental psycho-linguistics. In C. A. Ferguson and D. I. Slobin, eds., *Studies of child language development*. New York: Holt, Rinehart and Winston.

Smith, C., and A. van Kleeck. 1986. Linguistic complexity and performance. *Journal of Child Language* 13, 389–408.

Smith-Lock, K. M. 1992. Morphological skills in normal and specifically language-impaired children. Doctoral dissertation, University of Connecticut, Storrs.

Smith-Lock, K. M. 1993. Morphological analysis and the acquisition of morphology and syntax in specifically language-impaired children. In *Haskins Laboratories status report on speech research*, SR-114. Haskins Laboratories, New Haven, Conn.

Snedecor, G., and W. Cochran. 1980. *Statistical methods*. 7th ed. Ames: Iowa State University Press.

Snodgrass, J. G., and M. Vanderwort. 1980. A standardized set of 260 pictures: Norms for name agreement, image agreement, familiarity, and visual complexity. *Journal of Experimental Psychology: Human Learning and Memory* 6, 174–215.

Snyder, R. T., and P. Pope. 1970. New norms for an item analysis of the Wepman test at the 1st grade 6-year level. *Perceptual and Motor Skills* 31, 1007–1010.

Snyder, W. 1987. Grammatical and processing factors in the first language acquisition of complex structures in Japanese. Doctoral dissertation, Cornell University.

Snyder, W., and K. Stromswold. To appear. The structure and accquisition of English dative constructions. *Linguistic Inquiry.*

Solan, L. 1983. *Pronominal reference: Child language and the theory of grammar.* Dordrecht: Reidel.

Solan, L. 1986. Language acquisition data and the theory of markedness: Evidence from Spanish. In F. Eckman, E. Moravcsik, and J. Wirth, eds., *Markedness.* New York: Plenum.

Solan, L. 1987. Parameter setting and the development of pronouns and reflexives. In T. Roeper and E. Williams, eds., *Parameter setting.* Dordrecht: Foris.

Solan, L., and T. Roeper. 1978. Children's use of syntactic structure in interpreting relative clauses. In H. Goodluck and L. Solan, eds., *Papers in the structure and development of child language.* GLSA, University of Massachusetts, Amherst.

Spelke, E. 1979. Perceiving bimodally specified events in infancy. *Developmental Psychology* 15, 626–636.

Starkey, P., E. Spelke, and R. Gelman. 1983. Detection of intermodal correspondences by human infants. *Science* 222, 179–181.

Steckol, K., and L. Leonard. 1979. The use of grammatical morphemes by normal and language-impaired children. *Journal of Communication Disorders* 12, 291–301.

Stern, C., and W. Stern. 1907. *Die Kindersprache: Eine psychologische und sprachtheoretische Untersuchung.* Leipzig: Barth.

Stetzer, A. 1992. Listening to your mother: The effects of exaggerated pitch and pitch range on young children's sentence comprehension. Senior honors thesis, State University of New York, Buffalo.

Stevenson, R., and M. Pickering. 1987. The effects of linguistic and non-linguistic knowledge on the acquisition of pronouns. In P. Griffiths, ed., *Proceedings of the Child Language Seminar.* York University, England.

Stevenson, R., and C. Pollitt. 1987. The acquisition of temporal terms. *Journal of Child Language* 14, 533–545.

Strange, W., and P. A. Broen. 1981. The relation between perception and production of /w/, /r/, and /l/ by three-year-old children. *Journal of Experimental Child Psychology* 31, 81–102.

Strohner, H., and K. E. Nelson. 1974. The young child's development of sentence comprehension: Influence of event probability, nonverbal context, syntactic form, and strategies. *Child Development* 45, 567–576.

Stromswold, K. 1988a. Linguistic representations of children's *wh*-questions. *Papers and Reports on Child Language Development* 27, 107–114.

Stromswold, K. 1988b. The structure of children's *wh*-questions. Paper presented at the 13th Annual Boston University Conference on Language Development, Boston, October.

Stromswold, K. 1989a. Children's knowledge of tense. Paper presented at the 60th Annual Meeting of the Eastern Psychological Association, Boston, April.

Stromswold, K. 1989b. How conservative are children? *Papers and Reports on Child Language Development* 28, 148–155.

Stromswold, K. 1989c. Using naturalistic data: Methodological and theoretical issues (or How to lie with naturalistic data). Paper presented at the 14th Annual Boston University Conference on Language Development, Boston, October.

Stromswold, K. 1990a. The acquisition of language-universal and language-specific aspects of Tense. Paper presented at the 15th Annual Boston University Conference on Language Development, Boston, October.

Stromswold, K. 1990b. Learnability and the acquisition of auxiliaries. Doctoral dissertation, MIT.

Stromswold, K. 1994. The nature of children's early grammar: Evidence from inversion errors. Paper presented at the annual meeting of the Linguistic Society of America, Boston, January.

Stromswold, K. 1995a. The acquisition of inversion and negation in English: A reply to Déprez and Pierce (1993). Ms., Rutgers University.

Stromswold, K. 1995b. The acquisition of subject and object *wh*-questions. *Language Acquisition* 4, 5–48.

Stromswold, K. In preparation. The acquisition of argument and adjunct questions. Ms., Rutgers University.

Stromswold, K., and S. Pinker. 1986. Some questions about *wh*-questions. Paper presented at the 11th Annual Boston University Conference on Language Development, Boston, October.

Stromswold, K., and W. Snyder. 1995. Acquisition of datives, particles, and related constructions: Evidence for a parametric account. In D. MacLaughlin and S. McEwen, eds., *Proceedings of the 19th Annual Boston University Conference on Language Development*. Vol. 2. Somerville, Mass.: Cascadilla Press.

Sudhalter, V., and M. D. S. Braine. 1985. How does comprehension of the passive develop? A comparison of actional and experiential verbs. *Journal of Child Language* 12, 455–470.

Sully, J. 1896. *Studies of childhood.* New York and London.

Suzman, S. 1985. Learning the passive in Zulu. *Papers and Reports on Child Language Development* 24, 131–137.

Swinney, D. 1979. Lexical access during sentence comprehension: (Re)consideration of context effects. *Journal of Verbal Learning and Verbal Behavior* 18, 645–659.

Swinney, D., W. Onifer, P. Prather, and M. Hirshkowitz. 1979. Semantic facilitation across sensory modalities in the processing of individual words and sentences. *Memory and Cognition* 7, 165–195.

Swinney, D., and P. Prather. 1989. On the comprehension of lexical ambiguity by young children: Investigations into the development of mental modularity. In D. S. Gorfein, ed., *Resolving semantic ambiguity*. Berlin: Springer-Verlag.

Szabolsci, A., and F. Zwarts. 1990. Islands, monotonicity, composition and heads. Paper presented at GLOW Colloquium, Leiden.

Takahashi, M. 1991. Children's interpretation of sentences containing *every*. In T. L. Maxfield and B. Plunkett, eds., *Papers in the acquisition of wh*. GLSA, University of Massachusetts, Amherst.

Tallal, P., and M. Piercy. 1973. Defects of non-verbal auditory perception in children with developmental aphasia. *Nature* 241, 468–469.

Tavakolian, S. 1977. Structural principles in the acquisition of complex sentences. Doctoral dissertation, University of Massachusetts, Amherst.

Tavakolian, S. 1981a. The conjoined-clause analysis of relative clauses. In S. Tavakolian, ed., *Language acquisition and linguistic theory*. Cambridge, Mass.: MIT Press.

Tavakolian, S., ed. 1981b. *Language acquisition and linguistic theory*. Cambridge, Mass.: MIT Press.

Templin, M. C. 1957. *Certain language skills in children*. Minneapolis, Minn.: University of Minnesota Press.

Tenny, C. 1987. Grammaticalizing aspect and affectedness. Doctoral dissertation, MIT.

Thornton, R. 1990. Adventures in long-distance moving: The acquisition of complex *wh*-questions. Doctoral dissertation, University of Connecticut, Storrs.

Thornton, R. 1993. Children who don't raise the negative. Paper presented at the annual meeting of the Linguistic Society of America, Los Angeles, January.

Thornton, R. 1995. Referentiality and *wh*-movement in child English: Juvenile *D-link*uency. *Language Acquisition* 4, 139–175.

Thornton, R., and S. Crain. 1994. Successful cyclic movement. In T. Hoekstra and B. Schwartz, eds., *Language acquisition studies in generative grammar*. Amsterdam: John Benjamins.

Tomblin, J. B. 1993. The genetic epidemiology of specific language impairment. Paper presented at Merrill Advanced Studies Conference, Toward a Genetics of Language, University of Kansas, Lawrence, November.

Townsend, D., D. Ottaviano, and T. G. Bever. 1979. Immediate memory for words from main and subordinate clauses at different age levels. *Journal of Psycholinguistic Research* 8, 83–101.

Travis, L. 1984. Parameters and effects of word order variation. Doctoral dissertation, MIT.

Travis, L., and J. Morgan. 1989. Limits on negative information in language input. *Journal of Child Language* 16, 531–552.

Tyack, D., and D. Ingram. 1977. Children's production and comprehension of *wh*-questions. *Journal of Child Language* 4, 211–224.

Tyler, L. K. 1983. The development of discourse mapping processes: The on-line interpretation of anaphoric expressions. *Cognition* 13, 309–341.

Tyler, L. K., and W. D. Marslen-Wilson. 1981. Children's processing of spoken language. *Journal of Verbal Learning and Verbal Behavior* 20, 400–416.

Valian, V. 1991. Syntactic subjects in the early speech of American and Italian children. *Cognition* 40, 21–81.

Valian, V. 1994. Children's postulation of null subjects: Parameter setting and language acquisition. In B. Lust, G. Hermon, and J. Kornfilt, eds., *Syntactic theory and first language acquisition: Cross-linguistic perspectives*. Vol. 2, *Binding, dependencies, and learnability*. Hillsdale, N.J.: Lawrence Erlbaum.

Valian, V., and R. Wales. 1976. What's what: Talkers help listeners hear and understand by clarifying sentential relations. *Cognition* 4, 155–176.

van Kleeck, A. 1982. The emergence of linguistic awareness: A cognitive framework. *Merrill-Palmer Quarterly* 28, 237–265.

Wason, P. C. 1961. Responses to affirmative and negative binary statements. *British Journal of Psychology* 52, 133–142.

Wason, P. C. 1965. The contexts of plausible denial. *Journal of Verbal Learning and Verbal Behavior* 4, 7–11.

Wasow, T. 1972. Anaphoric relations in English. Doctoral dissertation, MIT.

Weissenborn, J. 1994. Constraining the child's grammar: Local well-formedness in the development of verb movement in German and French. In B. Lust, M. Suñer, and J. Whitman, eds., *Syntactic theory and first language acquisition: Cross-linguistic perspectives*. Vol. 1, *Heads, projections, and learnability*. Hillsdale, N.J.: Lawrence Erlbaum.

Weissenborn, J., T. Roeper, and J. G. de Villiers. 1991. The acquisition of *wh*-movement in French and German. In T. L. Maxfield and B. Plunkett, eds., *Papers in the acquisition of wh*. GLSA, University of Massachusetts, Amherst.

Weissenborn, J., T. Roeper, and J. G. de Villiers. 1995. *Wh*-acquisition in French and German: Connections between case, *wh*-features, and unique triggers. In C. Jakubowicz, ed., *Grammaire universelle et acquisition du langage. Recherches linguistiques de Vincennes* 24, 125–155.

Wepman, J. 1960. Auditory discrimination, speech and reading. *Elementary School Journal* 60, 325–333.

Werker, J. F., J. E. Pegg, and P. J. McLeod. 1994. A cross-language investigation of infant preference for infant-directed communication. *Infant Behavior and Development* 17, 323–333.

Werner, E., and J. Kresheck. 1983. *Structured Photographic Expressive Language Test – II*. Sandwich, Ill.: Janelle Publications.

Wexler, K. 1994. Optional infinitives. In D. Lightfoot and N. Hornstein, eds., *Verb movement*. New York: Cambridge University Press.

Wexler, K., and Y.-C. Chien. 1985. The development of lexical anaphors and pronouns. *Papers and Reports on Child Language Development* 24, 138–149.

Whitman, J. 1994. In defense of the strong continuity account of the acquisition of verb-second. In B. Lust, M. Suñer, and J. Whitman, eds., *Syntactic theory and first language acquisition: Cross-linguistic perspectives*. Vol. 1, *Heads, projections, and learnability*. Hillsdale, N.J.: Lawrence Erlbaum.

Wijnen, F., E. Krikhaar, and E. den Os. 1994. The (non)realization of unstressed elements in children's utterances: A rhythmic constraint? *Journal of Child Language* 21, 59–83.

Wilcox, M. J., and L. Leonard. 1978. Experimental acquisition of *wh*-questions in language-disordered children. *Journal of Speech and Hearing Research* 21, 220–239.

Williams, E. 1987. Introduction. In T. Roeper and E. Williams, eds., *Parameter setting*. Dordrecht: Reidel.

Winzemer, J. 1981. A lexical expectation model for children's comprehension of *wh*-questions. Doctoral dissertation, City University of New York.

Young, E., and J. Perachio. 1981. *Patterned Elicitation Syntax Test*. Tucson, Ariz.: Communication Skill Builders.

Younger, B. A., and L. B. Cohen. 1986. Developmental changes in infants' perception of correlations among attributes. *Child Development* 57, 803–815.

Ziesler, Y., and K. Demuth. 1995. Noun class prefixes in Sesotho child-directed speech. In E. Clark, ed., *Proceedings of the Twenty-Sixth Annual Child Language Research Forum*. Stanford, Calif.: CSLI Publications. Distributed by Cambridge University Press.

Index